THE THOUGHT OF THOMAS AQUINAS

The Thought of Thomas Aquinas

BRIAN DAVIES

CLARENDON PRESS · OXFORD

OXFORD
UNIVERSITY PRESS

Great Clarendon Street, Oxford OX2 6DP

Oxford University Press is a department of the University of Oxford.
It furthers the University's objective of excellence in research, scholarship,
and education by publishing worldwide in

Oxford New York

Athens Auckland Bangkok Bogotá Buenos Aires Calcutta
Cape Town Chennai Dar es Salaam Delhi Florence Hong Kong Istanbul
Karachi Kuala Lumpur Madrid Melbourne Mexico City Mumbai
Nairobi Paris São Paulo Singapore Taipei Tokyo Toronto Warsaw
with associated companies in Berlin Ibadan

Oxford is a registered trade mark of Oxford University Press
in the UK and in certain other countries

Published in the United States
by Oxford University Press Inc., New York

British Library Cataloguing in Publication Data

Data available

Library of Congress Cataloging in Publication Data
Davies, Brian, 1951–
The thought of Thomas Aquinas / Brian Davies.
Includes bibliographical references and index.
1. Thomas, Aquinas, Saint, 1256–1274. 2. Theology, Doctrinal—
History—Middle Ages, 600–1500. 3. Catholic Church—Doctrines—
History I. Title.
B765.T54D35 1992
230'.2'092—dc20
ISBN 0–19–826753–3 (pbk)

7 9 10 8 6

Printed in Great Britain
on acid-free paper by
Bookcraft (Bath) Ltd
Midsomer Norton, Avon

For
Richard Finn, James Claffey,
Mark Wynn, and Sean Fernandez

Preface

In the late 1270s rumours of theological controversy reached the ears of Pope John XXI. He responded by asking the bishop of Paris (Stephen Tempier) to set up an inquiry and to produce a full report. The bishop set up a commission to examine 'errors' current in the Arts Faculty at the University of Paris. On 7 March 1277 he condemned a long list of propositions supposed to derive from the faculty.[1] Attention was subsequently focused on the work of certain theologians, one of whom was Thomas Aquinas.

A commission of Masters of Theology, with only two exceptions, agreed to condemn a series of propositions derived from his writings. The scene was set for a formal censure, though none, in fact, occurred. But on 18 March 1277 the archbishop of Canterbury (Robert Kilwardby) issued a list of condemned propositions. These did not mention Aquinas by name, but some of them were clearly thought to derive from him.[2] Kilwardby's successor at Canterbury, John Pecham, reiterated the condemnation and also excommunicated at least one of Aquinas's followers.[3]

As things turned out, Aquinas was canonized in 1323. And he subsequently came to be ranked among the greatest of Christian writers. His influence on Christian thinking is second only to writers like St Paul and St Augustine. In one modern dictionary of Christian theology he rates more references than anyone except Jesus of Nazareth.[4] Nor has his stature been recognized only by Christians. Speaking from the viewpoint of secular philosophy, Anthony Kenny can say:

[1] The Parisian condemnation is documented in *Chartularium Universitatis Parisiensis*, ed. H. Denifle, OP and E. Chatelain, i (Paris, 1889), 543 ff. English text in Arthur Hyman and James J. Walsh (eds.), *Philosophy in the Middle Ages* (2nd edn., Indianapolis, 1987), 584 ff.

[2] For the Oxford condemnation see Daniel A. Callus, OP, *The Condemnation of St Thomas at Oxford* (London, 1955). For a discussion of the Parisian and Oxford condemnations, see Simon Tugwell, OP, *Albert and Thomas: Selected Writings* (New York, 1988), 237 ff.

[3] The person excommunicated by Pecham was Richard Knapwell. For an account of him see Frederick J. Roensch, *Early Thomistic School* (Dubuque, 1a. 1964), 34 ff.

[4] Alan Richardson and John Bowden (eds.), *A New Dictionary of Christian Theology* (London, 1983).

Aquinas is, I believe, one of the dozen greatest philosophers of the western world. His philosophy of nature has been antiquated, in great part, by the swift progress of natural science since the Renaissance. His philosophy of logic has been in many respects improved upon by the work of logicians and mathematicians in the last hundred years. But his metaphysics, his philosophical theology, his philosophy of mind and his moral philosophy entitle him to rank with Plato and Aristotle, with Descartes and Leibniz, with Locke and Hume and Kant.[5]

The same note is struck by the author of a recent editorial comment in *Philosophy*, a journal which cannot be accused of being in the pay of the Christian Church. 'St Thomas Aquinas', so our author declares, 'is a genius whose claim to that accolade is barely debatable.'[6]

In this book I aim to give a general and introductory overview of Aquinas's teaching. There is, however, a problem with such a project. His writings run to thousands of pages. One simply cannot do justice to them in one volume.

To a large extent, Aquinas himself comes to the rescue here. For, though there are significant developments in his thinking, there is also enormous continuity. His major conclusions can all be found in his first important work, the *Commentary on the Sentences*. He shifted in his emphases, but he did not change his mind radically. One cannot seriously speak of an 'Early Aquinas' and a 'Later Aquinas'. He was a man of many thoughts, but he always had a single vision, albeit one presented with varied nuances and with different degrees of attention to detail.[7] On that count he is relatively easy to expound.

But the details in Aquinas are important. And the problem of quickly doing him justice is augmented by a feature of his writings which can be fully appreciated only by someone who has worked through them in detail. For he is enormously systematic. What he says on one topic almost always needs clarification in terms of what he says about something else. Expounding him on one subject can quickly lead to one feeling the need to expound him on almost

---

[5] Anthony Kenny (ed.), *Aquinas: A Collection of Critical Essays* (London, 1969), 1.

[6] *Philosophy*, 65 (1990), 116.

[7] Cf. James A. Weisheipl, OP, *Friar Thomas d'Aquino* (Oxford, 1974; republished with Corrigenda and Addenda, Washington, DC, 1983), x: 'Early in life Thomas grasped certain fundamental philosophical principles that never changed. Always there was development, deeper understanding, and even rejection of earlier views. But there was never a metamorphosis in his approach to reality. There was never a "conversion" or violent rejection of earlier thought, but only corrections and modifications that led to a fuller, more human, and more divine appreciation of the basic problems of life.'

everything he writes about, as the reader may appreciate if only from the number of times I have in this book sought refuge in expressions like 'as we have seen' and 'as we shall see'.

I have therefore decided to follow him broadly in accordance with the scheme he provides in the *Summa theologiae*, which is his greatest achievement, and which is also the best-known synthesis of his thinking. It presents the essentials of a lifetime's reflection in an order which he felt appropriate, so I presume that one will hardly be doing him an injustice if one tries to introduce him with that text, those essentials, and that order in mind. To suit my own purposes, however, I shall sometimes depart from the order in which topics I turn to are discussed in the *Summa theologiae*. And I shall be noting ways in which the contents of that work differ from the teaching of Aquinas as presented by him elsewhere. Inevitably, I shall also have to be selective in the topics on which I try to indicate what Aquinas thought. Readers will notice that, for example, I do not deal with details of Aquinas on politics and aesthetics—though some of the matters I turn to have a bearing on these subjects.[8] I have also omitted discussion of Aquinas's contribution to thirteenth-century debates about the legitimacy and running of certain religious orders in the Catholic Church (a question which much engaged him but is now of merely historical interest).

Aquinas wrote in Latin, though his first language was a Neapolitan dialect. Many of his works are available in English, and, where the translation is not misleading, I quote from available English editions, though sometimes with modifications, and not always from the same edition even in the case of quotations from a single work. Most quotations from the *Summa theologiae* come from the sixty-one-volume Blackfriars edition,[9] which is, overall, probably the best English version, even if it fares ill on certain counts when compared with the more literally accurate translation published by the English Dominican Fathers in 1911/1920, which has been recently reprinted,

---

[8] For introductions to Aquinas on politics, as well as for basic texts by Aquinas on politics, see William P. Baumgarth and Richard J. Regan, SJ (eds.), *Saint Thomas Aquinas on Law, Morality and Politics* (Indianapolis, 1988) and Paul E. Sigmund (ed.), *St Thomas Aquinas on Politics and Ethics* (New York, 1988). For Aquinas on aesthetics, see Umberto Eco, *The Aesthetics of Thomas Aquinas* (London, 1988) and Armand A. Maurer, *About Beauty: A Thomistic Interpretation* (Houston, Tex., 1983).

[9] London, 1964–80.

and which is also often used in what follows.[10] Quotations from the
Bible are from the RSV edition except when they occur as part of
quotations from Aquinas.

B. D.

[10] Westminster, Md. 1981.

Acknowledgements

MANY friends and colleagues have helped me by reading and commenting on material which has found its way into this book. But I am especially indebted to David Burrell, CSC, James Claffey, OP, John Marenbon, James McEvoy, Simon Tugwell, OP, Christopher Williams, and Mark Wynn. I must also thank Hilary O'Shea for being a most gracious and encouraging OUP editor. Over many years Herbert McCabe, OP has taught me more about Aquinas than I can now remember. Perhaps it is true that, in the language of Aquinas, he is the most significant secondary cause of my text. He will not like it. But that is only to be expected.

Contents

Abbreviations   xii

1. THE SHAPE OF A SAINT   1
   Early Years   1
   From Student to Teacher   4
   Paris to Naples   5
   The Last Phase   8
   Aquinas's Character   10
   Reading Aquinas Today   16

2. GETTING TO GOD   21
   Ways not to Get to God   22
   God and His Effects: The Five Ways   25
   The Existence Argument   31
   Creation   33
   The Beginning of the World   35

3. WHAT GOD IS NOT   40
   Not Knowing What God is   40
   The Doctrine of Divine Simplicity: Preliminaries   44
   The Doctrine of Divine Simplicity: Details   51

4. TALKING ABOUT GOD   58
   Background to Aquinas   58
   Aquinas on God-Talk   60
   The Doctrine of Analogy   70
   Real and Notional Relations   75

5. PERFECTION AND GOODNESS   80
   God is Perfect   80
   God is Good   84
   God and Evil   89

6. UBIQUITY TO ETERNITY   98
   God's Presence in Things   98
   God is Changeless   101

God is Eternal 103
Aquinas on Eternity Today 109

7. ONENESS TO KNOWLEDGE 118
God is One 118
God has Power 121
God's Knowledge 124

8. WILL TO MERCY 139
Will in God 140
Love in God 149
God's Justice and Mercy 152

9. PROVIDENCE AND FREEDOM 158
Providence as God's Governing of Creatures 158
Miracles 169
Human Freedom 174
Prayer 178

10. THE ETERNAL TRIANGLE 185
Aquinas and the Doctrine of the Trinity 185
The Trinity and Philosophy 187
Processions in the Trinity 193
Relations and the Trinity 198
The Persons Taken Individually 202

11. BEING HUMAN 207
Me and My Body 207
Soul and Body 211
Death and the Soul 215
Desire and Action 220

12. HOW TO BE HAPPY 227
Happiness and God 227
Happiness and Need 231
Practical Reasoning 232
Virtues 239
Natural Law 244

13. HOW TO BE HOLY 250
The Human End and Human Nature 250
The Start of the Human Race 253

The Old Law 257
The New Law 260
Grace 262
The Cause and Kinds of Grace 266

14. THE HEART OF GRACE 274
Faith 274
Hope 285
Charity 288

15. GOD INCARNATE 297
The General Nature of Aquinas's Christology 297
The Union of Divinity and Humanity 300
What was Christ Like? 307

16. THE LIFE AND WORK OF CHRIST 320
The General Picture 320
Sin and the Incarnation 321
Satisfaction 324
Merit 332
Justification 335
The Resurrection and Ascension of Christ 339

17. SIGNS AND WONDERS 345
Sacraments 346
The Crowning Sacrament: The Eucharist 361

Select Bibliography 377
Index 385

Abbreviations

Comp.	*Compendium theologiae*
De aeter. mundi	*De aeternitate mundi*
De ente	*De ente et essentia*
De pot.	*De potentia*
De prin. nat.	*De principiis naturae*
De ver.	*De veritate*
De virt.	*De virtutibus in communi*
In De an.	*In Aristotelis librum De anima commentarium*
In De caelo	*Commentarium in libros Aristotelis De caelo et mundo*
In Eth.	*Sententia libri Ethicorum*
In Meta.	*In Metaphysicam Aristotelis commentaria*
In peri herm.	*Commentarium in Aristotelis libros peri hermeneias*
In Phys.	*In octo libros Physicorum Aristotelis expositio*
Quodl.	*Quaestiones quodlibetales*
Sent.	*Scriptum super libros Sententiarum*
SG	*Summa contra Gentiles*
Super ad Rom.	*Super epistolam ad Romanos lectura*
Super De Trin.	*Expositio super librum Boethii De Trinitate*
Super ev. Joh.	*Super evangelium S. Ioannis lectura*
Super Isaiam	*Postilla super Isaiam*
Super I ad Thess.	*Super primam epistolam ad Thessalonicenses lectura*
Super I ad Cor.	*Super primam epistolam ad Corinthios lectura*
Super sym. apos.	*Expositio super symbolo apostolorum*

I give references to the *Summa theologiae* without giving the title but simply by citing part, question, and article. Thus, 1a. 3. 3 means *Summa theologiae, prima pars* (part 1), question 3, article 3.

I

The Shape of a Saint

SCHOLARS are at odds about the details of Aquinas's life.[1] They even disagree about the date of his birth. The year usually given is 1224/5, but 1226 is also possible, and a very good case has been made in its favour.[2] The general picture is clear, however. Aquinas came on the scene some ten years after Magna Carta, within a year or so of the death of St Francis of Assisi (1181/2–1226), and within five years of the death of St Dominic (c.1170–1221), whose Order he joined and with whom he is therefore naturally associated. At the time of his birth, Roger Bacon (c.1214–c.1292) was about 22 years old. Robert Grosseteste (c.1170–1253) was roughly 51. St Albert the Great (c.1200–80) was only in his twenties.

Early Years

Aquinas was born in what was then the Kingdom of Naples, ruled by the Emperor Frederick II (*Stupor Mundi*). His family were local gentry. His birthplace was probably their main residence, the castle of Roccasecca. His father, who was one of Frederick's barons, was called Landulf d'Aquino. His mother's name was Theodora. At the age of 5 he was sent to the Abbey of Monte Cassino 'in order to be trained in good morals and taught his letters'.[3] His parents may have intended him to become abbot of the monastery,[4] but the place was a strategic site in a conflict between the emperor and the pope, and in

---

[1] The most important sources for Aquinas's life are works by William of Tocco and Bernard Gui. Also to be reckoned with are documents relating to Aquinas's canonization process. See A. Ferrua (ed.), *Thomae Aquinatis vitae fontes praecipuae* (Alba, 1968).

[2] See Simon Tugwell, OP (ed.), *Albert and Thomas: Selected Writings* (New York, 1988), 291 ff.

[3] Kenelm Foster, OP (ed.), *The Life of Saint Thomas Aquinas: Biographical Documents* (London, 1959), 26.

[4] See Ferrua, *Thomae Aquinatis . . .* 313.

1239 it was occupied by imperial troops. So he was removed to
further his studies at the University of Naples while he was still a
teenager.

The University of Naples (known at the time as a *studium generale*)
was something of a novelty when Aquinas went to study there.
Established by Frederick II, and highly cosmopolitan, its origins were
secular rather than ecclesiastical. It was founded as a rival to the
papal university in Bologna and was the first university established
by civil charter. It was also a place where the works of Aristotle
(384–322 BC) were studied seriously.

By 'the works of Aristotle' I mean 'the full range of his writings'.
Aristotle was known on the European scene long before Aquinas
came to Naples. But he was not long known as Naples knew him
when Aquinas arrived there. St Augustine (354–430) read and discussed him. The highly influential Boethius (*c.*480–*c.*524) did likewise, and provided the Latin West with translations of some of his
writings. For a long time, however, his works were not available as a
whole, and medieval thinkers in Europe thought of him primarily as a
logician. The writings for which he is probably best known nowadays,
his so-called 'physical', 'metaphysical', and 'ethical' treatises, became
available in translation from Greek and Arabic only in the second half
of the twelfth century and the first part of the thirteenth century.
And, during this time, they were disapproved of in some powerful
academic quarters. They were, for example, banned in the Faculty of
Arts at the University of Paris in 1215.[5]

So Aquinas was treading on controversial ground in finding
himself in a place where Aristotle was known and appreciated for
more than his logic. Intellectually speaking, he was entering a new
world. But it was one which he embraced with considerable fervour.
Aristotle became for him a paradigm of sound reasoning. He became
'the Philosopher', as Aquinas often calls him in the fashion commonplace at the time.

It has often been said that it was Albert the Great who introduced
Thomas to Aristotle. One can understand why this theory arose, for
Albert and Thomas were related as teacher and student, the former
evidently influencing the latter. And Albert has been described as
'the first theologian of the Middle Ages who looked Aristotle squarely

---

[5] *Chartularium Universitatis Parisiensis*, ed. H. Denifle, OP and E. Chatelain, i
(Paris, 1889), 78 f.

in the face'.[6] He was brought into the Dominican Order by its second Master General, Jordan of Saxony (d. 1237). He taught, travelled widely, and was at one time bishop of Regensburg. He commented on the range of Aristotle's writings and, though judgements on the nature of his Aristotelianism vary, his familiarity with and his enthusiasm for the philosopher are not in doubt. But, given the situation at Naples when Aquinas arrived there, it cannot be the case that it was Albert who introduced him to Aristotle. He must have encountered the latter's work before he met Albert. One of his teachers at Naples, Peter of Ireland, was a noted disciple and interpreter of Aristotle.[7]

We may therefore conclude that the seeds of much of Aquinas's later career were sown in Naples from 1239 onwards. But it was also decisively affected by another influence he encountered at that period. For at Naples he met members of the Dominican Order of friars. And he joined them in 1242 or 1243.

The Dominicans were still a new phenomenon in the early 1240s. Together with the Franciscan friars, founded around the same time as the Dominicans, they stood in marked contrast to the ancient and stable religious orders in the Church with which people were then familiar (orders of monks and canons). They were mendicants, who kept themselves by begging. By certain contemporary standards, they were not very respectable. Why, then, should Aquinas have been attracted to them?

Perhaps he joined them just because they were there when he decided to enter religious life (many people enter religious orders on that basis; personal relationships may often weigh more heavily than theory when it comes to a choice of vocation). He was befriended by the Dominican John of S. Giuliano, who encouraged him to enter the Order.[8] He knew the Neapolitan Dominicans. So his decision to enter the Dominican order is not very astonishing. It can be explained simply in terms of mere human contact. But we might also surmise that Aquinas was attracted to the Dominicans by the fact that

[6] Josef Pieper, *Scholasticism* (New York, 1964), quoting Martin Grabmann, *Mittelalterliches Geistesleben*, ii (Munich, 1936), 70. For a study of Albert's life see Tugwell, *Albert and Thomas*. See also James A. Weisheipl (ed.), *Albertus Magnus and the Sciences* (Toronto, 1980). For the relationship between Albert and Thomas see James A. Weisheipl, *Thomas d'Aquino and Albert His Teacher* (Toronto, 1980).

[7] Michael Bertram Crowe, 'Peter of Ireland: Aquinas's Teacher of the ARTES LIBERALES', in *Arts libéraux et philosophie au Moyen Âge* (Paris, 1969).

[8] See Ferrua, *Thomae Aquinatis . . .* 46 f.

they were especially committed to study, teaching, and preaching.[9] This supposition certainly squares with his subsequent career. It also fits with what he came to say when writing about religious orders. In the *Summa theologiae* he asks: 'Is a religious order devoted to the contemplative life better than one devoted to the works of the active life?' He replies that 'the active life has two different kinds of work', one of which 'flows from the fullness of contemplation, such as teaching and preaching'. Then he says that 'this is better than mere contemplation' since 'it is a greater thing to give light than simply to have light, and... it is a greater thing to pass on to others what you have contemplated than just to contemplate'. His conclusion, therefore, is that 'the highest rating among religious orders must be awarded to those which are geared to teaching and preaching'.[10] Such a line of thinking, if he had it in the 1240s, would certainly make sense of Aquinas's decision to join the Dominicans at that time.[11]

From Student to Teacher

From Naples, Aquinas was sent by his religious superiors to the priory of Santa Sabina in Rome. And, from there, he was dispatched to Paris. For one reason or another, however, his family tried to interfere with his choice of a Dominican vocation at this time. As he travelled to Paris in 1244, they waylaid him and detained him for about two years, first at the family castle of Montesangiovanni, then (probably) at Roccasecca. There is evidence that during this time he was able to read, and even to have contact with Dominicans, and he rejoined his brethren probably in the early months of 1246. The details of his movements straight after this are a matter of controversy, but we are entitled to conclude that, having spent a short time at Naples, he was next sent to Paris, where he transcribed the lectures of Albert on the anonymous author known as Denys (or Dionysius) the Areopagite.[12] On this supposition, we have to say that

---

[9] For an introduction to the first Dominicans, see Simon Tugwell, OP (ed.), *Early Dominicans* (New York, 1982). Standard histories of St Dominic include M. H. Vicaire, OP, *Saint Dominic and His Times* (London, 1964) and Guy Bedouelle, OP, *Saint Dominic: The Grace of the Word* (San Francisco, 1987).

[10] 2a2ae. 188. 6.

[11] See Tugwell, *Albert and Thomas*, 290.

[12] See ibid. 208. The best introduction to Denys is Andrew Louth, *Denys the*

Albert and Aquinas were in Cologne within a year or so, where the lectures on Denys continued and were supplemented by ones on the *Ethics* of Aristotle, which Aquinas also transcribed. At this time too Aquinas may have produced his text *De principiis naturae*, a short treatise dealing with some of the key ideas in Aristotle's *Physics*.[13]

Albert was evidently impressed by his young student and colleague. And others were also. For Aquinas was next sent to prepare to teach at the University of Paris, which, at that time, was one of Europe's chief centres of learning and a well-established training ground for students of theology and philosophy. According to one tradition, while he was at Cologne Aquinas was nicknamed 'the Dumb Ox'. This was because he was physically large and heavy (an impression conveyed by the best-known artistic impressions of Aquinas), and also because he was reserved, silent, and therefore thought to be stupid. Tradition also has it that, when Aquinas once performed well in the classroom, Albert observed: 'We call this lad a dumb ox, but I tell you that the whole world is going to hear his bellowing!'[14] The truth of these traditions is open to question, but there is no doubt at all that, from the time he arrived in Paris, Aquinas embarked on a literary output which finally grew to staggering proportions.

Paris to Naples

He received a licence to teach at Paris in 1256, and he may have arrived in the city as early as 1251. To begin with, he worked as an apprentice professor (*baccalaureus biblicus*) lecturing on Scripture. He then became a *baccalaureus Sententiarum*, which meant commenting on the *Sentences* of Peter Lombard (*c.*1095–1160), a work which was recommended by the Lateran Council in 1215 and which came to be accepted as the official university textbook for theological instruction.[15]

In 1256 Aquinas was made a professor (or Master) in theology.

Areopagite (London, 1989). For an excellent essay on Denys and Aquinas, see appendix 3 ('The Dionysian Corpus') to vol. xiv of the Blackfriars edition of the *Summa theologiae*.

[13] Cf. Tugwell, *Albert and Thomas*, 210.

[14] Foster, *Life of Aquinas*, 33.

[15] Lombard's *Sentences* were written around the end of the 1140s. The work was intended as an aid to the study of Scripture and the Fathers, excerpts from which it reproduced.

Between then and 1259 he lectured on the Bible and worked on a series of discussions based on classroom debates ('disputations') dealing with topics such as truth, providence, grace, freedom, and prophecy. The result is known as the *Disputed Questions on Truth* (*De veritate*), which was the first of several so-called Disputed Questions written by Aquinas. Others include *On the Power of God* (*De potentia*), *The Soul* (*De anima*), and *On Spiritual Creatures* (*De spiritualibus creaturis*).

In addition to these works Aquinas's complete writings include biblical commentaries, a series of commentaries on Aristotle, and a collection of polemical tracts on a variety of controversial matters such as the status of mendicants, the nature of the intellect, and the eternity of the world. But he is particularly famous as the author of two enormous treatises covering the whole range of Christian doctrine and its philosophical background. Commonly referred to by their Latin names, they are the *Summa contra Gentiles* and the *Summa theologiae*.

A 'summa' ('summary') was an extended treatment of doctrinal matters set out in an orderly and comprehensive manner. It was a standard literary genre for medieval writers from around the early twelfth century. The proper title of the *Summa contra Gentiles* is *De veritate catholicae fidei contra Gentiles*, which we can translate as *On the Truth of the Catholic Faith against Unbelievers*. On the basis of a fourteenth-century life of St Raymund of Peñafort (c. 1178–1275), tradition holds that it was commissioned as an aid for Dominican missionaries preaching against Muslims, Jews, and heretical Christians in Spain and North Africa. This theory has been subject to recent criticism, but it has also been recently defended.[16]

The *Summa theologiae* was begun in 1266, and it ranks as Aquinas's major achievement, though it remained unfinished at his death. It contains three long treatises (or 'parts') divided into subsections called 'questions' and 'articles'. And it ranges over topics such as God, creation, angels, human nature and happiness, grace, virtues, Christ, and sacraments. But, in spite of its impressiveness, its purpose seems to have been pretty down to earth. For, as has been

---

[16] See *Summa contra Gentiles*, i, text and French translation, with an Introduction by A. Gauthier (Paris, 1961), and A. Patfoort, *Thomas d'Aquin: Les Clés d'une théologie* (Paris, 1983). Gauthier criticizes the traditional story. Patfoort writes in its favour. In *Albert and Thomas*, Simon Tugwell develops Patfoort's points in a way which suggests a reconciliation with Gauthier's main contention. See 251 ff.

plausibly argued by Leonard Boyle, there is reason to think that, in writing the *Summa theologiae*, Aquinas 'had young and run-of-the-mill Dominicans primarily in mind and not a more sophisticated, perhaps university audience'. The work, we may say, was 'his own very personal contribution to a lopsided system of theological education in the Order to which he belonged'.[17] Considered from this viewpoint, the *Summa theologiae* is original for more than its teaching. As Boyle puts it:

All Dominican writers of *summae* previous to Thomas had valiantly covered various aspects of learning for their confrères in the pastoral care ... Now Thomas went further than anything hitherto attempted. He provided a *summa* of general theology, a manual which dealt with God and Trinity and Creation and Incarnation as well as with man, his strengths and weaknesses.[18]

In other words, with the *Summa theologiae* Aquinas was filling a gap. He was putting practical theology in a full theological context.

By any standards the *Summa theologiae* is a *tour de force*, and one wonders at the mental life of someone able to produce both it and the many other things written by Aquinas. His contemporaries were clearly quite fascinated by his capacity for thinking and writing, for we find much in their accounts which relates either to his literary output or to his attitude to study and reflection. According to one story he is said to have been asked if he would like to be lord of Paris. He is supposed to have replied that he would not know what to do with the city and that he would rather have the (presumably lost) homilies of St John Chrysostom (*c*.347–407) on the Gospel of St Matthew.[19] According to another report, he dictated to more than one secretary on different subjects at the same time.[20] One tradition even insists that he composed in his sleep.[21]

Aquinas was certainly a great worker, and not all the work was literary. He taught at Paris, not only between 1256 and 1259, but also between about 1269 and 1272. During both periods he was involved in a defence of the mendicant orders against critics from amongst the

[17] Leonard E. Boyle, *The Setting of the Summa Theologiae of Saint Thomas*, Étienne Gilson Series, 5 (Toronto, 1982), 17 and 30.
[18] Boyle, *The Setting of the Summa Theologiae*, 15 f.
[19] Cf. Ferrua, *Thomae Aquinatis ...*, 318.
[20] Ibid. 58.
[21] Ibid.

secular clergy (i.e. clerics who were not members of religious orders) such as William of Saint-Amour (d. 1272), Gérald d'Abbeville (*c.* 1220/5–1272), and Nicholas of Lisieux (active *c.*1272), who objected to the presence of Dominican and Franciscan professors at the University of Paris, and who wrote tracts designed to counter their influence.[22]

The details of Aquinas's movements from around 1259 to 1269 are a matter of dispute, but we know that he taught at Orvieto, where Pope Urban IV lived, and at Rome, where he was assigned to establish a house of studies in 1265. In 1272 he moved to Naples, where he became responsible for studies at the priory of San Domenico. And still the writing continued. At Orvieto, for instance, Aquinas worked on the *Golden Chain* (*Catena aurea*), a continuous commentary on the four Gospels composed of quotations from the Church Fathers, and *Against the Errors of the Greeks* (*Contra errores Graecorum*), a set of opinions on certain Greek Orthodox theologians. He continued with the *Summa theologiae*, and he composed a treatise on politics (*De regno*) as well as an edition of a liturgy for the newly created feast of Corpus Christi.

Relating to this time we have yet more allusions to his tendency to abstraction or concentration. One of the most famous concerns an occasion in 1269 when he was dining with King Louis IX of France. According to his biographer Bernard Gui, Aquinas, who seemed often to be 'rapt out of himself' when thinking, spent most of the meal pondering on the Manichees (a religious sect dating from the third century AD). Suddenly he struck the table and exclaimed, 'That settles the Manichees!', whereupon he called for his secretary to come and take dictation. He explained to the alarmed dinner guests, 'I thought I was at my desk.'[23]

The Last Phase

By 1274, however, Aquinas was suffering from more than abstraction. On 6 December 1273 he celebrated the Mass of St Nicholas. Then he suddenly abandoned his usual routine and neither wrote nor dictated anything else. His long-serving companion (*socius*),

[22] See James A. Weisheipl, OP, *Friar Thomas d'Aquino* (Washington, DC, 1983), 80 ff. and 263 ff.
[23] Foster, *Life of Aquinas*, 44. The historical credentials of the story have, however, been challenged. See Gauthier, *Summa contra Gentiles*, i. 23 ff.

Reginald of Piperno, urged him to return to work. The reply given was: 'Reginald, I cannot, because all that I have written seems like straw to me.'[24]

Exactly what had happened is uncertain, though the explanation normally given nowadays is that Aquinas suffered a stroke or a physical and emotional breakdown caused by overwork.[25] It is sometimes suggested that he underwent a 'mystical experience'. Whatever the truth of the matter is, the crisis of 1273 was clearly the beginning of the end for Aquinas. By the afternoon of 7 March 1274 he was lying dead in the Cistercian abbey of Fossanova, south of Rome.

Late in 1273 he was instructed to attend the Second Council of Lyons in his professional capacity as a theologian. He set out for Lyons, but became seriously ill and lodged for a while with his niece at the castle of Maenza. He is reported to have said here: 'If the Lord is coming for me, I had better be found in a religious house than in a castle.'[26] So he was carried to Fossanova, where he died in a guest-room a week or two later.[27]

The cause of his death is unknown. One account tells us that, on the journey to Lyons, Aquinas struck his head against a tree that had fallen across the road and that this left him half stunned and hardly able to stand.[28] On the basis of this report it has been suggested that he died of a haemorrhaged blood clot.[29]

The funeral rites were celebrated at Fossanova and the body was buried before the high altar. But it did not stay there, for there were a number of exhumations. It seems that these were brought about by fear on the part of the Cistercians that Aquinas's brethren would demand his remains. And that, in the end, is what happened. In 1369 the Dominicans retrieved what was left of Aquinas and the relics

---

[24] Ferrua, *Thomae Aquinatis . . .*, 318 ff. The comment has sometimes been viewed as a rejection of his ideas. But we have no reason to accept this interpretation. As we shall see, Aquinas's official position is that God is fundamentally incomprehensible and that all our talk of him fails badly to represent him as he is. And 'straw' is a conventional image for the literal sense of Scripture which, though limited, is still worth having (cf. Tugwell, *Albert and Thomas*, 266).

[25] See Weisheipl, *Friar Thomas d'Aquino*, 322 f.

[26] Ferrua, *Thomae Aquinatis . . .*, 213.

[27] Visitors can still visit the guest-room. When they do so, they might wonder, as I do, how Aquinas was brought to it, given his illness, his reputed size, and the way one has to get up to the room by means of an exceedingly steep and narrow winding stairway.

[28] Ferrua, *Thomae Aquinatis . . .*, 317.

[29] Weisheipl, *Friar Thomas d'Aquino*, 329.

were transferred to Toulouse, where they are now in the church of the Jacobins.

Aquinas's Character

What sort of man was Aquinas? As we have seen, reputation has it that he was reserved, scholarly, and given to abstraction. And it is obvious that he was thoroughly dedicated to teaching and writing. But he had many parts. He is chiefly thought of as a writer. Yet he was much more than that. He was a friar and priest. He was an administrator, a university lecturer, and a teacher of Dominican students. As a Dominican, he was also a preacher, though most of his preaching was delivered in Latin and confined to educated audiences.[30] He was also, of course, a student. And the range of his studies was considerable, as was that of his teaching. It covered Scripture, philosophy, theology, and science.

1. Philosopher or Theologian?

This last fact has led to a certain amount of debate among readers of Aquinas concerning the question 'How do we categorize him as a thinker?' More precisely, should we call him a philosopher or a theologian? Aquinas is sometimes viewed *either* as a philosopher *or* as a theologian—as if these titles signify easily distinguishable roles. But is it correct to pigeon-hole him in this way?

As we shall see below, some of his critics have felt that Aquinas really does not deserve to be called a philosopher. But this is a judgement which has also been reached by many of Aquinas's fans, some of whom insist that he is a theologian and that what he writes is theology rather than philosophy. Such was the view of, for example, Étienne Gilson (1884–1978), who did more than most to recommend Aquinas to twentieth-century readers. In recent years it has been reiterated by medieval scholars such as Anton Pegis and Armand Maurer. Gilson does not deny that there is philosophy in the works of Aquinas. But, he says, it is there as part of theology, from which it is indistinguishable.[31] Pegis makes the same point and,

---

[30] See Tugwell, *Albert and Thomas*, 259.

[31] For an exposition of Gilson on this matter see John F. Wippel, 'Étienne Gilson and Christian Philosophy', in John F. Wippel, *Metaphysical Themes in Thomas Aquinas* (Washington, DC, 1984).

referring to the *Summa theologiae*, so does Maurer. 'In this compendium of theology', he explains,

everything is theological, even the philosophical reasoning that makes up such a large part of it. The water of philosophy and the other secular disciplines it contains has been changed into the wine of theology. That is why we cannot extract from the *Summa* its philosophical parts and treat them as pure philosophy.[32]

There is much to be said in defence of this reading. The first topic raised in the *Summa theologiae* is that of what Aquinas calls *sacra doctrina* (sacred teaching).[33] And he clearly wishes to stress that this comprises the revealed content of Christian faith understood as truth which we cannot arrive at by merely philosophical argument.

It was necessary for man's salvation that there should be a knowledge revealed by God, besides philosophical science built up by human reason ... It was therefore necessary that, besides philosophical science built up by reason there should be a *sacra doctrina* learned through revelation.[34]

One sometimes encounters the idea that Christian doctrine is rational in the sense that it is grounded on demonstrations which any thinking person ought to accept. But this is not Aquinas's view. For him, rational arguments in defence of Christian doctrine cannot claim to be probative. Christian doctrine has to be taught by God.[35] Hence the need for sacred *teaching*, i.e., *sacra doctrina*.[36]

---

[32] *St Thomas Aquinas: Faith, Reason and Theology: Questions I–IV of his Commentary on the* De Trinitate *of Boethius*, translated with Introduction and Notes by Armand Maurer (Toronto, 1987), xv. Pegis elaborates his position in 'Sub Ratione Dei: A Reply to Professor Anderson', *New Scholasticism*, 39 (1965). Pegis is here responding to James Anderson's 'Was St Thomas a Philosopher', *New Scholasticism*, 38 (1964). Anderson asked whether Aquinas was a philosopher and replied that he was.

[33] Readers of Aquinas sometimes translate *sacra doctrina* as 'theology'. This is highly misleading. See my 'Is Sacra Doctrina Theology?', *New Blackfriars*, 71 (1990). See also James A. Weisheipl, 'The Meaning of Sacra Doctrina in Summa Theologiae I, q. 1' (*Thomist*, 38 (1974)), 79 f.: '*Sacra doctrina* ... can be called "theology" only in the etymological sense of the term as *Sermo de Deo*, which every believer has.'

[34] 1a. 1. 1. Cf. 1a. 12. 1, 1a. 12. 11–13, 1a. 32. 1, 2a2ae. 1. 5; *Super De Trin.* 1, 4.

[35] Aquinas allows that one can cite reasons which might be held to carry *some* weight with respect to truths of faith. But for him they are no more than pointers or ways of drawing attention to what coheres with truths of faith. 'Arguments from human reason cannot avail to prove what must be received on faith' (1a. 1. 8 ad. 1). If *sacra doctrina* contains human reasoning, says Aquinas, that is 'to make clear other things that are put forward in this teaching' and to provide 'extrinsic and probable arguments' (ibid.).

[36] In fact, Aquinas does not exclusively identify *sacra doctrina* with 'teaching that philosophy cannot uncover', for he says that it also contains 'those truths about God

Another fact to be reckoned with in this connection is that, as we have seen, Aquinas's first teaching job was that of *baccalaureus biblicus*, a position which required him to study and expound the Bible. The same demand was laid upon him in 1256 when he became *magister in sacra pagina*. For Aquinas, as for the other professors at Paris in his day, the Bible was the word of God, and, therefore, something in the light of which other teaching was to be judged.[37] And he thought that it is here that *sacra doctrina* is to be found. For him, *sacra doctrina* and *sacra scriptura* can be used interchangeably.[38] In his view, access to revelation is given in the words of canonical Scripture, and especially in the teaching of Christ contained there. Christ, he says, is 'the first and chief teacher of the faith' (*fidei primus et principalis Doctor*) who, being God, knows divine truth without benefit of revelation. With him come the prophets and apostles (including the evangelists). And from all of them, and from nothing else, comes the matter of revelation.

> *Sacra doctrina*...uses the authority of the canonical Scriptures as an incontrovertible proof...for our faith rests upon the revelation made to the apostles and prophets, who wrote the canonical books...Faith adheres to all the articles of faith by reason of one mean, viz. on account of the First Truth proposed to us in the Scriptures, according to the teaching of the Church who has the right understanding of them.[39]

In this sense, *sacra doctrina* is, for Aquinas, the content of Scripture. It is also the content of the Christian creeds since, in his view, these basically amount to a restatement of what is in Scripture—a pocket Bible, so to speak. The Old and New Testaments need to be studied with care, he argues, since 'the truth of faith is contained in Holy

---

which human reason could have discovered' (1a. 1. 1). But throughout his discussion of *sacra doctrina* the emphasis falls on it being a matter of revelation *qua* teaching given to those unable to come to the truth without it. Even where *sacra doctrina* is a matter of what human reason can discover, says Aquinas, it consists of truth 'which would only be known by a few, and that after a long time, and with the admixture of many errors' (ibid.).

[37] Aquinas calls God the author of Scripture (*auctor sacrae scripturae est Deus*: 1a. 1. 10). For Aquinas and Scripture, see J. van der Ploeg, 'The Place of Holy Scripture in the Theology of St Thomas', *Thomist*, 10 (1947); B. Smalley, *The Study of the Bible in the Middle Ages* (Oxford, 1941); B. Smalley, *The Gospels in the Schools c.1100–c.1280* (London, 1985), v. 5; M.-D. Chenu, *Toward Understanding Saint Thomas* (Chicago, 1964); Per Erik Persson, *Sacra Doctrina: Reason and Revelation in Aquinas* (Oxford, 1970).

[38] See 1a. 1. 1, 1a. 1. 8, and 1a. 1. 9.

[39] 1a. 1. 8 ad. 2 and 2a2ae. 5. 3 ad. 2. Cf. 1a. 36. 2 ad. 2.

Writ diffusely, under various modes of expression, and sometimes obscurely, so that, in order to gather the truth of faith from Holy Writ, one needs long study and practice'.[40] The creeds are needed to make the truth of faith quickly accessible to everyone. But they add nothing to what is already contained in Scripture. They merely summarize or highlight with a view to the needs of those who hear them.[41]

Teaching such as this, central as it is to Aquinas's thinking, clearly marks him out as a theologian.[42] But there is also much in his writings which allows us to approach him as a philosopher on a level with other philosophers. For one thing, as we saw above, he wrote commentaries on philosophical texts. And these are widely held to be fine examples of their kind. He also drew on the writings of philosophers, and he offered arguments for conclusions which, in his view, could be reached without benefit of special revelation—conclusions about the existence and nature of God, for example, and conclusions about matters of logic, politics, ethics, and the nature of human beings. Much that he has to say on these matters can be studied on its own terms by anyone, whether Christian or not. And it has, in fact, been studied in this way. Even when Aquinas is directly engaged with what we might take to be theology rather than philosophy (when he is discussing matters such as the Christian doctrines of the Trinity and the Incarnation, for instance), his regular method involves reasoning on the basis of data revealed. And he thinks of this reasoning as conforming to standards acceptable by anyone, whether Christian or not.

The treatment of *sacra doctrina* is again relevant at this point. For, though Aquinas thinks of *sacra doctrina* as revealed and, on that score, above reason, he also calls it a science (*scientia*) more noble (*dignior*) than other sciences and especially to be called wisdom (*sapientia*), a

---

[40] 2a2ae. 1. 9 ad. 1.

[41] 2a2ae. 1. 9 ad. 2.

[42] Cf. Walter H. Principe, *Thomas Aquinas' Spirituality* (Toronto, 1984), 9: 'Thomas Aquinas always was and always intended to be a theologian. If he was open to nature and to reason, his very original philosophy of *esse*, the act of existing, and his use of reason as well as of Greek and Arabic philosophy, were all within a rich theology—a theology working within faith and trying to get some further understanding of the mysteries of faith. Even his commentaries on Aristotle and his philosophical treatises were preparatory to their use in his theological writings, which form the great bulk of his works. His disputed questions and his great *summae* are theological works, and it is often forgotten that his regular, constant teaching consisted of commentaries on sacred scripture.'

science whose subject is God and in which proof can be said to be involved. By this he means that we can draw out what is implicit in revelation by a formally valid process of inference. On his account, therefore, argument is possible with regard to *sacra doctrina*. We are, so he thinks, in no position to argue with someone who accepts nothing in the body of revealed truth. But we can argue with someone who accepts some of it. Since revealed truth is certainly true, we can also presume that objections levelled against it can somehow be shown to be unfounded.

Since faith rests upon infallible truth, and since the contrary of a truth can never be demonstrated, it is clear that the arguments brought against faith cannot be demonstrations, but are difficulties which can be answered.[43]

So one might just as well say that Aquinas was both a theologian and a philosopher. Much of what he says can be read either as philosophy or as theology. It is, perhaps, most accurate of all simply to call him a Christian thinker, though this should not be taken to mean that his thought can be divided into two: a system of philosophy, founded solely on reason, and—based on and completing this—a system of revealed theology. He thinks as a Christian, and he uses his ability to think in a way which, in his view, does all that it can to show that the revelation given in Christianity is not just a creed for those who cannot think and give reasons for what they believe.

2. Saint and Thinker

He was also, of course, a Christian saint. He gave his life to God and he did so wholeheartedly in a way which came to inspire others. But it is worth remarking that he did not altogether conform to conventional notions of sanctity. As Simon Tugwell observes:

For one thing, he did not work miracles. At the time of his canonization so few miracles could be found in his life that it was raised as an objection against canonizing him, apparently, and John XXII is said to have retorted that every question he answered was a miracle.[44]

According to Martin Grabmann, Aquinas seems to have been the first person canonized chiefly for being a theologian and teacher.[45]

---

[43] 1a. 1. 8.
[44] Tugwell, *Albert and Thomas*, 259.
[45] Martin Grabmann, 'Die Kanonisation des heiligen Thomas', *Divus Thomas*, 1 (1923), 241 f. It should, however, be noted that the process of canonization by the

The records testify that Aquinas was devoted to prayer, and to the life of a religious order bound by vows of poverty, chastity, and obedience. He had a special love of the Mass, and he was famous for a commitment to poverty and austerity. His writings are clearly those of one in love with God and the Word Incarnate. But, even by the standards of religious orders, there is no particular reason for thinking him unusually austere or ascetic. If he was extreme about anything, it seems to have been work. So it is in his writings that we glimpse him best. And what emerges of his character from them is chiefly twofold.

First, it is clear above all that Aquinas was enormously inquisitive. He did not share St Albert's interest in the nuts and bolts of the world around us. Albert could tramp around studying flies and ostriches, while Aquinas was hard to coax from his room.[46] But in matters more abstract he moves from question to question with a breathtaking eagerness. He is always asking 'Why?' or 'What?' One might even say that Aquinas's whole system rests on a question. This is because the most important element in his thinking is God, and because God, for him, is an answer to puzzlement (*admiratio*), an answer which leaves us with yet more questions. Aquinas is not content simply to say that God is. He wants to explore the divine in as many ways as possible.

Second, Aquinas seems to have been very much concerned to communicate ideas. This is clearly manifest in the style of his prose. He has been condemned from the standpoint of literary criticism, as we shall see below, and it is fair to say that he does not compare with those theological authors whose prose can at times be justifiably counted as outstanding literature—authors like St Augustine, for example. But he writes with impeccable clarity, which says much for his cast of mind. It shows him to be someone wanting us to see what he is talking about rather than wanting us to see him talking about it. It shows him to be concerned with what is being said rather than who is saying it.

Contrary to an impression had by many, Aquinas's writings also

papacy had only been established shortly before the time of Aquinas by Innocent III. So the fact that Aquinas was the first person canonized chiefly for being a theologian and teacher does not mean that theologians and teachers had not been regarded as saints before this time. It merely means that they had not been canonized before then.

[46] A. Borgnet (ed.), *Alberti Magni opera omnia* (Paris, 1890-9), xiv. 88 and 118. Ferrua, *Thomae Aquinatis ...*, 315.

indicate that he was very open-minded. Unlike many of his followers, he was a cautious thinker not given to supposing that any one authority has all the answers. He quotes eminent sources, but he can also see fit to disagree with them on occasion. He even disagrees with Aristotle, so it would be wrong to say, as has often been said, that Aquinas is just an Aristotelian. Even when he supports Aristotle, the emphasis is not: 'Aristotle said it, so it must be true.' His usual line is: 'It is true and Aristotle made the point well.' Readers of Aquinas in the late nineteenth and early twentieth centuries were taught that he was an 'Aristotelian' rather than a 'Platonist'. But, as well as being influenced by Aristotle, he was also indebted to elements in the thought of Plato and to later writers of a Platonic caste of mind (Neoplatonists). He commented, for instance, on the *Book of Causes* (*Liber de causis*), an excerpted and adapted version of the *Elements of Theology* by the late Neoplatonist Proclus (*c*.410–85).[47] Like Albert before him, he also commented on Denys the Areopagite. As Josef Pieper says, the truth is that 'Thomas was neither Platonist nor Aristotelian; he was both'.[48] Far from thinking that all wisdom resides in a single school of thought, his desire seems to have been to draw, with gratitude for diversity, on as much as was available to him.

Reading Aquinas Today

Aquinas has been read by thousands of people. And his impact has been considerable, especially on theology. St Pius V called him 'the most brilliant light of the Church'. According to Pope Paul V he was the 'defender of the Catholic Church and the conqueror of heretics'. St Ignatius of Loyola (*c*.1491–1556) made him compulsory reading for early aspirants to the Jesuits. His influence can be clearly seen in the teachings of numerous Church Councils and in the writings

---

[47] For a detailed discussion of Aquinas and his Platonic background see Edward Booth, OP, *Aristotelian Aporetic Ontology in Islamic and Christian Thinkers* (Cambridge, 1983), chs. 2 and 6. See also R. J. Henle, *Saint Thomas and Platonism* (The Hague, 1956) and W. J. Hankey, *God in Himself: Aquinas' Doctrine of God as Expounded in the Summa Theologiae* (Oxford, 1987). Aquinas used William of Moerbecke's translation of the *Elements of Theology*, for which one may consult *Proclus: Elementatio theologica*, trans. William Moerbecke and ed. Helmut Boese (Louvain, 1987). An English edition of the *Elements* is edited by E. R. Dodds (2nd edn., Oxford, 1963).

[48] Josef Pieper, *Guide to Thomas Aquinas* (Notre Dame, Ind., 1987), 22.

of many subsequent theologians.[49] In the 1917 Code of Canon Law his is the only name mentioned in the canon on the training of priests, where it is said that Catholic priests should receive their philosophical and theological instruction according to his 'method, doctrine and principles'.[50] According to the 1983 Code, echoing the teaching of the Second Vatican Council,[51] he is to be taken 'in particular as their teacher'.[52]

To modern readers, however, Aquinas may seem rather off-putting for a number of reasons. To begin with, there is the fact that he wrote in Latin, and in prose packed with technical terms and allusions to authors of which most people nowadays have never heard. Another possible source of aversion is his style of writing. Though he writes clearly, his text does not sparkle. As Thomas Gilby says, when commenting on the *Summa theologiae*:

Passages of fine writing are rare, and these tease you with the feeling that elsewhere he was humdrum by choice ... The pace seldom quickens from a steady jog, the movement is not lissom, the syntax not versatile, the vocabulary is more spare than the ideology. There is no ornamentation, no attempt at elegant variation, no subtlety of tint; the sentences as they stand are like a scientist's jottings in basic English. Treat the *Summa* as a lexicon for a philosophy of religion, and it will not be surprising if the ideas delivered straight from it taste like food from a deep-freeze.[53]

This hardly amounts to a recommendation. Nor does the fact that Aquinas often deals with questions which cannot now be taken very seriously. Should Christ have been born in winter? Did the star which appeared at his birth belong to the heavenly system, or was it

[49] For a concise account of Aquinas's impact on those influenced by him, see Gerald McCool, *The Neo-Thomists* (*forthcoming*).

[50] Canon 589.

[51] Vatican II's 'Decree on the Training of Priests' lays down that Aquinas should be seriously studied. Cf. Austin Flannery, OP (ed.), *Vatican Council II: The Conciliar and Post Conciliar Documents* (Leominster, 1981), 719 ff.

[52] Canon 252.

[53] Appendix 3 of vol. i of the Blackfriars *Summa*, 52. Cf. Beryl Smalley commenting on the difference between Albert's writings on Scripture and Aquinas's commentaries: 'To read him [Aquinas] after Albert is like passing from a Victorian salon, littered with furniture and ornaments, to a white-washed "functional" living room' (*The Gospels and the Schools*, 261). One might, however, note that some have found aesthetic merit in Aquinas's way of writing. Cf. Pieper, *Guide to Thomas Aquinas*, who cites *Summa contra Gentiles*, 2, 3 ('sic ergo patet ... Deo sententiam') and observes: 'This sentence, it seems to me, has a distinct kinship to the last bars of a Bach organ fugue. Beauty of language, then, certainly exists in the works of Aquinas. But it is not really the beauty of a work of art. This language is beautiful as a perfect tool is beautiful' (110).

specially created? Why do fat men produce little semen? These are all issues in the *Summa theologiae*,[54] but they surely do not warrant much discussion today.

The difficulty which all this might seem to present is also compounded by two other facts. The first is that Aquinas has nothing to say on many subjects which currently engage modern readers. The second is that some of his views now appear generally unacceptable, if not plainly absurd. For example (though inevitably), he offers no discussion of issues which have arisen in religious studies only in the course of the last fifty years or so—the message of Christianity after Auschwitz or Hiroshima, for instance. Since he wrote before the rise of modern biblical criticism, he also has a dated approach to the Scriptures. And he has little to say on the subject of women. He certainly talks about them. But modern feminists will recoil from some of his observations.[55] Should woman have been created in the beginning? Yes, replies Aquinas. But only to help man in the work of procreation.[56] Women, he suggests, are naturally defective. They are 'by nature subordinate to man, because the power of rational discernment is by nature stronger in man'.[57] They 'seldom keep a firm grip on things',[58] and they must be especially sober since 'they are not tough enough to withstand their longings'.[59]

This is not the stuff of which modern theology is made. And Aquinas's philosophical agenda is also somewhat different from that of thinkers in recent years. Philosophers since the seventeenth century have been much preoccupied with questions concerning the possibility of knowledge. They have typically asked questions like 'Can we know anything?', or 'Is there a world distinct from our ideas?' But, though Aquinas has views about knowledge, he has no great interest in such issues. We may say of him what C. C. W. Taylor says of Aristotle.

While Aristotle was certainly aware of sceptical challenges to claims to knowledge, whether in general or in specific areas, the justification of knowledge claims in response to such challenges, which has been central to most

---

[54] 3a. 35. 8; 3a. 36. 7; 1a. 119. 2.
[55] Modern feminists *do* recoil from some of his statements about women. See for example, Uta Ranke-Heinemann, *Eunuchs for Heaven: The Catholic Church and Sexuality* (London, 1990), ch. 16.
[56] 1a. 92. 1.
[57] 1a. 92. 1 ad 1 and 3.
[58] 2a2ae. 156. 1 ad. 1.
[59] 2a2ae. 149. 4.

epistemology since Descartes, is at best peripheral to Aristotle's concerns ...
In particular, the central problem of post-Cartesian epistemology, that of
showing how our experience may reasonably be held to be experience of an
objective world, is hardly a problem for Aristotle. The problem for the post-
Cartesian philosopher is how, once having retreated in the face of Cartesian
doubt to the stronghold of private experience, he or she can advance sufficiently far beyond that experience to recover the objective world. Aristotle,
never having made the retreat, does not have the problem of the advance.[60]

In this respect, as in many others, Aquinas also differs considerably
from influential philosophers such as Descartes (1591–1650), Locke
(1632–1704), Hume (1711–76), and Berkeley (1685–1753). Some
modern philosophers have been positively dismissive of him—a
classic example being Bertrand Russell (1887–1970). While there
are theologians who find fault with Aquinas because of his philosophical interests, Russell condemned him for being a theologian.

There is little of the true philosophic spirit in Aquinas. He does not, like the
Platonic Socrates, set out to follow wherever the argument may lead. He is
not engaged in an inquiry, the result of which it is impossible to know in
advance. Before he begins to philosophize, he already knows the truth; it is
declared in the Catholic faith ... The finding of arguments for a conclusion
given in advance is not philosophy, but special pleading.[61]

Yet, as Anthony Kenny observes, Russell's remark 'comes oddly
from a philosopher who [in *Principia Mathematica*] took three hundred
and sixty dense pages to offer a proof that $1 + 1 = 2$'.[62] And, in spite
of misgivings which one might have in approaching Aquinas, there is
more to attract than to repel in him.

The point made by Gilby concerning his style cuts both ways. This
is because readers of Aquinas generally know what he is trying to say
precisely because of the way he writes. He is much easier to read
than many philosophers and theologians. One of his early advocates
claimed that

people of all sorts can easily benefit from his writings according to whatever
little intellectual capacity they have, and that is why even the laity and people
who are not very bright look for his writings and desire to have them.[63]

---

[60] 'Aristotle's Epistemology', in Stephen Everson (ed.), *Companions to Ancient
Thought, i: Epistemology* (Cambridge, 1990).
[61] Bertrand Russell, *A History of Western Philosophy* (London, 1946), 484 f.
[62] Anthony Kenny (ed.), *Aquinas: A Collection of Critical Essays* (London, 1969), 2.
[63] Ferrua, *Thomae Aquinatis ...*, 327.

Most serious readers of Aquinas will readily take the point.[64] And anyone will find that, though he wrote in an age of assumptions and questions different from those of today, he is chiefly concerned with perennial problems which are still at the centre of everyone's basic interests. God, truth, existence, people and their destiny: these are topics which are as fascinating now as ever they were. And they form the core of Aquinas's subject-matter. And, at his hands, they are treated with a skill that few authors can rival. Russell gave Aquinas low marks. Much more representative of philosophical opinion now, however, is the verdict offered by Anthony Kenny quoted above in the Preface.

It is, of course, true that Aquinas is dogmatic. But only in the sense that he never abandoned the view that there is teaching to be handed on.[65] His dogmatism is not that of someone who refuses to say why he thinks as he does. And, even in his concern to explain what his teaching comprises, he is constantly striving for enlightenment, not for a blind acceptance—as he indicates when describing the purpose of the university disputation. This, he says, is

> to instruct those who are listening, so that they will be brought to an understanding of the truth envisaged. Here one must rely on arguments which probe the root of truth and make people know how what is said is true; otherwise, if the Master decides the question simply by using sheer authorities, the hearer will certainly be left in no doubt that such and such is the case, but he will acquire no knowledge or understanding and will go away empty.[66]

At the outset, then, we may suggest that Aquinas has much to offer people who are anxious to think and understand. In subsequent chapters we will be seeing something of what it amounts to.

---

[64] It is worth adding that, though some attack Aquinas from the standpoint of literary criticism, others would defend him on the ground that his style is apposite to the matter in hand and the intent of the author. We should not, they would argue, confuse style with stylishness.

[65] His inaugural lecture of 1256 is a kind of meditation on the theme of teaching. The text is translated in Tugwell, *Albert and Thomas*, 355–60.

[66] *Quodl.* 9, 3.

2

Getting to God

AQUINAS holds that God is the Creator of everything and that human beings hold a special place in creation since they are redeemed or brought back to God by God himself in the person of Jesus Christ. Hence it is that, at the start of the *Summa theologiae*, he declares that he intends to set forth *sacra doctrina* by treating 'first, of God, secondly, of the journey to God of reasoning creatures, thirdly, of Christ, who, as man, is our road to God'.[1] The vision at work here, which in many ways echoes themes in Platonic thinking, is one in which God is the beginning and end of all things who draws us to himself as the one from whom we come. As M.-D. Chenu famously put it, the *Summa theologiae* has an *exitus–reditus* structure which Aquinas conceives of as reflecting the way things are in reality. It deals with a coming from God (*exitus*) and a return to him (*reditus*).[2]

But from where do we get the idea of God? Aquinas is famous for thinking that the existence of God can be proved by rational argument. That he thought this is about the only thing many people know of him. For them Aquinas is the great (or misguided) champion of the view that belief in God is something which can be vindicated by demonstration. It is therefore worth noting immediately that, in one sense, Aquinas is not at all worried about making out a case for God's existence. He knows of those with no Christian faith (ancient philosophers and 'infidels' as he calls them), but he does not really doubt the reality of God. It is most unlikely that he ever encountered an atheist in the modern sense. Nor does he maintain that anyone has an obligation to weigh up the evidence for theism. There is nothing, he says, 'to stop someone accepting on faith some truth which that person cannot demonstrate, even if that truth in itself is such that demonstration could make it evident'.[3] In common with some

---

[1] Introduction to 1a. 2.
[2] M.-D. Chenu, *Toward Understanding Saint Thomas*, trans. A. M. Landry and D. Hughes (Chicago, 1964), ch. 11.
[3] 1a. 2. 2 ad. 1.

modern philosophers, he thinks it perfectly proper for someone to start by taking God's existence for granted.[4] At the end of the day, his basic position is roughly that of St Anselm (*c.*1033–1109): 'I do not seek to understand so that I may believe; but I believe so that I may understand.'[5]

In spite of the dubious uses to which it has been put, however, the tradition of associating Aquinas with attempts to argue for God's existence is, indeed, legitimate. For, he does think it possible to state rational grounds for believing in God, and in various texts he tries to say what these are.[6] Though at one level he insists that one need not worry about the question 'Does God exist?', at another level he takes it very seriously. And his answer is unequivocal. His view is that God exists and that reasons can be given for saying so—reasons which ought to be acceptable to any fair-minded or impartial person. It has been claimed that Aquinas never really believed that God's existence is provable. But that is exactly what he did believe. This is clear from *Summa theologiae*, 1a. 2. 2 and *Summa contra Gentiles*, 1. 9, where he says that 'we can demonstrate . . . that God exists' and that God can be made known as we 'proceed through demonstrative arguments'. 'Demonstrative arguments' here means what it does for Aristotle— i.e. arguments which proceed from premiss(es) which entail a given conclusion on pain of contradiction.

Ways not to Get to God

What might these arguments be? Perhaps the first thing to note in turning to this question is that Aquinas always approaches it in an oblique manner—by noting how, in his view, we *cannot* defend belief in God's existence. He denies, for example, that God's existence is evident to us in the sense that logically self-evident propositions are, i.e. propositions which clearly cannot be false. We cannot doubt that if all men are mortal and if Socrates is a man then Socrates is mortal. To do so would be to land ourselves in contradiction. According to

---

[4] Cf. Alvin Plantinga, 'Reason and Belief in God', in Alvin Plantinga and Nicholas Wolterstorff (eds.), *Faith and Rationality* (Notre Dame, Ind., 1983).

[5] *Proslogion*, 1. Anselm's position on faith and reason is outlined by R. W. Southern in *Saint Anselm: A Portrait in a Landscape* (Cambridge, 1990), 123 ff.

[6] The best survey of Aquinas's arguments for the existence of God is Fernand van Steenberghen, *Le Problème de l'existence de Dieu dans les écrits de S. Thomas d'Aquin* (Louvain-La-Neuve, 1980).

Aquinas, however, there is no contradiction in saying that there is no God.

Nobody can think the opposite of a self-evident proposition, as Aristotle's discussion of first principles makes clear. But the opposite of the proposition 'God exists' can be thought, for *the fool* in the psalms *said in his heart: There is no God.*[7]

Some have argued that we cannot doubt God's existence since God is Truth and one cannot consistently disbelieve in truth (one cannot consistently say, 'It is true that there is no truth'). But, Aquinas replies, though it is evident that truth exists, one may doubt whether there is a 'First Truth', i.e. God.[8] There is, he says, a connection between truth and existence, so we can hold that there is truth because it is clear that there are things. However, he continues,

that there is a first being which is the cause of every being is not immediately evident . . . [and] . . . neither is it self-evident that the truth of all things derives from some first truth.[9]

St Augustine held that in order to know any truth the human mind requires special assistance from God. Such a position might furnish an argument from Truth to God, but Aquinas rejects it in his commentary on Boethius's *De Trinitate*. Here he asks whether 'the human mind needs a new illumination by the divine light in order to know the truth' and he cites Augustine as a supporter of the view that 'no one can learn from others unless God teaches one's mind from within'.[10] He replies by insisting, in contradistinction also to writers such as Avicenna (980–1037), that people by nature have the necessary equipment for knowledge without special outside assistance.[11]

He is also unhappy with the idea that everyone has an innate knowledge of God in the sense of possessing an explicit awareness of God's existence which all of us have by nature. There is, he concedes, a sense in which everyone has knowledge of God. St Paul teaches that 'ever since the creation of the world [God's] invisible nature, namely his eternal power and deity, has been clearly per-

---

[7] 1a. 2. 2. In Aristotle, cf. *Metaphysics*, 4. 3. 1005^{b}11 and *Posterior Analytics*, 1. 10. 76^{b}23 ff.

[8] 1a. 2. 1 ad. 3.

[9] *De ver.* 10. 12.

[10] Augustine, *De magistro*, 12. 40 and 14. 45.

[11] *Super De Trin.* 1. 1.

ceived in the things that have been made'.[12] In his commentary on this teaching, Aquinas agrees.[13] He also accepts that in everyone, 'there is naturally implanted something from which one can arrive at knowledge of the fact of God's existence'[14] and that we desire by nature a happiness which can only be found in God. Yet, he adds, 'the existence of God is not implanted in us by nature in any clear or specific way', and the knowledge which everyone has of God 'is not, simply speaking, awareness that there is a God, any more than to be aware of someone approaching is to be aware of Peter, even if it should be Peter approaching'.[15]

In pressing this line of thinking Aquinas is even led to reject one of the most famous arguments for God's existence—the so-called 'Ontological Argument', most commonly associated with St Anselm.[16] Proponents of this argument hold that God, by de-finition, is something than which nothing greater can be thought. They then urge that anything matching this definition has real or extra-mental existence since existing in reality as well as in the understanding is greater than existing in the understanding alone. But, in common with most modern philosophers, that is not how Aquinas sees things. According to him:

Even if the meaning of the word 'God' were generally recognized to be 'that than which nothing greater can be thought', nothing thus defined would thereby be granted existence in the world of fact, but merely as thought about. Unless one is given that something in fact exists than which nothing greater can be thought—and this nobody denying the existence of God would grant—the conclusion that God in fact exists does not follow.[17]

---

[12] Rom. 1: 20.

[13] *Super ad Rom.* 6. 117.

[14] *De ver.* 10. 12.

[15] 1a. 2. 1 ad. 1.

[16] Cf. Anselm, *Proslogion*, 2 and 3, and Descartes, *Meditations on First Philosophy*, 5. The name 'Ontological Argument' derives from Immanuel Kant. For a brief introduction to and discussion of the argument, see my *An Introduction to the Philosophy of Religion* (Oxford, 1982), ch. 4. In what follows I am not purporting to explain how Anselm viewed his *Proslogion* argument. What I expound is often said to be Anselm's argument, but one may take leave to doubt that. See my '*Quod vere sit Deus*: Why Anselm Thought that God Truly Exists', *New Blackfriars*, 72 (1991), and G. E. M. Anscombe, 'Why Anselm's Proof in the *Proslogion* is not an Ontological Argument', *Thoreau Quarterly*, 17 (Winter/Spring 1985).

[17] 1a. 2. 1 ad. 2. It has often been observed that Aquinas's treatment of the Ontological Argument does not seem to engage fully with the argument as found in Anselm. Insofar as this is true, the reason might lie in the fact that the version of the argument discussed by Aquinas was not so much Anselm's as a version of Anselm's

In any case, Aquinas adds, there is a problem concerning our knowledge of God's nature. We know, for example, what a man is. So we can safely maintain that man, by definition, is an animal. But, says Aquinas, we cannot be sure that God exists from our knowledge of what he is by definition.

> The proposition 'God exists' is self-evident in itself (*per se nota secundum se*), for ... its subject and predicate are identical, since God is his own existence. But because what it is to be God is not evident to us, the proposition is not self-evident to us, and needs to be made evident [it is *per se nota secundum se* but not *per se nota quoad nos*].[18]

How, then, can it be made evident? On what basis can we claim knowledge of God's existence? Aquinas's reply is that we can know of God only on the basis of what is evident to us. And that, he thinks, is what we perceive by means of our senses. According to him we must proceed from world to God, from effect to cause. This, he observes, is the sense of the passage from St Paul noted above. We do not start with a knowledge of God. We begin as knowing the world in which we live. So we will have to be content with reasoning to God's existence from that.

> There are two types of demonstration. One showing 'why', follows the natural order of things among themselves, arguing from cause to effect; the other, showing 'that', follows the order in which we know things, arguing from effect to cause ... Now any effect of a cause demonstrates that that cause exists, in cases where the effect is better known to us, since effects are dependent upon causes, and can only occur if the causes already exist. From effects evident to us, therefore, we can demonstrate what is not evident to us, namely that God exists.[19]

God and His Effects: The Five Ways

1. Preliminaries

Aquinas's best-known defence of this conclusion comes in his so-called 'Five Ways' (*Quinque Viae*) found in the second question of

argument current in the 13th century and offered by writers such as Alexander of Hales (*c.*1186–1245). For a discussion of the matter, see Jean Chatillon, 'De Guillaume d'Auxerre à saint Thomas d'Aquin: l'Argument de saint Anselme chez les premiers scholastiques du XIIIe siècle' in Jean Chatillon, *D'Isidore de Séville à saint Thomas d'Aquin* (London, 1985). I know of no evidence proving that Aquinas read Anselm's *Proslogion*.

[18] 1a. 2. 1.   [19] 1a. 2. 2.

the *Summa theologiae*. So at this point I need to say something about these. Before I descend to details, however, I ought to make three introductory points.

The first is that the arguments of the Five Ways are by no means original. They are heavily indebted to the work of authors earlier than Aquinas—to Aristotle, for example, and to Jewish and Arabic authors such as Maimonides (1135–1204), Avicenna, and Averroës (1126–98).[20] Aquinas is not a slave of his sources in the Five Ways. This is clearest of all with respect to the manner in which he draws in them on Aristotle. For, though it can be said that in some sense Aristotle believed in God, and though his arguments for God are used by Aquinas in the Five Ways, his notion of God differs strikingly from that of Aquinas. But it still remains that a detectable set of arguments lies behind the Five Ways. They do not come out of the blue.

Secondly, although Aquinas says that the Five Ways are arguments for the existence of God, they are not intended as an exhaustive defence of belief in God's existence. Contrary to what is sometimes supposed, they are only a first stage. More precisely, they do not purport to show that God exists with all the attributes traditionally ascribed to him. All they explicitly argue is that there is (1) 'some first cause of change not itself being changed by anything', (2) 'some first cause', (3) 'something which must be and owes this to no other thing than itself [and is] the cause that other things are', (4) something 'which causes in all other things their being, their goodness, and whatever other perfection they have', and (5) something 'with understanding' by which 'everything in nature ... is directed to its goal'. If we read the Five Ways in context, we will find that Aquinas builds on them and develops an account of what must be true of God in the light of further considerations and questions. Their purpose is to set the ball rolling, not to bring the game to an end. They comprise the first phase of a discussion which stretches well beyond them. As William Lane Craig observes:

Thomas's proofs for the existence of God encompass the whole of 1a. 2–11 in the *Summa theologiae*. Modern readers, used as they are to anthologised versions of Aquinas's Five Ways, all too often fail to grasp this important

---

[20] For introductions to Maimonides and Averroës see Oliver Leaman, *Averroës and His Philosophy* (Oxford, 1988) and *Moses Maimonides* (London, 1990). Concise documentation of the 'sources' of Aquinas's Five Ways can be found in Leo J. Elders, SVD, *The Philosophical Theology of St Thomas Aquinas* (Leiden, 1990), ch. 3.

point. Aquinas is sometimes criticised for what is thought to be his over-hasty conclusion: '... and this is what everybody understands by God'; but this misunderstanding only arises by tearing Aquinas's proofs out of their proper context. It is not until the finish of question 11 that the existence of what we mean by 'God' has been demonstrated.[21]

The third point to note concerns what we may call the role of chronology in the Five Ways. To understand it, the best thing to do is to begin by drawing a distinction between different kinds of causal relations.

I was produced by my parents. And they were produced by their parents. So, in a sense, I was produced by my grandparents. But my grandparents were not doing anything as I was being born. They were dead. I came from them not in the sense that my coming to be required my dependence on them as I came to be. I came from them in the sense that they in the past did something which finally resulted in my coming to be.

Let us put this by saying that the causal relationship in which I stand to my grandparents is a chronological one. With that terminology in mind, we can now go on to observe that not all causal relationships are chronological.

Consider, for instance, the statue of Nelson standing on Nelson's Column in Trafalgar Square in London. It can be attributed to the fact that someone put it there in the past. So it can be accounted for in something like the way my coming into being depended on my grandparents. But it also depends on the column supporting it. Remove the column and Nelson will fall. The position of his statue depends on the column's support all the time it stands there for the tourists to photograph.

With all that behind us we can now note that it is causal relationships belonging to this second type with which Aquinas is concerned in the Five Ways. How his concern bears fruit should become evident presently. For the moment, though, we may say that his view is that there are phenomena which depend on God in something like the way the statue of Nelson depends for its support on the column. In the Five Ways, God is not a cause who at some time past set a process going which then in time had certain effects. He is the cause of effects which depend on him *as they occur.*

---

[21] William Lane Craig, *The Cosmological Argument from Plato to Leibniz* (London, 1980), 159.

2. The Five Ways: The Arguments

In general, Aquinas's Five Ways employ a simple pattern of argument. Each begins by drawing attention to some general feature of things known to us on the basis of experience. It is then suggested that none of these features can be accounted for in ordinary mundane terms, that we must move to a level of explanation which transcends that with which we are familiar.

Another way of putting it is to say that, according to the Five Ways, questions we can raise with respect to what we encounter raise further questions the answer to which can only be thought of as lying beyond what we encounter.

Take, for example, the First Way, in which the influence of Aristotle is particularly prevalent.[22] Here the argument starts from change or motion in the world.[23] It is clear, says Aquinas, that there is such a thing—he cites as an instance the change involved in wood becoming hot when subjected to fire.[24] How, then, may we account for it?

According to Aquinas, anything changed or moved is changed or moved by something else. *Omne quod movetur ab alio movetur.* This, he reasons, is because a thing which has changed has become what it was not to begin with, which can only happen if there is something from which the reality attained by the thing as changed somehow derives.[25] Therefore, he concludes, there must be a first cause of things being changed or moved. For there cannot be an endless series of things changed or moved by other things since if every change in a series of connected changes depends on a prior changer,

---

[22] Aristotle presents an argument like that of Aquinas in *Physics*, 7. Aquinas acknowledges his debt to Aristotle's argument in *SG* 1. 13 where he offers a longer version of what appears in the *Summa theologiae* as the First Way.

[23] Aquinas here is concerned with what he calls *motus*. For him this includes change of quality, quantity, or place (hence the legitimacy of translating *motus* as 'change' or 'movement').

[24] Aquinas calls the First Way 'the most obvious' (*manifestior*) proof. That, I presume, is chiefly because what he calls *motus* is something which impinges on us all the time. Maimonides and Averroës are two other authors who thought that the truth of the reasoning which surfaces in the First Way is particularly evident. Cf. Maimonides, *The Guide for the Perplexed*, 1. 70 and Averroës, *Epitome of Metaphysics*, 4.

[25] Aquinas does not mean that the world does not contain things which can be thought of as changing themselves. He does not, for example, deny that people initiate change in themselves or that animals can do so. He would say, however, that nothing in the world is wholly the source of its own change. See *The Philosophy of Thomas Aquinas*, ed. Christopher Martin (London, 1988), 61. Cf. *SG* 1. 13.

the whole system of changing things is only derivatively an initiator of change and still requires something to initiate its change. There must be something which causes change or motion in things without itself being changed or moved by anything. There must be an unchanged changer or an unmoved mover.

Anything which is moved is moved by something else ... To cause motion is to bring into being what was previously only able to be, and this can only be done by something that already is ... Now the same thing cannot at the same time be both actually *x* and potentially *x*, though it can be actually *x* and potentially *y*: the actually hot cannot at the same time be potentially hot, though it can be potentially cold. Consequently, a thing which is moved cannot itself cause that same movement; it cannot move itself. Of necessity therefore anything moved is moved by something else ... Now we must stop somewhere, otherwise there will be no first cause of the movement and as a result no subsequent causes ... Hence one is bound to arrive at some first cause of things being moved which is not itself moved by anything, and this is what everybody understands by God.

The pattern of the First Way is repeated in the rest of the Five Ways. According to the Second Way, there are causes in the world which bring it about that other things come to be. There are, as Aquinas puts it, causes which are related as members of a series. In that case, however, there must, he adds, be a first cause, or something which is not itself caused to be by anything. For causes arranged in series must have a first member.

In the observable world causes are found to be ordered in series; we never observe, nor ever could, something causing itself, for this would mean it preceded itself, and this is not possible. Such a series of causes must however stop somewhere; for in it an earlier member causes an intermediate and the intermediate a last ... Now if you eliminate a cause you also eliminate its effects, so that you cannot have a last cause, nor an intermediate one, unless you have a first.

According to the Third Way[26] there are things which are perishable (e.g. plants) and things which are imperishable (in Aquinas's

---

[26] Aquinas's sources for the Third Way have been a subject of some scholarly controversy. Some of its key concepts are found in Aristotle. Maimonides offers an argument very similar to that of the Third Way in *The Guide for the Perplexed*, 2. 1. One can also compare the Third Way with a proof of God's existence given by Avicenna (cf. Arthur J. Arberry, *Avicenna on Theology* (London, 1951), 25 for the text in English). But Aquinas's Third Way is a distinct argument and not just a straightforward repetition of earlier arguments with which it may be compared.

language, imperishable things are 'necessary' beings or things which 'must be').[27] But why should this be so? The answer, says Aquinas, has to lie in something imperishable and dependent for its existence on nothing.[28]

Now a thing that must be, may or may not owe this necessity to something else. But just as we must stop somewhere in a series of causes, so also in the series of things which must be and owe this to other things.

In the Fourth and Fifth Ways Aquinas turns to different questions. Why are there things with varying degrees of perfection?[29] And how does it come about that in nature there are things which, while not themselves intelligent, operate in a regular or goal-directed way?[30] Perfections in things, Aquinas suggests, imply a source of perfections. Where there are degrees of perfection, there must, he thinks, be something that has maximum perfection, and this must account for the occurrence of the perfection in other things. And the goal-directed activity of non-rational things suggests that they are governed by what is rational.

Some things are found to be more good, more true, more noble, and so on, and other things less. But such comparative terms describe varying degrees of approximation to a superlative; for example, things are hotter and hotter the nearer they approach to what is hottest. Something therefore is the truest and best and most noble of things. Now *when many things possess some property*

---

[27] See Patterson Brown, 'St Thomas' Doctrine of Necessary Being', in Anthony Kenny (ed.), *Aquinas: A Collection of Critical Essays* (London, 1969).

[28] There is a textual problem concerning the Third Way which my brief account of it bypasses. For a discussion of the issues and for a treatment of different interpretations of the Third Way see Steenberghen, *Le Problème de l'existence de Dieu*, 188–201 and Craig, *Cosmological Argument*, 182 ff.

[29] In the Fourth Way the background to the argument seems chiefly Platonic. Aquinas holds that perfection admits of degrees, a notion found in Plato, St Augustine, St Anselm, and many others. The Platonic theory which seems to lie behind the Fourth Way is expounded with reference to the Way in Anthony Kenny, *The Five Ways* (London, 1969), ch. 5.

[30] Here Aquinas invokes the notion of final causality or teleological explanation, which can be found in book 2 of Aristotle's *Physics*. For Aristotle, a final cause or a teleological explanation was an answer to the question 'To what end or purpose is this happening?' For an exposition and discussion of Aristotle on purpose in nature, see Richard Sorabji, *Necessity, Cause and Blame: Perspectives on Aristotle's Theory* (London, 1980), chs. 10 and 11. The argument of the Fifth Way is given in more detail by Aquinas in *De ver.* 5. 2. Teleological arguments for God are common in antiquity and in early Christian authors and medieval Arabic, Islamic, and Jewish writers. See Herbert A. Davidson, *Proofs for Eternity, Creation and the Existence of God in Medieval Islamic and Jewish Philosophy* (New York, 1987), ch. 7.

in common, the one most fully possessing it causes it in the others: fire, to use Aristotle's example, *the hottest of all things, causes all other things to be hot.* There is therefore something which causes in all other things their being, their goodness, and whatever other perfections they have.

Some things which lack awareness, namely bodies, operate in accordance with an end . . . Nothing however that lacks awareness tends to a goal except under the direction of someone with awareness and with understanding . . . Everything in nature, therefore, is directed to its goal by someone with understanding.

The Existence Argument

Though Aquinas distinguishes at least five ways of demonstrating God's existence, however, in arguing for the truth of theism he places special emphasis on one argument, which I shall call 'The Existence Argument'. It appears again and again in his writings, and it is often presupposed in contexts where it is not given explicitly. It is fleshed out in *De potentia* 7 and *Summa contra Gentiles*, 1. 22 and 2. 52. It also occurs in *De ente et essentia*, 4. But it is particularly concisely stated in *Summa theologiae*, 1a. 65. 1.

Whenever different things share something in common, there must be some cause of this sharing; precisely as different, they themselves do not account for it. Thus it is that whenever some one element is found in different things, these receive it from one cause, just as different hot bodies get their heat from one fire. Existence, however, is shared by all things, however much they differ. There must therefore be a single source of existence from which whatever exists in any manner whatsoever, whether invisible and spiritual or visible and material, obtains its existence.

In various places, Aquinas distinguishes different senses in which something can be said to be.[31] Here, though, his meaning is that the fact of there being actual subjects, real objects or individuals, ultimately means that something exists independently of any cause outside itself, something which accounts for the existence of everything else. Why? Aquinas's reasoning can be indicated as follows.

Suppose we forget about God for a moment. In that case we can simply note that various things exist. You and I continue to be. And the Taj Mahal does likewise. So much seems evident.

[31] For example, 1a. 3. 4 ad. 2.

Now the existence of things, Aquinas maintains, cannot be deduced from what they are by definition (from what Aquinas calls their 'nature' or 'essence'). You can know what a dog is without knowing that there are dogs (definitions of 'dog' would not cease to be valid even if dogs became extinct). It is not part of the nature or essence of a dog that it should exist. In this sense, Aquinas argues, existence is something different from nature or essence, and the actual existence of something cannot be explained simply on the basis of a knowledge of its nature or essence. It 'has' existence but 'is' not existence, as we might put it.

Well, says Aquinas, still forgetting about God for the moment, we can ask of anything having existence how it comes about that it does have existence. How come the thing exists? Confronted by something in the world, we can ask how it comes to be there—meaning not just 'What got it started?' but 'What keeps it going?'

It cannot, says Aquinas, be because the thing in question causes itself to exist. To do that it must, though not necessarily temporally, pre-exist itself, which is impossible.[32] For to cause existence is already to exist. So 'if a thing's existence differs from its nature, that existence must be externally caused'.[33]

Aquinas therefore maintains that there is a first source of existence—by which he means God. For, he adds, if the existence of everything depends on something which in turn depends for its existence on something else, the series of existing things will not be accounted for at all. There cannot be a never-ending series of things caused to be and causing to be. If each cause of A's existence were itself in need of a cause of its existence, then no cause of A could exist, and A itself could not exist. Since A does exist, and does need a cause, it follows that not all of A's causes are in need of a cause.

In other words, the need for causes of existence must come to an end: there must be a cause the existence of which is not itself in need of a cause. Given that there are things in whose nature or essence existence is not included, there is something which produces their being, something which makes them to be though nothing makes it to be.[34]

---

[32] 1a. 2. 3.

[33] 1a. 3. 4.

[34] Once again we have here an argument with antecedents. The existence argument in Aquinas is especially reminiscent of thinking propounded by Avicenna, for an

What you have here is the view that belief in God is to be taken seriously since, as well as asking what it is that causes some particular thing or class of things (as well as asking, 'What is the cause of there being Brian Davies?' or 'What is the cause of there being human beings?'), one can ask, 'Why is there anything at all?' or 'Why is there something rather than nothing?'[35] In Aquinas this view is stated by saying that all things apart from God share in or 'participate' in existence, while God *is* Existence—in Aquinas's Latin, that all things apart from God share in or participate in *esse* while God is *Esse* itself. 'We are bound to conclude that everything that is at all real is from God . . . All things other than God are not their own existence but share in existence.'[36] The ancient philosophers, says Aquinas, asked causal questions about things in the world. But some, he adds, 'climbed higher to the prospect of being as being' and 'observed the cause of things inasmuch as they are beings, not merely as things of such a kind or quality'.[37] These philosophers, Aquinas continues, were right. If something exists, either its existence follows from its nature (it cannot but exist), or it is brought about by something other than itself. Yet there cannot be an endless series of things bringing about the existence of others while themselves being brought about by something else. There has to be something which exists by nature. And this, for Aquinas, is God.

Creation

So God, for Aquinas, is the reason or cause of there being anything apart from himself. Or, as we may also say, God, for him, is the Creator. Some of the things which need to be said about Aquinas on the notion of creation will emerge in later chapters, for the notion of creation pervades his writings. But we can still at this point note the essentials of his teaching about it.

---

exposition of whom see Craig, *Cosmological Argument*, 86 ff. and Davidson, *Proofs for Eternity*, ch. 9. In chapter XII. 2 of his book Davidson traces the influence of Avicenna on later medieval writers including Aquinas. Connections between Aquinas and Avicenna (as well as Maimonides) are explored in David B. Burrell, *Knowing the Unknowable God: Ibn-Sina, Maimonides, Aquinas* (Notre Dame, Ind., 1986).

[35] Cf. Herbert McCabe, OP, *God Matters* (London, 1987), 2 ff.
[36] 1a. 44. 1.
[37] 1a. 44. 2.

To begin with, for example, we can note that creation by God (the act of creating) is, for Aquinas, the making of something from nothing. When things come to be in the world they always do so against a background where things already exist. They come to be from something, as, for example, I came to be from the sperm and egg which turned into me when I was conceived. According to Aquinas, however, with God's act of creating we have something different. We have the coming to be of things with no background of existing things, a coming to be which is not from anything. The only thing presupposed to creation is God. In creation, what is not (period) comes to be (period).

We must consider not only the emanation of a particular being from a particular agent, but also the emanation of all being from the universal cause which is God; and this emanation we designate by the name of creation. Now what proceeds by particular emanation is not presupposed to that emanation; as when a man is generated, he was not before, but man is made from *not-man*, and white from *not-white*. Hence if the emanation of the whole universal being from the first principle be considered, it is impossible that any being should be presupposed before this emanation. For nothing is the same as no being. Therefore, as the generation of a man is from the *not-being* which is *not-man*, so creation, which is the emanation of all being, is from the *not-being* which is nothing.[38]

Hence, not surprisingly, Aquinas can add (1) that a distinction must be drawn between creating and changing,[39] and (2) that only God can create. I can create a picture by moving bits of paint around and shaping it on a canvas, i.e. by bringing about a change in things. According to Aquinas, however, God, in creatively bringing something into existence, is not acting on anything so as to modify things somehow. He is effecting no alteration on what already exists before he creates. He makes things to be *ex nihilo* (from nothing), and only he can do this. Or as Aquinas himself puts it (drawing on the Existence Argument):

Creation is the proper activity of God alone. Effects which are more universal need to be taken to more universal and original causes. Among all effects the most universal is existence itself, which should accordingly be the proper effect of the first and most universal cause, which is God . . . Now to produce existence absolutely, not merely of this thing or that sort of thing,

---

[38] 1a. 45. 1.
[39] 1a. 45. 2.

belongs to the meaning of creation. Manifestly creation is the proper action of God himself.[40]

This means that all things depend on God for their continued existence. In saying that God is the Creator of something, Aquinas is not just saying that God just got it going at some time past. He means that God sustains it in being. In this sense his doctrine of creation is also a doctrine of continuous preservation.

There are two ways in which one thing may be kept in being by another. The first is indirect and incidental, as when one who removes a destructive force is said to preserve a thing in existence; for example, one who watches over a child lest it fall into a fire is said to preserve the child's life. The second is a *per se* and direct way of preserving a thing in existence, in so far, namely, as the thing preserved is so dependent that without the preserver it could not exist. This is the way that all creatures need God to keep them in existence.[41]

Strictly speaking, it goes contrary to Aquinas's language to talk of the continuing existence of things as a matter of God creating. 'It is true', he remarks, 'that *God worketh until now*—but by conserving and governing the creation he has made, not by making new creatures.'[42] The fact, however, remains that the conservation of things by God is, for Aquinas, closely related to their first coming into being. Both depend on God's activity as they come about.

The Beginning of the World

In short, it is important to recognize that God, for Aquinas, is not just an answer to the question 'What started the world?' He certainly holds that if the world had a beginning, then God must be the ultimate reason for this. But, as I indicated above, his arguments for God's existence are unconcerned with chronology. He thinks that God accounts for change (the First Way). But he also thinks that God would do this even if change had no beginning. And, in his view, even if the world had no beginning, God would be just as much the cause of things being (the Second Way), being such that they 'must be' (the Third Way), being more or less perfect (the Fourth

[40] 1a. 45. 5.
[41] 1a. 104. 1.
[42] 1a. 73. 2 ad. 1.

Way), and being governed in their behaviour by intelligence (the
Fifth Way). His line is that the world as it is now would not be there
if it were not for the fact that the world now depends on God
bringing it about. 'We have to imagine, not a linear or horizontal
series, so to speak, but a vertical hierarchy, in which a lower member
depends here and now on the present causal activity of the member
above it.'[43]

A good indication of how Aquinas thinks on the matter comes in
his treatment of the question 'Can we prove that the world had a
beginning?', to which he returns in several places. He discusses it in
the *Summa theologiae*, the *Commentary on the Sentences*,[44] the *Summa
contra Gentiles*,[45] and the *De potentia*.[46] He also has a whole work
devoted to it (*De aeternitate mundi contra murmurantes*). For our purposes, the main thing to note is that his solution to the question is
agnostic. In common with Maimonides,[47] whose views on the beginning of the world were also shared by St Albert,[48] Aquinas thinks
that the world's having had a beginning can be neither proved nor
disproved.

Aristotle took a different view. Like Aquinas in his First Way, he
held that there must be an unchanged changer or unmoved mover.
But he also argued that there was no temporally first event—that the
world had no beginning in time.[49] In common with everyone in
European antiquity outside the tradition of Judaism and Christianity,
he denied that matter ever began. Aquinas, on the other hand,
interprets the book of Genesis as teaching that the world had a
beginning, and he believes in a beginning of the world on that basis.
Yet he also holds that, from the viewpoint of philosophy, it cannot be
proved that the world had a beginning. He thinks that, as far as
philosophy can show, the world could have a history going back
indefinitely. 'That God is the creator of a world that began to be is an
article of faith', he says. It 'is held through revelation alone, and
cannot be demonstrated'.[50]

---

[43] F. C. Copleston, *Aquinas* (Harmondsworth, 1955), 123.
[44] *Sent.* 2. 1. 1. 5.
[45] 2. 32 ff.
[46] 3. 17.
[47] *The Guide for the Perplexed*, 2. 16 and 23.
[48] *Summa theologiae*, 2, tr. 1, q. 4, a. 5.
[49] Cf. *Physics*, 8. 1. 251.
[50] 1a. 46. 2.

In our own day, of course, there are people who deny this conclusion. And there were many who did the same both before and during the time of Aquinas. The sixth-century Christian writer John Philoponus tried to prove that the world had a beginning in *De aeternitate mundi contra Proclum* (529).[51] So did some famous Islamic thinkers.[52] The question of the world's beginning was much discussed at the University of Paris during the thirteenth century,[53] and no less a figure than St Bonaventure (*c*.1217–74) came out on the side of the view that reason can demonstrate that the world must have started a finite time ago.[54] Aquinas, however, is simply unconvinced by the arguments in favour of this thesis.[55] He thinks that there is no contradiction involved in saying that the world never had a beginning, for he holds that 'the world' is not definable so as to rule out its always having existed. And he denies that the contrary conclusion follows from what we know of God. As we shall see in Chapter 7, in his view, God causes things by virtue of his will. So we cannot, he thinks, deduce that God must will a certain kind of world (e.g. one which had a beginning).

The newness of the world cannot be demonstrated on the part of the world itself. For the principle of demonstration is the essence of a thing. Now everything according to its species is abstracted from *here* and *now*; whence it

---

[51] An English edition of this work, with introduction, is *Philoponus: Against Aristotle on the Eternity of the World*, trans. Christian Wildberg (London, 1987).

[52] Al-Ghazali (b. 1058/9) tried to do this in his *Tahafut al-Falasifa* (ed. M. Bouyges (Beirut, 1927)); English translation in *Averroës' Tahafut al-Tahafut*, trans. S. van den Bergh (London, 1954). Cf. William Lane Craig, *The Kalam Cosmological Argument* (London, 1979) and Davidson, *Proofs for Eternity*. A philosophically lively discussion of ancient and medieval authors on the beginning of the world can be found in Richard Sorabji, *Time, Creation and the Continuum* (London, 1983), chs. 13 ff.

[53] See John F. Wippel, *Metaphysical Themes in Thomas Aquinas* (Washington, DC, 1984), 192 f. Texts on the beginning of the world by Aquinas and Bonaventure, together with a text by Siger of Brabant, can be found in Cyril Vollert, Lottie H. Kendzierski, and Paul M. Byrne (eds.), *St Thomas Aquinas, Siger of Brabant, St Bonaventure: On the Eternity of the World* (Milwaukee, 1964). I should add that in the work just cited Wippel maintains that prior to writing *De aeternitate mundi* Aquinas's view was that one cannot prove or disprove the thesis of the world having had a beginning while in *De aeternitate mundi* he thinks of a beginningless world as possible.

[54] This was also the position of John Pecham and Henry of Ghent (d. 1293). For an introduction to the 13th-century controversy concerning the beginning of the world, see F. van Steenberghen, *Thomas Aquinas and Radical Aristotelianism* (Washington, DC, 1970).

[55] So also was Boethius of Dacia, a master in the Arts Faculty at Paris *c*.1270. See *On the Supreme Good, On the Eternity of the World, On Dreams*, trans. John F. Wippel (Toronto, 1987).

is said that universals are everywhere and always. Hence it cannot be demonstrated that humanity, or heaven, or a stone were not always. Likewise it cannot be demonstrated on the part of the efficient cause, which acts by will. For the will of God cannot be investigated by reason, except as regards those things which God must will of necessity; and what he wills about creatures is not among these.[56]

His point about the 'essence of a thing' is that definitions of objects (whether real or imaginary) tell you what they are like in a timeless sense. You can know what a dog is without knowing when dogs came into being or even whether there are dogs. By the same token, so Aquinas reasons, you can know what the world is without knowing whether or not it had a beginning.

Or could it be that there really are cogent arguments for the world having a beginning? One argument Aquinas considers states that it must have had a beginning simply because it is made and 'everything that is made has a beginning to its duration'. But, he replies, the world could be made by God without there being a time before it was made. 'In the event of the action being instantaneous and not successive, it is not required for the maker to be prior in duration to the thing made.'[57]

An objector might observe that if God made the world, the world was made from something or nothing. It cannot have been made from something, otherwise the world's matter would have preceded it. So it was made from nothing. In that case, however, it has being after non-being. So it began.

But, again, Aquinas finds the case unproved. To say that the world was made from nothing is, he insists, simply to say that it is not made from anything, not that it was made at some first clockable moment of time. 'Those who hold the eternity of the world would agree that it was made by God from nothing, in the sense that it was not made from anything, not that it was made after nothing.'[58]

A popular argument with defenders of the world's non-eternity is that if the world has existed always, there would have elapsed an infinite number of days before the present one. But it is impossible to

---

[56] 1a, 46, 2. By an 'efficient cause' Aquinas means something which operates so as to bring about a change or another thing. According to this terminology, which derives from Aristotle, parents can be called the efficient causes of their children or gin can be the efficient cause of a hangover. On the topic of God's will and necessity, see below.

[57] 1a. 46. 2 ad. 1.

[58] 1a. 46. 2 ad. 2.

traverse an actual infinite. So if the world were without beginning, the present would never have arrived. Here, however, Aquinas detects a fallacy. We should not, he argues, suppose that between two extremes there is an infinite number of finite lengths of equal size. So between two instants there cannot be an infinite number of days. Whatever past day we choose to focus on, there is merely a finite number of days between it and today. And there is thus no difficulty in supposing that the present could have arrived though the world's history is infinite. 'A passage is always from one term to another, and whichever day from the past we pick on, there is only a limited number between then and today, and this span can be traversed.'[59]

And thus Aquinas continues with respect to many other arguments. We have reason to believe in God, he thinks. That God exists is a judgement well grounded in sound philosophical thinking. But the existence of God does not follow from what we must suppose to have happened in the past. Philosophically speaking, God is required to account for what we can now observe, and he accounts for it in its presentness as we observe it. In this sense, P. T. Geach is right to say that Aquinas thinks of God as the Maker of a world which can, if you like, be viewed as 'a great big object' equally dependent on God at all times. Geach is also right to say that Aquinas's view is that, if the world is an object, it 'seems natural to ask about it the sort of causal questions which would be legitimate about its parts. If it began to exist, what brought it into existence? In any case, what keeps it from perishing, as some of its parts perish? And what keeps its processes going? And to what end?'[60] Hence the Five Ways.

For Aquinas, then, things as we find them give rise to causal questions, ones which we can frequently answer by appealing to the activity of what is in the world. But our efforts to cope with certain causal questions like 'Why is this thing changing?', or 'Why is this thing here at all?', imply the need to raise further questions. We can ask why the water turned brown or why there are donkeys, but this ought to lead us to ask why there is change at all or why there is a world at all. Insofar as he believes that questions like these have an answer, Aquinas believes in God. In the next few chapters we shall be looking more closely at what he takes God to be.

[59] 1a. 46. 2 ad. 6.
[60] G. E. M. Anscombe and P. T. Geach, *Three Philosophers* (Oxford, 1973), 112.

3

What God is not

AQUINAS is often thought of as someone with a precise or definite concept of God, someone who thinks he can explain just what God is. And it is not surprising that this is how he has struck people. An early biographical source states that even as a child he was fascinated by the question 'What is God?'[1] And the question was one to which he came to offer a series of systematic answers. His writings are crammed with assertions about God and his nature.

Yet a presiding thesis of Aquinas is that, though we can know *that* God exists (*an est*), we cannot know *what* God is (*quid est*). One might expect that, once he has argued for the existence of God, Aquinas would next proceed to offer a systematic and positive account of God's nature, properties, or attributes. But that is not what he does. In a passage immediately following the text of the Five Ways, he writes:

Having recognized that a certain thing exists, we have still to investigate the way in which it exists, that we may come to understand what it is that exists. Now we cannot know what God is, but only what he is not; we must therefore consider the ways in which God does not exist, rather than the ways in which he does.

The same move is made in the *Summa contra Gentiles*. Book 1, chapter 13 of the treatise is called 'Arguments in Proof of the Existence of God'. Chapter 14 begins with the assertion: 'The divine substance surpasses every form that our intellect reaches. Thus we are unable to apprehend it by knowing what it is.'

Not Knowing What God is

1. *Aquinas's Basic Position*

What does Aquinas mean by saying this? To start with, it is important to note that he does not mean what the casual reader is likely to

---

[1] Kenelm Foster (ed.), *The Life of Saint Thomas Aquinas* (London, 1959), 59 n. 5.

suppose from the extracts just cited. 'We cannot know what God is' could easily be taken to suggest that we know no truths about God. But that is not Aquinas's view. His approach to God has been called 'agnostic', but it is not entirely negative. As we shall see, he maintains that we can know many things about God—that he is living, good, powerful, and so on. He certainly does not think that we can make no true predications concerning God.[2]

To grasp his position, we need to understand that according to him we know what something is when we can define it. More precisely, we know what something is when we can locate it in terms of genus and species.[3] In saying that we cannot know what God is, therefore, he is chiefly denying that God can be defined or placed in a class.[4] He means that our knowledge of God is not comparable to that which a scientist has of things. As John Wippell explains:

From the beginning of his career until its end Thomas consistently denies to man in this life quidditative knowledge of God ... One should define quidditative knowledge or knowledge of what God is very strictly, even as Thomas himself has done. He has made it clear, for instance, in the *De Potentia* and in the First Part of the *Summa Theologiae*, that when he agrees with John Damascene that we cannot know what God is, what he is thereby excluding is comprehensive and defining knowledge of God.[5]

Aquinas does not mean us to believe that we have no knowledge of God. At the same time, however, he thinks that the nature of God is, in a sense, incomprehensible to us—that God defies our powers of understanding. People often say that God is mysterious, and Aquinas would agree. But the mystery of God is more radical for him than it is for many who proclaim it. As Herbert McCabe writes, in his view,

when we speak of God, although we know how to use our words, there is an important sense in which we do not know what they mean ... We know how to talk about God, not because of any understanding of God, but because of what we know about his creatures.[6]

---

[2] P. T. Geach properly draws attention to this point in G. E. M. Anscombe and P. T. Geach, *Three Philosophers* (Oxford, 1973), 117.

[3] Cf. *Sent.* 1. 37. 3. 3, 1. 43. 1. 1.

[4] Cf. *Comp.* ch. 26.

[5] John F. Wippel, *Metaphysical Themes in Thomas Aquinas* (Washington, DC, 1984), 239.

[6] Herbert McCabe, OP, appendix 3 to vol. iii of the Blackfriars edition of the *Summa theologiae*.

God, for Aquinas, transcends our attempts to picture or describe him. Having said that he is, we must also admit that we do not know what he is.

2. Theological Background

One source of this conclusion undoubtedly lies in the theological tradition to which Aquinas was heir. For there was much in that which could be readily summed up in the words 'We do not know what God is.' Biblical authors regularly speak of God as hidden or elusive. St John, for example, insists that 'no man has ever seen God'.[7] Of primary importance here at the post-biblical level, however, is Neoplatonism and its impact on Christians influenced by it, especially writers such as Denys the Areopagite.

In Neoplatonic thinking one finds much complicated analysis of the divine, but also much agnosticism.[8] Neoplatonists distinguished divine names (such as 'One', 'Being', 'Life', and 'Intelligence'), but they did not always suppose that what the names signified was intelligible or comprehensible. Plotinus (*c.*205–70) spoke of the One as a first principle beyond determination and limitation and therefore transcendent or beyond being and understanding.[9] A similar way of talking occurs in Proclus, for whom it cannot even be said of the One that it is the One.[10] In this world of thought, divinity is readily conceived of as thoroughly inconceivable.

By the middle of the thirteenth-century, this theme of divinity beyond the grasp of language had become an important part of respectable Christian discourse And a major cause of it becoming so was Denys. In reality a fifth- or early sixth-century Christian, probably writing in Syria, he was taken to be the convert of St Paul referred to in the Acts of the Apostles (17: 34). So his standing was virtually that of an apostolic authority. His background, however, was Neoplatonism, especially the Neoplatonism of Proclus. So he

---

[7] John 1: 18. The theme of God's hiddenness in the Bible is explored in Robert Davidson, *The Courage to Doubt* (London, 1983).

[8] For a survey of Neoplatonic thinking, see R. T. Wallis, *Neoplatonism* (London, 1972) and A. H. Armstrong (ed.), *The Cambridge History of Later Greek and Early Medieval Philosophy* (Cambridge, 1967).

[9] For an account of Plotinus see Armstrong, *Cambridge History*, chs. 12 ff. and J. M. Rist, *Plotinus: The Road to Reality* (Cambridge, 1967).

[10] *Proclus' Commentary on Plato's Parmenides*, trans. Glenn R. Morrow and John M. Dillon (Princeton, NJ, 1987), 589 ff.

was also profoundly agnostic. He distinguished between cataphatic theology and apophatic theology (i.e. talk about God in which we affirm things of him, and talk which denies things of him). And he stressed that, however cataphatic our talk of God is, it must also be strongly apophatic. As Andrew Louth explains, according to Denys:

God reveals something of himself. We can affirm that: this is cataphatic theology. But what God reveals of himself is not himself; as we seek to understand God as he is in himself, we must go behind the affirmations we make, and deny them of God, and thus engage in apophatic theology.[11]

To cut a long story short, the point to note now is that Aquinas was definitely much indebted to the line of thinking represented by authors such as Denys. In fact, he was clearly directly influenced by Denys himself. As we saw in Chapter 1, he commented on Denys, like Albert his teacher.[12] And he frequently quotes Denys as an authority. An undoubted source of Aquinas's agnosticism concerning God, therefore, is the tradition of Denys.[13]

3. *The Range of Human Knowledge*

But there are other sources as well, one of which consists in what Aquinas thinks about human knowledge in general. Like many philosophers since the seventeenth century, Aquinas is a kind of empiricist. In his view, our knowledge derives from and is dependent on the fact that we are sensing beings. It is a consequence of the fact that we are acquainted with material objects. And, since God is not a material object, Aquinas concludes that he is unknowable in his essence or nature.

The knowledge that is natural to us has its source in the senses and extends just so far as it can be led by sensible things; from these, however, our understanding cannot reach to the divine essence . . . In the present life our intellect has a natural relation to the natures of material things; thus it understands nothing except by turning to sense images . . . In this sense it is obvious that we cannot, primarily and essentially, in the mode of knowing that we experience, understand immaterial substances since they are not

---

[11] *Denys the Areopagite* (London, 1989), 87 f.
[12] For an account of the Dionysian tradition and Albert's connection with it, see Simon Tugwell, *Albert and Thomas: Selected Writings* (New York, 1988), 39 ff.
[13] For an English edition of Denys see *Pseudo-Dionysius: The Complete Works*, trans. Colm Luibheid and Paul Rorem (London, 1987).

subject to the senses and imagination... What is understood first by us in
the present life is the whatness of material things... [hence]... we arrive at
a knowledge of God by way of creatures.[14]

In other words, God is beyond our understanding since he is not
an object of sense experience. As we saw in the last chapter, Aquinas
defends belief in the existence of God in terms of the fact that the
objects of sense experience raise certain questions. But the answer to
these questions is not, in his view, something we understand in the
way that we understand the things which give rise to them. We can
know that there is an answer, but we cannot comprehend it. So it
follows, says Aquinas, that what we know best is what God is not. In
trying to speak of him we will need to proceed by distinguishing him
from things that we do know, by employing what Aquinas calls 'the
method of remotion', by denying this, that, or the other of God.

Now, in considering the divine substance, we should especially make use of
the method of remotion. For... the divine substance surpasses every form
that our intellect reaches. Thus we are unable to apprehend it by knowing
what it is. Yet we are able to have some knowledge of it by knowing what it is
not. Furthermore, we approach nearer to a knowledge of God according as
through our intellect we are able to remove more and more things from
him.[15]

But what is it that God is not? Here we come to yet another main
source of Aquinas's theistic agnosticism. This is his version of what is
commonly called the 'doctrine of divine simplicity', a doctrine which
forms the core of his teaching about God, who, so he declares
(quoting St Augustine), 'is the most truly simple thing there is' (*vere et
summe simplex est*). God, so he argues, 'is altogether simple'.[16]

The Doctrine of Divine Simplicity: Preliminaries

The assertion that God is simple is very much part of classical
theological reflection on God and his nature.[17] It is present in the
work of influential Arabic and Jewish writers such as Ibn-Sina

---

[14] 1a. 12. 12, 88, 1, 88, 3.
[15] *SG* 1. 14.
[16] 1a. 3. 7.
[17] For a brief history of the notion of divine simplicity see the article by W. J. Hill in
vol. xii of the *New Catholic Encyclopedia* (New York, 1967).

(980–1037) and Maimonides. It is taught by the Catholic Church, according to which God is 'one, singular, completely simple and un- changeable spiritual substance... inexpressibly loftier than any- thing besides himself which either exists or can be imagined'.[18] It is also solidly embedded in the work of numerous major Christian authors such as Augustine and Anselm. So it is not, perhaps, surprising that Aquinas accepts it as well. The interesting question, though, is why he finds it acceptable.

In saying that God is simple, he is not, of course, suggesting that God is stupid or unintelligent. His main purpose is to stress that certain truths about creatures are not truths about God. According to him, God is simple since he is (1) unchangeable, (2) not an individual, (3) not created. To grasp his meaning, however, we will first have to note some of the things he says about change and individuality.

1. Change

Aquinas recognizes two kinds of change—'accidental' change and 'substantial' change. The significance of the distinction can be brought out by means of example.

Suppose there is a cow standing in a field. It could, of course, leave the field. It could be taken to a barn. And this would be a kind of change. In moving from field to barn a cow undergoes change of a sort, for it shifts its location.

But this movement would not make any difference to the kind of thing it is—a cow. As Aquinas would say, being in a field or a barn does not belong to what a cow is by 'nature'. It does not belong to being a cow that it should be in a field or in a barn. And there are other changes open to cows of which the same can be said. Daisy might be docile. But she will still be a cow if she becomes frisky. She might become lame or pregnant. But this, again, will not abolish the fact that she is a cow.

In Aquinas's language, changes like these are 'accidental changes'. They are changes which things can undergo without turning into things of a different kind, without changing in what Aquinas calls their 'essence', 'substance' or 'nature'. Things, he says, may be

---

[18] Vatican I, *Dogmatic Constitution on the Catholic Faith*, ch. 1. See *Decrees of the Ecumenical Councils*, ed. Norman P. Tanner (London, 1990), ii. 805.

modified. They may, as he puts it, be 'potentially' different (i.e. they may have a capacity to be other than they are). But in changing as they do (in ceasing to be 'actually' what they are) their fundamental constitution need not be removed. A cow in a field is 'actually' in a field and 'potentially' in a barn. Let us suppose it moves to a barn. In that case it is actually in the barn and, in a sense, has changed. But it has not turned into something else. It has not ceased to be a cow. A cow in a barn is just as much a cow as one in a field, and vice versa.

On the other hand, however, things can change in a more drastic fashion than they do by changing their location and the like. A cow will still be a cow when it moves from the field to the barn. But what of the butcher waiting to turn it into beef?

On Aquinas's account, when a cow dies it does not just lose some 'accidental' feature (which he sometimes calls an 'accidental form'). When a cow dies it becomes a different kind of thing. As Aquinas puts it, it loses its 'substantial form'. In terms of this view, beef (a dead cow) is not a *kind* of cow (like a Jersey or a Friesian). It is what used to be a cow but is now something else—namely a corpse.

This kind of change, when something goes out of existence by turning into a new thing, is called by Aquinas 'substantial change'. And he calls the capacity (or 'potentiality') a thing has for changing substantially its 'matter'. For him, therefore, things in the world can be spoken of as having, or being, both 'form' and 'matter'.

'Form' is a term with a long philosophical history. It occurs, for example, in Plato, who thought that there were subsisting 'forms' or 'ideas' over and above the world of things in which things in the world participated, as he put it. In the words of Anthony Kenny: 'In many cases where we would say that a common predicate was true of a number of individuals Plato will say that they are all related to a certain Form or Idea: where A, B, C are all F, they are related to a single Form of F.'[19] For Aristotle, however, forms exist only because distinct things exist. On his account, the form of redness, say, exists because *A* is red and *B* is red and *C* is red. And in this he is followed by Aquinas, who explicitly declares a preference for Aristotle over Plato on the subject.

Plato believed that the forms of things exist separately, and that individual things are named after these separate forms in which they participate in some way: Socrates, for example, is called a 'man' by reference to some separate

19 *The Five Ways* (London, 1969), 71.

form of man. And just as he believed in separate forms of man and horse, calling them Man Himself and Horse Itself, so also Plato believed in separate forms of being and unity, called Being Itself and Unity Itself, by participating in which everything was said to be or to be one. The existent Good Itself and Unity Itself he believed to be the supreme God, by reference to which all things were said to be good by participation. [But] Aristotle repeatedly proves [that] the part of this opinion which postulates separate, self-subsistent forms of natural things appears to be absurd.[20]

For Aquinas, a form is that by which something actually is what it is, whether substantially or accidentally—a cow, for example ('substantial form') or brown ('accidental form'). 'What brings about substantial existence in actual fact is called substantial form; what brings about accidental existence in actual fact is called accidental form.'[21] Roughly speaking, we have form when we have a definite thing or a property or attribute predicable of things.

Aquinas's notion of 'matter' (or 'prime matter', *materia prima*, as he sometimes calls it) is a harder notion to understand. For, in his teaching, matter, in a sense, is nothing at all. It is potentiality, not actualization. It is that by which something having a nature might cease to have it and turn into something else, as a cow can turn into beef. It is that which allows us to speak of things having a capacity for substantial change. It is that factor by which quite distinct individual things are historically connected in a substantial change so that *this* individual is made out of *that* one.

Matter, for Aquinas, is therefore not some nondescript 'body' or 'stuff'. He does allow for a sense of 'matter' in which it corresponds to our English 'stuff', for he speaks of the matter (e.g. bronze) of which a statue is made.[22] But he also thinks that, if there were the same body or same actual stuff in Daisy and the beef she turns into, then the change involved in her death would be no more radical than the one involved when she moves from field to barn. Nothing substantial would have gone out of existence or come into being. The body or stuff would simply have changed accidentally. In this sense Aquinas thinks of matter as different from what we mean by 'stuff'. He also denies that it is some aspect or feature shared by two things (e.g. the cow and the beef it turns into). For any such aspect there would be a form which actually belonged to the things (as brownness

---

[20] 1a. 6. 4.
[21] *De prin. nat.* ch. 1.
[22] Ibid. ch. 2.

or being in the barn can actually belong to two cows), whereas the matter of a thing is the opposite of its actuality. It is what makes it liable not to be actual. It is what makes it liable to perish.

Matter, for Aquinas, is opposed to form. Form is that by which something actually *is* (e.g. a cow), while matter is that by which what it is might *not be* (that by which a cow can become a corpse). According to Aquinas, it is because we have a material world that the food a cow's mother eats, while actually food, is potentially a cow (could cease to be food and be turned into an embryo cow in the womb, with the same matter). It is because we have a material world that a cow can cease to be a cow and be turned into beef, with the same matter, which, in turn, might be turned into something else. As Kenny puts it: 'Prime matter is matter which as such is not any particular kind of stuff; not that there is any matter which is stuff of no particular kind, but that matter *qua* matter, is not stuff of any particular kind, and can be stuff of any kind whatever.'[23]

In other words, in thinking of matter Aquinas has in mind a historical line (though not a quantity of actual imperishable stuff) running through a series of perishings and comings to be. Matter, he says, 'achieves actual existence through the form which determines it' (1a. 50. 5). As such, it 'exists potentially only',[24] or is 'being potentially',[25] and is neither a substance nor a property or attribute.[26]

This is not to say that matter is a kind of existing bare potentiality, a substance without a nature or qualities. Aquinas holds that a thing is actual by virtue of its form, and that not even God can make pure unformed matter. So he does not try to answer the question 'What is there throughout the process of something changing substantially?' All he says is that first we have what is wholly a thing of this kind (e.g. a cow); then we have what is wholly something else (e.g. a corpse). Since matter is nothing nameable or thinkable (like a substance or a quality), it is not, for Aquinas, even intelligible. 'Because all definition and all knowledge relies on form', he remarks, 'first matter cannot be known or defined in itself, but only by means of composite things containing it.'[27] But it is, he adds, of crucial import-

---

[23] 'Intellect and Imagination in Aquinas', in Anthony Kenny (ed.), *Aquinas: A Collection of Critical Essays* (London, 1969), 280.
[24] 1a. 76. 7.
[25] 1a2ae. 55. 2.
[26] 1a. 76. 7.
[27] *De prin. nat.* ch. 2.

ance. For not only is it that by which things are able to change substantially. It is also that by which they are distinguishable as individuals or distinct substances.

2. *Individuals*

In its most common modern use, the word 'individual' signifies an instance of a class or group of which there is or could be more than one member. On this basis we speak of James and John as individual men. But what makes them *two* rather than one? What makes them a *couple* rather than a unit?

Some would here appeal to what Aquinas calls accidental forms. Suppose that James is short, pale, and abrasive while John is tall, tanned, and placid. On the account now in question James is distinct from John because of his size, colour, and temperament.

Aquinas, however, rejects this answer. It may, he thinks, be true that *A* is different from *B* because *A* is short, pale and abrasive while *B* is tall, tanned and placid. But, so he reasons, in pointing to such differences as differences between *A* and *B* we are already pre-supposing that *A* and *B* are distinct. Features which belong to things accidentally cannot, he thinks, serve to distinguish between one individual and another.

And to this point he adds another. For he also holds that individuation is not effected by what things are by nature. If individuals are not constituted as such by their accidental forms (features which they may acquire or lose without ceasing to be things of the kind to which they belong), it might be thought that their individuality lies in their essence or nature, in what they can only lose by ceasing to exist altogether. But that, says Aquinas, cannot be true either. For, where things share a nature, it cannot be their nature which distinguishes them from each other. If James and John are both human beings, it cannot be their humanity which distinguishes them from each other. This is something they share.

In the end, Aquinas concludes that it is by virtue of matter that two things of the same kind can coexist. We have to say that for James to exist is for him to be *this* man, and for John to exist is for him to be *that* man, where 'this' and 'that' do not signify formal characteristics but simply go along with gestures of pointing. The connection between pointing and individuation arises for Aquinas since, in his view, geometrical attributes are self-individuating or individuated in their own right.[28] His idea is that individuation in the present sense occurs by virtue of dimensive quantity, by virtue of what Aquinas calls 'designated matter' (*materia signata*).[29] As Joseph Bobik puts it: 'This individual is a determinate 'this' individual, and is unique by virtue of designated matter, by reason of matter considered under determined dimensions.'[30] Or, as Aquinas writes: 'Since dimensive quantity alone possesses by its nature that whereby the multiplication of individuals in a same species can take place, the primary source of such multiplication appears to be rooted in dimension.'[31]

An objector might reply that this must be false since we can individuate between non-material things so as to understand there being more than one of them. Aquinas, however, would say that, if we are to understand there being individual items of the same kind, we must at least know on what principle they are to be counted. And he would have found it hard to say what such a principle could be without reference to what is material.

Some have argued that the notion of a non-material individual is clear to us from our own case. On their account, and as Descartes, for instance, held, we are non-material since we are persons whose nature is immaterial.[32] But Aquinas would not have agreed. Like many philosophers today, he would have said that it is just not clear how sense can be attached to the notion of a non-material human person.[33] His view is that we distinguish between people insofar as they are nameable, observable entities, that in the absence of material differences there seems to be no way of distinguishing between one human being and another.[34]

One might reply that things can be distinguished from each other

---

[28] See 3a. 77. 2.

[29] *De ente* 2. 23.

[30] *Aquinas on Being and Essence: A Translation and Interpretation* (Notre Dame, Ind., 1965), 76.

[31] *SG* 4. 65.

[32] This thesis is often called 'Cartesian Dualism'. It is defended by Descartes in his *Meditations on First Philosophy* and elsewhere. For a good introduction, see John Cottingham, *Descartes* (Oxford, 1986).

[33] Aquinas does not want to say that people can in no sense be said to exist as individuals in the absence of matter, for he believes that human souls can exist independently of the bodies whose souls they are. We shall be returning to this point below.

[34] This is now a point commonly levelled against Descartes. See e.g. P. F. Strawson, 'Self, Mind and Body', in *Freedom and Resentment* (London, 1974) and G. E. M. Anscombe, 'The First Person', in *Collected Philosophical Papers*, i (Oxford, 1981).

if they can just be described differently. But Aquinas would say that things will not be there to be so described unless they are distinct to begin with. To make the point as Peter Geach does, his argument would be that, for example,

Two pennies that coexist may in fact differ in all sorts of respects—one may be in mint condition and the other bent, defaced and stained—but these cannot be what make the pennies two: if there were not in any case two pennies, they could not acquire these differences. What makes the two pennies two is that they are two pieces of matter.[35]

For Aquinas, therefore, matter is 'the principle of individuation within a species'.[36] And for him that means that things in the world are distinct because they are physical, bodily, or corporeal.[37]

The Doctrine of Divine Simplicity: Details

1. Phase One: Form, Matter, Individuality, and Nature

Moving on now to the details of Aquinas on divine simplicity, the first thing to note is that part of it boils down to the thesis that nothing in the section above applies to God. Simplicity, for Aquinas, is the opposite of compositeness (*compositio*). And to begin with, he declares, God is simple (lacking in *compositio*) since he is incapable of accidental or substantial change and is not an individual of form and matter.

God cannot undergo accidental and substantial change for he is the cause of all the changes there are and cannot, therefore, exemplify such change. So there can be no potentiality in God, no capacity to be other than he is whether accidentally or substantially. He is purely actual, which, for one thing, means that he is not a body.[38]

---

[35] Anscombe and Geach, *Three Philosophers*, 73. Cf. P. T. Geach, *God and the Soul* (London, 1969), 22 f.

[36] 1a. 56. 1 ad. 2.

[37] For a brief indication of development in Aquinas's view of individuation, see Robert A. O'Donnell, CSP, 'Individuation: An Example of the Development in the Thought of St Thomas Aquinas', *New Scholasticism*, 33 (1959).

[38] As we shall be seeing later, in the light of the doctrine of the Incarnation Aquinas is prepared to countenance statements like 'God is a body'. But he never does so in a way that suggests that the divine nature is something bodily.

In the first existent everything must be actual; there can be no potentiality
whatsoever. For although, when we consider things coming to exist, potential
existence precedes actual existence in those particular things; nevertheless,
absolutely speaking, actual existence takes precedence over potential existence. For what is able to exist is brought into existence only by what already
exists. Now we have seen that the first existent is God. In God then there can
be no potentiality. In bodies, however, there is always potentiality, for the
extended as such is potentially divided. God, therefore, cannot be a body.[39]

This, of course, implies for Aquinas that in God there can be no
composition of form and matter. For 'the very existence of matter is a
being potential; whilst God, as we have seen, contains no potentiality,
but is sheer actuality'.[40] God, so Aquinas holds, is nothing but form,
which means that he is not in the ordinary sense an individual.

In the language of Aquinas, this point is expressed in the teaching
that God is the same as his essence or nature, and that there is no
composition of *suppositum* and nature or essence in God. For Aquinas,
a *suppositum* is a distinct subject or individual—*this* particular thing as
opposed to *that* particular thing, James as opposed to John. As we
have seen, according to Aquinas things in the world are constituted
as individuals by virtue of matter. So, since he has argued that God is
not a body, and is form without matter, he naturally concludes that
God is not an individual as something in the world can be. He is not
an instance of a class whose members share a common nature. He is
indistinguishable from his nature.

James and John are the same sort of thing. Since they are both
human beings, they share the same nature or essence. But James is
not John, and John is not James. They are individuals (individual
human beings), and their being such is not something which follows
from their nature. Let us put this by saying that as individuals they
have a certain nature but are not *identical with* it. In that case, so
Aquinas is saying, we will now have to hold that God does not *have* a
nature. It is better to say that he *is* his nature or that *who* God is (the
individual God is) and *what* God is (the divine nature) amount to
the same, or cannot be distinguished. James is not his nature, for
humanity is something possessed by people other than him. The
same goes for John. In this sense, therefore, a distinction can be
drawn between James and his nature, and John and his nature. In the

[39] 1a. 3. 1.
[40] 1a. 3. 2.

judgement of Aquinas, however, this is not so with God. He is *what* he is. Insofar as he is an individual, he is only so by virtue of being a distinct nature—as James or John would be if either of them were Human Nature considered as a sort of abstract entity.

God is to be identified with his own essence or nature. We shall understand this when we see why things composed of matter and form must not be identified with their natures or essences. Essence or nature includes only what defines the species of a thing: thus human nature includes only what defines human beings, or what makes human beings to be human beings, for by 'human nature' we mean that which makes humans human. Now the species of a thing is not defined by the matter and properties peculiar to it as an individual; thus we do not define 'human being' as that which has this flesh and these bones, or is white, or black, or the like. This flesh and these bones and the properties peculiar to them belong indeed to this human being, but not to that person's nature. An individual human being then possesses something which one's human nature does not, so that a human being and a human being's nature are not altogether the same thing. 'Human nature' names, in fact, the formative element in people; for what gives a thing definition is formative with respect to the matter which gives it individuality. The individuality of things not composed of matter and form cannot however derive from this or that individual matter, and the forms of such things must therefore be intrinsically individual and themselves subsist as things. Such things are thus identical with their own natures. In the same way, then, God, who, as we have seen, is not composed of matter and form, is identical with his own godhead, with his own life and with whatever else is similarly said of him.[41]

This is not to say, as, for example, Alvin Plantinga seems to think, that properties which are different are not different when God has them, and that God is nothing but a property.[42] It is to say that, though we speak of God by means of sentences which differ in meaning, the reality to which our talk of God latches on is not something to be literally believed to be distinct from its nature. A modern analogy for what Aquinas has in mind here is provided by Geach.

'The square of—' and 'the double of—' signify two quite different functions, but for the argument 2 these two functions both take the number 4 as their value. Similarly, 'the wisdom of—' and 'the power of—' signify different forms, but the individualizations of these forms in God's case are not distinct

[41] 1a. 3. 3.
[42] Alvin Plantinga, *Does God Have a Nature?* (Milwaukee, 1980) 47.

from one another; nor is either distinct from God, just as the number 1 is in no way distinct from its own square.[43]

This is no more than an analogy, but it ties up well enough with what Aquinas writes. He does not deny that, for example, 'God is wise' means something different from 'God is powerful'. In this sense he accepts that God has different properties. What he denies is that what is signified by 'the wisdom of God' is possessed by God as a property distinct from that of being powerful. He also denies that 'the wisdom of God' and 'the power of God' refer to something other than what is signified by means of the word 'God'.

2. *Phase Two: Essence and Existence*

For Aquinas, then, God is simple in that he has no *compositio* of form and matter, and none of *suppositum* and nature. He is pure form. And he is his nature. But there is another crucial element involved in Aquinas's notion of divine simplicity. For God, he says, is also simple since he lacks *compositio* of essence and existence. In him these amount to the same thing, and 'the substance of God is therefore his existence'.[44] In this respect, God is unique.

To see what Aquinas is driving at here, one needs to recall something of what we saw in Chapter 2. According to Aquinas, things in the world are not 'just there'. Their existence derives from God and 'we are bound to conclude that everything that is at all real is from God'.[45] As Aquinas sees it, therefore, things in the world are potential in a further sense from those senses noted above. They are potentially *non-existent*—not just because they can change substantially or accidentally, but also because there might not be any world at all.

James is pale, but potentially tanned. He is also, alas, potentially a corpse. So he can be modified and he can perish. But in being like this he has not, Aquinas thinks, exhausted the depths of his potentiality. If there were no world, there would be no James to be modified and nothing for him to turn into. As Aquinas puts it, he is not just form and matter and not just an individual sharing a nature with others (like John). He is a mixture or *compositio* of essence and existence. He exists all right, but nothing about him is enough

---

[43] *Three Philosophers*, 122. Cf. *God and the Soul*, 49 f.
[44] 1a. 3. 4.
[45] 1a. 44. 1.

by itself to ensure his existence. We may know what he is. We may understand his nature. But, though he cannot exist without his nature, not even this will bring him into being or keep him in existence. In this sense, he is totally dependent on God.

Well, Aquinas now adds, this kind of *compositio* does not apply to God either. And that is because he is the first cause, the reason why there is a world and the reason why there is anything apart from himself. Considered as such, says Aquinas, God is not something with the potentiality of not being. If he were that, then he would himself be something whose existence is derived. The conclusion Aquinas therefore draws is that God is his own existence. He is *Ipsum Esse Subsistens*, 'Existence Itself' or 'Underived and non-relative Existence'. To put it another way, God is not a creature. Creatures, Aquinas thinks, 'have' existence, for their natures (*what* they are) do not suffice to guarantee their existence (*that* they are). But with God this is not so. He does not 'have' existence; his existence is not received or derived from another. He is his own existence and the reason why other things have it.

Properties that belong to a thing over and above its own nature must derive from somewhere, either from that nature itself . . . or from an external cause . . . If therefore the existence of a thing is to be other than its nature, that existence must either derive from the nature or have an external cause. Now it cannot derive merely from the nature, for nothing with derived existence suffices to bring itself into being. It follows then that, if a thing's existence differs from its nature, that existence must be externally caused. But we cannot say this about God, whom we have seen to be the first cause. Neither then can we say that God's existence is other than his nature.[46]

In Aquinas's view, this would be true even if the created order contained things which are not material. For suppose there were immaterial beings other than God—sheer forms which were not the actualization of any matter, as, in fact, Aquinas held angels to be.[47] They would differ from material things since they would have no in-built tendency to perish. In the language of Aquinas, they would be 'necessary' beings rather than 'contingent' ones. They would also be identical with their natures, for Aquinas held that there are no two angels of the same kind or 'species'. But they would still be potentially non-existent since they would receive their existence from

---

[46] 1a. 3. 4.
[47] 1a. 50. 2.

God. And, though they could not decay or perish at the hands of other creatures, it would be possible, absolutely speaking, for God to de-create (annihilate) them. They would not therefore exist simply by being what they are. They would be whatever they are, of course. But they would also be held in being by God, and, in their case too, there would be a distinction between essence and existence. 'Without doubt', says Aquinas, 'the angels, and all that is other than God, were made by God. For only God is his existence; in all else essence and existence are distinct.'[48] Or, as he explains it elsewhere:

Some things are of a nature that cannot exist except as instantiated in individual matter—all bodies are of this kind. This is one way of being. There are other things whose natures are instantiated by themselves and not by being in matter. These have existence simply by being the natures they are: yet existence is still something they *have*, it is not what they are—the incorporeal beings we call angels are of this kind. Finally there is the way of being that belongs to God alone, for his existence is what he is.[49]

This is not to say that if we knew God's nature we could deduce his existence from it (as the Ontological Argument is traditionally credited with supposing). Nor is it to say that existence is a property identical with God, as some readers of Aquinas take him to be arguing.[50] It is to say that God depends on nothing for his existence—that creatures are made by God while God is made by nothing. Aquinas, in fact, does not think of existence as a property at all, let alone one identical with God. In some passages he comes close to writing as if existence were a property of individuals, one with which God can be identified, for there he seems to be saying that existence is caused by God and shared by all things as heat is shared by all hot things and is caused by fire—with the proviso that while a hot thing is not identical with heat, God is identical with existence.[51] But appearances here are deceptive. In Aquinas's view, for a thing to be is not for it to have a property common to all individuals. The being of something is, for him, a function of it having a certain nature. Existence, he states, is given by 'form'.[52] On this account, dogs and cats, for instance, exist, not because they share

---

[48] 1a. 61. 2.
[49] 1a. 12. 4.
[50] Terence Penelhum, 'Divine Necessity', *Mind*, 69 (1960), reprinted in Basil Mitchell (ed.), *The Philosophy of Religion* (Oxford, 1971). I quote from Mitchell, 184 f.
[51] See 1a. 2. 3, 1a. 3. 4, and *De pot.* 7. 2.
[52] See 1a. 9. 2, 1a. 50. 4, 1a. 90. 3.

a single property, but because they are dogs and cats (in the language of Bertrand Russell, because '*X* is a dog' and '*X* is a cat' are sometimes true).[53] For Aquinas, heat will exist only if something is or has the form of heat. And in the passages now in question he is saying that, if the existence of a form depends on nothing outside it, it will not be possible to distinguish between the form and its existence. If heat were a subsisting thing rather than a property shared by subsisting, hot things, it would be 'heat itself', not a hot 'such and such' dependent on heat for being hot. By the same token, Aquinas maintains, as the subsisting, uncaused cause of everything other than himself, God is 'existence itself', *Ipsum Esse Subsistens*.

Once again, then, we find Aquinas saying what God is not. Whatever God is, he is *not* dependent on anything for his existence. By now, however, it should be clear to the reader that if we label Aquinas 'agnostic', we are not using the word in its common, modern sense. As Victor White once put it:

St Thomas's position differs from that of modern agnostics because while modern agnosticism says simply, 'We do not know, and the universe is a mysterious riddle', a Thomist says, 'We do not know what the answer is, but we do know that there is a mystery behind it all which we do not know, and if there were not, there would not even be a riddle. This Unknown we call *God*. If there were no God, there would be no universe to be mysterious, and nobody to be mystified.'[54]

God, for Aquinas, may be unknowable. But he is still there. If he is not an ordinary kind of thing, he is not a nothing either, which would seem to suggest that we should now consider what else Aquinas thinks should be said of him.[55]

---

[53] Bertrand Russell, *Logic and Knowledge* (London, 1965), 230 f.
[54] Victor White, OP, *God the Unknown* (London, 1956), 18 f. Cf. also F. C. Copleston, *Aquinas* (Harmondsworth, 1955), 139.
[55] Cf. Ludwig Wittgenstein, *Philosophical Investigations*, trans. G. E. M. Anscombe (Oxford, 1968), para. 304, where Wittgenstein says of the sensation of pain what Aquinas, were he writing today, might say of God: 'It is not a *something*, but not a *nothing* either!'

4

Talking About God

WE have now seen that Aquinas thinks of God as incomprehensible. We know something about God, he says. We know that God exists and is the cause of his creatures. We also know that he is simple. And yet, Aquinas adds, 'we cannot know what God is'.[1] Only God can 'know subsistent existence itself', and 'no created mind can see the essence of God unless he by his grace joins himself to that mind as something intelligible to it'.[2] Or, as Aquinas writes in the *De potentia*: 'Human intelligence is not equal to the divine essence' and 'one reaches the highest point of one's knowledge about God when one knows that one does not know him.'[3]

In that case, however, how can we think or say anything about him? Does our talk of God make sense? Does it convey information? It may be all very well sharply to distinguish between God and his creatures. It may not seem strange to insist that God is mysterious. But are we therefore to conclude that God eludes us entirely? Do we have no positive notion of him at all?

Background to Aquinas

Christian theologians earlier than Aquinas adopted apparently con-flicting answers to these questions. Some, for example, said that, though God is indeed transcendent, we still have quite a positive knowledge of him. St Augustine, for instance, spoke of the mind as

---

[1] An interesting symptom of this view in Aquinas is the fact that he speaks of the Tetragrammaton (conventionally rendered as 'Jehovah' or 'Yahweh') as the most appropriate name of God, better even than 'He Who Is'. He does this in 1a. 13. 12 ad. 1, though not elsewhere, and his reason is that the Tetragrammaton 'is used to signify the incommunicable', i.e. applying to God alone and thereby suggesting his hiddenness or ineffability. See Armand Maurer, 'St Thomas on the Sacred Name', *Medieval Studies*, 34 (1972), reprinted in Armand Maurer, *Being the Knowing: Studies in Thomas Aquinas and Later Medieval Philosophers* (Toronto, 1990).

[2] 1a. 12. 4.

[3] *De pot.* 7. 5 ad. 14.

rising to a vision of God, the major obstacle to the fullness of which seems to be moral rather than intellectual weakness.[4] While Plotinus maintained that God, or the One, is beyond being, Augustine, along with many other Christians, held that God is being. Centuries later, Peter Abelard (1079–1142) observed that God is unique and 'calls for a unique way of talking'. But he also declared that, by virtue of Christ and revelation, God has given us knowledge of himself and 'has himself manifestly disclosed to us what he is'.[5] The idea seems to be that, though there is a sense in which God is unknowable, he is somehow knowable in faith, the language of which somehow does do justice to him.

Other writers before Aquinas were, however, much less confident of our ability to capture divinity in language and understanding. John Damascene's *De fide orthodoxa* opens by strongly denying that any created intellect can grasp God. The same teaching emerges in Denys and his influential translator John Eriugena (*c.*810-*c.*877). God, affirms Denys, 'is beyond all being and knowledge'.[6] 'Just as the senses can neither grasp nor perceive the things of the mind', he says, 'just as corporal form cannot lay hold of the intangible and incorporeal, by the same standard of truth beings are surpassed by the infinity beyond being, intelligences by that oneness which is beyond intelligence.'[7] According to Eriugena, Denys is right and negative or apophatic theology is a primary means of talking about God.

And this is the prudent and catholic and salutary profession that is to be predicated of God: that first by the Cataphatic, that is by affirmation, we predicate all things of Him, whether by nouns or verbs, though not properly but in a metaphorical sense (*translative*); then we deny by the Apophatic, that is, by negation, that He is any of the things which by the Cataphatic are predicated of Him, only (this time) not metaphorically but properly—for there is more truth in saying that God is not any of the things that are predicated of Him than in saying that He is.[8]

Nor was such agnosticism common only to Christian writers. The Jewish Avicebron (*c.*1021-*c.*1058), speaking of the 'First Essence'

---

[4] *Confessions*, 7. 9 f., 18 ff.
[5] *Theologia Christiana*, 3. 116.
[6] *The Mystical Theology*, ch. 1.
[7] *The Divine Names*, ch. 1.
[8] *Periphyseon* (*De divisione naturae*), ed. I. P. Sheldon Williams (Dublin, 1978), 1. 522.

which is the goal of human beings, says that we can know 'that' it is, not what it is.[9] More famously, Maimonides held that no positive attributes can be predicated of God.

> There is no necessity at all for you to use positive attributes of God with the view of magnifying Him in your thoughts ... I will give you ... some illustrations, in order that you may better understand the propriety of forming as many negative attributes as possible, and the impropriety of ascribing to God any positive attributes. A person may know for certain that a 'ship' is in existence, but he may not know to what object that name is applied, whether to a substance or to an accident; a second person then learns that a ship is not an accident; a third, that it is not a mineral; a fourth, that it is not a plant growing in the earth; a fifth, that it is not a body whose parts are joined together by nature; a sixth, that it is not a flat object like boards or doors; a seventh, that it is not a sphere; an eighth, that it is not pointed; a ninth, that it is not round shaped; nor equilateral; a tenth, that it is not solid. It is clear that this tenth person has almost arrived at the correct notion of a 'ship' by the foregoing negative attributes ... In the same manner you will come nearer to the knowledge and comprehension of God by the negative attributes ... I do not merely declare that he who affirms attributes of God has not sufficient knowledge concerning the Creator ... but I say that he unconsciously loses his belief in God.[10]

Aquinas on God-Talk

1. False Moves

In spite of what we have already seen of his thinking, Aquinas does not wholly agree with the view that our talk about God should be construed as chiefly or primarily negative. We do not know what God is, he believes. But he also holds that talk of God is not always saying what something is not. For example, he observes: 'When a man speaks of the "living God" he does not simply want to say that God ... differs from a lifeless body.'[11] We do not just deny things of God, says Aquinas. We ascribe various kinds of noble attributes, or perfections, to God. We say that he is 'good' or 'wise' and the like. And here we speak positively or affirmatively.

---

[9] *Fons vitae*, 5. 24.
[10] *The Guide for the Perplexed*, trans. M. Friedlander (London, 1936), 86 ff.
[11] 1a. 13. 2. Cf. *De pot.* 7. 5.

Another position Aquinas rejects is one which tries to make sense of what we say of God only in causal terms. According to this view, which is also represented by Maimonides and is a variation on the theme 'By their fruits you shall know them', to say, for example, that God is good is just to say that he *causes good things*. But that, replies Aquinas, will not do, for at least two reasons.

First, he states, if 'God is good' only means that God causes good things, we would not have any particular reason to apply one term to God rather than another.

God is just as much the cause of bodies as he is of goodness in things; so if 'God is good' means no more than that God is the cause of goodness in things, why not say 'God is a body' on the grounds that he is the cause of bodies?[12]

Second, if 'God is *X*' only means 'God causes *X*-ness', it would follow 'that everything we said of God would be true only in a secondary sense, as when we say that a diet is "healthy", meaning merely that it causes health in the one who takes it, while it is the living body which is said to be healthy in a primary sense'. Aquinas holds that God would be some of the things we say he is even if he caused nothing. He therefore concludes that speaking of God as we do cannot just be saying what God has brought about.

Since, as our faith teaches and as Maimonides also grants, creatures have not always existed, it follows [on his account] that we could not say that God was wise or good before the existence of creatures. For it is evident that before creatures existed he did nothing as regards his effects, neither as good nor as wise.[13]

2. *Aquinas's Answer*

The solution which Aquinas adopts, therefore, is that in talking of God in an apparently positive way (in saying that he *is* thus and so, not just that he is *not* such and such), we do, in a sense, describe God. His line is that, though God is above naming, our statements about him can signify the divine nature. 'God', he writes, 'is said to have no name, or to be beyond naming because his essence is beyond what we understand of him and the meaning of the names we use.'[14]

---

[12] 1a. 13. 2.
[13] *De pot.* 7. 5.
[14] 1a. 13. 1 ad. 1.

So the language we use to speak of God is at one level inadequate
and we do not know what God is. But in speaking of God we can,
says Aquinas, speak truly. And we can know that we are doing so. In
other words, his view is that what we say of God can be literally true,
though the full reality signified by our words defies our comprehension. We can speak of God and mean what we say, but we cannot
comprehend the reality which makes our statements true. Words
such as 'good' and 'wise' truly characterize God, but they 'fail to
represent adequately what he is'.[15]

3. Details

One reason Aquinas has for making this suggestion lies in a notion
which he shares with Denys. What I have reported of Denys so far
may leave the reader feeling that, for him, the last word about God
must be negative. But there is a sense in which the feeling would not
be fully justified. For, though he believes that God is indescribable,
Denys also wants to say that God can and should be described as his
creatures can be described. For he holds that God is the cause of his
creatures, and that a cause of something shows itself in its effects so
that these reflect it somehow. Since all creatures are God's effects,
Denys asserts, it can be said that they all resemble God, or are all
somehow like him, and that things which can be said of them can also
be said of God. 'What has actually to be said about the Cause of
everything', he writes, 'is [that] since it is the Cause of all beings, we
should posit and ascribe to it all the affirmations we make in regard
to beings.'[16] As causing all and as transcending all, says Denys, God
'is rightly nameless'. But he also 'has the names of everything that is'
since 'he is their cause' which 'actually contains everything before-
hand within itself'.[17]

In this, Aquinas agrees with Denys.[18] He contends that, since
creatures are caused to be by God, they resemble him, or are somehow like him in so far as they display perfections.

---

[15] 1a. 13. 2.
[16] *The Mystical Theology*, ch. 1.
[17] *The Divine Names*, 1. 7.
[18] Some medieval authors influenced by Denys distorted his teaching somewhat by
ignoring his subtle blend of negative and positive when it comes to the issue of talk
about God. Aquinas, however, is remarkably Dionysian in his conclusions and in 1a.
13 alone Denys is cited no less than eight times. The very title of 1a. 13 is adapted
from Denys.

We speak of God as we know him, and since we know him from creatures we can only speak of him as they represent him. Any creature, in so far as it possesses any perfection, represents God and is like him, for he, being simply and universally perfect has pre-existing in himself the perfections of all his creatures.[19]

To the modern reader this may seem to suggest that God literally resembles things to be found in the world. Yet such is not Aquinas's view. He does hold that effects are *like* their causes. But he does not mean by this that, for example, eggs look like chickens or that bakers look like bread. As McCabe puts it, his point is that a cause is 'a thing exerting *itself*, having its influence or imposing its character on the world'.[20] On this account, to know that *A* has caused *B* is to understand *B* as something which flows from the nature of *A*, something brought about by *A* insofar as it is acting in its characteristic way.

For Aquinas, a cause and its effect are intimately connected. They are not simply instances of objects or events which we observe to be constantly conjoined, as the philosopher David Hume suggested.[21] An effect, for Aquinas, flows from its cause (rather than from something else) because the cause is a thing of a certain kind with a definite way of being or working. In McCabe's words:

St Thomas's whole theory of causal explanation is based on the idea that things have certain natures and that having these natures they have certain activities which are natural to them. When you know what something is you already know what it is likely to do—it is indeed the same thing fully to understand the nature of a thing and to know what it will naturally do . . . Thus a causal explanation is one in terms of the natural behaviour of things. When you have found the cause there is no further question about why this cause should produce this effect, to understand the cause is just to understand that it naturally produces this effect.[22]

It is in this sense that Aquinas thinks of effects as resembling their causes.[23] Effects are like their causes, he holds, because they are that

---

[19] 1a. 13. 2.

[20] Appendix 2 to vol. iii of the Blackfriars edition of the *Summa theologiae*, 102.

[21] David Hume, *A Treatise of Human Nature*, ed. L. A. Selby-Bigge (2nd edn., Oxford, 1978) and *An Enquiry Concerning Human Understanding*, ed. L. A. Selby-Bigge (3rd edn., Oxford, 1975).

[22] Herbert McCabe, *God Matters* (London, 1987), 101.

[23] The notion that effects resemble their causes is not original to either Denys or Aquinas. It can be traced back at least as far as Aristotle. See *Metaphysics*, 7. 7 ff.,

in which the operation and nature of their causes is played out or is manifest. Because they come from what their causes are, they reveal what brought them about, 'for what a thing does reflects what its active self is'.[24] Or, as we might say, 'You cannot give what you have not got.'

And thus it is, Aquinas maintains, with God and his effects. Things in the world reflect or reveal something of what he is because they come from him, because he is their cause or that from which they flow. On this basis, God can be named from his creatures, i.e. spoken of by means of words which we use in describing them. For Aquinas, therefore, we are not equivocating when we say, for example, 'I am good' and 'God is good'. In this sentence, he maintains, 'good' is not being used as, say, 'jam' is used in 'I adore strawberry jam' and 'There was a terrible jam on the motorway this evening' (i.e. equivocally). Indeed, says Aquinas, we cannot think of terms applied to God and to creatures as being used equivocally. For if they were so used, they would just lack content so far as they apply to God. If 'good' in 'I am good' and 'God is good' is like 'plane' in 'A carpenter uses a plane' and 'I'm frightened of travelling in a plane', then to be told that God is good is not to be told anything of significance.

A name is predicated of some being uselessly unless through that name we understand something of the being. But, if names are said of God and creatures in a purely equivocal way, we understand nothing of God through those names; for the meanings of those names are known to us solely to the extent that they are said of creatures. In vain, therefore, would it be said or proved of God that He is a being, good, or the like.[25]

As Aquinas goes on to note, however, what God and creatures share cannot be exemplified by God as it is by creatures. God, for Aquinas, belongs to no genus or species. So he does not resemble his creatures as, for example, I can resemble you.

---

especially 9. 1034ᵃ22 and *Metaphysics*, 12. 4. 1070ᵇ30 ff. See also: *Physics*, 2. 7. 198ᵃ26 f. *De anima*, 2. 5. 417ᵃ18 ff.; *De generatione et corruptione*, 1. 7. 324ᵃ9 ff.

[24] 1a. 4. 3.

[25] *SG* 1. 33. 6. Readers should not be confused by Aquinas's use of the word 'name' in this quotation. 'Name' here translates 'nomen', which, for present purposes, we can take as equivalent to the English word 'term'. For Aquinas, a *nomen* predicated of God is a term used in making true affirmative predications concerning him.

A creature is not like God as it is like to another member of its species or genus, but resembles him as an effect may in some way resemble a transcendent cause although failing to reproduce perfectly the form of the cause.[26]

In Aquinas's view, therefore, we need to embrace two apparently opposing conclusions. We may say that terms can be applied to God as well as to creatures. We may say, for example, that I am good and that God is good. But we must also insist that properties or attributes ascribable to God and creatures differ in the way they are exemplified.

Suppose I know of two faithful things. If I say nothing but this, you cannot know what I am talking about. For 'thing' is a kind of dummy word and it does not serve to identify anything. But you can still have some idea about what is meant by calling the things I speak of (whatever they are) faithful. At the same time, since you do not know what things I am talking about, you do not know the exact form taken by their fidelity, i.e. what it is like for each of them to be faithful. What is involved in a dog being faithful is different from what is involved in a husband being faithful to his wife. And that, again, is different from, say, a society being faithful to its traditions.

In the language of Aquinas, the point made here can be expressed by saying that there is a difference between the *res significata* (that which is signified) of a descriptive word (e.g. faithful) and its *modus significandi* (mode of signification).[27] The word 'faithful' has meaning regardless of what is being called faithful. Or, as Aquinas would say, it has a *res significata*. But faithfulness can be exhibited in different ways depending on what it is that is faithful. So Aquinas would also say that we must allow for the way in which what is said of something can be true in the case of that thing. We need to allow for what is actually involved in something being thus and so. And, in order to refer to that, Aquinas uses the phrase *modus significandi*. With reference to God, therefore, he argues:

We have to consider two things ... in the words we use to attribute perfections to God, firstly the perfections themselves that are signified—goodness, life and the like—and secondly the way in which they are signified.[28]

The point that Aquinas is getting at here is that one can understand something of what is meant when a thing is said to be thus and

---

[26] Ibid.
[27] The distinction between *res significata* and *modus significandi* goes back at least as far as the work of 12th-century grammarians.
[28] 1a. 13. 3.

so without understanding exactly what it is like for the thing itself to be thus and so. One can, for example, understand the sentence 'Marmaduke is faithful' without knowing whether Marmaduke is someone's husband or someone's cat. According to Aquinas, though we might not be able to understand what it is like for God to be as he may be said to be, it is still, in principle, possible for us to understand what is meant when he is said to be thus and so or such and such. In other words, it is, he thinks, possible to agree that certain words can signify something that is really in God, that we can understand something of what is signified by these words, while it is also true that the way in which God is as he is said to be is not something we can understand.

To put it another way, Aquinas's position is that, while I, for example, exemplify goodness by being a good *man*, God exemplifies it by being *God*. We can both be called 'good' (there is no equivocation in 'I am good' and 'God is good'), but we cannot be good as two things in the same class are good—by having goodness in exactly the same way. 'Good', as Aquinas says, cannot be used 'univocally' (in exactly the same sense) when applied to God and creatures. That is because of God's non-composite nature as grasped by means of the doctrine of divine simplicity. Since I am not my nature or existence, I and my nature are distinguishable and my nature is distinct from my existence. With God, however, such is not the case. He is indistinguishable from his nature and existence, and it follows from this that his way of being differs from that of anything else.

When we say that a man is wise, we signify his wisdom as something distinct from the other things about him—his essence, for example, his powers or his existence. But when we use this word about God we do not intend to signify something distinct from his essence, power or existence. When 'wise' is used of a man, it so to speak contains and delimits the aspect of man that it signifies, but this is not so when it is used of God; what it signifies in God is not confined by the meaning of our word but goes beyond it. Hence it is clear that the word 'wise' is not used in the same sense of God and man, and the same is true of all other words, so they cannot be used univocally of God and creatures.[29]

In short, in speaking of God we use words which are normally employed with respect to things in the world. But, insofar as we speak truly, we will be latching on to something (God) whose way of

---

[29] 1a. 13. 5.

being what we say it is differs from that of anything else we describe in the same manner. In this sense, we both do and do not understand what we are saying when we talk about God.

As Dionysius says, when the scriptures state that nothing is like to God, *they are not denying all likeness to him. For the same things are like and unlike God: like in so far as they imitate as best they can him whom it is not possible to imitate perfectly; unlike in so far as they fall short of their cause.*[30]

Yet Aquinas is clear that some things we say of God are to be understood literally. We would badly misunderstand him if we took him to be arguing that our talk of God is metaphorical. 'Not all words are used of God metaphorically; some are used literally', he notes.[31] He is, of course, happy to say that some words are used of God metaphorically. For Scripture is full of metaphors used to characterize God. It tells us, for example, that God is a rock. But metaphor, for Aquinas, is not a literal mode of discourse. And, in his view, our talk of God is sometimes to be understood literally.

To follow him here it helps to note that he has a kind of test for discriminating between terms applied to God metaphorically and terms applied literally. This involves taking a statement about God and asking, 'Is that really true?' If a negative answer is possible, then the statement is metaphorical. Otherwise the statement must be understood literally.

Consider for example 'God is a rock'. Is that *really* true? Aquinas would reply that it is true in a sense. Rocks are firm and stable, as God can be said to be. But God is not made of the substance of which a rock is formed. He is not even corporeal. So, Aquinas would say, 'God is not *really* a rock', it makes sense to deny that he is a rock, and to call him a rock is to indulge in metaphor.

But what of the statement 'God is good'? Is that really true? Aquinas would here reply that it is unreservedly true, true without qualification. While it makes sense to deny that God is a rock, for Aquinas it makes no sense to deny that God is good. So 'God is good' must be understood literally.

Some words that signify what has come forth from God to creatures do so in such a way that part of the meaning of the word is the imperfect way in which the creature shares in the divine perfection. Thus it is part of the meaning of

---

[30] 1a. 4. 3 ad. 1. The reference is to *The Divine Names*, ch. 9.
[31] 1a. 13. 3.

'rock' that it has its being in a merely material way. Such words can be used of God only metaphorically. There are other words, however, that simply mean certain perfections without any indication of how these perfections are possessed—words, for example, like 'being', 'good', 'living' and so on. These words can be used literally of God.[32]

We can use them in talking of God because, says Aquinas, God must contain the perfections of his creatures. The trick, however, is to recognize that he contains them as their Maker, not as a creature.

This, in turn, suggests to Aquinas that we need to be flexible in the way we speak about God. Since God is totally simple, we must speak of him as if he were both straightforwardly an individual (like a mundane object) and also as if he were abstract (like a pure form).

God is both simple, like a form, and subsistent, like a concrete thing, and so we sometimes refer to him by abstract nouns to indicate his simplicity and sometimes by concrete nouns to indicate his subsistence and completeness; though neither way of speaking measures up to his way of being, for in this life we do not know him as he is in himself.[33]

In other words, it is just as true to say 'God is Goodness' as it is to say 'God is good'. In fact, we need both ways of talking. Since he is not an individual material thing, God is not a mixture (*compositio*) of form and matter, *suppositum* and nature. But he is real enough. So we have to talk of him in the best way we can, which means talking of him as we do of material individuals. Since dangers of misrepresentation follow from this, however, we need to compensate for the practice. One way of doing so is to talk of God as if he were whatever it is that some material things share in being describable individuals—their 'forms' in Aquinas's terminology. You and I may be good, and God is good. But God is also Goodness. And since he is, for example, wise and powerful, God is also Wisdom and Power.

Notice, however, that in taking this line Aquinas is not, as some have supposed, asking us to believe that words used in talking of God (words like 'good' and 'wise') are synonymous. Since he holds that God is simple, he takes God to be the same as (indistinguishable from) his attributes, which, in turn, are the same as (indistinguishable from) himself (all that is in God *is* God). But Aquinas does not

---

[32] Ia. 13. 3, ad. I.
[33] Ia. 13. I ad. 2.

maintain that, for example, 'God is good' *means* the same as 'God is wise'. His point is that, since God is simple, the reality signified by 'the wisdom of God' is the same thing as that signified by 'the goodness of God'. What we mean by a word, he contends,

is the concept we form of what the word signifies. Since we know God from creatures we understand him through concepts appropriate to the perfections creatures receive from him. What pre-exists in God in a simple and unified way is divided amongst creatures as many and varied perfections. The many perfections of creatures correspond to one single source which they represent in varied and complex ways. Thus the different and complex concepts that we have in mind correspond to something altogether simple which they enable us imperfectly to understand. Thus the words we use for the perfections we attribute to God, although they signify what is one, are not synonymous, for they signify it from many different points of view.[34]

In other words, and in the language of Gottlob Frege (1848–1925), expressions like 'the wisdom of God' and 'the goodness of God' have the same 'reference'. They signify one thing—God himself. But they have different 'senses'.[35] Or as McCabe observes, commenting on 1a. 13. 4:

The different predicates we might use of, say, a man—that he is wise, for example, and poor, and intoxicated, are heteronymous in spite of the fact that they all apply to the one man and they all apply to the whole of him, for each one means a different aspect of him. But this cannot be the case with God; the words we use of him cannot be heteronymous because they mean different aspects of him, for there are no different aspects to God. What these words mean in God is entirely one, nevertheless they have different meanings. This is because the meaning of the words—what controls our use of them—is their meaning in application to creatures. When we use them of God we are trying to mean more than this.[36]

---

[34] 1a. 13. 4. For another passage where Aquinas clearly denies that terms applied to God are synonymous, see *Comp.* ch. 25.

[35] See *The Philosophy of Thomas Aquinas*, ed. Christopher Martin (London, 1988), 14. Frege notes that the expressions 'The Morning Star' and 'The Evening Star' clearly differ in sense. They are not synonymous. Yet both signify one and the same thing (the planet Venus). As Frege, therefore, puts it, they differ in sense but not in reference. See Gottlob Frege, 'On Sense and Meaning', in *Collected Papers on Mathematics, Logic and Philosophy*, ed. Brian McGuiness (Oxford, 1984), 157 ff. The term in Frege which I render as 'sense' is *Sinn*. My 'reference' renders Frege's *Bedeutung*, but 'meaning' may be a better rendering—as one of Frege's translators now argues. See P. T. Geach, 'Reference and Buridan's Law', *Philosophy*, 62 (1987).

[36] Appendix 3 to vol. iii of the Blackfriars edition of the *Summa theologiae*, 105.

The Doctrine of Analogy

Though I have avoided the expression, what I have just reported is what commonly goes by the name of 'the doctrine of analogy', the teaching that 'words are used of God and creatures in an analogical way'.[37] Together with the Five Ways, it is probably the thing for which Aquinas is best known, though it is not original to him.[38] As I hope the reader can now see, it is not vastly complicated, though many have made it seem so.[39] All it fundamentally maintains is (1) that terms applied to God and to things in the world are never applied univocally (because creatures are composite and God is simple), but (2) that we need not equivocate when we apply a term to God and a creature (in saying, for example, 'I am good' and 'God is good' we use a word in the same sense to state what is true both of me and of God).[40] To flesh out the nature of Aquinas's doctrine of analogy, however, it is worth adding a few points which will help us to understand it better.

1. Analogy and the Literal

Aquinas's distinction between univocal, equivocal, and analogical is a distinction between literal modes of discourse. Students of Aquinas sometimes suppose that this is not the case. They often think that, when, for example, Aquinas says that 'good' is applied to God and to creatures 'analogically', his meaning is that God is only good 'so to speak' or 'after a fashion'. But this is by no means true.

---

[37] 1a. 13. 5.

[38] The notion that terms can be applied to God and to creatures analogically is one to be found in a number of 13th-century authors indebted, in this respect, to Aristotle.

[39] Thomas de Vio, OP, Cardinal Cajetan (1469–1534), is particularly famous as a scholastic theologian who, in commenting on Aquinas, made heavy weather of his appeal to analogy. See his *The Analogy of Names*, trans. E. A. Bushinski (Pittsburgh, 1953). I am inclined to think that discussions of analogy later than Aquinas attribute to him a position he never had. In this sense I agree with David Burrell when he says: 'Aquinas is perhaps best known for his theory of analogy. On closer inspection it turns out that he never had one' (*Aquinas, God and Action* (London, 1979), 55).

[40] This, at any rate, is the substance of Aquinas's mature position on analogy. It has been argued, however, that his views underwent some development between the *Commentary on the Sentences*, where it is discussed, and the three main texts where it is later treated by him—the *Summa contra Gentiles*, the *De potentia*, and the *Summa theologiae*. Cf. B. Montagnes, OP, *La Doctrine de l'analogie de l'être d'après S. Thomas d'Aquin* (Louvain, 1963).

'I have a red rose' and 'I have a red car' use 'red' in exactly the same sense (univocally). Both uses are literal. 'I was struck by a rake' (said of a garden tool and a lecherous man) uses 'rake' with unconnected meanings, so is equivocal. But it still uses the word literally. And literal use of one and the same word would, in Aquinas's view, be what is involved in the case of a term applied analogically to God and to a creature. On his account, we may, for example, say that Solomon and God are both wise. And, for him, that is because both Solomon and God really are wise. In 'Solomon is wise' and 'God is wise' the word 'wise', Aquinas thinks, is used in different but related ways. And both uses are literal.

2. *Applying Primarily*

Aquinas thinks that words used analogously of God and creatures apply primarily to God and secondarily to creatures. This may seem a curious line for him to take since he believes that we name God from creatures and, therefore, that we speak of him using words by which we describe things which we know better than we know him. That might lead us to expect Aquinas to say that terms applied to God and creatures apply primarily to creatures and secondarily to God. Yet his view is the opposite of this.

When we say God is good or wise we do not simply mean that he causes wisdom or goodness, but that he possesses these perfections transcendently. We conclude, therefore, that from the point of view of what the word means it is used primarily of God and derivatively of creatures.[41]

For Aquinas, wisdom in creatures derives from God, and therefore from what 'the wisdom of God' signifies. In this sense, Solomon's wisdom, for instance, is something that waits on the wisdom of God, something that would not exist if God were not there as Wisdom itself. In Aquinas's view, therefore, God is primarily what his creatures are insofar as they are perfect. We speak of him by means of a language appropriate to talking of creatures. And we judge it to serve as a way of speaking truly of God. But creatures derive from God, and, insofar as they resemble him, they do so as things which show forth what is in God before it is in them.

The idea which Aquinas is presenting here can also be viewed as

---

[41] 1a. 13. 7.

expressing a notion found in Denys. According to Denys, when we
say that God is not thus and so, we are not asserting that it is simply
or unqualifiedly false that he is thus and so. His view is that negations
concerning God must themselves, in a sense, be negated. For, as we
have seen, he holds that God can be 'named' from everything (compared to anything) because he is the creator of everything. This, in
turn, leads him to be fond of the prefix 'hyper' ('above'). We may
deny that God is good, but not in order baldly to assert, 'It is not the
case that God is good', for we may say, 'God is hyper-good', meaning that his goodness transcends the goodness of created things while
at the same time being reflected in that.

What has actually to be said about the Cause of everything is this. Since it is
the Cause of all beings, we should posit and ascribe to it all the affirmations
we make in regard to beings, and, more appropriately, we should negate all
these affirmations. Now we should not conclude that the negations are simply
the opposites of the affirmations, but rather that the cause of all is considerably prior to this, beyond privations, beyond every denial, beyond every
assertion.[42]

For Denys, 'God is good' is not false. But it is inadequate—in
something like the way 'Mozart is musical' is inadequate, or is an
understatement, though not false.[43] And just as we might say that
Mozart and figures of musical genius comparable with him set standards of musicality with reference to which the musicality of the
average musician can be judged, so Aquinas will say that words used
analogously of God and creatures apply primarily to God and
secondarily to creatures. For him, for example, goodness in creatures
derives from and is but a pale reflection of the goodness exemplified
by God. Considered as such, it is goodness in a derived or secondary
sense. His conclusion, therefore, is that

because we come to a knowledge of God from other things, the reality in the
names said of God and other things belongs by priority in God according to
his mode of being, but the meaning of the name belongs to God by pos-
teriority. And so he is said to be named from his effects.[44]

We call God good and the like having first learned to call creatures
good and the like. In this sense God's goodness and the like is

---

[42] *The Mystical Theology*, ch. 1.
[43] I owe this example to Simon Tugwell. See *Albert and Thomas: Selected Writings*
(New York, 1988), 42 f.
[44] *SG* 1. 34.

secondary to what is found in creatures. But it is also prior, since what is found in creatures derives from God, whose way of being what we say he is makes creatures who are like him nothing more than imitators of something lying beyond them.

3. Analogy and Other Arguments

Since Aquinas holds that God can be named from his creatures because he is their Maker, one could say that his doctrine of analogy provides a self-contained method for constructing a language in which to talk of God. Roughly speaking, the rule would be: take any property and ascribe it to God while denying of him any creaturely limitations. But it is also possible (and in some ways more useful) to think of Aquinas's comments on analogy somewhat differently. For they can also be read as a reflection on or description of what is going on with the language we use in talking of God before we construct a doctrine of analogy. E. L. Mascall observes: 'The function of the doctrine of analogy is not to make it possible for us to talk about God in the future but to explain how it is that we have been able to talk about him all along.'[45] And Mascall, I think, is right, for at least three reasons.

In the first place, in the *Summa theologiae* (as in other works) Aquinas only mentions analogy after he has explained why God must be spoken of in certain specific ways. 1a. 13 (the *locus classicus* for Aquinas on analogy) follows a set of questions in which Aquinas argues for the truth of a number of positive assertions concerning God—e.g. 'God is a cause', 'God is good', 'God is perfect', 'God is everywhere', and 'God is eternal'.

Second, Aquinas often gives reasons for ascribing certain attributes to God without having recourse to the 'God-is-like-his-creatures' argument which features in his discussion of analogy.

Third, viewed with the two facts just mentioned in mind, what Aquinas offers in 1a. 13 and in parallel texts is, effectively, a summary of much that emerges from arguments given elsewhere, which suggests that the contents of 1a. 13 and the like need to be read together with such arguments.

In short, fully to understand Aquinas on analogy, we will need to see how he reasons when not directly concerned with it as a distinct

---

[45] *Existence and Analogy* (London, 1949), 94.

topic. For, in his view (and as we shall be seeing in the next few chapters), while the doctrine of analogy shows that the way is open in principle for speaking of God truly and literally, particular statements about God can be justified individually and with no direct recourse to the doctrine.

4. Family Resemblances

There is a modern parallel to Aquinas's notion of analogy in the work of the philosopher Ludwig Wittgenstein (1889–1951). In his *Philosophical Investigations*, Wittgenstein speaks of what he calls 'family resemblances'. A word, he says, though it is not always used in the same sense, need not always be used in a sense unrelated to that which it has on a given occasion.

Consider for example the proceedings that we call 'games'. I mean board-games, card-games, ball-games, Olympic games, and so on. What is common to them all?—Don't say: 'There *must* be something common, or they would not be called "games"'—but *look and see* whether there is anything common to all.—For if you look at them you will not see something that is common to *all*, but similarities, relationships, and a whole series of them at that.[46]

As the members of a family can resemble each other without looking exactly like each other, so, affirms Wittgenstein, words can sometimes mean something different on different occasions without meaning something entirely different on the occasions in question. 'We see a complicated network of similarities overlapping and criss-crossing: sometimes overall similarities, sometimes similarities of detail.'[47] This is very close to what Aquinas teaches concerning the way in which terms are applied to God and creatures. We may say, for example, that Solomon is wise and that God is wise. We do not mean that God's wisdom is just what Solomon's wisdom amounts to. But nor do we mean that it is something wholly unlike this. Solomon and God are alike, even if they are also very different. In calling both of them wise we are not equivocating. But neither are we putting them on a level with each other.

One should not push the parallel between Aquinas and Wittgenstein too far. But it is worth observing that they complement each other in

---

[46] *Philosophical Investigations*, trans. G. E. M. Anscombe (Oxford, 1968), para. 66.
[47] Ibid.

at least this respect: both of them allow for literal talk using terms which differ in what Aquinas would call their *modus significandi*. Wittgenstein seems to be saying that knowing what is going on somewhere in being told that a tennis game is going on is knowing about something very different from what one would be knowing in knowing that, say, a game of patience is going on somewhere. But in each case one would know of a game taking place. In a similar way, Aquinas would argue, knowing what is true in knowing that I am good is knowing something very different from what one would know about in knowing that God is good. But we are not equivocating in speaking of me as good and of God as good.

Real and Notional Relations

So we now have before us the substance of Aquinas's teaching on the significance of our talk of God. To put it as simply as possible, he holds to three theses. (1) We do not know what God is, for he cannot be defined and he differs quite radically from the things to which we compare him. (2) As the source of his creatures, however, God may be said to resemble them, though he lacks all creaturely limitations. (3) There is room for arguing that certain specific predicates can be ascribed to him.

In the next few chapters I shall be trying to explain how Aquinas puts these theses to work in detail, and this will serve to round out the contents of this chapter and the last. As an appendix to what I have just been reporting, however, some comments are in order concerning a conclusion propounded by Aquinas in the course of his treatment of analogy in the *Summa theologiae*. This is the suggestion (a common one in Aquinas's day) that while creatures are really related to God, God is not really related to creatures—that, in Aquinas's words,

since God is altogether outside the order of creatures, since they are ordered to him but not he to them, it is clear that being related to God is a reality in creatures, but being related to creatures is not a reality in God.[48]

The suggestion certainly seems rather extraordinary when stated baldly. And some have attacked it with vigour. The commonest

---

[48] 1a. 13. 7. Cf. also *SG* 2. 11 and *De pot.* 7. 8 ff. For modern philosophical discussion of the suggestion, see Peter Geach, 'God's Relation to the World', *Sophia*, 8 (1969) and C. J. F. Williams, 'Is God Related to His Creatures?', *Sophia*, 8 (1969).

criticisms of it are (1) that God must be really related to his creatures since, if they are related to him, both are related to each other (if John stands in the relation 'father of' to Bill, Bill must stand in a corresponding relation to John), and (2) God must be really related to his creatures since the contrary suggestion implies that God is detached or distant from his creation. It is therefore important to recognize that Aquinas does not deny these rebuttals. If one reads him in detail on the question of God's relation to creatures, one will, in fact, find him endorsing all of the following propositions. (1) We can speak of God as related to his creatures in view of the purely formal point that if one thing can be said to be related to another, then the second thing can be said to be related to the first. (2) Since God can be compared to creatures, since he can be spoken of as being like them, he can be thought of as related to them. (3) Since God knows creatures, he can be said to be related to them. (4) Since God moves creatures, he can be said to be related to them. (5) Since God can be spoken of as 'first', 'highest', and so on, he can be said to be related to creatures since these terms are relational ones.[49]

What, in fact, Aquinas is saying in his (curious sounding) teaching on God's relation to the world is that God is not something alongside his creatures. For Aquinas, God is the source of his creatures and, for this reason, is distinct from and different from them. Given the difference between God and creatures, Aquinas reasons, it can be said that being a creature is something in the creature but not something in God. Or, to put it another way, the fact that there are creatures is a fact about creatures, not God.

This may sound terribly esoteric and deeply confused, which is how it has seemed to numerous readers of Aquinas and of those who in his day and earlier said the same thing. But what he is driving at is really quite intelligible and not particularly incredible. To see this, consider the following example.

Suppose I go to Australia and spend a long time there as a tourist. In these circumstances, I could be said to acquire a knowledge of Australia or, simply, to know Australia. I could also be said to stand in a certain relation to Australia—i.e. one of knowledge. It is the case that I know Australia. It is the case that Australia is known by me.

On the other hand, however, my knowing Australia is nothing in

---

[49] *De pot.* 7. 10.

Australia. Of course it is true that logicians who know that I know Australia can infer that Australia is known by me. But logicians who know that Australia is known by me need be no better informed about Australia than non-logicians who have never been there.

Or consider another example. The money in your pocket, so the government might say, is worth more than it was worth a year ago. So the money in your pocket now is more valuable than the money in your pocket a year ago. From this we can conclude that your money of a year ago was less valuable than it is now. But this 'being more valuable' or 'being less valuable' is not something in the stuff which is in your pocket. Our talk of value here does not describe what is in your pocket. It is a way of indicating how we think of it, of what it means for our purposes.

This, Aquinas reasons, is the way it is with respect to God and his creatures. Creatures, he thinks, are created by God, and the fact that they are created is part and parcel of them being what they are. They are creatures, just as Australia is an enormous island and just as the money in your pocket weighs so many ounces or has such and such a chemical structure. To think of creatures as uncreated would be simply false—just as to think that Australia was not an island would be false, or just as to think that a coin had such and such a weight might be false. In this sense, Aquinas reasons, being related to God is a reality in creatures.[50]

And yet, he adds, there is nothing comparable in God. Of course we can say that God is the Creator of his creatures. But, Aquinas wants to suggest, God being the Creator of his creatures is like Australia being known by me or like the money in my pocket being now worth more than it was a year ago. For Aquinas, the fact that there are creatures makes no difference to God—just as the fact that I know Australia makes no difference to Australia, and just as the fact that my coming to be able to buy more with my coins and notes makes no difference to them. In Aquinas's view, God is unchangeably himself and he remains this way even though it is true that there are creatures created and sustained by him.

Another way of making the point is by employing some terminology invented by Peter Geach—a distinction between 'Cambridge changes' and 'merely Cambridge changes'.[51]

---

[50] For an account of Aquinas and other medieval authors on the topic of relations, see Mark G. Henninger, SJ, *Relations: Medieval Theories 1250–1325* (Oxford, 1989).

[51] P. T. Geach, *Logic Matters* (Oxford, 1972), 321 f. and *God and the Soul*, 71 f.

Suppose that Fred is outgrown by Bill. Someone might observe that Fred has become shorter than Bill. Let us say that this observation reports a 'Cambridge change' in Fred—for it squares with a criterion of change given by some well-known Cambridge philosophers of the early twentieth century (e.g. Russell). According to this criterion, a thing has changed if at one time it is describable thus and so, while it is later describable differently.[52]

Are we now to say that Fred must have really changed in himself? He might have done, for he might have shrunk. But there is another possibility. 'Fred has become shorter than Bill' could be true simply because Bill has grown taller than Fred. We can put this by saying that, in that case, we are here dealing with a 'merely Cambridge change'—something that counts as a Cambridge change without involving a real change in the subject we are talking about.

The thing to note now is that, in his discussion of God's relations to the world, one of Aquinas's principal concerns is to insist that, when ascribing 'Cambridge change' to God, we are, in fact, only reporting 'merely Cambridge changes'—that statements relating God and his creatures so as apparently to predicate real change of him are true only because of real changes in creatures. In reporting what goes on here we speak of God as acquiring new relational properties (as undergoing genuine change). But this is only a way of speaking, for God acquires nothing and is unchanging.

Since God is altogether outside the order of creatures . . . it is clear that being related to God is a reality in creatures, but being related to creatures is not a reality in God; we say it about him because of the real relation in creatures. So it is that when we speak of his relation to creatures we can apply words implying temporal sequence and change, not because of any change in him but because of a change in the creatures; just as we can say that the pillar has changed from being on my left to being on my right, not through any alteration in the pillar but simply because I have turned around . . . God's temporal relations to creatures are in him only because of our way of thinking about him, but the opposite relations of creatures to him are realities in the creatures. It is quite admissible to attribute a relation to God because of something that takes place in the creature, for we cannot express the reality in creatures without talking as though there were matching relations also in God, so that God is said to be related to a creature because the creature is related to him.[53]

[52] In Geach's formulation: 'The thing called "*x*" has changed if we have "*F(x)*" at time *t* true and "*F(x)*" at time *t1*" false, for some interpretation of "*F*", "*t*" and "*t1*"' (*God and the Soul*, 71 f.).
[53] 1a. 13. 7.

We can connect these remarks with what Aquinas says about tenses and God. We use tensed statements with God as subject, he notes. So we seem to imply that God undergoes change. But what makes the statements true, says Aquinas, is changes not in God but in creatures. We can date God's actions. But only because there is history in which events occur successively. Or, as we can say today, God became the giver of victory to William of Normandy in 1066, not because God somehow changed in 1066, but because William conquered England in that year. More of this in Chapter 6, however.

5

Perfection and Goodness

AQUINAS thinks that God defies our comprehension. But, as we have seen, he also holds that we are still able to make true statements about him. So far, however, we have only looked at how he defends this thesis in general terms, and it is now time to descend to particulars. What exactly does he think we can say of God? His remarks on the matter deal with assertions of two types: (1) Those which can be made and defended on rational grounds without recourse to special (Christian) revelation; (2) those which derive from revelation. The second group will concern us later in this book. In this chapter, and the three chapters following, we shall consider Group (1), starting with the assertions 'God is perfect' and 'God is good'.

God is Perfect

Aquinas is not insensitive to objections to calling God perfect. For example, so he notes, on grounds of etymology we should think of a 'perfect' thing as something that is 'thoroughly made' (from the Latin *perficere*). But God is not made. He is the unmade Maker of everything other than himself. How, then, can he be called 'perfect'?

'Perfect' does not seem a suitable term to apply to God, for etymologically it means 'thoroughly made'. Now since we would not say that God is made, we should not say that he is perfect.[1]

Then again, says Aquinas, God's nature is to exist. But every existing thing, no matter how lowly, exists, while to say that something is perfect seems to imply that it is special in some sense. So should we not say that the fact that God's nature is to exist means that he is nothing special and, therefore, not perfect? How could he be this if he is what anything manages to be?

---

[1] 1a. 4. 1 obj. 1.

The nature of God is simply to exist. Now simply to exist is seemingly most imperfect: the lowest common denominator of all things. God then is not perfect.[2]

But God, Aquinas holds, certainly is perfect, as the Bible teaches. 'We read in *Matthew: be ye perfect, as your heavenly Father is perfect.*'[3] And he argues that the truth of this teaching is evident in the light of two arguments, the background to which should be clear in the light of the last two chapters.

The first is that God is perfect because he is fully actual. Aquinas thinks that perfection is the opposite of imperfection. He also thinks that imperfection is present when something which is potentially perfect is actually imperfect. As he sees it, an imperfect thing (e.g. a rotten egg) is something which is lacking what ought to be there (we object to rotten eggs because they are not what we expect eggs to be). In this sense, something imperfect fails because it is not what it could be, because, in Aquinas's language, it lacks a certain sort of actuality.[4] And, since he takes God to be wholly actual, Aquinas therefore concludes that God can be thought of as perfect.

The first origin of all activity will be the most actual, and therefore the most perfect, of all things. For things are called perfect when they have achieved actuality, the perfect thing being that in which nothing required by the thing's particular mode of perfection fails to exist . . . Because things that are made are called perfect when the potentiality of them has been actualized, we extend the word to refer to anything that is not lacking in actuality, whether made or not.[5]

To cast things in the manner of negative theology, God must be perfect since he is in no way potential—since there is nothing which he could be but is not. Since God, for Aquinas, has no potentiality, he cannot be modified and cannot, therefore, be either improved or made worse. There is with him no 'could be thus and so but is not'. For God to be, therefore, is for God to be as divine as it takes divinity to be. It is for God to be fully God and, therefore, perfectly God.

---

[2] 1a. 4. 1 obj. 3.
[3] 1a. 4. 1.
[4] Cf. *Comp.* ch. 20: 'Imperfection occurs in a thing for the reason that matter is found in a state of privation. On the other hand, perfection comes exclusively from form.'
[5] 1a. 4. 1.

Each thing is perfect according as it is in act, and imperfect according as it is in potency and lacking act. Hence, that which is in no way in potency, but is pure act, must be most perfect. Such however, is God. God is, therefore, most perfect.[6]

Second, says Aquinas, God is perfect because he is the cause of his creatures and must therefore contain their perfections. As we saw in the last chapter, Aquinas thinks that causes are reflected in their effects. On this basis he reasons that God contains in himself all the perfections of his creatures and is therefore properly called perfect. Once again, we need to note that Aquinas does not here mean that God has the perfections of his creatures in the way that they have them. He does not, for example, suppose that a perfect tadpole or a perfect house *look* like God. For him, God does not have the perfections of creatures in the mode possessed by them (as a woman might have the perfections of her daughter because she has equivalent intelligence or a similar physical appearance). But he does hold that, insofar as a creature is perfect, its perfection exists in God as its cause as, for example, 'a teacher has in his own mind the knowledge he hands on to others'.[7] The perfections of creatures flow from God and therefore express something of what he is.

God is self-subsistent being itself, and therefore necessarily contains within himself the full perfection of being. For clearly a hot thing falls short of the full perfection of heat only because it does not fully partake of the nature of heat; to a self-subsistent heat nothing of the virtue of heat could be lacking. Nothing therefore of the perfection of existing can be lacking to God, who is subsistent existence itself. Now every perfection is a perfection of existing, for it is the manner in which a thing exists which determines the manner of its perfection. No perfection can therefore be lacking to God.[8]

So, says Aquinas, 'we echo the heights of God as best we can', and we call God perfect because of what his creatures are and because of what he cannot be. For this reason, we may even say that creatures resemble God. For they share a form (a 'whatness') with God according to their mode of being as things created. They cannot bear likeness to God of the same specific or generic type as the form of God. They cannot be exactly what God is because he is not in any

---

[6] *SG* I. 28. 6.
[7] *Comp.* ch. 21.
[8] Ia. 4. 2.

creaturely class. But, as having existence, they resemble the primary and universal source of existence.[9]

In speaking of creatures as resembling God, Aquinas is not denying what we saw him to be saying in Chapter 3. He is still concerned with what God is not. We can, he declares, admit that creatures are like God. But only *aliquo modo* (in a way). And, he adds, it is inappropriate to say that God resembles creatures.

Although we may admit in a way that creatures resemble God, we may in no way admit that God resembles creatures; for, as Dionysius points out, *mutual likeness obtains between things of the same order, but not between cause and effect* [*The Divine Names*, 9, 6]: thus we would call a portrait a likeness of a man, but not vice-versa.[10]

At the same time, however, Aquinas also thinks that creatures resemble God in quite specific ways. As we will see later, he thinks of some people as being like God by virtue of grace, for this makes us sharers in the divine nature. But he also thinks it possible to argue that there are definite ways in which creatures resemble God even without reference to grace. He thinks, for example, that human beings resemble God since they are made in God's image, as is taught in Genesis 1: 26. *X* is an image of *Y*, says Aquinas, if *X* is copied from *Y* and if *X* is like *Y* in a more than passing way. Human beings, he adds, are copied from God, since all that they are comes from what he is.[11] And, like God, they have knowledge and understanding.[12] So human beings are in God's image, albeit that they are not God's perfect image.

It is plain that people bear some likeness to God that is derived from God as its original, though this likeness does not amount to equality, since this particular original infinitely surpasses the thing modelled on it. So then we say that God's image is to be found in people, though not his perfect image. This is indicated by Scripture when it says that people were made *after* God's image; for the preposition 'after' signifies the sort of approximation which is attainable by an essentially distant object.[13]

---

[9] Cf. 1a. 4. 3.
[10] 1a. 4. 3 ad. 4; cf. *SG* 1. 29. 5.
[11] 1a. 93. 1.
[12] 1a. 93. 2.
[13] 1a. 93. 1.

God is Good

Turning now to Aquinas on God's goodness, the first thing to note is that his view differs from one that has been widely espoused, especially in modern times—i.e. the view that God is good because he is *morally good*, because he is decent and virtuous, or because he has a firm grasp of the duties and obligations bearing on any right-minded individual (or god) and always acts in keeping with them.[14] Aquinas does not believe that God has virtues. Nor does he think of God as subject to duty or obligation. He certainly thinks that terms signifying human moral perfections can be predicated of God. He is clear that we can speak of God as just, truthful, or loving, for instance. But words which designate moral perfections in human beings do not, for him, signify God's moral integrity. And, to the often-repeated argument that this cannot be true since God is a good person, Aquinas would simply deny the implied premise. For him, God is not a person—not, at least, if 'person' means what it usually does for those who insist that God is a person, i.e. an instance of a kind, a mind with many and changing thoughts. There is a sense in which he would agree that God is a person. He says that if we take 'person' to signify 'that which is most perfect in the whole of nature, namely what subsists in rational nature', then God can be spoken of as a person since he has all perfections. And he stands by this conclusion even though he recognizes that there are objections to it (e.g. that the word 'person' is not used in the Bible to refer to God).[15] But he also insists that, if God is to be God, he cannot be a person as you and I are persons. He thinks that 'person', as applied to God, is an honorific term, not one designed to indicate that God is in any way potential, as people are.

1. *Good as Relative and Desirable*

To understand Aquinas's position on the goodness of God we must first know something about his view of goodness in general. And here there are two main points to note, the first of which we can introduce by means of a distinction between what have been called logically 'attributive' adjectives and logically 'predicative' ones.

---

[14] For a modern statement of a contrary view see Richard Swinburne, *The Coherence of Theism* (Oxford, 1977), 179 f.

[15] 1a. 29. 3 ad. 1.

Following an analysis offered by Peter Geach, let us say that 'in a phrase "an *AB*" ("*A*" being an adjective and "*B*" being a noun) "*A*" is a (logically) predicative adjective if the predication "is an *AB*" splits up into a pair of predications "is a *B*" and "is *A*"'. Let us also say that, if such is not the case, '*A*' is a (logically) attributive adjective.[16] On this account, 'big' and 'small' are attributive adjectives and 'red' is predicative. As Geach suggests:

'*X* is a big flea' does not split up into '*X* is a flea' and '*X* is big', nor '*X* is a small elephant' into '*X* is an elephant' and '*X* is small'; for if these analyses were legitimate, a simple argument would show that a big flea is a big animal and a small elephant a small animal . . . On the other hand, in the phrase 'a red book', 'red' is a predicative adjective . . . for 'is a red book' logically splits up into 'is a book' and 'is red'.[17]

With this distinction in mind we can note that 'good', for Aquinas, is logically attributive. He does not think of it as signifying a common property shared by everything which has it. He holds that its use on a given occasion cannot be understood unless one knows to what it is being applied. In this sense, he thinks of goodness as relative. For him, 'good' works like 'big' and 'small', and differs from 'red'. To appreciate what is meant when told that something is good, one needs to know which noun the adjective is qualifying.

On the other hand, however (and coming to the second point), Aquinas does think that some general account can be given of what it means to call something good. For, following Aristotle, he maintains that 'good is what all things desire',[18] and that the desired goal for a thing is its perfection, which is a matter of actuality. On his account, therefore, goodness is the same as actuality, and to be good is to exist. 'To be good is really the same thing as to exist . . . What a thing is, as a being and a substance, is a definite good.'[19]

The fundamental thought governing this thesis is that goodness is what is aimed at or sought, that good things are things which are wanted or attractive, that a good *X* is an *X* which has whatever features are desirable in that kind of thing. Or, as Aquinas also says, a good *X* is an *X* which achieves a degree of perfection considered as

---

[16] P. T. Geach, 'Good and Evil', reprinted in Philippa Foot (ed.), *Theories of Ethics* (Oxford, 1967), 64.
[17] Ibid.
[18] *Ethics*, I. I. 1094ª3.
[19] Ia. 5. I and Ia2ae. 8. I.

the kind of thing it is. In this sense, being a good X is *being* something—i.e., a thing exhibiting what is desirable considered as the kind of thing it is. Being a good word processor, for instance, is being something with the features we look for in word processors.

For Aquinas, then, goodness is connected with being. In his view, the goodness of a thing lies in perfection actualized. A thing is good insofar as it is desirable, and insofar as it *is* in some sense.

The goodness of a thing consists in its being desirable ... Now clearly desirability is consequent upon perfection, for things always desire their perfection. And the perfection of a thing depends on how far it has achieved actuality. It is clear then that a thing is good inasmuch as it exists, for ... it is by existing that everything achieves actuality.[20]

Aquinas does not think that 'good' and 'existing' are synonymous. For he concedes that something can exist without being wholly perfect. But he also argues that, even if something is not good without qualification (even if it is not wholly actual), it must be actual, and therefore good, simply by virtue of existing. In this sense, he concludes, everything that exists is good.

For everything, inasmuch as it exists, is actual and therefore in some way perfect, all actuality being a sort of perfection. Now ... anything perfect is desirable and good. It follows then that, inasmuch as they exist, all things are good.[21]

This optimistic sounding theory is very much at the heart of Aquinas's thinking. He explicitly rejects the view that creation, *qua* creation, is or contains evil.[22] He also denies that there can be anything which is purely evil. 'Nothing can be essentially evil', he affirms, 'since evil must always have as its foundation some subject, distinct from it, that is good.'[23] On his account, not even the Devil is all bad. 'There cannot be a being which is supremely evil, in the way that there is a being that is supremely good because it is essentially good.'[24]

2. How is God Good?

With Aquinas's general account of 'good' behind us, we can now turn directly to why he thinks of God as good. To put it in a nutshell,

---

[20] 1a. 5. 1.
[21] 1a. 5. 3.
[22] Cf. 1a. 65. 2. and 3. Also 2a2ae. 25. 5.
[23] *Comp.* ch. 17.   [24] Ibid.

God, for Aquinas, is good because he is *desirable* and because he is perfectly actual. In the *Nicomachean Ethics* Aristotle suggests that the good is 'that at which all things aim'.[25] And that is what Aquinas wants to say.

Goodness should be associated above all with God. For goodness is consequent upon desirability. Now things desire their perfection; and an effect's perfection and form consists in resembling its cause, since what a thing does reflects what it is. So the cause itself is desirable and can be called 'good', what is desired from it being a share in resembling it. Clearly, then, since God is the primary operative cause of everything, goodness and desirability fittingly belong to him. And so Dionysius [*The Divine Names*, 4. 4] ascribes goodness to God as to the primary operative cause, saying that God is called good as the source of all subsistence.[26]

What Aquinas is driving at here might be clear from what is noted above. But we need to fill in the details. For he now seems to be saying that God is desirable since all things desire him, which seems false. There are people who know nothing of God, or who do not believe in him. Why should we think that they desire God? And what about non-human creatures? What about dogs and fish? What about the cabbages in the garden? How can they be thought to desire God?

To understand Aquinas at this point, we need to note that, in the present context, 'desire' does not mean 'conscious desire'—implying an awareness of what is desired by people who would agree that they have a given desire. When Aquinas speaks of desire, he is thinking of what we might also call 'inclination' or 'tendency' (*inclinatio* or *appetitus* in Aquinas's Latin). His idea is that all things desire goodness ('good is what all things desire') in the sense that they are naturally drawn to their perfection, whatever that may consist in, and however varied its exemplification from case of case.

In his view, each thing has by nature an appetite for or tendency to its perfection and good. Or, bearing in mind the connection he sees between being and goodness, his suggestion is that everything naturally tends *to be* itself. Left to themselves, he thinks, things just are what they are by nature. They may be interfered with, and may, therefore, be thwarted or defective, considered as the kind of thing they are. But, in the absence of interference, things simply realize their natures. They 'seek' to be themselves.

[25] I. I. 1094^{a}3.
[26] Ia. 6. I.

With this point in mind, Aquinas now asks the following question. Given that every creature naturally seeks its perfection, is what it seeks something which lies in itself, or is it something to be found elsewhere? And the answer he gives is that the perfection sought by creatures lies outside them.

Here, an analogy might help. Suppose we have a good alarm clock. In being what it is, does it tend towards being what it has determined for itself? Since it has a maker, the answer would seem to be 'No'. Left by itself, a good alarm clock continues to be what it is. But that is something intended by the person who has constructed it. In this sense, the goodness of the alarm clock follows from its maker's intention (from what the maker has in mind) and its goodness is an embodiment of what first of all lies in its maker (albeit that the maker does not look in the slightest like a good alarm clock). The tendency of the clock to be what it is, and therefore to be good, is built into it by the maker who determined that it should be the kind of thing it is.

For Aquinas, this is how it is with everything created. In his view, created things are made by God, and they all seek to be themselves (they seek their good) by acting in accordance with what God intends (has in mind) for them. For this reason Aquinas suggests that in seeking (tending to) their good, creatures are manifesting a kind of blueprint in the divine mind, that 'all things are said to be good by divine goodness, which is the pattern, source and goal of all goodness'.[27] As he sees it, this means that they are seeking God. For their goal is something that lies in God as their Maker. God is that by virtue of which there is something instead of nothing. So he is the ultimate Maker, the ultimately desirable, the ultimate good. He is the omega because he is the alpha. He is the end (what is desirable) because he is the beginning.

That is what Aquinas is saying in the last quotation given above. It is also part of what he is driving at in his teaching that God contains the perfections of his creatures (see above, Chapter 4, to the account in which we have now therefore added). And, to round off his account of God's goodness, he basically has only two further things to say. The first is that God is not just good. He is *supremely* good. The second is that God alone is good by nature. He is supremely good because, not being in any class to which others belong, he is not so much 'a good such and such' as Goodness itself (see above,

[27] 1a. 6. 4.

Chapters 3 and 4). And he alone is good by nature since, unlike everything other than himself, (1) he has no risk of failing to exist (and hence of failing to be what he is by nature), (2) he has no potentiality for change (and hence improvement), and (3) he has no goal of perfection outside himself to which he is drawn.

Since it is as first source of everything not himself in a genus that God is good, he must be good in the most perfect manner possible. And for this reason we call him supremely good . . . he alone exists by nature, and in him there are no added accidents (power, wisdom and the like which are accidental to other things belonging to him by nature, as already noted). Moreover, he is not disposed towards some extrinsic goal, but is himself the ultimate goal of all other things. So it is clear that only God possesses every kind of perfection by nature. He alone therefore is by nature good.[28]

God and Evil

At this point, however, we come to an ancient and much discussed problem. For it is obvious that there is a lot of badness around. The world contains a great deal of evil. How, then, do we square this fact with the teaching that God is good? If everything comes from God, as Aquinas holds, should we not properly conclude that God, in fact, is not good?

To put it as simply as possible, Aquinas's answer is that there can be no question of God's goodness being called into question because he has produced what is evil. Ultimately, says Aquinas, the explanation of evil is not to be found in what God has *done* or is *doing*. Rather, it lies in what he has *not* done or is *not* doing.

1. Evil and Privation

Aquinas's thinking here has a definite background, of which a very important element is the position on evil offered by St Augustine. Himself much influenced by Neoplatonists such as Plotinus, Augustine maintained that evil is negative and can be defined as a privation of goodness (*privatio boni*).

For what is that which we call evil but the absence of good? In the bodies of animals, disease and wounds mean nothing but the absence of health; for

---

[28] 1a. 6 and 7.

when a cure is effected, that does not mean that the evils which were present—namely, the disease and wounds—go away from the body and dwell elsewhere: they altogether cease to exist; for the wound or disease is not a substance, but a defect in the fleshly substance,—the flesh itself being a substance, and therefore something good, of which those evils—that is privations of the good which we call health—are accidents.[29]

For Augustine, God is the Creator and, as it says in the Bible, God looked on his creation and found it good. Augustine's view, therefore, is that creation as such is nothing but good, and what we call evil must be uncreated. It must be other than what God produces by creating.[30]

In this Aquinas agrees with Augustine. As we have seen, he thinks of goodness in creatures in terms of there *being* something. On his account, something is good since it has what it needs to be itself, since it is perfect or actual in some way. In that case, however, to say that something is bad (or evil) is to say, not that it *has* something, but that it *lacks* something. As Aquinas puts it, badness is nothing positive. It is a 'privation of form'.

Like night from day, you learn about one opposite from the other. So you take good in order to grasp what evil means. Now we have accepted the definition that good is everything that is desirable. Well, then, since each real thing tends to its own existence and completion, we have to say that this fulfils the meaning of good in every case. Therefore evil cannot signify a certain existing being, or a real shaping or positive kind of thing. Consequently, we are left to infer that it signifies a certain absence of a good.[31]

It is important to notice that Aquinas is not here asserting that evil simply does not exist. He is not, for example, telling us that evil is an illusion, as Mary Baker Eddy taught in her claim that 'all inharmony of mortal mind or body is illusion, possessing neither reality nor identity though seeming to be real and identical'.[32] Evil, he holds, can be said to be since judgements of the form '*X* is bad' can be true.[33] He is not saying without qualification that badness (or evil) is not there. Nor does he deny that the falling short which leads us to talk

[29] *Enchiridion*, ch. 11. For Plotinus on evil as privation see *Enneads*, 1. 8. 3.

[30] For a full account of Augustine and evil see G. R. Evans, *Augustine on Evil* (Cambridge, 1982).

[31] 1a. 48. 1.

[32] *Science and Health with Key to the Scriptures* (Boston, 1971), 275.

[33] 1a. 48. 2 ad. 2.

of badness (or evil) can be and is recognized as something of which one has to take account. He would agree, for example, that:

> If I have a hole in my sock, the hole is not anything at all, it is just an absence of wool or cotton or whatever, but it is a perfectly real hole in my sock. It would be absurd to say that holes in socks are unreal and illusory just because the hole isn't made of anything and is purely an absence. *Nothing* in the wrong place can be just as real and just as important as *something* in the wrong place. If you inadvertently drive your car over a cliff, you will have nothing to worry about; it is precisely the nothing that you will have to worry about.[34]

He would also agree that something can be bad because something is there. He does not mean that what is bad always lacks some bit or part. In his view, a thing may be bad because it has unwanted extras. As he might say today, a bad word processor can be one that, as well as having all the pieces you expect to find in it, also has a pint of glue installed.

His point is that a thing is only bad because something which *ought* to be there is not there. This is the sense in which he thinks, evil can be said not to be. Just as to say, 'There is nothing here', is not to say of *something* that it is here, so, in Aquinas's view, to say that there is evil is not to say that there is any real thing.

> The word 'being' is used in two senses. In the first to signify the entity of a thing, and so taken it is . . . equivalent to what is real. And in this sense no privation is a being, and consequently no evil either.[35]

There is evil. And there is gold in them there hills. But, so Aquinas thinks, we must distinguish between there being evil and there being gold. In the case of the gold, we have an independently existing substance, something there to talk about, something to which we can assign properties. In the case of evil, we have the opposite of good. We have what ought to be there but is not—a kind of non-being which only exists because something is failing in some respect.

For Aquinas, therefore, the question to ask when confronted by evil is not, 'Why does God produce so much evil?' It is, 'Why is there less good than there might be?' He thinks that God produces being (*esse*). He conceives of God as the cause of everything other than

---

[34] Herbert McCabe, OP, *God Matters* (London, 1987), 29.
[35] 1a. 48. 2 ad. 2.

himself and, therefore, as the cause of their goodness. But, he says, since evil is a failure in being (an absence of *esse*), God cannot stand in the same causal relationship to evil as he does to what he produces. He cannot make or sustain evil as he can make or sustain mountains and elephants. We will therefore have to account for it in some other way.

2. *Accounting for Evil*

(*a*) Two Kinds of Evil

In trying to account for evil, Aquinas starts by distinguishing between two kinds of evil: (1) *malum poenae* and (2) *malum culpae*. (1) is 'evil consisting in the loss of a form or part required for a thing's integrity'. (2) is 'the evil of withdrawal in activity that is due, either by its omission or by its malfunctioning according to manner and measure'.[36]

The terminology used by Aquinas here may seem very foreign to modern readers, but the distinction he is making with it is a familiar one. In speaking of *malum poenae*, he is simply thinking of what modern writers sometimes call 'natural evil'—as when someone falls ill or loses a limb (we can call this 'evil suffered'). In speaking of *malum culpae*, on the other hand, he is thinking of what is often called 'moral evil' or 'sin', as when people fail to do what they ought to do, or as when someone does what simply should not be done (let us call this 'evil done').[37]

So the problem for Aquinas lies in explaining how there can be both 'evil suffered' and 'evil done'. And his answer to the problem is twofold. First, something is the victim of 'evil suffered' because there is deficiency caused by the flourishing activity of something else. Strictly speaking, therefore, it is parasitic on goodness. Second, we have 'evil done' because there is sheer failure. Strictly speaking, therefore, it is not a thing which has been brought about by something else.

---

[36] 1a. 48. 5.

[37] 'Evil suffered' also corresponds to what some have called 'non-moral evil' or 'metaphysical evil'. In Aquinas's thinking, *malum poenae* and *malum culpae* are ills which are bound up with sin. He inherits the distinction from St Augustine. Cf. Augustine's *De libero arbitrio*, 1. 1. 1.

(b) Evil Suffered

The first answer here is a version of the view that much evil is to be explained as part of the good of the whole natural order. In Aquinas's judgement, when we are faced with 'evil suffered' (e.g. a sick child), we must presume that it exists because something is interfering with its victim somehow, because something is acting so as to render its victim thwarted or defective in some way, because something, in short, is being itself, and therefore flourishing, at the expense of something else. And, since Aquinas thinks that this is so, he concludes that 'evil suffered' always occurs because something else is good in its own way. As Herbert McCabe nicely expounds it, Aquinas's view is that 'there can never be a defect inflicted on one thing except by another thing that is, in doing so, perfecting itself'.

When I suffer from a disease it is because the bacteria or whatever are fulfilling themselves and behaving exactly as good bacteria should behave. If we found a bacterium which was not engaged in inflicting disease on me we should have to judge that, like a washing machine that did not wash clothes, it was a defective or sick bacterium. The things that inflict evil on me, therefore, are not themselves evil; on the contrary, it is by being good in their way that they make me bad in my way... There is no mystery about my headache. Similarly with my cancer or my influenza—always there is a natural explanation and always the explanation is in terms of some things, cells or germs or whatever, doing what comes naturally, being good. Sometimes, of course, and rather more often than he admits, the doctor is baffled. But he puts this down to his own ignorance; he says: 'Well eventually we may hope to find out what is causing this, what things are bringing it about simply by being their good selves, but for the moment we don't know'. What he does *not* say is this: there is no explanation in nature for this, it is an anti-miracle worked by a malignant God.[38]

So with 'evil suffered' there are always two points of view to be considered. As McCabe puts it: 'The lion is being fulfilled, indeed he is being filled, precisely by what damages the lamb... Being eaten by a lion is undoubtedly bad for the lamb... On the other hand, it actually is good from the lion's point of view.'[39] The 'evil suffered' which can be attributed to some things is due to the fact that other things achieve their good. Or, in Aquinas's words:

[38] McCabe, *God Matters*, 32 f.
[39] Ibid. 31.

God's principal purpose in created things is clearly that form or good which consists in the order of the universe. This requires, as we have noticed, that there should be some things that can, and sometimes do fall away. So then, in causing the common good of the ordered universe, he causes loss in particular things as a consequence and, as it were, indirectly.[40]

(c) Evil Done

It should, I hope, be obvious from this account that there is a sense in which Aquinas thinks of God as the cause of 'evil suffered'. For evil such as this is, for him, an effect of there being goodness, and he thinks of goodness in things as an effect of God. With respect to 'evil done', however, he takes a different line and it is this which we must now try to understand.

As I noted above, in speaking of 'evil done', Aquinas is thinking of moral evil or sin. But his view of this differs from that of many people today. It is often said that in trying to decide whether or not people are morally evil we should concentrate on what they bring about. And it will often be said that if they harm nobody or do damage to nothing, then we need not think of them as morally bad. The idea here is that the evil of moral evil or sin lies in those on whom we inflict evil or to whom we behave badly. Yet this is not what Aquinas believes.

He does, of course, accept that, if I choose to murder Fred, then I cause him to suffer evil and I am therefore morally bad. And he agrees that wicked people can bring about evil consequences. But the death of Fred (an undoubted evil) could just as well be brought about by a falling tree as by me. So, if we think of what is involved in me murdering Fred as more than just a case of 'evil suffered', we must be thinking of more than what happens to Fred. Or so Aquinas would say. He therefore concludes that, in murdering Fred, *I* suffer too. In acting as I do, I undergo a kind of diminishment, and it is here that moral evil is to be located.

Aquinas holds that human goodness consists in human well-being. The good man or woman is one who is fully human. We shall return to the details of this position later, but for the moment we can note that one of the things which it entails for Aquinas is that morally wicked people or sinners are not just damaging their victims. Such

[40] 1a. 49. 2.

people are also thwarting themselves. They are failing to be what they need to be. They are falling short of their end as human beings. For Aquinas, therefore, 'evil done' is an absence of goodness (and therefore of being) in the one to whom it can be ascribed. In this respect it resembles 'evil suffered'. On Aquinas's account, a morally wicked person is like someone suffering from a physical disease.

Yet he also thinks that the cases are not quite parallel. With 'evil suffered' there is always an explanation in terms of goodness and (ultimately) in terms of God as the Maker of good things. But with 'evil done', says Aquinas, there is no similar explanation. My murdering Fred has no cause exerting itself and being good at my expense. The evil involved here has no concomitant good. It is nothing but a case of privation, absence, or defect. The agent inflicting the harm is the same as the one who suffers it.[41]

For this reason, Aquinas argues that the evil involved in 'evil done' must at one level be accounted for simply in negative terms—as a matter of there being an absence of an existing good and an absence of any good operating cause. For him, moral evil is even more a matter of privation than 'evil suffered', for, unlike 'evil suffered' it is not the obverse of some good. On the other hand, however, he also has a somewhat less negative explanation of 'evil done'. The evil of moral evil is not, in his view, something positive, so it cannot be an effect of God as an independently existing substance must be. But it can be said to have a cause, Aquinas holds, since it is willed by agents who exhibit 'evil done'. 'With voluntary causes', he writes, 'the deficient action proceeds from an actually deficient will, that is a will not submitted to its rule and measure.'[42]

Here, as should be evident, Aquinas is presuming that with moral evil we have agents who can be held to be genuinely responsible. For him, 'evil done', is only attributable to free creatures. He therefore maintains that one can speak of it as caused—caused by those to whom it is attributable. But he quickly adds that this is not to say that 'evil done' is in any sense caused by God. He holds that, if I am morally defective, it is I who am responsible for my state, not God.

The obvious objection to this conclusion would seem, of course, to

---

[41] It has been held that moral evil is bad because it somehow harms God. But Aquinas has no time for this suggestion. As we shall see below, God cannot be causally affected by what his creatures do. For Aquinas, all actions of creatures are an effect of God.

[42] 1a. 49. 1 ad. 3.

be that it contradicts Aquinas's notion of God as Maker and sustainer of everything. And Aquinas notes the objection himself. In his formulation it runs: 'The effect of a secondary cause goes back to the first cause. Now good is the cause of evil ... Therefore, since he is the cause of all good ... it follows that all evil is from God.'[43] In other words, if evil is parasitic on good, then all of it must be caused by God since he is the cause of the goodness of things. But Aquinas argues that the conclusion does not follow. He concedes that failure can be traced to God as the efficient cause of all the real and the good which must be there for evil to exist. He also agrees that God can be said to have a causal role when it comes to moral evil since he makes sinners and keeps them in being. His conclusion, however, is that defective activity, or effects resulting from this, are properly and primarily ascribable only to the agent in whom the defect lies.

The effect of a deficient secondary cause is derived from a non-deficient first cause with respect to what is real and complete there, not to what is defective. For example, all the motion in the act of limping comes from a person's vitality, but not the ungainliness which comes from the crooked leg. Likewise all that is real and active in a bad action comes from God as its cause, yet the defect there arises from a deficient secondary cause.[44]

The goodness involved in being a voluntary creature capable of falling short and doing so comes from God, Aquinas seems to be saying. But failure in a creature's voluntary action comes only from the fact that the creature is not acting as it should. And for this lack of action only the non-acting creature can be held accountable.

According to Aquinas, then, evil is a lack of good which comes about either because of the presence of goodness or because something is simply failing. And on this basis he continues to maintain that God is good, not bad. He would be bad, Aquinas thinks, if he willed evil directly and for its own sake. But his creation does not show him to be doing this. What it presents us with is (1) a world in which natural evil is always a matter of there being nothing but good derived from God, and (2) a world in which moral evil, always an absence of good, is attributable only to those who engage in wickedness or sin. On this account, God does not creatively will evil. All he wills is good. And he can only be said to will evil in the sense of permitting

---

[43] 1a. 49. 2 obj. 2.
[44] 1a. 49. 2 ad. 2.

it, not in the sense of causing it directly. Aquinas accepts that, since God is the efficient cause of all the real and good which must be there for evil to exist, there is a sense in which evil can be traced to God. But only because (1) in making a world in which some things flourish at the expense of others, God is making what is good and (2) because in making a world in which there is moral evil, God is not doing something (i.e. bringing about more moral good than there is) and certain creatures are failing in some respect.

One might object that God should bring about more good than he does and that he is therefore bad because he is blameworthy or guilty by neglect. But, from what has been said above, it should be clear that Aquinas would find the objection intolerable. He thinks that we may indeed blame people for not doing something or other. He agrees that failure to act can be a sign of badness. But God, for him, is wholly good as the source and pattern of all creaturely goodness, from which it follows that there are no standards over and against him in the light of which he must conduct himself. In this sense, and as I said above, God's goodness for Aquinas is not moral goodness, though the full implications of his teaching on this matter have yet to be drawn out.

6

Ubiquity to Eternity

CONTINUING with the theme of what can be known of God apart from Revelation, I now want to turn to three beliefs which are absolutely fundamental to Aquinas's thinking. These are: (1) God is everywhere; (2) God is unchangeable; (3) God is eternal. When we have seen what Aquinas has to say in presenting and defending these theses, we shall, in Chapters 7 and 8, consider his teaching on seven further related topics: God's oneness, power, knowledge, will, love, justice, and mercy.

God's Presence in Things

The belief that God is everywhere, sometimes known as the doctrine of divine ubiquity, has always been part and parcel of Judeo-Christian theism. So it is hardly surprising that Aquinas subscribes to it. As a Dominican friar he would often have chanted the words of Psalm 139:

> Whither shall I go from thy Spirit?
> Or whither shall I flee from thy presence?
> If I ascend to heaven, thou art there!
> If I make my bed in Sheol, thou art there!

In his scheme of things, however, belief in God's omnipresence takes on a special importance. For he invokes it constantly, and it is much more prominent in his system that it is in the thinking of many other theistic writers. As he understands it, it also means something different from what it does to some theists. For he does not think that God is present just in the sense of knowing what is going on everywhere and being able to interfere. He thinks that God exists in everything and is in every place. He also thinks that God is *wholly* in everything and that being everywhere *only* applies to God.

The intellectual foundation of his position here lies in something we noted in Chapter 2: the notion that God is the cause of the existence of everything other than himself. God's proper effect, says Aquinas, is existence (*esse*), which he causes, not only when creatures begin to exist, but as long as they are preserved in being. In speaking of existence as God's 'proper effect', I mean 'effect which he produces by virtue of being what he is essentially'—his characteristic effect, if you like. Aquinas's idea is that just as, say, it belongs to sulphuric acid to have such and such effects to be listed by scientists (effects which they can note, and from which they can conclude that sulphuric acid has been at work), so it belongs to God to have the effect of creating and sustaining things in being (though, as we shall see presently, Aquinas does not take this to mean that God *has* to create and sustain things). There *being* things is what you get when God, so to speak, goes out of himself and acts. On this basis Aquinas concludes that God is present to everything as an agent is present to that upon which it works. He is in all things because he makes and sustains them.

God exists in everything; not indeed as part of their substance or as an accident, but as an agent is present to that in which its action is taking place . . . Since it is God's nature to exist, he it must be who properly causes existence in creatures, just as it is fire itself that sets other things on fire. And God is causing this effect in things not just when they begin to exist, but all the time they are maintained in existence . . . Now existence is more intimately and profoundly interior to things than anything else, for everything as we said is potential when compared to existence. So God must exist and exist intimately in everything.[1]

As we shall see later, from this teaching Aquinas derives a whole theology of God's providence and grace. For the moment, however, I want only to flesh it out briefly by noting three general points which he makes concerning it.

One is that God is in every place simply because he makes all places. Since Aquinas denies that God is a material object, one might wonder how he can seriously hold that God may be said to have physical location. And Aquinas, himself, agrees that God, in a sense, is nowhere. He is not *here* as opposed to *there*. He is not *there* as opposed to *here*. On the other hand, Aquinas adds, we can speak of places (and therefore of 'here' and 'there') because there are things with physical locations, things which therefore result in there being

---

[1] ia. 8. i.

places. And since God is actively present to these things by making and sustaining them, he is where these places are.

First, he is in every place giving it existence and the power to be a place, just as he is in all things giving them existence, power and activity. Secondly, just as anything occupying a place fills that place, so God fills all places. But not as bodies do (for bodies fill places by not suffering other bodies to be there with them, whilst God's presence in a place does not exclude the presence there of other things); rather God fills all places by giving existence to everything occupying those places.[2]

Second, says Aquinas, God is whole and entire in every place. It is not just that God is in a place by being partly there, as I can be partly in the garden by sticking my head out of the garden window. Drawing on his doctrine of divine simplicity, Aquinas maintains that God has no parts. He therefore concludes that, if divinity is present anywhere, it is there entire and undivided. He also concludes that, since only God is wholly undivided (since only God is entirely simple), and since only God is the maker and sustainer of everything, only God can be wholly everywhere. If it were the only thing that existed, a given physical thing might be said to be everywhere, for its constitution would be that by virtue of which there was any place. If there was nothing but a single grain of wheat, say, it could be said to be everywhere, since places would be established only in terms of its make-up. But it would not, says Aquinas, be everywhere as God is. Even a solitary grain of wheat would be divisible. Being composed of parts, it would not exist entirely in every part of itself, and, therefore, it would not be wholly everywhere. God, however, is indivisible, and, if he is present at a place, he is entirely present there. Or, as Aquinas suggests, he is 'everywhere essentially'.

By being everywhere essentially I mean not just happening to be everywhere in certain circumstances, as a grain of wheat would be everywhere if no other bodies existed. When a thing is such that it would exist everywhere in any circumstances, it exists everywhere essentially. Now this belongs to God alone. For no matter how many places one may think up, even infinitely more than now exist, God would necessarily exist in them all, since nothing can

---

[2] 1a. 6. 2. C. J. F. Williams asks me whether this commits Aquinas to the independent existence of 'places'. As far as I can see, Aquinas is not so committed, though he does not offer an analysis of place-statements in a way clearly designed to rule out any commitment to belief in the existence of places as distinct things, as Williams does in *Being, Identity and Truth* (Oxford, 1992).

exist except he cause it to do so. And so to be everywhere outright and essentially belongs to God and to God alone, for no matter how many places one may think up God himself will necessarily exist in them, and not just parts of him.[3]

Finally, Aquinas contends, since God is in all things in the manner explained above, it follows that all things are subject to his control. More precisely, God's ubiquity entails that nothing acts independently of God, that he is operating in the activity of anything whatsoever, and that the working of his creatures derives from him.

But just as God has not only given being to things when they first began to exist, but also causes being in them as long as they exist, conserving them in being, as we have shown, so also has he not merely granted operative powers to them when they were originally created, but he always causes these powers in things. Hence, if this divine influence were to cease, every operation would cease. Therefore, every operation of a thing is traced back to him as to its cause.[4]

Aquinas believes that God is causally at work in the entire history of his created order, that he is absent from nothing, and that everything that happens is an expression of his will. Later in this book we shall see how he develops this conclusion. At this point, however, we may note that, according to Aquinas, God is not just present to everything. He is *changelessly* present to everything.

God is Changeless

According to Aquinas, God is unchangeable or immutable.[5] He also thinks that only God is unchangeable. 'Only God is altogether unchangeable', he writes. 'Creatures can all change in some way or other.'[6] In his judgement, this conclusion follows from the fact that God is the first cause of change in things (as the first of the Five Ways argues). It is also part and parcel of the doctrine of divine simplicity.

---

[3] 1a. 6. 4.
[4] *SG* 3. 1. 67. 3.
[5] For an excellent and very thorough account of Aquinas on God's changelessness see Michael J. Dodds, OP, *The Unchanging God of Love: A Study of the Teaching of St. Thomas Aquinas on Divine Immutability in View of Certain Contemporary Criticism of This Doctrine* (Fribourg, 1986).
[6] 1a. 9. 2.

With respect to the point about God as cause of change, Aquinas's basic position is that only an unchanging and unchangeable God can account for there being a world in which change occurs. A mutable individual, he reasons, would simply be part of the changing world and, as such, would point to something beyond it, something wholly unchanging. Why? Because, he affirms, a first cause of change cannot, by definition, be mutable. If it were mutable it would either be changed by something other than itself, which means that it would not be a first cause of change, or both be and not be in some specified state (it would be simultaneously potential and actual in some respect), which is impossible. It might be thought that a first cause of change could be both unchanging and changing since its unchanging part or parts could bring about changes in another part or parts of it. But that, Aquinas thinks, would make it a changing thing, not the first cause of change.

God who changes all things, must himself be unchangeable. If he, being the first changer, were himself changed, he would have to be changed either by himself or by another. He cannot be changed by another, for then there would have to be some changer prior to him, which is against the very idea of a first changer. If he is changed by himself, this can be conceived in two ways: either that he is a changer and changed according to the same respect, or that he is a changer according to one aspect of him and is changed according to another aspect. The first of these alternatives is ruled out. For everything that is changed is, to that extent, in potency, and whatever moves is in act. Therefore if God is both changer and changed according to the same respect, he has to be in potency and in act according to the same respect, which is impossible. The second alternative is likewise out of the question. If one part were causing change and another were being changed, there would be no first changer himself as such, but only by reason of that part of him which causes change ... Accordingly the first changer must be altogether unchangeable.[7]

As for the bearing on God's changeableness of the doctrine of divine simplicity, we only need to remind ourselves that, according to that doctrine, God can undergo no accidental or substantial change. He cannot be modified, and he cannot perish. It is not just that, as a matter of fact, God is identical with what he is (that he is the same as his nature). Aquinas thinks that there can be no attribute added to what he is by nature or essence. And this, he says, means that God is

---

[7] *Comp.* ch. 4.

immutable or unchangeable and not just (as a matter of fact) un-changing. He is sheerly actual, unmixed with potentiality, while any changing thing is always somehow potential. Changing things are composite since they persist over time as being *first* like this, and *then* like that. But God is not composite. Changing things acquire some-thing previously not attained, but God is fully actual, which means, once again, that he cannot change.

Our findings so far prove God to be altogether unchangeable. First, because we have proved that there must be some first existent, called God, sheerly actual and unalloyed with potentiality, since actuality, simply speaking, pre-cedes potentiality. Now any changing thing, whatsoever the change, is some-how potential. So it clearly follows that God cannot change in any way. Secondly, because anything in change partly persists and partly passes, as a thing changing from white to black persists in substance. Things in change are therefore always composite. Now God we have shown to be not at all composite, but altogether simple. Clearly then he cannot change. Thirdly, because anything in change acquires something through its change, attaining something previously not attained. Now God, being limitless and embracing within himself the whole fullness of perfection of all existence, cannot acquire anything, nor can he move out towards something previously not attained. So one cannot in any way associate him with change.[8]

And, in Aquinas's judgement, all of this has a further important implication. For, in his view, it points to the conclusion that God is eternal.

God is Eternal

In medieval theology, there is a virtually constant tradition according to which eternity is distinct from time. This tradition owed a great deal to earlier Greek thinking about eternity, especially to that of Neoplatonism. According, for example, to Plotinus, things subject to time are changing things, which may, therefore, be contrasted with Intelligence (*nous*), which is not subject to time and is therefore eternal. Time, says Plotinus, is 'the life of soul in a movement of passage from one way of life to another',[9] and eternity is the life of the intelligible world without successiveness.

---

[8] 1a. 9. 1.
[9] *Enneads*, trans. A. H. Armstrong (Cambridge, Mass., 1980), vol. iii: 3. 7. 11.

One sees eternity in seeing a life that abides in the same, and always has the all present to it, not now this, and then again that, but all things at once (*hama ta panta*), and not now some things, and then again others, but a partless completion, as if they were all together in a point, and had not yet begun to go out and flow into lines; it is something which abides in the same in itself and does not change at all but is always in the present, because nothing of it has passed away, nor again is there anything to come into being, but that which it is, it *is*; so that eternity is not the substrate but something which, as it were, shines out from the substrate itself in respect of what is called its sameness, in speaking about the fact that it is not going to be but is already, that it is as it is and not otherwise, for what could come to be for it afterwards, which it is not already? For there is nothing starting from which it will arrive at the present moment, for that could be nothing else but what is [now]. Nor is it going to be what it does not now contain in itself. Necessarily there will be no 'was' about it, for what is there that was for it and has passed away? Nor any 'will be', for what will be for it? So there remains for it only to be in its being just what it is. That, then, which was not, and will not be, but *is* only, which has being which is static by not changing to the 'will be', nor ever having changed, this is eternity.[10]

In the Latin West, this conception of eternity emerges very clearly in Augustine and Anselm,[11] and it was classically formulated by Boethius. In his famous slogan: 'Eternity is the complete and total possession of unending life all at once' (*Aeternitas est interminabilis vitae tota simul et perfecta possessio*).[12] Boethius himself is here echoing Plotinus, and also Proclus, for whom eternal existence 'is simultaneously present in its entirety', so that 'there is not one part of it which has already emerged and another which will emerge later, but as yet is not'.[13]

Aquinas's teaching on eternity needs to be located against the background of this tradition (he quotes the Boethian formula in 1a. 10. 1). So he thinks that God is eternal in the sense of being distinct from time. As he puts it, 'time and eternity clearly differ'.[14] To understand the significance of his view of God's eternity, however, we must first consider how he conceives of time.

---

[10] Ibid. 3. 7. 3.

[11] See Anselm, *Proslogion*, 9, and Augustine, *Confessions*, 11. 13.

[12] *The Consolation of Philosophy*, 5. The quotation might just as well, I think, be rendered 'Eternity is the complete and total possession of unending life without successiveness.'

[13] *The Elements of Theology*, prop. 52.

[14] 1a. 10. 4.

1. Aquinas on Time

His ideas on the subject must surely have been influenced by many writers. Augustine, for instance, treats of time at length, and Aquinas will have been familiar with his discussion of the subject, as well as with those of others later than Augustine, writers such as Boethius and Anselm.[15] But the primary source for his teaching about time is undoubtedly Book 4 of Aristotle's *Physics*, on which he commented in detail, and on which he draws for his account of God's eternity.

Aristotle argues that time is essentially connected with change, that it measures change. He does not think that it is identical with change, since many things change while 'time is equally everywhere and with everything', and since change may be fast or slow while 'what is fast and what is slow is defined by time'. But he does maintain that without change there is no time.

When we ourselves do not alter in our mind or do not notice that we alter, then it does not seem to us that any time has passed . . . If the now were not different but one and the same, there would be no time . . . It is manifest, then, that time neither is change nor is apart from change, and since we are looking for what time is we must start from this fact, and find what aspect of change it is.[16]

The solution Aristotle arrives at is that time is 'a number of change in respect of the before and after'.[17] The precise nature of this theory is a matter of some controversy, but it certainly seems clear that, for Aristotle, change is a criterion of time passing, and we cannot understand what it would be for time to pass in the absence of change. And that is what Aquinas believes. In his view, we can only think of a thing as being in time insofar as we can think of it as being first like this and then like that.

For since succession occurs in every movement, and one part comes after another, the fact that we reckon before and after in movement makes us apprehend time, which is nothing else but the measure of before and after in movement.[18]

---

[15] Cf. *Confessions*, 11. For a careful philosophical appraisal of Augustine on time see Christopher Kirwan, *Augustine* (London, 1989), chs. 8 and 9.

[16] *Physics*, 218^{b}21 f.

[17] Ibid. 218^{b}9 ff. I quote from *Aristotle's Physics, Books III and IV*, trans. with notes by Edward Hussey (Oxford, 1983), 42 ff.

[18] 1a. 10. 1.

Or, as we find in the commentary on the *Physics*: 'We say that time passes when we sense a before and after in change. It follows, therefore, that time is consequent upon change in respect to before and after.'[19]

2. *Why God is Eternal*

For Aquinas, then, our concept of time is parasitic on our recognition of change. And, from this premise, he works towards the conclusion that God is eternal in the sense of being unmeasured by time. For, as we have seen, he thinks that God is unchangeable.

Just as we can only come to know simple things by way of composite ones, so we can only come to know eternity by way of time, which is merely the numbering of before and after in change ... Now something lacking change and never varying its mode of existence will not display a before and after. So just as numbering antecedent and consequent in change produces the notion of time, so awareness of invariability in something altogether free from change produces the notion of eternity.[20]

In other words, in God there is no successiveness. We live our lives by undergoing a history consisting of change following change. But, says Aquinas, the life of God is different from ours in this respect. With him there is no before and after. As Boethius would have said, God has his life *tota simul* (all at once). In the sense in which we understand history (as what happens to people or things), God, for Aquinas, has no history, and those who would try to write his biography have no subject-matter. 'The notion of eternity', he states, 'derives from unchangeableness in the same way that the notion of time derives from change. Eternity therefore principally belongs to God, who is utterly unchangeable.'[21]

Aquinas suggests that it follows from all this that God also has no beginning or end. According to him, a thing which changes is always something to which one can assign a before and after in terms of change. For the notion of change is bound up with the notions of 'before' and 'after'. Something wholly unchanging, therefore, will have no before and after, and will have no beginning or end. For

[19] Lecture 17. 579.
[20] 1a. 10. 1.
[21] 1a. 10. 2.

anything with a beginning or end is something with a before or after (it begins before it ends, if it ends; and it ends after it began, if it began). So 'anything existing in eternity is *unending*, that is to say, lacks both beginning and end (for both may be regarded as ends)'.[22]

3. Eternity, Duration, and Temporal Location

So Aquinas thinks that God is eternal because non-temporal. And from this one might conclude that eternity, for him, is equivalent to timelessness. On the other hand, however, though many readers of Aquinas have taken him to be saying that God is timeless,[23] there is some reason for caution on the matter. That is because his way of talking about eternity does not quite square with what one might expect of the view that God is timeless.

In speaking of the view that God is timeless, I am now referring to the claim that God has no duration or temporal location, which is what 'God is timeless' means for many people. According to this claim, though we might say that such and such is now true of me, or that such and such was true, or will be true, it is wrong to say that such and such is now true of God, or that such and such was true, or will be true of him. As Paul Helm, for instance, puts it, 'there is for him no past and no future . . . [and] . . . it makes no sense to ask how long God has existed, or to divide up his life into periods of time'.[24] God's eternity, says Helm, is to 'be explained in terms of time-freeness . . . from which both the notions of duration and instantaneousness are banished'.[25]

This, however, is arguably not Aquinas's view of eternity. As we have noted, he thinks of time as relative to change. And he concludes that God is non-temporal because he is unchangeable. At one level, therefore, it is perfectly proper to say that God, for Aquinas, transcends time. We might even say that God, for him, is timeless. But we should be wary of ascribing to him the notion of timelessness just introduced. I say this for several reasons.

The first is that Aquinas defends belief in God's eternity by citing with approval the view of eternity found in Book 5 of Boethius's

---

[22] 1a. 10. 1.

[23] Here I include myself. See 'A Timeless God', *New Blackfriars*, 64 (May 1983) and *Thinking about God* (London, 1985).

[24] Paul Helm, *Eternal God: A Study of God without Time* (Oxford, 1988), 24.

[25] Ibid. 36.

The Consolation of Philosophy (quoted above). Though Boethius distinguishes between time and eternity, however, he does not unequivocally say that God lacks duration. He tells us that what is eternal does not pass from a past state to a present state, that it does not grasp tomorrow and lose yesterday, that it has all its life in a motionless way. This need only mean that God undergoes no distinguishable real changes. Boethius says that if the world lacked beginning or end it would still be only *perpetuus* (everlasting) not *aeternus* (eternal). But that, he explains, is because it would fail to be like God who 'stays still', i.e. 'does not change'.[26]

Second, it goes against the language of Aquinas to speak of God as having no duration. Like Boethius, he distinguishes between time and eternity, as we have seen. But he also accepts that eternity is 'a measure of duration . . . measuring abiding existence',[27] that the eternity of God 'embraces (*includit*) all times',[28] that eternity is 'present to all time and embraces all time' (*toti tempori adest, et ipsum concludit*),[29] and that 'God exists always' (*Deus semper est*).[30] Far from thinking of God as unequivocally durationless and as absolutely out of relation to past, present, and future, Aquinas seems to hold both that God has duration and that he exists at all times (from which we might be forgiven for inferring that God always existed, that he exists now, and that he will always exist).[31]

It may be, as Christopher Hughes has recently suggested, that Aquinas's talk of God's duration is merely a way of indicating that God is not a fleeting or transient being.[32] He may indeed hold

---

[26] Richard Sorabji argues that Boethius is pretty unequivocal in denying duration to God. See *Time, Creation and the Continuum* (London, 1983), 115 ff. For what I take to be a better exposition of Boethius on eternity see Eleonore Stump and Norman Kretzmann, 'Eternity' (reprinted in Thomas V. Morris (ed.), *The Concept of God* (Oxford, 1987)).

[27] 1a. 10. 1. Cf. also 1a. 14. 13 and 1a. 42. 2.

[28] 1a. 10. 2 ad. 4.

[29] 1a. 57. 3.

[30] *Comp.* ch. 7.

[31] For some analysis of Aquinas on eternity as duration see Carl J. Peter, *Participated Eternity in the Vision of God: A Study of the Opinion of Thomas Aquinas and His Commentators on the Duration of the Acts of Glory* (Rome, 1964).

[32] *On a Complex Theory of a Simple God: An Investigation in Aquinas' Philosophical Theology* (Ithaca, NY, 1989), 116 ff. I do not, however, see how something can be said to be non-transient or non-fleeting unless it is also said that the thing continues to be and, in this sense, has duration. One might hold that numbers or logical truths are non-transient and non-fleeting though also lacking duration. But God, for Aquinas, has substantial existence and is, in this respect, quite unlike a number.

that eternity is equivalent to timelessness, and I may be making a fuss about nothing in the last few paragraphs. I may, indeed, be seriously misrepresenting Aquinas. But, as far as I can see, his distinction between time and eternity is simply a distinction between what undergoes real change and what, though enduring, really changes in no respect. This, of course, squares with the fact that his primary argument for God being eternal is that God is unchangeable. On his account, a thing falls short of eternal existence the more it is bound up with change, whether actual or potential.[33] For this reason, we may suggest that he does not in fact subscribe to the view that God is timeless in the sense defined above. His teaching that God is eternal amounts to the view that the life of God cannot be measured in terms of successive states and is equivalent to the claim that God is wholly immutable.

Others came to the knowledge of God by way of his eternity. They saw that whatever exists in things is changeable, and the nobler anything is in the scale of things the less changeable it is. For instance, lower bodies are changeable both in their substance and in their location, but the heavenly bodies, which are nobler, are unchangeable in their substance and undergo only change of place. Along these lines it can obviously be inferred that the first principle of all things, the highest and most noble of all, is immutable and eternal. And this eternity of the Word is implied by the prophet when he says 'sitting', that is, presiding in eternity with absolutely no change at all. 'Your seat, O God, is forever' [Ps. 44: 7]. 'Jesus Christ, yesterday and today, the same forever' [Heb. 13: 8]. It is to display this eternity that John says, 'In the beginning was the Word' [John 1: 1].[34]

Aquinas on Eternity Today

Aquinas's view of God's eternity stands, as I have said, in a definite tradition of Western theology. It is also solidly supported by Christian creeds and professions of faith, for it is tied to the belief that God is wholly immutable, which, as I have said, is standard Christian teaching.[35] Modern writers, however, very often deny that God is

---

[33] That Aquinas conceives of God's eternity principally in terms of changelessness emerges with particular clarity in the *Compendium of Theology*, ch. 8. Cf. also 1a. 10. 5.

[34] *Super ev. Joh.*, Prologue.

[35] See G. L. Prestige, *God in Patristic Thought* (2nd edn., London, 1952).

changeless, and a consequence of this is that many of them also reject what Aquinas believes about eternity—bearing in mind that eternity, for him, is bound up with immutability. Before I move on to other matters, therefore, I ought, perhaps, to say something about his views on eternity in the light of contemporary criticism. I cannot here give a summary of what this amounts to in detail, but I shall try to indicate the objections most frequently levelled against Aquinas's position, and I shall briefly try to indicate what I think he would say in reply to them. If nothing else, this will help the reader to a better understanding of what Aquinas means by calling God eternal.

1. *God's Character and Activity*

Eternity, in Aquinas's sense, involving immutability, is often equated with being unable to act, with being indifferent or aloof, and with being inert or static. God cannot, so the argument goes, be any of these things. So he cannot be eternal as Aquinas says that he is. Hence, for example, we find Grace Jantzen arguing:

A living God cannot be static: life implies change and hence temporality. This means that the doctrine of immutability cannot be interpreted as absolute changelessness, which would preclude divine responsiveness and must rather be taken as steadfastness of character.[36]

A similar view can be found in the work of Richard Swinburne and Nelson Pike, who focus their criticism on the suggestion that God can act or create while being, in Aquinas's sense, outside time, i.e. while lacking successiveness. According to Swinburne:

If we say that P brings about X, we can always sensibly ask *when* does he bring it about? If we say that P punishes Q, we can always sensibly ask *when* does he punish Q... If P at t brings about X, then necessarily X comes into existence (simultaneously with or) subsequently to P's action... And so on.[37]

If God is to act, so Swinburne seems to be saying, he must do so as you and I do—by engaging in a process which involves him being first like this and then like that. And Pike adopts a similar line of argument. According to him, if God creates, then he produces or sustains, but

---

[36] Alan Richardson and John Bowden (eds.), *A New Dictionary of Christian Theology* (London, 1983), 573.
[37] *The Coherence of Theism* (Oxford, 1977), 221.

the specialized verbs we use when describing a case of deliberate or intentional production ... seem to carry with them identifiable implications regarding the temporal positions of the items produced and the creative activity involved in their production.[38]

In Pike's view, temporal implications 'seem to be there in every case; they seem to be part of the "essence" of "produce" '.[39]

In reply to these objections, Aquinas would make a number of points. In some of them he would be drawing on what he teaches concerning Christian doctrine based on revelation (e.g. that God is involved in the world by virtue of the Incarnation). We will return to such matters later. For the moment we can note what he would say simply from the viewpoint of philosophy and apart from appeal to revelation.

First, he would I think, deny that his doctrine of God's eternity is rightly interpreted as the teaching that God is static. To say that something is static can be understood as asserting something positive about it, to describe it. But when Aquinas tells us that God is eternal he is primarily telling us what God is not, namely not changing. And, in holding to the view that God is immutable, he is chiefly denying that certain creaturely limitations are found in God. He is denying that God is lacking in actuality, and that anything acts on him so as to introduce change in him. From the nature and the context of Aquinas's treatment of God's immutability, it seems clear that he would sympathize with Herbert McCabe when he writes:

It is extremely difficult for readers of Aquinas to take his agnosticism about the nature of God seriously. If he says 'Whatever God may be, he cannot be changing' readers leap to the conclusion that he means that what God is is static. If he says that, whatever God may be, he could not suffer together with (*sympathise* with) his creatures, he is taken to mean that God must by nature be unsympathetic, apathetic, indifferent, even callous. It is almost as though if Aquinas had said that God could not be a supporter of Glasgow Celtic, we supposed he was claiming God as a Rangers fan.[40]

One might reply that there is little difference between 'God is static' and 'God is immutable'. And, insofar as one agrees with that suggestion, one will find no problem in ascribing to Aquinas the

---

[38] *God and Timelessness* (London, 1970), 106.
[39] Ibid. 107.
[40] *God Matters* (London, 1987), 41.

conclusion that God is static. But his modern critics who attack him for holding this thesis take him to be saying that God is static as inanimate things, such as rocks, are static. And that is certainly not his view. If he thinks of God as static, he is thinking of God as statically exemplifying absolute perfection, including that associated with mind, activity, and the like.

Second, Aquinas would deny that life should be defined to include the notion of undergoing change. For him, living things are 'automobiles', i.e. things with a principle of movement lying in themselves. Since he thinks that God is the first cause and unchanged changer (or mover), with a principle of movement in himself whether or not he creates, Aquinas concludes that God is the ultimate 'automobile', and is therefore supremely alive.

God has life in the truest sense. To see this we must note that life is attributed to certain things because they act of themselves and not as moved by other things; hence the more perfectly this is verified in a thing the more perfectly does it possess life . . . That Being, then, whose own nature is its act of knowledge, which also does not have what belongs to it by nature determined for it by another, is the Being which has life in the highest degree. Such a Being is God.[41]

In reply to authors such as Jantzen, therefore, Aquinas would say that, far from lacking life, the unchanging God exemplifies life more fully than anything. And, with respect to the point that a changeless God cannot act, he would challenge the suggestion that nothing can be said to act unless it undergoes change in itself. 'We agree', he comments,

that an efficient cause which works through change must precede its effect in time, for the effect enters as the term of the action whereas the agent is its start. Yet in the event of the action being instantaneous and not successive, it is not required for the maker to be prior in duration to the thing made.[42]

To understand Aquinas here, we can start with an analogy. Suppose we ask how people manage to teach each other. It seems natural to say that they do it by uttering words or by using blackboards and so on (and therefore by undergoing various changes). For that is how teaching is effected by people. But teaching cannot be defined as going through certain motions. I can utter true statements until I am

---

[41] 1a. 18. 3.
[42] 1a. 46. 2 ad. 1.

blue in the face. I can fill a thousand blackboards with letters and diagrams. But none of these processes will count as teaching unless somebody actually learns something. For this reason it seems necessary to say that, when interested in whether or not I have taught somebody, we are interested, not in changes occurring in me, but in changes occurring in somebody else. I cannot teach you except by undergoing change of some kind. But my undergoing these changes does not constitute my teaching you. Unless you actually learn something, they are simply fruitless bits of behaviour on my part. Teaching occurs when learning occurs, when someone changes from a state of ignorance to a state of knowledge concerning some truth.

Aquinas puts this point by saying that some activity (of which teaching would be an example) is 'transitive' as opposed to 'immanent'. Citing Aristotle,[43] he observes that there are two kinds of activity.

There is that which takes effect in some external thing, altering it in some way; for example, burning or cutting [transitive activity]. And there is that which does not pass on to anything external but remains within the agent; such are sensation, understanding and willing [immanent activity].[44]

In Aquinas's view, therefore, the action of an agent may lie only in changes brought about in that on which it is acting. It need not be defined in terms of changes in the agent.

So, in reply to authors like Swinburne and Pike, Aquinas would say that, even though God is unchanging, he can act. For he can and does act transitively, namely by bringing about changes in creatures. With this point in mind, Aquinas (as I noted in Chapter 4) would even add that we can date God's actions. For changes in the world can be dated and, since they are brought about by God, his act of bringing them about can be similarly dated. Suppose we say that such and such has been brought about by God. Then we ask, 'When?' Suppose the answer is, 'At 2 o'clock last Friday'. Does that mean that God must have been undergoing some process at 2 o'clock last Friday? Aquinas would say, 'Not at all'. It need only mean that at 2 o'clock last Friday such and such came to pass by virtue of God. Whether God changes in bringing it about is another question.

<hr />

[43] *Metaphysics*, 9. 8. 1050ᵃ23.
[44] 1a. 54. 2. Cf. also 1a. 14. 2, 1a. 18. 3. ad. 1, 1a. 27. 1, 1a2ae. 22. 1.

2. The Bible and God's Change

A further popular modern objection to Aquinas on eternity is that
what he says on the subject conflicts with the teaching of the Bible.
Here the argument shifts from philosophical considerations and rests
on the fact that the biblical God is depicted as a temporal, changing
individual. Its advocates hold that, since Aquinas thinks of God's
eternity as non-temporal and immutable, his teaching is unscriptural
and therefore untenable. According, for example, to John Lucas, 'the
whole thrust of the biblical record' implies that God changes. The
Bible

> is an account of God both caring and knowing about the world, even the five
> sparrows, which at one time had not yet been, and later had been, sold for
> two farthings, and intervening in the world, doing things, saying things,
> hearing prayers, and sometimes changing his mind.[45]

'The changelessness of God', says Lucas, 'is not to be naturally read
out of the Bible, but rather was read into it in the light of certain
philosophical assumptions about the nature of God.'[46] Here Lucas
agrees with Swinburne, according to whom:

> The God of the Old Testament, in which Judaism, Islam and Christianity
> have their roots, is a God in continual interaction with men, moved by men
> as they speak to him . . . If God did not change at all, he would not think now
> of this, now of that . . . The God of the Old Testament is not pictured as
> such a being . . . The doctrine of divine timelessness is very little in evidence
> before Augustine. The Old Testament certainly shows no sign of it . . . The
> same applies in general for New Testament writers.[47]

Since Aquinas was obviously concerned to be loyal to Christian
tradition, one might suppose that he would find such objections to be
extremely telling against him. In this, however, one would be wrong,
as Aquinas himself indicates when considering what are evidently the
same objections (albeit cast in a medieval mould). For he thinks that
what he has to say about the changelessness of God can be perfectly
well held by someone who also respects what the Bible has to say.

To begin with, he would agree with the premise of Lucas and
Swinburne's position: that the Bible speaks of God as undergoing

---

[45] *The Future* (Oxford, 1989), 214.
[46] Ibid. 215.
[47] *The Coherence of Theism*, 214 ff.

change or as being temporal. In his discussion of prayer in the *Summa contra Gentiles* he cites Isaiah 38: 1 ff. and Jeremiah 18: 7 ff. as places in the Bible where change is ascribed to God.[48] He makes a similar move in his treatment of divine immutability in the *Summa theologiae*. In 1a. 9. 1 obj. 3, for instance, he notes that 'Drawing near and drawing away are descriptions of movements' and that 'scripture applies them to God' in James 4: 8. And in obj. 4 to 1a. 10. 2 we find: 'Past, present and future do not exist in eternity, which, as we have said, is instantaneously whole. But the Scriptures use verbs in the present, past and future tenses, when talking of God.' In his replies to these objections Aquinas does not dispute the facts to which they draw attention.

On the other hand, however, he would not regard such facts as forcing us to conclude that God is mutable and temporal. He notes, for example, that though Scripture speaks of God as changing, it also speaks of him as unchanging. He cites Malachi 3: 6 ('I am God, I change not'). He also cites Numbers 23: 19 and 1 Samuel 15: 29. More significantly, he also notes that sense must be exercised in reading Scripture and that this must be borne in mind by anyone invoking its letter as a way of settling what we should and should not say of God.

In Aquinas's view, Scripture is not a dead thing wearing its full significance on its face. He thinks that we must treat it as contemporary, and that we need to engage with it using our best available resources, so that there is a kind of dialogue between the words of Scripture and the believing Church which makes use of them and draws its life from them. This in turn means that, for him, the truths conveyed by Scripture can be other than surface indications might suggest. He thinks that Scripture has to be interpreted in the light of what we know.

One thing this means for him is that we need to distinguish between a literal and a non-literal reading of scriptural texts.[49] A biblical text, for him, can be read literally when it tells us what we could not know otherwise and/or when it tells us something not incompatible with what we know to be the case. When Scripture

---

[48] *SG* 3. 96.
[49] For St Thomas on Scripture and the interpretation of it see, in addition to the works cited in ch. 1 n. 37, Thomas Gilby, OP, 'The Summa and the Bible', appendix 11 to vol. i of the Blackfriars *Summa theologiae* (London, 1964).

tells us that God became incarnate, we can take the statement literally (more of this below). When, on the other hand, it tells us that God breathes, we have to interpret in a non-literal sense. Breath, in the literal sense, is what we and other animals produce through our mouths and noses. So bodily creatures alone can be said literally to breathe, and biblical talk about the breath of God has to be understood accordingly.

And, Aquinas thinks, it is the same with biblical statements implying a real change in God. According to him, we know that change is a creaturely thing which is brought about by God who cannot, as first mover and pure act, be said literally to change in himself. Biblical statements about God changing therefore have to be understood accordingly. Hence we find that the reply to obj. 1 of 1a. 9. 1 (above) runs:

The scripture is here talking of God in metaphors. For just as the sun is said to enter or depart from a house by touching the house with its rays, so God is said to draw near to us when we receive an influx of his goodness, or draw away from us when we fail him.

The reply to obj. 4 of 1a. 10. 2 is: 'Verbs of different tenses are used of God, not as though he varied from present to future, but because his eternity comprehends all phases of time.' In each case Aquinas wants both to respect the truth of Scripture, to take its words seriously, and also to be faithful to truths we know of God apart from what Scripture says.

In short, he thinks that the Bible (and Christian teaching based on it) will contain metaphor or figurative or symbolical language which needs to be read as such. And he thinks that this is thoroughly appropriate since we arrive at knowledge by means of senses, and since speaking of God as if he were a creature in the world is a help to us thinking about him. In 1a. 1. 9 he writes:

Holy Scripture delivers divine and spiritual realities under bodily guises. For God provides for all things according to the kind of things they are. Now we are of the kind to reach the world of intelligence through the world of sense, since all our knowledge takes its rise from sensation. Congenially, then, holy Scripture delivers spiritual things to us beneath metaphors taken from bodily things.

This teaching of Aquinas is worth noting since it throws light on his view of the Bible and its language. He wants to say that the Bible is trying to teach about what is not part of this world, yet it has to do so by using the normal methods of communication used to talk about things or persons—the method in which we talk about bodily, worldly things or embodied realities.

7

Oneness to Knowledge

AQUINAS accepts the Christian doctrine of the Trinity, so he believes that divinity somehow contains distinction within itself. He thinks, as we might put it, that there are three who are God. He also thinks that, if we ask, 'three what?', the answer is, 'three persons'. 'In the Creed of Athanasius', he writes, 'we say: "One is the person of the Father, another of the Son, another of the Holy Ghost".'[1] But, also in line with Christian orthodoxy, Aquinas is a monotheist. He believes that there is but one God. 'It is written, "Hear, O Israel, the Lord our God is one Lord"', he says, citing Deuteronomy 6: 4.[2] We shall be turning to his treatment of the Trinity in Chapter 10. As background to that chapter, however, we need first to see why Aquinas takes the resolutely monotheistic position which he everywhere adopts.

God is One

Many have argued that there is only one God since the world can only have been made by a single intelligence. St Augustine, for instance, does this in *De libero arbitrio*, where he declares that creatures reflect the eternal form of God, and that the order and unity of nature shows forth the unity of the creator.[3] The same view occurs in Abelard's *Introductio* and *Theologia Christiana*.[4] And Aquinas accepts this line of thinking. For he holds that the world has a unity since things fit together and since diverse things come into an order only when they are ordered by a single cause.

We find that all the parts of this world are ordered to one another according as some things help some other things. Thus, lower bodies are moved by

---

[1] 1a. 29. 3.
[2] 1a. 11. 3.
[3] *De libero arbitrio*, 3. 23. 70.
[4] *Introductio*, 3. col. 1088; *Theologia Christiana*, 5. col. 1318[a].

higher bodies, and these by incorporeal substances . . . Nor is this something accidental, since it takes place always or for the most part. Therefore, this whole world has only one ordering cause and governor. But there is no other world beyond this one. Hence, there is only one governor for all things, whom we call God.[5]

He also subscribes to a version of another common argument for God's unity, one invoking the principle known as Occam's razor, according to which one should not postulate more causes than are needed to account for a given effect. This argument holds that one God would be enough to account for what we observe, and that we should therefore presume that there is but one God.

That which is accomplished adequately through one supposition is better done through one than through many. But the order of things is the best it can be, since the power of the first cause does not fail the potency in things for perfection. Now, all things are sufficiently fulfilled by a reduction to one first principle. There is, therefore, no need to posit many principles.[6]

Aquinas's fundamental argument for the oneness of God is, however, bound up with his belief in God as the first cause of created things and with his doctrine of divine simplicity. More precisely, it derives from his teaching (1) that God and his nature are indistinguishable, (2) that God is wholly perfect because wholly actual, and (3) that God is Existence Itself.

If the first teaching is true, says Aquinas, then monotheism is also true, because it does not make sense to speak of there being more than one of a particular individual. There may be many men, and there may be many men called 'Socrates'. But there can only be one Socrates (i.e. the teacher of Plato). 'There are many men' makes sense; but 'There are many Socrates' is nonsense. By the same token, Aquinas argues, if *who* God is and *what* God is cannot be distinguished (if there is no distinction in God of *suppositum* and nature), there can only be one God.

No individual can share with others its very singularity. Socrates can share what makes him human with many others, but what makes him this human being can belong to one alone. So if Socrates were this human being just by being a human being, there could no more be many human beings than there can be many Socrates. Now in God this is the case, for as we showed God is

[5] *SG* 1. 42. 7; cf. 1a. 11. 3.
[6] *SG* 1. 42. 4.

his own nature. So to be God is to be this God. And it is thus impossible for there to be many Gods.[7]

Aquinas does not mean that 'God' is the proper name of God as 'Socrates' is of Socrates, as my above analogy might be thought to imply. Some, indeed, have construed 'God' as a proper name—the proper name of some person.[8] But Aquinas does not do this. Quoting St Ambrose (*c*.339–97), he asserts that 'God' is a *nomen naturae*, a term signifying a nature—the divine nature.[9] And with reference to the oneness of God, the point he wishes to make is that this nature is necessarily non-multipliable. The divine nature, he maintains, is as individual as the bearer of a proper name and, as such, it is not subject to multiplication. He concedes that we speak as though more than one thing could be God, as when we speak of 'other gods', or as when the Psalmist writes, 'I say you shall be gods.'[10] But that, he adds, is to communicate by metaphor, and is an inevitable by-product of the fact that nouns regularly signify things which are not indistinguishable from their natures.[11]

With respect to the claim that God's oneness follows from his perfection or actuality, Aquinas's position is that if there were many Gods, they would have to differ somehow and could not all be infinitely perfect or wholly actual. For Aquinas, if A differs from B, then A lacks something B has, or vice versa. He therefore suggests that, if the difference between Gods A and B meant A lacking something which B possessed, A would not be altogether perfect (and hence not God). And, if the difference between A and B meant A having a perfection lacked by B, then B would not be God.

God, as we have seen, embraces in himself the whole perfection of existence. Now many Gods, if they existed, would have to differ. Something belonging to one would not belong to the other. And if this were a lack the one God would not be altogether perfect, whilst if it were a perfection the other God would lack it. So there cannot be more than one God.[12]

Finally, Aquinas reasons, the oneness of God follows from his being Existence Itself since (1) 'to be one is to exist undivided' and

---

[7] 1a. 11. 3.

[8] Instances are alluded to by Michael Durrant in *The Logical Status of 'God'* (London, 1973), ch. 1, which also discusses the theory that 'God' is a proper name.

[9] 1a. 13. 8.

[10] Ps. 81: 6.

[11] 1a. 13. 9.

[12] 1a. 11. 3.

(2) since God is Existence Itself, he is supremely existent (because he has not acquired existence) and supremely undivided (since he is simple).

Since to be one is to exist undivided, anything supremely one must be both supremely existent and supremely undivided. Both characteristics belong to God. He exists supremely since he has not acquired an existence which his nature has then determined, but is subsistent existence itself, in no way determined. He is also supremely undivided, because as we have seen he is altogether simple, not divided in any way, neither actually nor potentially.[13]

Notice, however, that, in propounding all these arguments for God's oneness, Aquinas is not suggesting that God is one in the sense of being one *such and such* (as Socrates is one *human being* or Fido is one *dog*). God, for Aquinas, is not one instance of a class of which there could be many members. He is one in the sense that he is subsistent, something existing undivided, something for which to be and to be a unity (one thing) are effectively equivalent. As Geach observes, for Aquinas, 'all that "there is *one* God" signifies over and above "there is (a) God" is *indivisio*—that it is *not* the case, for any *x* and *y*, that *x* is a *different* God from *y*'.[14]

God has Power

So the one God exists undivided as the simple source of all created perfection and existence. And as such, Aquinas adds, he also has power. In fact, he is all powerful or omnipotent. What this means for Aquinas, however, needs to be spelled out in some detail.

1. What Omnipotence does not Mean

We can start by noting what it does not mean. And here there are three points worth making.

1. When we say that something has power (meaning that it *can* do or be such and such, or that it is *able* in some respect), we may be thinking of active power or passive power. Thus, I can play tennis (active power) and I can be kissed (passive power). We should there-

---

[13] Ia. 11. 4.
[14] G. E. M. Anscombe and P. T. Geach, *Three Philosophers* (Oxford, 1973), 119.

fore be clear that, in ascribing power to God, Aquinas is thinking only of active power—of what God can do as an agent in his own right taking the initiative. For him, there is no passive power in God because he is wholly active and entirely lacking in potentiality. This means that he cannot be acted on or affected by something other than himself.

2. Unlike some thinkers, Aquinas does not understand God's omnipotence to mean that God can do absolutely anything you care to mention. In contrast to Descartes, for example, he does not think that God can bring about what is contradictory.[15] As we shall see in a moment, for Aquinas, God's power can only intelligibly be said to range over what can be, over what is possible absolutely speaking. Since he also believes that what is contradictory cannot be (is simply impossible), he concludes that what is contradictory does not fall within the range of omnipotence.

Now it is incompatible with the meaning of the absolutely possible that anything involving the contradiction of simultaneously being and not being should fall under divine omnipotence. Such a contradiction is not subject to it, not from any impotence in God, but because it simply does not have the nature of being feasible or possible. Whatever does not involve a contradiction is in that realm of the possible with respect to which God is called omnipotent. Whatever involves a contradiction is not held by omnipotence, for it just cannot possibly make sense of being possible.[16]

So, for example, God, cannot square circles. And he cannot change the past.

Anything that implies a contradiction does not fall under God's omnipotence. For the past not to have been implies a contradiction; thus to say that Socrates is and is not seated is contradictory, and so also to say that he had and had not been seated ... Hence for the past not to have been does not lie under divine power.[17]

---

[15] Descartes holds that laws of logic and mathematics depend on God's will. In a letter to his friend Mersenne he writes: 'Mathematical truths ... were established by God, and depend on him entirely, like all other created beings ... In general we may affirm that God can do everything we can comprehend, but not that He cannot do what we cannot comprehend ... Not even the so-called eternal truths, like *a whole is greater than its part*, would be truths, if God had not established things so' (*Descartes: Philosophical Writings*, trans. and ed. Elizabeth Anscombe and Peter Thomas Geach (Milton Keynes, 1970), 259 ff.). Descartes, however, does say that we cannot conceive how God's decrees might have been otherwise once made. See *Descartes' Conversation with Burman*, trans. John Cottingham (Oxford, 1976), 22 and 90.

[16] 1a. 25. 3.   [17] 1a. 25. 4 and 5.

On this account, God cannot even restore Miss X's virginity once it has been lost, as Aquinas himself points out while quoting St Jerome (*c*.342–420) as an authority.[18]

3. Aquinas also denies that God can do everything that other agents can do. I can get drunk, but Aquinas does not think that this power belongs to divinity since he denies that God is corporeal and potential. Or, as he puts it, God cannot do all things that are possible to created natures.[19] Among other things, this means that God cannot sin because sin involves a failure in act. 'To sin is to fall short of full activity. Hence to be able to sin is to be able to fail in doing, which cannot be reconciled with omnipotence.'[20] It has been suggested that if God cannot sin, he cannot be omnipotent.[21] But Aquinas takes exactly the opposite line and echoes writers like St Anselm, who also argue that being able to sin is incompatible with omnipotence.[22] 'It is', he observes, 'because God is omnipotent that he cannot sin.'[23] According to Aquinas, being able to sin implies mutability and a falling short of the perfect good which God is by nature. In his view 'God can sin' is as contradictory as 'God can square circles' or 'God is not God'.

2. *Omnipotence for Aquinas*

For Aquinas, God's power needs to be understood in the light of the fact that his proper effect is existence. He (rightly) denies that God is all-powerful where that means 'God can do everything possible to his power', for he finds this formula circular, 'repeating no more than that God is almighty because he can do all that he can do'.[24] But we can, he thinks, say that God is all-powerful because he can do what is possible, where that means 'God can bring about whatever can exist without any logical impossibility being involved'.

God is almighty because he can do everything that is absolutely possible ... Something is judged to be possible or impossible from the

---

[18] 1a. 25. 5 ad. 3. Jerome is not the only writer Aquinas could have quoted to the same effect. Anselm, for example, also speaks of God being unable to undo the past. See *Proslogion*, 7.

[19] 1a. 25. 3; cf. *De pot.* 1. 1. 6.

[20] 1a. 25. 3.

[21] Cf. Nelson Pike, 'Omnipotence and God's Ability to Sin', *American Philosophical Quarterly*, 6 (1969).

[22] *Proslogion*, 7.

[23] Ibid.   [24] Ibid.

implication of the terms: possible when the predicate is compatible with the subject, for instance, that Socrates is seated; impossible when it is not compatible, for instance, that a human being is a donkey.[25]

In other words, to say that God is omnipotent is to say that there is no definite limited range of possibilities in what he can bring about. Things belonging to a distinct genus and species are limited in what they can bring about, for they can only produce effects which are characteristic of things in that genus and species. But God, Aquinas holds, is not limited in this way. A man and a woman can bring it about that something is a human being. Two dogs can bring it about that something is a dog. But God can bring it about that something is, *period*. So, says Aquinas, if it *could be*, then God can bring it about, and his power is relative to the bringing about of what can be.

Since every agent enacts its like, every active power has a possible objective corresponding to the nature of that activity which the active power is for . . . The divine being, on which the notion of divine power is founded, is infinite existence, not limited to any kind of being, but holding within itself and anticipating the perfection of the whole of existence. Whatever can have the nature of being falls within the range of things that are absolutely possible, and it is with respect to these that God is called all-powerful.[26]

An implication of this position, we should notice, is that from God's world we can deduce nothing about his character, not as we would normally deduce character, anyway. Something quite different from what we find could, in fact, have been God's world.

God's Knowledge

In the *Summa theologiae*, Aquinas moves from an exposition of why we can say that God is one to a general discussion of the way in which we use language concerning him. There then follows a consideration of the claim that knowledge can be ascribed to God, so it will be convenient for us to turn now to what Aquinas has to say about that claim.

He holds that there is knowledge or understanding in God. But his grounds for this conclusion differ from those sometimes given by

---

[25] 1a. 25. 3.
[26] 1a. 25. 3.

theists. For these often argue that knowledge can be ascribed to God just because his effects suggest that their cause is intelligent, which is not quite Aquinas's line. He certainly thinks that the nature of the world suggests an intelligent cause behind it (cf. the fifth of the Five Ways). But he rests his case for the truth that God has knowledge chiefly on an item of our negative knowledge of God—namely that God is not material. To follow him on this point, however, we will first need to note more of what he says on the subject of knowledge in people.

1. Human Knowledge

As I noted in Chapter 2, Aquinas is a kind of empiricist. He believes that our knowledge depends on sense experience. But he also holds that, though our knowledge takes its rise from sense experience, and though we can speak of there being sensory knowledge or sensible cognition, bare sense experience of things will not give us intellectual knowledge of them. His view is that the human intellect understands or thinks of things by abstracting from sense data (*phantasmata*) and that the mind, in coming to knowledge, is not purely passive. It has, he contends, two powers: the 'agent intellect' (*intellectus agens*) and the 'receptive intellect' or 'possible intellect' (*intellectus possibilis*).

One and the same soul . . . has a power called an agent intellect . . . abstracting from the conditions of individual matter, and another to receive ideas of this kind, which is called the receptive intellect as having the power to receive such ideas.[27]

The expressions 'agent intellect' and 'possible intellect' have a history in medieval thinking going well beyond that of Aquinas. Ultimately derived from Aristotle's *De anima*, they were in common use among those who had read Aristotle or read about him as tools for explaining how we come to know. But they were not always understood in the same way.

Some, such as Alexander of Hales and Robert Grosseteste, held, or were thought to hold, that the agent intellect is God himself or something strongly dependent on God for its operation. In their view, our intellectual knowledge does not arise simply on the basis

---

[27] 1a. 19. 4 ad. 4.

of natural human powers. It requires a kind of illumination or enlightenment from beyond.[28]

Others (including most of the masters in the Parisian Arts Faculty between about 1225 and 1250) held that the agent intellect is something in human beings, something natural or proper to them. And this is the position of Aquinas, who in this respect thought himself to be faithful to Aristotle.[29] According to him, the agent intellect abstracts from sense experience of particular things to form universal ideas. The receptive (or possible) intellect is, in Anthony Kenny's neat phrase, 'the storehouse of those ideas once abstracted'.[30] And, if one were to ask Aquinas why there must be an agent intellect, his answer would be that it is required since material objects are, of themselves, not intelligible. In his view, you do not understand what a thing is just by coming across instances of it which impinge on the senses. For him, nothing material is actually understandable, and it therefore follows that we must have an ability to grasp what the senses deliver in a way that allows us to understand what gives rise to sense impressions.

Plato thought that the forms of natural things existed apart without matter and are therefore thinkable: because what makes something actually thinkable is its being non-material. These he called species or ideas. Corporeal matter, he thought, takes the form it does by sharing in these, so that individuals by this sharing belong in their natural kinds and types; and it is by sharing in them that our understanding takes the forms it does of knowledge of the different kinds and types. But Aristotle did not think that the forms of natural things existed independently of matter, and forms existing in matter are not actually thinkable. Nothing passes from potentiality to actuality except by something already actual, as sense perception is actuated by something which is actually perceptible. So it was necessary to posit a power belonging to the intellect to make actually thinkable objects by abstracting ideas (species) from their material conditions. This is why we need to postulate the agent intellect.[31]

For Aquinas, then, the world is potentially intelligible, and it becomes intelligible to us as we abstract from sense data and thus

---

[28] Details providing background to this sketchy generalization can be found in James McEvoy, *The Philosophy of Robert Grosseteste* (Oxford, 1982).
[29] See *De ver.* X. 6 and 1a. 84. 6.
[30] Anthony Kenny, *Aquinas* (Oxford, 1980), 69.
[31] 1a. 79. 3.

come to understand things. On this account, it is form which is the real object of human knowledge. For Aquinas, therefore, the model for knowing is not so much *seeing* as *talking*. Though he often uses the image of intellectual vision in speaking about knowledge, his argument is that to know or understand is to be able to deploy meanings or concepts. Knowledge, he affirms, is not of *individuals* but of *forms*.[32]

As we saw in Chapter 3, a form is that by which something actually is what it is, whether substantially or accidentally. A form exists when there is a definite thing or a property or attribute predicable of things. Though he believes that there are subsisting non-material forms (e.g. God), Aquinas holds that, as we understand them, forms exist in matter and are attributable to particular individuals. But he also thinks that, on the basis of acquaintance with particulars, we gain ideas or concepts in terms of which particulars can be classed, understood, or talked about. When we do this, he says, the forms of things come to be in a different sense from the way they exist as exemplified by the individuals whose forms they are. When knowledge or understanding occurs, forms come into being which are, not the forms of individual material things, but the forms of these things considered as objects of knowledge. Such forms are the 'intelligible species', as Aquinas calls them. And they come to be in us. They are the result in us of our minds getting to work on the data of sense experience and transforming it from a 'big, booming, buzzing confusion' to a world of meaning or understanding.

On this account, to understand what, for example, a dog is means having in oneself what it takes to be a dog (the form of a dog) without actually being a dog. Fido is a dog and he has his form because what it is to be a dog is exemplified by him. Or, as Aquinas would say, Fido has his form 'materially' (*materialiter*). But what of me understanding what Fido is? Aquinas's answer is that when I begin to do this the form which gave existence to Fido the individual in the world now comes to function as a meaning in the mind. Or, as Aquinas puts it, I understand what Fido is because the form of a dog

[32] Aquinas's teaching on human knowledge ultimately derives from Aristotle's *De Anima*. But it differs in significant ways from that of other medieval writers also influenced by Aristotle. For background on the history of Aristotle's theory of knowledge in the Middle Ages, see chapters 29 ff. of Norman Kretzmann, Anthony Kenny, and Jan Pinborg (eds.), *The Cambridge History of Later Medieval Philosophy* (Cambridge, 1982).

comes to exist 'intentionally' (*intentionaliter*) instead of 'materially' (*materialiter*). Aquinas holds that forms can be received in the intellect immaterially. The form of a dog, say, exists individualized and materialized in Fido. But it exists universal and immaterial in the mind. In the one case, as Aquinas puts it, it has *esse naturale*. In the other case it has *esse intentionale*. And he thinks that knowledge occurs when there is form which is not received in matter. If it were received in matter it would be a material thing—e.g. a dog. But knowledge of dogs occurs when the form of a dog occurs without being received in matter. It occurs when the form of a material thing comes to have *esse intentionale* as opposed to *esse naturale*.

The perfection of one thing cannot be in another according to the determined act of existence which it has in the thing itself. Hence, if we wish to consider it in so far as it can be in another, we must consider it apart from those things which determine it by their very nature. Now, since forms and perfections of things are made determinate by matter, a thing is knowable in so far as it is separated from matter. For this reason, the subject in which these perfections are received must be immaterial; for, if it were material, the perfection would be received in it according to a determinate act of existence. It would, accordingly, not be in the intellect in a state in which it is knowable, that is, in the way in which the perfection of one thing can be in another . . . A thing must be received by a knowing intellect in an immaterial way. For this reason, we observe, a nature capable of knowing is found in things in proportion to their degree of immateriality.[33]

2. Divine Knowledge

According to Aquinas, then, knowing and being known is nothing but existence unlimited by matter. Knowledge, for him, involves the receiving of forms immaterially. With knowing and intelligibility there is a liberation from matter, from which it would seem to follow that the more a knower can liberate something from materiality, the more knowing it is. And it is with this point in mind that Aquinas moves to the conclusion that there is knowledge in God. Indeed, he argues, God's knowledge is unlimited.

God has knowledge, and that in the most perfect way. This will become evident if we note that the difference between knowing and non-knowing subjects is that the latter have nothing but their own form, whereas a

---

[33] *De ver.* 2. 2.

knowing subject is one whose nature it is to have in addition the form of something else. Thus, clearly, the nature of a non-knowing subject is more confined and limited by comparison with knowing subjects; the latter have a greater scope and extension; hence Aristotle says that the soul is in a manner all things. Now form is limited by matter: for which reason we said above that the freer forms are from matter the more they approach to a kind of infinity. It is clear, then, that a thing's freedom from matter is the reason why it is able to know; and the capacity to know is in proportion to the degree of freedom from matter. Thus plants are said to have no knowledge because of their materiality. But the senses are able to know because they are able to receive the likenesses of things without the matter; and intellect is still more capable of knowing because it is freer from matter and unmixed, as we read in Aristotle. Hence since God is immaterial in the highest degree, as is clear from what we have said above, it follows that he has knowledge in the highest degree.[34]

Here it may appear that Aquinas is offering the fallacious argument: 'If something knows, it is immaterial. God is immaterial. So God knows.' But that is not what Aquinas is saying. Drawing on his view of knowledge as expounded above, his argument is:

1. Given two things, one with knowledge and the other without, the thing without knowledge is more restricted than the thing with knowledge.
2. This is because a thing without knowledge has only its own form, while a knowing thing has more than its own form.
3. Being material means having only one form.
4. Non-materiality implies having more than one form.
5. If the possession of form is restricted by matter, the less material something is the less restricted it is when it comes to the possession of form immaterially.
6. The possession of form immaterially is knowledge. So the less material something is the less restricted it is when it comes to knowledge.
7. Something completely unrestricted materially will be completely unrestricted when it comes to knowledge.
8. So God, being completely immaterial, must not only know; he must be unrestricted with respect to knowledge.

This conclusion, Aquinas also wants to say, follows from God's perfection as well. St Anselm dealt with the topic of divine knowl-

---

[34] Ia. 14. 1.

edge by suggesting that God has knowledge because he is 'that than which nothing greater can be conceived' and because it is greater to know than to be ignorant.[35] And Aquinas here takes the same line as Anselm. 'Among the perfections of things', he observes, 'the greatest is that something be intelligent, for thereby it is in a manner all things, having within itself the perfections of all things. God is, therefore, intelligent.'[36]

But what does God know, and what does his knowledge imply? Answers to these questions abound in Aquinas's writings, though, in keeping with what we have already seen of him, they have a negative air since they concentrate mainly on differences between God's knowledge and human knowledge. At this point I shall simply note how he expands his general account of God's knowledge by drawing attention to five major assertions which he defends. These are (1) God knows himself, (2) God knows creatures through his essence, (3) God knows individuals, (4) God knows future contingents, and (5) God's knowledge is the cause of creatures.

(a) God's Self-Knowledge

We should be quite clear that when he says that God knows himself Aquinas is not thinking of anything like introspection. He does not mean that God somehow looks inward and identifies what he finds there, as Descartes thought we can do.[37] His idea is that God and what God knows are indistinguishable. He thinks that the subject and object of divine knowledge cannot be thought of as two different things and that God knows himself simply by being God.

As we have seen, God, for Aquinas, has no accidents and is identical with his nature. In Aquinas's view, all that is in God is God. Since there is knowledge in God, Aquinas therefore concludes that, in God's case, the subject/object distinction involved when we know disappears, that God's knowing and what he knows are the same.

Since God has no potentiality but is pure actuality, in him intellect and what is known must be identical in every way: thus he is never without the knowledge-likeness, as our intellect is when it is only potentially knowing;

---

[35] *Proslogion*, 6.
[36] *SG* 1. 44. 6.
[37] *Meditations on First Philosophy*, 2.

and in him the knowledge-likeness is not different from the substance of the divine intellect, as in ourselves the knowledge-likeness is different from the substance of our intellect when we are actually knowing; but in him the knowledge-likeness itself is the divine intellect itself. And thus he knows himself through himself.[38]

The expression translated here as 'knowledge-likeness' is *species intelligibilis*, which is what I referred to above as 'intelligible species', i.e. forms received by the mind. What Aquinas is saying, therefore, is that though people are different from the content of their knowledge or from the fact that they are actually knowing (since they learn and can become ignorant), God and his knowledge are not thus distinct. God's actual knowledge (the existence of form without matter) is not different from himself, so he and his knowledge are the same. It follows from this, of course, that God is not just supremely knowing. He is also supremely intelligible or understandable. Since God is unchangeable, it also follows that his knowledge is not discursive— i.e. (1) that God does not first know this and then know that, and (2) that he cannot pass from ignorance to knowledge. Or, as Aquinas writes: 'God sees everything in one, that is, in himself . . . Hence he sees everything at once and not successively.'[39]

(b) God's Knowledge of Creatures

According to Aquinas, we know things because something else acts on us so that our knowledge results as a consequence. He thinks that human knowledge is, at least partly, a case of potentiality being actualized by virtue of causes outside the knower. God's knowledge, however, cannot be anything like this, he says. In his view, God is fully actual, and is the first cause of things being acted on. It follows, he concludes, that knowledge in God is not the actualization of a potentiality by virtue of something outside himself. It should rather be thought of on the model of self-knowledge.

In conceiving of God as self-knowing, Aquinas stands in line with Aristotle, for whom the life of God is an act of self-knowledge. In Aristotle's thinking, however, the object of divine thought must be the best thing there is, namely itself, from which it would seem to follow that God has no knowledge of what is not divine.[40] Aquinas,

---

[38] 1a. 14. 2.
[39] 1a. 14. 7.
[40] *Metaphysics*, 1074^{b}33 ff.

on the other hand, stoutly maintains that God must have knowledge of things other than himself. And he actually grounds his thesis on the conclusion that God has self-knowledge.

For if God knows himself, Aquinas contends, then he knows himself as Creator and sustainer of things other than himself, since that is what he is. And knowing himself as this involves him in knowing his creatures. For if God knows himself perfectly, he knows his power perfectly. And, since his power extends to other things, he knows these too.

God must know things other than himself. For evidently he knows himself perfectly: otherwise he would not be perfect, since his being is his act of knowledge. But if something is known perfectly, its power must be known perfectly. Now the power of a thing cannot be known perfectly unless the objects to which the power extends are known. Hence, since the divine power extends to other things by being the first cause which produces all beings . . . God must know things other than himself. And this will be still more evident if we add that the very being of God, the first efficient cause, is his act of knowing. Hence whatever effects pre-exist in God as in the first cause must be in his act of knowledge; and everything there must be in the condition of intelligibility; for all that is in another is therein according to the condition of that in which it is.[41]

This, of course, does not mean that God and creatures are identical. It means that God knows himself as the cause of his effects, which therefore exist in him as an object known exists in any knower, namely 'intentionally' or immaterially. Creatures are in God as known by him, but they are still distinct from him.

(c) God's Knowledge of Individuals

When he says that God knows individuals, Aquinas means that God knows what exists in the world, not just in the sense of knowing what things in the world have in common, but also in the sense of knowing their differences. He thinks that God must know individuals as the individuals they are because his knowledge of creatures would otherwise be imperfect.

To know something generically and not specifically is to know it imperfectly . . . If, therefore, God's knowledge of other things were merely universal and not specific, it would follow that his act of knowledge—and consequently his

---

[41] 1a. 14. 5.

existence also—would not be in every way perfect . . . We must therefore say that he knows things other than himself in what is proper to each; not only in what they have in common as beings, but in the ways in which they are different from one another.[42]

Aquinas also thinks that God must know individuals as individuals since we know them as such and since 'all the perfections found in creatures are found first in God in a higher way'.[43]

But Aquinas has something of a problem on his hands in saying how this is so, one which arises from the fact that, on his account, matter is the principle of individuation and human knowledge of individuals derives from sensory experience. As we have seen, he thinks that individuals, as such, are not intelligible. We cannot express in words what it is that makes Fido to be Fido or Davies to be Davies, for their individuality is constituted by matter (cf. Chapter 3). But we can, Aquinas thinks, be said, in a sense, to know them as individuals—to know them as 'this thing' and 'that thing'. For we can clearly be acquainted with Fido and Davies. This, Aquinas says, is because we can bump into them and the like, because they can impinge on us at the level of sense. Given, however, that God is not material, he has no senses by which to encounter and become acquainted with individuals and, on that basis, to know them in their individuality as we can. How, then, can he know them?

Aquinas's answer is that God knows individuals (*singularia*) because he is the reason why there are things other than himself. More precisely, God knows material individuals because he is the Maker, not just of forms, but of the matter in which they are received, because he actualizes forms received in matter. For Aquinas, God's knowledge and power are identical. So his knowing what his power brings about means him knowing *all* that it brings about—which includes the reception of this form in this matter, matter being from God as much as anything else.[44]

God's active power extends not only to forms which provide the universal factor, but also to matter . . . His knowledge, then, must necessarily extend to

---

[42] 1a. 14. 6.
[43] 1a. 14. 11.
[44] Aquinas is clear that God must be the cause of matter (*materia prima*). He argues for this in 1a. 44. 2, where he says that matter makes individual things individuals and, in this sense, is part of what they are (cf. 1a. 75. 4). Their being what they are derives from God as the source of all being. So matter comes from God.

individuals, which are individuated by matter. He knows things other than himself through his essence ... therefore his essence must be the sufficient principle for knowing all things that come into existence through him, not merely in their universal natures but in their individuality. The same would be true of the craftsman's knowledge if it produced the whole thing and not merely the form.[45]

In other words, God knows himself not just as the cause of it being true that 'X is a dog' is sometimes true. He also knows himself as cause of the fact that 'X is a dog' is true for given values of X. He knows himself as cause of the fact that Fido is a dog and Rover is a dog. If carpenters could plan, not just the look of their chairs, but also their matter (in Aquinas's sense of 'matter'), they would know them through and through. By the same token, says Aquinas, God knows his creatures through and through, as material individuals and not just as things that can be described in general terms.

(*d*) Future Contingents

By 'future contingents' I mean 'things to come which are not now necessitated in their causes'. Let us suppose that in the year 2000 someone truly writes 'Davies wrote a book in 1995'. Let us also suppose that nothing in the world in 1989 made it inevitable that Davies would write a book in 1995. In that case, my writing of 1995 would be what Aquinas would call a future contingent. And, he affirms, God changelessly knows all future contingents. 'God knows all things ... and some of these are contingent events in our future, [so] it follows that God knows contingent future events.'[46]

Aquinas's reason for saying this lies in his view that God change-lessly knows himself as the Maker and sustainer of his creatures. The world may not now contain whatever might be involved in me writing a book. But Aquinas thinks that, if I will write a book, then my doing so is changelessly known to God because any writing I may achieve will only come about by virtue of God. So knowledge of the future is actual in God even though the future is (by definition) not itself actual.

Many philosophers have observed that this thesis is problematic.[47]

[45] 1a. 14. 11.

[46] 1a. 14. 13.

[47] For recent discussions of the matter see Jonathan L. Kvanvig, *The Possibility of an All-Knowing God* (London, 1986) and William Hasker, *God, Time, and Knowledge*

For to them it seems to imply that the future is thoroughly determined. If someone knows that-*p*, it follows that-*p*. It is true of necessity that if Fred knows that I drink port, then I drink port. How, then, can God know that such and such *will* happen without it being true that such and such *must* happen? And if such and such *must* happen, how can it be thought of as anything other than necessary or inevitable?

Though he is aware of it, however,[48] Aquinas does not regard this line of reasoning as undermining his thesis that God knows future contingents. For, in his view, God's changeless knowledge is best compared with the knowledge we have of a fact before us in the present, not with the knowledge we have that such and such must happen in the future. Though events succeed each other in time, he says, God knows them all at once. And this, he adds, is quite compatible with their being contingent.

Suppose that I know that you will die in five minutes. Aquinas would say that I can only be said to have knowledge here because I am aware of factors at work necessitating your imminent death (because, for example, I know that someone has turned off your life-support system). He thinks that if I genuinely know that such and such will happen, the such and such in question is inevitable because it is determined in its causes. Otherwise I cannot know that it will happen.

But now change the example. Suppose I know that you are talking to me. Aquinas does not think that my knowledge now entails that your talking to me is in any way necessitated. For him, '*X* knows that-*p*' does not mean that *p* is necessary in the sense that it cannot be otherwise. And, with this kind of analogy in mind, he argues that God's 'all at once' knowledge of contingent events does not rob them of their contingency.

God is wholly outside the order of time, standing, as it were, in the high citadel of eternity, which is all at one time. The whole course of time is subject to eternity in one simple glance. So at one glance he sees everything that is done in the course of time; he sees everything as it is in itself, not as if it were future relative to his view. It is only future in the ordering of its causes—though God does see that ordering of causes. In a wholly eternal

(Ithaca, NY, 1989). For a survey of ancient and medieval views see William Lane Craig, *The Problem of Divine Foreknowledge and Future Contingents from Aristotle to Suarez* (Leiden, 1988).

[48] See 1a. 14. 3 obj. 2.

way he sees everything that is the case at any time, just as the human eye sees
the sitting down of Socrates as it is in itself, not in its causes. The fact that
some human being sees the sitting down of Socrates does not take away the
contingency of this event ... Nevertheless, the human eye does see the sitting
down of Socrates most certainly and without any possibility of error while he
is sitting down ... We are left, then, with the conclusion that God knows
everything which happens in time most certainly and without possibility of
error; but in spite of this the things that happen in time are not necessarily
but contingently the case, and do not necessarily come to be the case, but
contingently.[49]

In other words, God's knowledge is not a matter of him first
knowing that something will happen, and then knowing that it has
happened, where that implies a change in God. Some have expressed
the point by saying that, for Aquinas, God does not have foreknowledge. But that reading does not quite square with what Aquinas
actually says. He does not deny that God has foreknowledge. In 3a.
46. 2, for example, he writes: 'It is impossible that God's foreknowledge should be erroneous.' But he does maintain that God knows
the whole course of time in an unchanging way. Or, as he puts it:

Although contingent events come into actual existence successively, God
does not, as we do, know them in their actual existence successively, but
all at once; because his knowledge is measured by eternity, as is also his
existence; and eternity, which exists as a simultaneous whole, takes in the
whole of time ... Hence all that takes place in time is eternally present
to God ... because he eternally surveys all things as they are in their
presentness.[50]

You and I come to know what happens as it happens, for we are
mutable and our knowledge grows. For Aquinas, however, it is not
like this with God. He knows the created order rather as we know
what we directly perceive on a given occasion.[51] And this, Aquinas

[49] *In peri herm.*, book 1, lectio 14.
[50] 1a. 14. 13.
[51] It has been said that this view of Aquinas entails the ludicrous conclusion that
events occurring at different times are really simultaneous with each other. Anthony
Kenny, for instance, argues that 'On St Thomas's view, my typing of this paper is
simultaneous with the whole of eternity. Again, on this view, the great fire of Rome is
simultaneous with the whole of eternity. Therefore, while I type these very words,
Nero fiddles heartlessly on' (*Aquinas: A Collection of Critical Essays* (London, 1969),
264; see also Richard Swinburne, *The Coherence of Theism* (Oxford, 1977), 220. But
this argument misrepresents Aquinas's position. Aquinas does not believe that God
knows events because they are all simultaneously present. He holds that God
changelessly knows all events.

reasons, allows us to say that God can know future contingents. It allows us to say that, though God knows what will be, not all that will be is necessitated or fated.

The contingent is opposed to the certitude of knowledge only so far as it is future, not so far as it is present. For when the contingent is future, it can not-be. Thus, the knowledge of one conjecturing that it will be can be mistaken: it will be mistaken if what he conjectures as future will not take place. But in so far as the contingent is present, in that time it cannot not-be. It can not-be in the future, but this affects the contingent not so far as it is present but so far as it is future. Thus, nothing is lost to the certitude of sense when someone sees a man running, even though this judgement is contingent. All knowledge, therefore, that bears on something contingent as present can be certain. But the vision of the divine intellect from all eternity is directed to each of the things that take place in the course of time, in so far as it is present. It remains, therefore, that nothing prevents God from having from all eternity an infallible knowledge of contingents.[52]

As many have noted, this is essentially the solution to the question of God's knowledge of what is future offered by Boethius in *The Consolation of Philosophy*.[53] God's knowledge, he contends, is not best compared with human foreknowledge. Rather it should be thought of as 'knowledge of a never passing instant' in that God sees future things 'present to him just such as in time they will at some future point come to be'. 'With one glance of his mind', says Boethius, God

distinguishes both those things necessarily coming to be and those not necessarily coming to be, just as you, when you see at one and the same time that a man is walking on the ground and that the sun is rising in the sky, although the two things are seen simultaneously, yet you distinguish them, and judge the first to be voluntary, the second necessary.[54]

(e) God's Knowledge as Causal

Aquinas's final main conclusion about God's knowledge is one which distances him sharply from various writers both ancient and modern. Origen (*c*.185–*c*.254), for example, maintained that 'A thing will not happen in the future because God knows it will happen, but because

---

[52] *SG* 1. 67. 2.
[53] A solid general introduction to Boethius is Henry Chadwick, *Boethius: The Consolations of Music, Logic, Theology and Philosophy* (Oxford, 1981).
[54] *The Consolation of Philosophy*, 5, trans. S. J. Tester (Cambridge, Mass., 1978).

it is going to happen therefore it is known by God before it does happen.'[55] Essentially the same view is found in modern writers who construe God's knowledge of creation as analogous to ours when it can be said that we have justified, true belief about the way things are.[56] Aquinas, however, takes exactly the opposite position. For instead of saying, as one might expect him to, that God's knowledge of his creation is dependent on the way it is, he argues that God's creation is the way it is because God knows it.

> The knowledge of the human intellect is in a manner caused by things. Hence it is that knowable things are the measure of human knowledge; for something that is judged to be so by the intellect is true because it is so in reality, and not conversely. But the divine intellect through its knowledge is the cause of things.[57]

The reason for this move should by now be apparent. Since there is no potentiality in God, and since God is the first cause of things being changed, his knowledge of creatures cannot be a case of them acting on him so as to bring it about that he knows them. It must rather be the case that creatures are as they are (and therefore known to God) by virtue of God. Augustine put this by saying that 'Not because they are does God know all creatures, spiritual and corporeal, but they are because He knows them.'[58] And Aquinas says the same.

> It cannot be said that what is known by God is the cause of his knowledge; for things are temporal and his knowledge is eternal, and what is temporal cannot be the cause of anything eternal. Similarly, it cannot be said that both are caused by one cause, because there can be nothing caused in God, seeing that he is whatever he has. Hence, there is left only one possibility: his knowledge is the cause of things.[59]

For Aquinas, the best model of God's knowledge of creatures is that of a craftsman's knowledge of what he makes, though, inevitably, the analogy limps.[60] It is, however, a natural one given Aquinas's firm insistence on the difference between God and creatures and given his belief in God as beginning and end of all things.

---

[55] *On Romans*, 7.
[56] See Swinburne, *The Coherence of Theism*, ch. 10, where a justified, true belief account of God's knowledge is maintained.
[57] *SG* 1. 61. 7.
[58] *De Trinitate*, 15. 13.
[59] *De ver.* 2. 14.
[60] The analogy is offered by Aquinas in 1a. 14. 8.

8

Will to Mercy

IT should now be obvious that, in spite of his agnosticism, Aquinas has plenty to say about what we need to affirm of God from a philosohical viewpoint and without explicit reference to, or dependence on, Christian revelation. According to him, we have good philosophical grounds for saying that God is the creator of the world *ex nihilo*. He also thinks that there are philosophical reasons for believing that God is perfect, good, ubiquitous, eternal, unique, powerful, and knowledgeable.

But people who believe in God usually want to assert more of him that this. Pious Christians who plan for the future say that they shall do such and such 'God willing'. They think of God as having will. As a Christian, Aquinas certainly agrees with them, but does he think that their position is philosophically defensible? Does he believe that there are philosophical grounds for ascribing will to God? And does he think the same of the equally prevalent belief that God rules the world with justice and mercy? The God of the Bible is said to be just and merciful. And Aquinas believes in the God of the Bible. But does he hold that there are extra-biblical reasons for ascribing justice and mercy to God?

The short answer is 'Yes', and in this chapter we shall see why. The thoroughly systematic nature of Aquinas's thinking should by now be apparent to the reader. But we have further evidence of it as we turn now to his philosophical treatment of God's will, love, justice, and mercy, for what he has to say presupposes and connects with much that he teaches concerning God's changelessness, power, and knowledge. His philosophical case for ascribing will to God rests, for example, on his view of God's knowledge or understanding. And he develops it by drawing on the conclusion that God is wholly immutable.

Will in God

I. Why God has Will

Jews, Christians, and Muslims take it for granted that there is will in God, or that will can somehow be ascribed to him. That there is will in God seems a fundamental tenet of theism. But it is, to begin with, well worth noting that some who have spoken the language of theism have not always held that will can be ascribed to God.

Take, for example, Aristotle. He was no Jew, Christian, or Muslim. But he subscribed to a form of belief in God. It would be misleading to say otherwise.[1] As we saw in Chapters 2 and 7, however, the God of Aristotle differs from that of Aquinas. And one of the reasons why he differs is because he does not have what, I presume, most people would mean by 'will'. The nature of will is a disputed matter, but all parties are agreed that, if you have will, then you *act* in some way, or you can *try to act*. You *do things voluntarily*. You *bring things about by choice*. Yet Aristotle does not think that this is true of God. He thinks that God is chiefly a knower whose object of knowledge is himself. According to Aristotle, there is indeed a sense in which God gets things done, for he is the unmoved mover or changer who accounts for movements and changes with which we are familiar. That is why it is true to say that Aquinas is particularly close to Aristotle in his First Way of proving God's existence. But Aristotle's God moves or changes by being what Aristotle calls a final cause. For him, God is that at which things aim. He is that to which things are drawn, and he causes their movement just by being this. Even as first mover or changer, therefore, there is a sense in which he does nothing. The iron filings drawn to the magnet are moved, we might say, by the magnet. But the magnet, so we can also say, does nothing when drawing the filings to it. And Aristotle seems to think that this is how it is with God and what is drawn to him. The God of Aristotle is like a great, transcendent magnet. There is a sense in which he causes or explains motion or change. But he does not preside over it as doing what he wants to do. He does not act voluntarily to get things done. He does not exercise will.

A similar line of thinking can be found in Neoplatonic writers such

---

[1] Cf. *Metaphsics*, 12. 6 ff. The best recent exposition of Aristotle's theism is L. P. Gerson, *God and Greek Philosophy* (London, 1990), ch. 3.

as Plotinus. For him, the supreme principle (the One) is what ultimately gives rise to the world, for from it come divine beings, or 'hypostases', from whom flow yet lower orders of beings. Yet the emergence of such orders is not the result of decision or will. The One, for Plotinus, lies beyond change and, therefore, beyond activity. The things which come from it do so by a kind of necessity, of which Plotinus speaks by invoking the image of emanation—the idea being that what comes from the One flows from it in view of its nature, rather as heat flows from fire, cold flows from snow, and light flows the sun.[2] Plotinus does not even think of the divine hypostases as creating by decision. For them, everything happens inevitably and for the best, and their activity is like spontaneous operations in nature rather than the process of making when a maker with a project is at work.[3]

For Aquinas, however, God acts voluntarily. He exercises will. Why? Because he has knowledge. Aquinas thinks that there is will in God because there is knowledge in God. For knowledge in God must include knowledge of what is good. And to know what is good is to will it.

From the fact that God is endowed with intellect it follows that He is endowed with will. For, since the understood good is the proper object of will, the understood good is, as such, willed. Now that which is understood is by reference to one who understands. Hence, he who grasps the good by his intellect is, as such, endowed with will. But God grasps the good by his intellect. For, since the activity of his intellect is perfect . . . He understands being together with the qualification of the good. He is, therefore, endowed with will.[4]

Is it really true that to know what is good is to will it? The obvious objection to the suggestion seems to be that we can know what is good and still back away from it. I can know that it is bad to smoke and good to go for walks in the country. Yet I might still smoke heavily and never take any exercise. But the move from knowledge to will seems natural to Aquinas since, in his view, though we might know that such as such is good for us and yet reject it, our rejecting it is not to be explained in terms of our knowledge. He would say that my smoking while knowing of the dangers of smoking has an

---

[2] *Enneads*, 5. 1. 6. 28 ff., 5. 3. 12. 39 ff., 5. 4. 1. 23 ff.
[3] Ibid. 3. 2. 2. 8 ff., 4. 3. 10. 13 ff., 4. 4. 11, 4. 4. 12, 5. 8. 7. 1 ff.
[4] *SG* 1. 72. 2.

explanation. It lies in my order of priorities—in what I rank first, second, third, etc. in order of desirability. And, for him, this means that, even when I do what I know to be bad in some way, I do what I do because I am willing a good of which I know. In his opinion, knowing something to be good goes with being drawn to it or attracted by it. And this 'being drawn to', this 'being attracted by', is what he has in mind when he speaks of will. For him, will is what you have when something is drawn to or attracted by goodness perceived, known, or understood. In this sense, it follows on knowledge. And, since God's knowledge is perfect, says Aquinas, it would seem that he too has will. He knows the good and is drawn to it.

As there is mind in God, so there is will; the one involves the other. A physical thing has its actual existence through its form of existence, and likewise a mind is actually understanding through having an intelligible form. Now the bearing of a thing to a form natural to it is this: that when not possessed it tends there, and when possessed it stays. Such is the case with any natural completion that is a good for the nature in question. When cognition is absent this bearing on good is called 'natural appetite'.

A thing of intelligence has a like attitude towards a good apprehended through an intelligible form, so that it makes for that good when it is still to be gained, and rests with it when it is gained: both are functions of willing. Accordingly anything with a mind has a will, just as a thing with sensation has emotional appetite.

Consequently there must be a will in God because he has mind.[5]

Notice that Aquinas is not here saying that will presupposes intellect and that since God has intellect he has will. His argument is that will is definable in terms of tending to, being attracted to, the good as perceived or known, and that perception of the good always goes with being drawn to it. So God, being supremely perfect and therefore most knowing, is attracted to the good supremely. As Aquinas puts it in the *Summa contra Gentiles*:

Since the understood good is the proper object of the will, the understood good is, as such willed . . . He who grasps the good by his intellect is, as such, endowed with will. But God grasps the good by his intellect . . . He is therefore endowed with will.[6]

Or as we read in the *Compendium of Theology*:

[5] 1a. 19. 1.
[6] *SG* 1. 72.

God must have volition. For he understands himself, who is perfect good...But good as apprehended is necessarily loved, and love operates through the will. Consequently God must have volition.[7]

2. *God as Willing Himself*

From the last quotation it will be clear that, according to Aquinas, God's will has a particular object, namely himself. It will also be clear that he thinks of God as willing himself of necessity. But we need to see why he thinks in this way and what it entails for him, and to do so we can start by digging a little deeper into his general concept of will.

The fundamental point to grasp is that he thinks of every intelligent agent as willing the good of necessity. To be sure, he notes, subjects with will (voluntary agents) do not of necessity will all possible goods. When I choose an ice-cream I am not choosing a curry or an artichoke. According to Aquinas, even when I choose an ice-cream I do not do so of necessity, for choice (involving will) must be unforced and, in this sense, not necessitated. At the same time, however, Aquinas sees the operation of will as a being drawn to what is desirable, attractive, and so on. And we cannot, he thinks, help ourselves doing that. We cannot but desire the desirable or attractive. 'Willing is rational appetition', he writes, 'and there is no appetition except for a good, because appetition is nothing other than a certain bent towards a thing that is wanted.'[8] His idea is that, just as we cannot but assent to logical truths and the like once we have understood them, we cannot but be drawn to what we see as good. If I am convinced that nothing but an ice-cream will help me to go on living, then, he would say, I will inevitably choose an ice-cream if I am able to.

So will moves towards the good of necessity. At any rate, it moves to what those with will conceive of as good. And Aquinas believes that this is just as true of God's will as it is of ours. God inevitably wills what is good. For he is omniscient. And because he is omniscient, says Aquinas, he knows what goodness is as such. He knows the source and exemplar of everything we can count as good, for he knows himself (Chapter 7 above). Aquinas therefore concludes that God necessarily wills himself, for he is the source and exemplar

---

[7] *Comp.* ch. 32.
[8] 1a2ae. 8. 1.

of everything we can count as goodness. He is goodness itself (Chapter 5 above), and his goodness is therefore the primary object of his will.

For each being endowed with a will the principal object willed is the ultimate end. For the end is willed through itself and through it other things become objects of will. But the ultimate end is God himself, since he is the highest good, as has been shown. Therefore God is the principal object of his will.[9]

In this scheme of things, therefore, God can delight in himself and rest in himself. Since will aims at what is good, and since God is goodness itself, the will of God is satisfied just by God himself. For this reason, Aquinas concludes that there is no need for God to will anything other than himself. He is perfectly happy and realized simply by being God.

3. God as Willing Other Things

Yet, as Aquinas himself has argued, there are things other than God which derive from him. For this reason, therefore, he also concludes that God wills things other than himself. God, for him, is both Aristotelian and Christian, as we might say. But what of these things which are other than God? Should we say that God must will them, that they have a kind of inevitableness or necessity? As we have seen, some writers earlier than Aquinas spoke of things arising by virtue of emanation. For them, God cannot but produce other things since the created order is a kind of natural spin-off from him. Aquinas, however, will have none of this notion for two main reasons.

First (as we have seen), he thinks that God is completely at rest in himself. God is perfectly happy just by being God. He does not need to go out of himself to produce anything to add to his contentment. In fact, Aquinas would say, God's contentment *cannot* be added to. For there is no potentiality in God and he is immutable.

Another way of making this point is to distinguish between means and ends, and ways in which means might be necessary to ends. And this, too, is something Aquinas does.

Suppose that I want to get to New York within twelve hours. Also suppose that I am presently in London. There is clearly no alternative open to me but to fly. Given that I have the goal of reaching

[9] *SG* 1. 74. 5.

New York within twelve hours, I am also bound to choose to fly. Here, I have an end which I will. I also have means which I will. And my willing the means is necessary if I am to achieve my end.

But suppose I only want to get to New York within a month or two. Then I am less restricted when it comes to willing certain means. I can still take a plane. But I could also travel by boat. In this case I am not constrained to will a given thing (taking a plane or using a boat) in order to reach the end I will.

Well, says Aquinas, that is how it is with God. He wills the good of necessity. And, for him, this means willing himself as the perfect good. But, in willing that, he is not constrained to will the existence of creatures, as I might be forced to take a plane in order to get to New York within a given time.

By willing an end we are not bound to will the things that lead to it, unless they are such that it cannot be attained without them (as when to preserve life we must take food or to cross the sea we must take a boat). Other things, however, without which the end can be attained, we do not will of necessity (thus a horse for a journey we can take on foot, and the same holds good in other cases). Hence, since God's goodness subsists and is complete independently of other things, and they add no fulfilment to him, there is no absolute need for him to will them.[10]

We can put all this by observing that, for Aquinas, there is nothing *in* God which forces him to produce anything other than himself. But he also holds that there can be nothing *apart from* God which forces him to produce other things. For Aquinas, God is the unchangeable first source of everything other than himself and of the operation of everything other than himself (Chapters 2 and 6 above). He is the immutable cause of the being of everything non-divine, and the activity of everything other than him derives from him as the unchanging first cause of change. On this basis Aquinas concludes that nothing can act on God and that nothing can nudge him into being anything other than he eternally is (i.e. content and wholly fulfilled in himself). It is, of course, true, says Aquinas, that if God wills the existence of certain creatures, then there is a kind of inevitability about them. For God's will is eternal. 'On the supposition that he does will a thing, it cannot be unwilled, since his will is immutable.'[11] But Aquinas thinks that the necessity here is hypothe-

---

[10] 1a. 19. 3.
[11] Ibid.

tical. That is to say: 'Granted that God wills whatever he does from eternity the inference is not that he has to, except on the supposition that he does.'[12]

For Aquinas, therefore, the existence of things apart from God derives neither from a need in God nor from the activity of something other than God. And that, he says, obliges us to conclude that the existence of what is not divine derives from God's will. For the whole point about will is that it is something uncoerced.

Necessity of coercion is totally incompatible with willing. For we call violent whatever is against the bent of a thing. But the movement of the will is a sort of bent towards something. And so just as something is called natural because it accords with a natural bent, so a thing is called voluntary when it accords with the bent of the will. And just as it is impossible for anything to be at once violent and natural, it is equally impossible for anything to be coerced, or subject to violence, and yet be voluntary.[13]

In short, given that God produces things, he does so voluntarily. Things other than God are there because he wills them. He wills the existence of you and me, for example. Yet in holding to this view, Aquinas adds what, for him, are two important qualifications.

The first is that God undergoes no change in willing things other than himself. This idea seems counter-intuitive for the simple reason that we find ourselves changing when we will different things. When I am putting the cat out for the night, I am doing and intending something different from what I am about when I am eating my supper. In the first case I am doing and thinking such and such. In the second case I am doing and thinking something different. With this point in mind, some have suggested that since God has will he must be changeable. The idea is that if such and such occurs by virtue of God's will, and if it is followed by something else, then God must be changing rather as I do when I move from putting the cat out to having my supper. Here, however, Aquinas would distinguish between changing one's will and willing a change. In his view, all changes occur by virtue of God's will. But this does not mean that God's will changes, or that God, therefore, changes in himself.

God's will is altogether unchangeable. All the same note that to change your will is one matter, and to will a change in some things is another. While remaining constant, a person can will this to happen now and the contrary to

---

[12] 1a. 19. 3 ad. 1.   [13] 1a. 82. 1.

happen afterwards. His will, however, would change were he to begin to will what he had not willed before, or cease to will what he had willed before . . . We have already shown that God's nature as well as his knowledge is altogether immutable. So, therefore, is his will also.[14]

Secondly, Aquinas maintains, God wills his creatures not as ends in themselves but as reflections of himself. On his account, the world God has made is willed as ordered to God, which again means that God is always and primarily willing his own goodness. According to Aquinas, God wills his creatures all right. We know that because the creatures are there and because nothing in or outside God can have forced him to make them. But since his will is directed to the ultimate good (i.e. himself), it is himself that he is ultimately engaged in willing even as he wills his creatures.

To put it another way, God's creatures are ultimately things directed to God, things drawn to the goodness which he is. 'He wills his own being and the being of others. However, he wills himself as the end, and others as to that end.'[15] In Chapter 5 we saw how Aquinas thinks that God is the alpha and omega because he is the source of his creatures and because all his creatures aim at what is first in him and secondly in them. Now we find Aquinas developing that point so as to suggest that *what God is* amounts to *what he wills* in willing his creatures. In making them, as Aquinas puts it, God wills himself and, in this sense, shares himself with them. But since his willing of creatures is voluntary (because neither his nature nor anything apart from him forces him to make them), we must, Aquinas adds, think of God's willing of creatures as wholly free and something for which we are in no position to assign causes.

By one act God understands everything in his essence, and similarly by one act he wills everything in his goodness. Hence, just as in God the understanding of the cause is not the cause of his understanding the effect, though he understands effects in their cause, so his willing the end does not cause his willing things subordinate to it, though he does will them to be ordered to that end. In other words, he wills this to be because of that, but he does not will this because he wills that.[16]

In willing me to exist, God wills his own goodness, and he always does this of necessity. But he can will his own goodness without willing me to exist and without being made to will my existence by anything acting on him. Like the existence of everything derived

[14] 1a. 19. 7.   [15] 1a. 19. 2.   [16] 1a. 19. 5.

from God, therefore, my existence is in no sense something we can deduce from a knowledge of what God is. It is something freely given.

For Aquinas, this, in turn, means that God could have made an entirely different world from the one he has made. God's creating is free, he says. So it is not explicable in terms of things having an effect on him. Nor is it explicable in terms of him needing to create. He gains nothing from there being creatures, and he therefore gains nothing from there being the creatures there are rather than others which might have been. Furthermore, says Aquinas, since God primarily wills the ultimate good, he could have made something which is more like it than the world which he has made. 'God could make other things than he has, or could add others to the things he has made; and this other universe would be better.'[17] Since Aquinas holds that everything existing is good and that God is in no way the creative or direct cause of evil (Chapter 5 above), he thinks that God makes the world as good as he can make it, i.e. that, granted that God makes this world, he makes it the best possible this-world. But since he also thinks that God can make whatever can exist without implying contradiction, and since he also thinks that there could be better things than we are familiar with in this world, he also maintains that God has not made as many good things as it is possible for him to make, i.e. he could have made a better world.

On the other hand, however, Aquinas does give some account of an end involved in God creating as he has. In 1a. 47. 1, for example, he suggests that

the distinction and multitude of things is from the intention (*ex intentione*) of the first cause, who is God. For he brought things into being in order that his goodness might be communicated (*propter suam bonitatem comunicandam*) to creatures, and be represented by them. And because his goodness could not be adequately represented by one creature, he produced many and diverse creatures.

That is to say, what God intends by creating is not his reason for creating, but God's intention in creating is the communication and representation of his goodness. Why? Because, so Aquinas answers, *bonum est diffusivum sui et esse* ('the good is diffusive of itself and being'):

[17] 1a. 25. 6.

The communication of being and goodness proceeds from goodness. This is clear both from the very nature of good and from its concept. For by nature, the good of anything whatever is its act and perfection. Now something acts insofar as it is in act, and by acting, it diffuses its being and goodness into other things ... For this reason it is said that 'the good is diffusive of itself and being'. This diffusion belongs to God, for ... He is the cause of being for other things.[18]

This, I think, means (1) that something acting is itself actual (and therefore good), and its effects express what it is, and (2) that, in creating, God may therefore be said to aim at expressing what he is.

On Aquinas's account, therefore, if we were to ask for God's reason in creating, all that could be said is that it lies in his goodness. Someone might object that this cannot be why God creates since it does not explain why he creates rather than not. It might be argued that there must be a reason why God creates rather than not and that, if his goodness is a reason for his creating, then he needs to create. But a reason for doing such and such does not have to be a compelling cause making one do such and such. I might have children for any number of reasons, but my actually choosing to have them need not be in any way necessitated. I might have them for various reasons, but I might also decline to have them while acknowledging the force of reasons for having them. By the same token, Aquinas seems to argue, God's diffusion of his goodness is a reason for him to create, but it is not a reason for him to create rather than not. It is a reason for him to create this world, but not a reason for him to create this world rather than some other. On the other hand, however, it is, says Aquinas, an instance of what we are talking about when we say that God is loving.

Love in God

Aquinas's view of God's love provides another example of his rigorous insistence that God is radically different from creatures, an insistence not shared by all theistic writers. For, when he says that God loves, or that there is love in God, he does not, speaking as a philosopher, mean what we usually have in mind when we think of people as loving. As we shall see later, he does hold that love

[18] *SG* 1. 37. 5.

between people has a counterpart or parallel in God. For he takes this teaching to be part of the doctrines of the Trinity and the Incarnation. He also thinks that there is a sense in which God and people share a kind of love, as we shall see when we look at his teaching on the theological virtues. Independently of revelation, however, his view of God's love is not what we tend to think of when we think of love in people.

When we attribute love to people we normally mean that they are preoccupied with each other and that they are emotionally involved with or affected by each other. We also tend to mean that they need each other somehow, or that they are lost or impaired without each other. In attributing love to God, however, Aquinas means none of this, for reasons which should be apparent in the light of what we have so far found him saying. Since he thinks of God as the eternal source of creatures who works in them and who is happy in himself, Aquinas would find it absurd or even blasphemous to suppose that God is affected by or in need of anything other than what is divine. The notion that God has feelings or emotions, implying that God is moved by something, would, for Aquinas, have to be treated as nothing but metaphor.[19] For him, there is love in God because there is *will*. 'We have shown that there is will in God, and therefore must affirm that there is love in him as well.'[20]

Why? Because, says Aquinas, will of its nature involves love. As we have seen, will, for Aquinas, is what we have when intellectual creatures are drawn to or attracted by good, known or understood. And this being drawn to or attracted by can, says Aquinas, be called love.

For the first motion of will, indeed of any power of appetition, is love . . . It is like their very root. No one desires an object or rejoices in it unless it be a good that is loved . . . On this account wherever there is appetite or will there must be love; take away the foundation and nothing else is left.[21]

Aquinas thinks that God loves simply by being God. Since God wills the good of necessity, and since this means him willing himself, there

---

[19] Cf. *SG* 1. 91. 15. Many 20th-century writers do not treat it as metaphor. They hold that God loves in that he literally undergoes emotion and is moved by what is distinct from him. For some introduction to this way of thinking see J. Van der Veken (ed.), *God and Change: Process Thought and the Christian Doctrine of God*, Louvian, 1987).
[20] 1a. 20. 1.
[21] Ibid.

is love as soon as there is divinity. While some would say that there can be love in God only because he is affected by other things, Aquinas would say that there being love in God follows immediately on the fact that, by virtue of his knowledge and will, God, so to speak, has found the ultimate object of love in himself alone. He does not need others in order to love. He loves just by being himself.

Yet Aquinas also agrees that God loves other things. For, as well as defining love as a matter of will, he also defines it as willing what is good. And, since he thinks that God wills good by making and preserving his creatures, he also believes that God loves his creatures. Insofar as a thing exists, says Aquinas, it is willed by God as its cause. Since Aquinas also thinks that existing things, simply by existing, are good (Chapter 5 above), he concludes that God therefore wills good to every existing thing, and that he therefore loves them all.

God loves all existing things. For in so far as it is real each is good; the very existence of each single thing is good, and so also is whatever it rises to. We have already shown that God's will is the cause of things, and consequently that in so far as it has reality or any goodness at all each thing must needs be willed by God. God therefore wills some good to each existing thing, and since loving is no other than willing good to someone, it is clear that God loves everything.[22]

The idea here, of course, is not that God stumbles across things to fall in love with, as we do. It is that God loves all things other than himself since he causes them to be and in doing so wills goodness. And, in saying that God loves all things here, Aquinas means exactly that. Hence, for example, he argues that God even loves sinners. He loves them insofar as they exist, for their existing is his love in operation. Insofar as they are sinners, says Aquinas, they lack something (they are not as good as they could be) and this lack is not made by/not loved by God (see above, Chapter 5). On this count, Aquinas argues, one may speak of sinners as hated by God. But he also insists that what is there can only be there because God has willed it. So if God can be said to hate sinners, he can also be said to love them, for the love of God is creative.

Since our will is not the cause of things being good but responds to that goodness as to its objective, our love in willing good for a thing is not the

[22] Ia. 20. 2.

cause of that goodness. Instead its goodness, real or only imagined, evokes our love, which cherishes the dearness it possesses and wishes to gain that which it is yet to have; to this purpose we bend our energies. God's love, however, pours out and creates the goodness in things.[23]

God's Justice and Mercy

1. Problems

Historically speaking, the notion that there is love in God has gone hand in hand with the idea that God is both just and merciful. In the Old Testament, for instance, God's love for his people is defined in terms of his covenant with them, which exemplifies his justice or 'righteousness'.[24] And Aquinas, too, sees justice and mercy in God as connected with God's love as well as with each other. In his view, however, the ascription of justice to God is problematic. For can we seriously attribute justice to God? And, if we say that God is just, how can we also think of him as merciful?

The first problem arises for Aquinas since, in his view, justice is a virtue, and virtue cannot be ascribed to God without qualification. According to Aquinas, virtues generally add to human perfection. They make us better people. But God, he reasons, is changelessly perfect and therefore does not need improving. Nor does he need to grow in perfection in ways appropriate to human beings. For God is not a human being.

The second problem is one which Aquinas shares with writers such as St Anselm. If God is just, then, presumably, he judges people according to their deserts. But how can he do this if he also waives or ignores their offences? Justice implies giving each what is due to him. But mercy implies giving what is not due. How then can God be all-just and all-merciful?[25] As Anselm writes: 'But how do You spare the wicked if You are all-just and supremely just? How does the

---

[23] 1a. 20. 2.

[24] See the entries for 'Justice', 'Love', 'Mercy', and 'Righteousness' in John L. McKenzie, SJ, *Dictionary of the Bible* (London, 1975).

[25] This, as I say, is a problem for Anselm and Aquinas. But some Christian authors earlier than Aquinas were evidently able, at least sometimes, to write as though there is no problem here. In his *Enchiridion*, for instance, St Augustine rather blandly asks: 'Now, who but a fool would think that God was unrighteous, either in inflicting penal justice on those who had earned it, or in extending mercy to the unworthy?' (ch. 98).

all-just and supremely just One do something that is unjust? Or what kind of justice is it to give everlasting life to him who merits eternal death?'[26] In Aquinas's formulation: 'Mercy is a relaxing of justice. However, God cannot leave undone what his justice demands.'[27]

2. *Answers*

To begin with, Aquinas makes it quite clear that he recognizes differences between God's justice and some of its human exemplifications. He notes, for example, that human justice is sometimes a product of transactions involving giving and receiving (following Aristotle, he speaks here of 'commutative justice').[28] I can be just because I give you what I owe you. But Aquinas does not think that God can be in anyone's debt. In his scheme of things, all that creatures have comes from God, who cannot, therefore, be just in accordance with standards of commutative justice. 'There is', he says emphatically, 'no question of this with God; as St Paul asks, *Who has first given to him and recompense shall be made to him?*'[29]

As well as commutative justice, however, there is also, says Aquinas, 'distributive justice'—as when some governor dispenses to each according to his or her worth. And God, he thinks, can be thought of as just if the justice we ascribe to him is distributive.

As this justice is displayed in a well-ordered family or community through its head, so the good order of the universe, manifested both in natural and moral beings, sets forth God's justice . . . Now we can mark a double ordering in things: one, ordering of all creatures to God, and two, their being ordered among themselves, thus of parts to wholes, of accidents to substances, and of each thing to its immediate purpose. Consequently throughout God's works we can consider a double due, namely what is owing to God and what is owing to the creature. Under both respects God gives what is due. It is his due that things should fulfil what his wisdom and will holds for them and that they should display his goodness; in this way his justice observes divine decency and renders to himself what is due to himself. It is the creature's due to have what is ordained for it, thus that human beings should have hands, and that the beasts should serve them; in this way God works

[26] *Proslogion*, 9.
[27] Ia. 21. 3, obj. 2.
[28] For the background in Aristotle, see *Ethics*, 5. 4. 113^{b}25.
[29] Ia. 21. 1; cf. Rom. 11: 35.

according to justice in giving to each what its constitution and condition require.[30]

Aquinas holds that God makes things with certain natures and sustains them in their natures. So he gives them what is proper to them.[31] In doing this, however, he is also honouring another kind of order since everything is directed to God. For, as we have seen, in Aquinas's scheme of things everything seeks the good and the good is God. In this sense, he says, God works to produce what is due to himself. For him, then, God can be said to be just since he orders all things to himself and, by doing so, operates to his own honour and in accordance with his nature. This, he adds, means that God's justice to himself is prior to his justice to creatures. For these conform to a standard which is in God before it is in them. Or, as Aquinas also explains, God is just in that, by virtue of him, things are ordered in accordance with an eternal law.

The notion of eternal law is most famously explored by Aquinas in 1a2ae. 93, itself part of a treatise on law running from 1a2ae. 90–108, to which we will later be returning. For the moment, however, and simply in order to understand what Aquinas is driving at when he speaks of God's justice in 1a. 21 and parallel texts, it will here suffice to draw attention to five points.

First, Aquinas thinks of law as having to do with government and goodness. The function of law is to lead things to what is good for them. Ultimately, then, all proper law is directed to the good of things.

Second, and as we have seen, Aquinas holds that the good of things depends on their fulfilment in accordance with their natures. For him, a good X is an X which has all that it needs to flourish as an X. Hence God is perfectly good since he lacks nothing (though he is not a good such and such) and creatures are good insofar as they flourish considered as what they are.

Third, according to Aquinas the natures of things come from God. He makes creatures, and their natures therefore flow from him and are in him as archetypes or patterns or exemplars. An architect conceives of what he proposes to build and then organizes the

---

[30] 1a. 21. 1.

[31] This notion can also be found in Denys, whom Aquinas quotes approvingly with respect to God's justice. See 1a. 21. 1 and *The Divine Names*, 8, 7.

building. In an analogous way, Aquinas holds, creatures and their natures are in God before they exist in themselves.

Fourth, since everything that is in God is God, Aquinas maintains that the being of creatures in God is not distinct from God and that there is therefore a kind of law in God, which, since God is eternal, must also be called eternal. For the standards by which things are judged good or bad lie in the very being of God.

Fifth, on the basis of all this, Aquinas argues that, in creating, God, so to speak, is obeying a law concerning the good of creatures (and hence giving them what is due to them) and obeying himself (in doing what the eternal law, identical with himself, dictates).

As an exemplar of the things he makes by his art pre-exists in an artist's mind, so an exemplar of the ordered actions to be done by those subject to his sway pre-exists in a governor's mind . . . Through his wisdom God is the founder of the universe of things, and . . . in relation to them he is like an artist with regard to the things he makes . . . [Also] he is the governor of all acts and motions to be found in each and every creature. And so, as being the principle through which the universe is created, divine wisdom means art, or exemplar, or idea, and likewise it also means law, as moving all things to their due ends. Accordingly the Eternal Law is nothing other than the exemplar of divine wisdom as directing the motions and acts of everything . . . Law is nothing but a dictate of practical reason issued by a sovereign who governs a complete community. Granted that the world is ruled by divine Providence . . . it is evident that the whole community of the universe is governed by God's mind. Therefore the ruling idea of things which exists in God as the effective sovereign of them all has the nature of law. Then since God's mind does not conceive in time, but has an eternal concept . . . it follows that this law should be called eternal . . . A human authority [by issuing laws] imparts a kind of inward principle of activity to its subjects; so also God impresses on the whole of nature the principles of the proper activities of things. Accordingly God is said to command the whole of nature . . . That is why every motion and every act in the whole universe is subject to the Eternal Law.[32]

Aquinas can therefore speak of God being just in a twofold sense. In creating, he conforms to the Eternal Law, which is himself. In conforming to it, he respects the good of creatures and he gives them their due. But, Aquinas maintains, in doing all this God also acts with mercy, which is therefore compatible with his justice. For the good of creatures, he says, is not something owed to them. It is a gift given to them independent of their merit.

[32] 1a2ae. 93. 1. 3 and 5.

The reasoning here derives from the principle that creatures have their being from God. If I cook a good meal, nobody could praise it as deserving its excellence at my hands. One might think the meal excellent, but one could not seriously suppose that its excellence was owed to it by anyone. In the same way, says Aquinas, nobody could suppose that the excellence or goodness of God's creatures is owed to them. At any rate, one could not say that it is owed to them by God. For, in relation to his creatures and all that they are, he is like a cook producing a meal (only more so). For Aquinas, the goodness or happiness of creatures, whatever that consists in, comes entirely from God. Simply by creating God is being merciful. For, in doing that, he is giving goodness to things which have no existence apart from his activity, things which therefore have no claim on him. Indeed, says Aquinas, God's mercy actually precedes his justice.

The work of divine justice always presupposes the work of mercy, and is based on it. Nothing is owed the creature except according to something pre-existing there or credited in advance... Since we cannot go back indefinitely we must arrive at something that depends solely on the generous goodness of the divine will... We might say, for instance, that to have hands is the right of human beings because of their rational soul, so also to have a rational soul in order that they be human, yet to be a human being is just because of God's goodness.[33]

So Aquinas maintains that there is no incompatibility between God's justice and mercy, as, in fact, Anselm claimed before him.[34] God's mercy, he says, is not contrary to his justice, for it is something that goes beyond justice.

God's mercy works above his justice, not against it. Take this illustration: a man is owed a hundred, and you give him two hundred from your own pocket; there is no injustice in the deal, and you are being tender-hearted and open-handed. So it is when you forgive an offence against yourself. For a pardon is a sort of present.[35]

---

[33] 1a. 21. 4.

[34] While Aquinas offers quite a complex and subtle explanation of how God is both just and merciful, Anselm seems to opt for a simpler solution. He writes: 'He who is good to both good and wicked is better than he who is good only to the good. And he who is good to the wicked by both punishing and sparing them is better than he who is good to the wicked only by punishing them" (*Proslogion*, 9). Yet Anselm, too, invokes the idea that God is just by acting in a way due to God. 'You are just not because You give us our due but because You do what befits You as the supreme good' (*Proslogion*, 10). Aquinas quotes Anselm with approval in 1a. 21, 1 ad. 3.

[35] 1a. 21. 3 ad. 2.

In other words, God always acts in accord with justice, but in being just he is always giving more than is owed or due. He is just because he creatively provides the goodness of creatures and therefore conforms to the eternal law and to himself. He is merciful because in giving goodness to creatures he is giving them themselves and is therefore giving them their only chance of meriting anything, whether from God or from anything else.[36]

But there is more to Aquinas's view of God's mercy than this. As we shall see when we come to what Aquinas has to say on the topic of the redemption wrought by Christ, he also holds that God is merciful since he shares his life with us. Inscrutable and distant though God may seem when viewed through the eyes of the philosopher, in Aquinas's thinking he offers us a chance to become divine. The mercy involved here is, for him, part of divine providence, so we shall next take a look at some of the things he says about that.

---

[36] For reasons which will now be apparent to the reader, however, Aquinas denies that God has mercy where that is understood in emotional terms, as a feeling of some sort. 'To feel sad about another's misery', he writes, 'is no attribute of God' (1a. 21. 3). For Aquinas, God's mercy lies in what he brings about, not in what something brings about in him. It lies 'in its effect, not in the affect of feeling (*secundum effectum, non secundum passionis affectum*) (ibid.)

9

Providence and Freedom

As I said at the end of the last chapter, Aquinas maintains that God's mercy and love are aspects of his providence. But he has more to say about providence than that. To start with, we shall look at his teaching on providence in general. We shall then turn to what, for him, are three implications of this—ones concerning chance, the action of created causes, and the topic of predestination. Finally, we shall see what he says on three topics which fall within the notion of providence as he understands it and as others have also, i.e. miracles, human freedom, and prayer.

Providence as God's Governing of Creatures

1. The General Thesis

The English word 'providence' derives from the Latin *providentia*. Strictly speaking, therefore, it means 'foresight' or 'protective care' ('provision'). So to ascribe providence to God is to say (and has always been understood as saying) that he tends to his creation or that he somehow looks after it. Though Aquinas thinks of providence in this sense, however, he mostly speaks of it while having in mind the way in which God governs or rules his created order. His teaching on God's providence is really equivalent to what he thinks about the relation of creatures to God. Essentially, therefore, it comprises the beliefs (1) that creatures are made by God *ex nihilo*, (2) that they depend on him entirely for their being or goodness, and (3) that they are moved by God both as efficient cause and as final cause (as alpha and omega). Indeed, it is with specific reference to these beliefs that Aquinas ascribes providence to God in the first place.

We have to declare that God has providence. He creates every goodness in things, as we have already shown. It is not only in the substance of created things that goodness lies, but also in their being ordained to an end, above all to their final end, which, as we have seen, is the divine goodness. This good order existing in created things is itself part of God's creation. Since he is the cause of things through his mind, and, as we have already made clear, the idea of each and every effect must pre-exist in him, the divine mind must preconceive the whole pattern of things moving to their end. This exemplar of things ordained to their purpose is exactly what Providence is.[1]

For Aquinas, then, to acknowledge God's providence is tantamount to accepting that everything that happens does so in accordance with what God intends. Or, as Aquinas would also say, it is tantamount to accepting that everything that happens does so in accordance with God himself, for God and his intention are not distinct. And when I say 'everything that happens' here, I mean exactly that. Aquinas thinks that providence is to be attributed to God since he orders *all* things to an end. He makes them to be and he directs them to their end. All things fall under providence since all things are directed to their end by God who accounts for their existence and knows them as individuals.

Things are said to be ruled or governed by virtue of their being ordered to their end. Now, things are ordered to the ultimate end which God intends, that is, divine goodness, not only by the fact that they perform their operations, but also by the fact that they exist, since, to the extent that they exist, they bear the likeness of divine goodness which is the end for things . . . God, through his understanding and will, is the cause of being for all things. Therefore he preserves all things in being through his intellect and will.[2]

2. *Chance*

One of the things this implies for Aquinas is that nothing is subject to chance—if to be subject to chance means falling outside the range of God's causal activity and therefore outside providence. He maintains that there is just no such thing as an event falling outside divine providence. In his view, to speak of such an event would be to speak of what cannot be.

Here he closely follows the reasoning of Boethius, who deals with the subject of chance in Book 5 of *The Consolation of Philosophy*. To start with, Boethius raises the question of chance in general terms.

---

[1] Ia. 22. 1.
[2] *SG* 3. 65. 2 f.; cf. *SG* 3. 67. 3, quoted above in Ch. 6.

'For I want to know whether you think chance is anything at all, and if so, what?' Hardly has the question been raised, however, than it is quickly made clear that in God's world there is no place for randomness. If a chance event is an uncaused event, says Boethius, there are no chance events. For all events spring from God's causal operation.

If indeed someone were to define chance as an event produced by random motion and not by any chain of causes, then I assert that chance is nothing at all . . . For what place can be left for randomness where God constrains all things into his order?

Yet Boethius does allow a sense in which an event can be called a matter of chance. There may, he says, be events which result from unrelated causes leading to an outcome which, strictly speaking, cannot be said to have a single, presiding cause. Citing Aristotle's *Physics*, he defines chance as occurring whenever

something is done for the sake of some given end, and another thing occurs, for some reason or other, different from what was intended . . . as, for example, if a man digging in the ground in order to till his field were to find he had dug up a quantity of gold.

Chance, says Boethius, is 'the unexpected event of concurring causes among things done for some purpose'. And yet, he insists, the outcome which we speak of as happening by chance is still the result of causes. It does not come from nothing,

for it has its proper causes, and their unforeseen and unexpected coming together appears to have produced a chance event. For if the man tilling his field were not digging the ground, and if the man who put it there had not hidden his money in that particular spot, the gold would not have been found.

That is what Aquinas wants to say. Yes, he agrees, there are chance events, as Boethius thinks.

A chance event does not have one proper cause . . . because what happens accidentally is not strictly speaking a single reality or event, for instance, as when a boulder falls and a landslide starts, or as when a man digs a grave and finds a cache.[3]

For Aquinas, however, even chance events have causes, and their causes (and therefore their effects) are always part of providence.

---

[3] 2a2ae. 95. 5; cf. 2a2ae. 43. 1 ad. 3.

'Thus the meeting of two servants, in their eyes unexpected because neither knew of the other's errand, was foreseen by their master who intentionally sent them where their paths would cross.'[4]

In short, Aquinas would contest the view that there are events which are completely uncaused. Some modern physicists say that certain natural processes may be completely random and completely uncaused. And some philosophers say the same. But Aquinas holds that, even if there are events which have no cause or causes in nature, there can be no coming into being and no change without the causal activity of God. He does not think that every natural process must be the inevitable outcome of causes operating in a deterministic way. For one thing, he believes in the reality of human freedom and would allow that if, for example, I freely kick a stone, then a process in nature occurs which is not inevitable given the way causes in nature work. As we saw in the last chapter, he certainly wants to say that there are contingent events. And for him, these can be events in the natural world. But he also thinks that they will fall under God's causality and that, for this reason, they will not be random events or matters of chance. They will fall within the scope of God's eternal will.

That events always fall within the scope of God's will is true, Aquinas adds, even when they can be viewed as in some sense bad. In the tradition which he inherits, the providence of God is regularly viewed as working for the good of things. And that is how Aquinas conceives of it. But he does not draw the conclusion that everything must therefore flourish or that harm can befall nothing. He is perfectly aware that some things fail, and in his view that fact is also part of providence. For, he argues, there cannot even be failure in created things unless they exist and unless they are what they are by virtue of God.

Take, for example, failure in the sense of physical frustration—as when people fall sick. Aquinas notes that this might be cited as an apparent refutation of the conclusion that everything is subject to divine providence.

Any wise guardian wards off harm and evil from his charges as much as he can. Yet we see many evils in things. Either God cannot prevent them, and so is not almighty, or he does not really care for all.[5]

---

[4] 1a. 22. 2 ad. 1.
[5] 1a. 22. 2 obj. 2.

But he replies that God is not a 'wise guardian', if that means being someone having charge of some particular thing. God is the maker of the world and, therefore, has charge of everything. A parent with charge of a child will naturally try to protect the child as far as possible. But, says Aquinas, instead of having limited responsibility, God has universal providence, which means having care for the goodness of more than one thing. And he exercises his providence by providing for some things at the expense of others.

Corruption and defects in natural things are said to be contrary to some particular nature; yet they are in keeping with the plan of universal nature; inasmuch as the defect in one thing yields to the good of another, or even to the universal good: for the corruption of one is the generation of another, and through this it is that a species is kept in existence. Since God, then, provides universally for all being, it belongs to his providence to permit certain defects in particular effects, that the perfect good of the universe may not be hindered, for if all evil were prevented, much good would be absent. A lion would cease to live if there were no slaying of animals; and there would be no patience of martyrs if there were no tyrannical persecution.[6]

In other words, and as we saw Aquinas saying in Chapter 5, 'evil suffered' is always explicable in natural terms. It is not contrary to providence. It falls within it.

The same, he thinks, goes for 'evil done', with reference to which he also recognizes a possible objection to the notion of providence. One might say, he notes, that 'a person left all on his own is not under the charge of a governing authority' and that 'God leaves people to fend for themselves', particularly when they act badly.[7] On this basis one might conclude that providence does not cover 'evil done'. And yet, Aquinas replies, even though people (unlike inanimate objects) can be responsible for what they do, and even if they are, in this sense, 'left on their own', they do not act independently of God.

Physical things are acted on in the sense that they are directed to an end by another; they do not act like self-determining agents who shape themselves to a purpose, in the manner of rational creatures who deliberate and choose by free judgement . . . Yet because the very act of freewill goes back to God as its cause, we strictly infer that whatever people freely do on their own falls under God's Providence.[8]

[6] 1a. 22. 2 ad. 2.
[7] 1a. 22. 2 obj. 4.
[8] 1a. 22. 2 ad. 4.

3. Secondary Causes

A second conclusion derived by Aquinas from his general view of providence is that God operates through secondary causes which are real causes. According to him, God is the first cause of all being and change. He is, therefore, the *primary* cause of everything that happens in the world. But Aquinas also thinks that God sometimes brings about events by arranging for them to be the effects of causes distinct from himself (though not independent of his causal activity). These causes are what Aquinas calls *secondary* causes. And for him, they are genuine causes.

The point to grasp here is that Aquinas must be distinguished from predecessors of his whom he calls 'some of the sages in the Moorish books of law'.[9] He must also be distinguished from later thinkers such as the French philosopher Malebranche (1638–1715). The 'sages in the Moorish books of law' were Muslim theologians such as Al Ash'ari (d. 936), who taught that at any given time the world consists of atoms which exist fleetingly and which are causally independent of past and future events. In the view of these thinkers, everything that happens is caused, not by created causes, but by God. This, too, was more or less Malebranche's position. He held that created things are in themselves causally inefficacious and that God is the sole true cause of change in the universe (a theory commonly known as Occasionalism).[10]

In Aquinas's view, however, there are created things which are in themselves causal. In his opinion, when the bat hits the ball it is indeed the bat which sends the ball flying, though both bat and ball exist and undergo change by virtue of God. 'Divine Providence', he argues, 'works through intermediaries. For God governs the lower through the higher, not from any impotence on his part, but from the abundance of his goodness imparting to creatures also the dignity of causing.'[11] It is true, he says, that God must be operative in every creaturely cause. So the actions of creatures are, in a sense, always God's action.

The divine power must needs be present to every acting thing . . . God is the cause of everything's action inasmuch as he gives everything the power to act,

---

[9] *De pot.* 3. 7.

[10] Nicholas Malebranche, *Entretiens sur la métaphysique et sur la religion*, trans. Willis Doney (New York, 1980), 7. 10.

[11] 1a. 22. 3.

and preserves it in being and applies it to action, and inasmuch as by his power every other power acts.[12]

Bats therefore hit balls by virtue of God. Or, as Julian of Norwich puts it, 'God does everything which is done.'[13] Yet the actions of creatures are, for Aquinas, still actions (or movements). And as such they are genuinely causal. Bats really send balls flying.

Why should we believe this? One of Aquinas's arguments is a commonsense one. He says that things in the world just do seem to bring about effects. Some writers on causality (e.g. Hume) speak as though causality were occult or invisible.[14] For them, we do not, strictly speaking, observe causality. Others, however, have urged that we perceive quite a lot of it. In the words of Elizabeth Anscombe:

As surely as we learned to call people by name or to report from seeing it that the cat was on the table, we also learned to report from having observed it that someone drank up the milk or that the dog made a funny noise or that things were cut or broken by whatever we saw cut or break them.[15]

With respect to God and causality, Aquinas, we may say, sides with Anscombe rather than Hume. Our senses, he argues, put us directly in contact with created things operating causally.

Since the senses do not perceive unless they are acted upon by the sensible object . . . it would follow that a man does not feel the fire's heat, if the action of the fire does not produce in the sensorial organ a likeness of the heat that is in the fire. In fact if this heat-species be produced in the organ by another agent, although the touch would sense the heat, it would not sense the heat of the fire, nor would it perceive that the fire is hot, and yet the sense judges this to be the case, and the senses do not err about their proper object.[16]

But Aquinas also argues that there are real created causes for other reasons. As he writes in the *Summa theologiae*:

---

[12] *De pot.* 3. 7; cf. ch. 6 above.

[13] *Julian of Norwich: Showings*, ed. Edmund Colledge, OSA, and James Walsh, SJ (London, 1978), 197. Cf. Simon Tugwell, OP, *Ways of Imperfection* (London, 1984), 192 f.: 'Julian, like St Thomas, has a strong doctrine of the complete efficacy and all-pervasiveness of God's creative act. God does everything that is done, even what is done by creatures. And because his will is unchanging, this means that creatures must indefectibly attain to their foreordained goal.'

[14] David Hume, *An Enquiry Concerning Human Understanding*, ed. L. A. Selby-Bigge (3rd edn., Oxford, 1975), 63 ff.

[15] G. E. M. Anscombe, *Collected Philosophical Papers*, ii (Oxford, 1981), 137.

[16] *De pot.* 3. 7; cf. *SG* 3. 69. 17.

There are some who have taken God's working in everything that acts to mean that no created power effects anything in the world, but that God alone does everything without intermediaries. For example, it would not be the fire giving heat, but God in the fire, and similarly in all other instances. But this is impossible, and first because it would deprive creation of its pattern of cause and effect, which in turn would imply lack of power in the creator, since an agent's power is the source of its giving an effect a causative capability. It is impossible, secondly, because if the active powers that are observed in creatures accomplished nothing, there would be no point to their having received such powers. Indeed, if all creatures are utterly devoid of any activity of their own, then they themselves would seem to have a pointless existence . . . God's acting in creatures, therefore, must be understood in such a way that they themselves still exercise their own operations.[17]

To judge by parallel discussions in the *Summa contra Gentiles* and the *De potentia*, Aquinas seems here to be making two main points.[18] The first is that to say that God produces nothing with genuine causal power is to say that his power is limited since the ability of a thing to produce what has active power is an indication of power. The second is that to think of created things as lacking in causal power is to think of God as, so to speak, wasting his time. If I can produce an effect without going through certain motions, then I might just as well dispense with the motions and get down to the business of producing the effect directly. If I can make an omelette without breaking eggs, I can spare myself the trouble of breaking the eggs. By the same token, Aquinas argues, if God alone brings about all changes in the universe, then there is no point in his bothering with what seem to us to be genuine causes of these changes.

If created things could in no way operate to produce their effects, and if God alone worked all operations immediately, these other things would be employed in a useless way by him, for the production of these effects.[19]

Aquinas, of course, is not saying that God cannot make an omelette without breaking eggs. He would agree that God can create a ready-to-eat omelette *ex nihilo*. His point is that if what I appear to do when making an omelette is not actually a case of me making an omelette, then it seems to be rather superfluous.

---

[17] 1a. 105. 5.
[18] See *SG* 3. 69 and *De pot.* 3. 7.
[19] *SG* 3. 69. 13.

4. Predestination

The next thing we need to note is that providence, for Aquinas, entails a doctrine of predestination.[20] The full nature of such a doctrine as he wants to expound it will only become evident as we turn to what he thinks of grace and the work of Christ. At this stage, though, there are still some points which can usefully be touched on.

The most important concerns what he fundamentally means by 'predestination'. And here we might start by noting that what he says reflects what others had said before him. In particular, it reflects what one can find in St Paul and St Augustine. Key texts here are Paul's letter to the Romans, Augustine's *De gratia et libero arbitrio* (*On Grace and Free Will*), and other related works of Augustine.

The issue of predestination arises in *Romans* following a long discussion of faith and its consequences. In speaking of 'faith', Paul is chiefly concerned with the faith of Christians, which, he says, brings them into a state of freedom. In this state, Paul adds, Christians are helped by 'the Spirit', who 'intercedes for the saints according to the will of God'.[21] This remark, in turn, leads Paul to speak about the working of God in those who are the saints according to his will. We read:

We know that in everything God works for good with those who love him, who are called according to his purpose. For those whom he foreknew he also predestined to be conformed to the image of his Son, in order that he might be the first-born among many brethren. And those whom he predestined he also called; and those whom he called he also justified; and those whom he justified he also glorified.[22]

The idea here seems to be that Christians who benefit from the fulfilment of Christ's work, those who are united with Christ, are what they are in accordance with God's eternal plan, purpose, or decree. Their salvation is a matter of God's ordination or predestination and, so Paul seems anxious to stress, they therefore have grounds for assurance. Nothing can tear them away from God.[23]

---

[20] In *De veritate*, 6. 1 we read: 'For two reasons, therefore, predestination is placed under providence as one of its parts, namely, because direction to an end ... pertains to providence, and because providence ... includes a relation to the future.' Aquinas derives 'predestination' from 'destination' which he understands as implying direction to an end. He takes 'pre' before 'destine' to imply reference to the future.

[21] Rom. 8: 27.

[22] Rom. 8: 28 ff.

[23] For a brief but balanced discussion of Paul on predestination, see D. E. H. Whiteley, *The Theology of St Paul* (Oxford, 1974), 89 ff.

The same teaching emerges in Augustine, though it is developed with an eye on intellectual problems which do not appear in Paul, even if they can be raised on the basis of what he writes. According to Augustine, the election or justification of the Christian is a consequence of God's eternal election. Augustine, however, famously dwells on predestination with an eye on those who do not, so to speak, make the grade as children of God. For why did God hate Esau, as Paul asserts in Romans 9: 13? And how are we to understand Paul's subsequent teaching that God 'hardens the heart of whomever he wills?'[24] According to Augustine, here we have to say that what happened was somehow a positive action on God's part based on his justice.

I think it is quite clear that God works in people's hearts to incline their wills to whatsoever way he wills: either to good in accordance with his mercy, or to evil in accordance with their evil merits, and this, indeed, by his own judgments, sometimes manifest, sometimes hidden, but always just.[25]

Between the time of Augustine and Aquinas, the notion of predestination caused controversy in the West, especially in the ninth century. For some developed it in a way which seemed to conflict with belief in human freedom, and some suggested (as Augustine never had) that Christ did not die for all people and that God predestines some to damnation, i.e. that he inexorably decrees damnation for some from eternity (the theory known as 'double predestination'). Hence, for example, the Second Council of Orange (529) was moved to condemn the teaching that God predestines some people to evil. And John Scotus Eriugena, in opposition to Godescalc of Orbais (*c*.804–*c*.869) contested the propriety of saying that God predestines the wicked to damnation.[26] In the teaching of Aquinas, however, predestination means very much what it does for Augustine.

To begin with, he always conceives of it as having to do with salvation or glory. For him, predestination is predestination to eternal life. 'The planned sending of a rational creature to the end which is eternal life', he explains, 'is termed predestination, for to predestine is to send.'[27] On the basis of this understanding, he holds that we can even speak of the predestination of Christ.

[24] Rom. 9: 18.
[25] *De gratia et libero arbitrio*, 11. 43.
[26] Henricus Denzinger and Adolfus Schönmetzer, *Enchiridion symbolorum definitionum et declarationum de rebus fidei et morum* (Freiburg, 1976), 397; John Scotus Eriugena, *De divina praedestinatione*.
[27] 1a. 23. 1.

Predestination in the strict sense ... is a divine pre-ordination, established from eternity, concerning events to be brought about in time through the grace of God. Now the fact that a man should be God and that God should be a man is an event brought about in time by God through the grace of union. Yet it is impossible to maintain that God did not decree from eternity that he was to bring this about in time, for this would be equivalent to asserting that the divine mind is subject to development. Consequently it must be held that the actual union of natures in the person of Christ falls under the eternal predestination of God.[28]

Aquinas thinks that Christ's predestination is a pattern of ours since we are predestined to be children of God, which means sharing in the sonship of Christ.[29] It is also a cause of our predestination since we are saved through Christ. 'For it is not only what is to happen in time that falls under the eternal predestination, but as well the manner and the temporal economy according to which it is to be brought about.'[30]

Secondly, Aquinas also maintains that we must believe in predestination if we believe that some will enjoy eternal life. Why? Because God, who is goodness itself, governs all things and is therefore responsible for the fact that some people achieve beatitude or eternal life. As we have seen, Aquinas holds that God operates in all creaturely operations and that his will is eternal or changeless. In his scheme of things, God changelessly wills (and knows) the whole course of the created order. Given, then, that some will rise to glory with God, he concludes that this can only be because God, from eternity, has willed it, or because it is predestined by him. Hence the connection between providence and predestination.

An implication of this conclusion is that human beings cannot gain eternal life with God by any action open to them *qua* human beings. Beatitude, or life with God, is a gift. And Aquinas is aware of the implication. For him, as we shall later see in more detail, eternal life does not go along with being human (it is not essential to being human). Nor can it be achieved just by what people do. It has to be brought about by God and may, therefore, be spoken of as a matter of predestination.

How right it is that God should predestine human beings. We have seen that everything falls under his Providence, also that the function of providence is

---

[28] 3a. 24. 1.
[29] 3a. 24. 3.
[30] 3a. 24. 4.

to arrange things to an end. Now the destiny to which creatures are ordained by God is twofold. One exceeds the proportion and ability of created nature, and this is eternal life which... surpasses the nature of any creature. The other is proportionate to it, and can be reached by its own natural powers. Now when a thing cannot reach an end by its own natural power, then it has to be lifted up and sent there by another, as when an archer flights an arrow to the target. So a creature of intelligence, capable of eternal life, is brought there, properly speaking, as sent by God. The idea of this sending pre-exists in God, as does the idea of ordering the whole of things to their end, which we have called Providence.[31]

Since predestination concerns those able to share in eternal life with God, Aquinas also presumes that it only concerns creatures with intellect and will, i.e. those capable of knowing and loving God.[32] It does not concern non-rational beings.[33] We might like to meet our goldfish in heaven. But beatified goldfish seem not to be included in Aquinas's reckoning. To those who find this a depressing thought, he would reply that the best thing for people is union with God, not fellowship with our pets, and that this can only be achieved as one knows and loves God. In the light of his theory of knowledge, this, for Aquinas, will involve the actualization of a state in which people are filled with and constituted by the divine nature so that God really is all in all. As Herbert McCabe observes, commenting on the *prima pars*:

It is an important theme of Question 12 that when, in beatitude, a man understands the essence of God, the mind is not realized by a form which is a likeness of God, but by God himself. God will not simply be an object of our minds, but the actual life by which our minds are what they will have become.[34]

Miracles

If we think of God's providence as a matter of him governing the course of his creation, however, and if we believe, as Aquinas does, that God brings about events by causes which operate in the world,

---

[31] Ibid.
[32] For Aquinas, this means people, of course; but also angels. Cf. 1a. 23. 1 ad. 3.
[33] See 1a. 23. 1 ad. 2.
[34] Appendix 2 to vol. iii of the Blackfriars edition of the *Summa theologiae*.

we might well wonder whether (1) he can bring about events which do not fit in with what we expect in the light of the way things normally behave and (2) whether he can bring about events without using created causes. In short, we might wonder what Aquinas thinks of miracles.[35] Writers who have discussed them have tended to ask two distinct questions. (1) Are they possible? (2) Have they occurred? Aquinas's view is that the answer to both questions is 'Yes'.

With respect to the possibility of miracles, he simply takes his stand on what we have already seen him saying on the topic of God's omnipotence. Since God can bring about whatever does not involve a contradiction, he can bring things about which would not be expected in terms of what normally happens, and he can do so directly and without the use of secondary causes. 'The divine will', says Aquinas, 'is not limited to this particular order of causes and effects [sc. those which obtain in the world] in such a manner that it is unable to will to produce immediately an effect in things here below without using any other cause.'[36] So he would think it absurd to say that, for example, our knowledge of the world is proof that miracles do not or cannot happen. His argument would be that our knowledge of the world is irrelevant as far as the possibility of miracles goes. What matters, he would say, is our knowledge of God.

On the question of the actual occurrence of miracles, he presumes that evidence exists to show that they have occurred. This would not be everyone's view in the twentieth century, but it is not surprising that Aquinas subscribes to it since miracles are reported in Scripture (which he and his Christian contemporaries took to be authoritative and historically reliable) and since belief in their occurrence was commonplace in the Middle Ages. You would have been considered positively odd in the thirteenth century if you did not believe in the occurrence of many miracles.[37] And with reference to belief in mir-

---

[35] 'Miracle', indeed, has been subject to different definitions. At this point I take it to mean something like 'event of an extraordinary kind brought about by God directly and without the operation of any secondary cause'. But, as we shall see, this definition is narrower than that of Aquinas.

[36] *SG* 3. 99. 6.

[37] In saying that miracles are reported in Scripture, I do not mean that the Bible has a theory of miracles which can be identified with that of Aquinas or any other post-biblical writer. I simply mean that events of the kind cited by Aquinas as miraculous are reported in the Bible. For biblical teaching on miracles see C. F. D. Moule (ed.), *Miracles* (London, 1965) and R. M. Grant, *Miracle and Natural Law in Graeco-Roman and Early Christian Thought* (Amsterdam, 1952). For a fine discussion of the historical

acles, Aquinas was not odd. He even thought it possible to distinguish between three kinds of miracle. There are, he says: (1) 'events in which something is done by God which nature could never do', (2) 'events in which God does something which nature can do, but not in this order', and (3) that which 'occurs when God does what is usually done by the working of nature, but without the operation of the principles of nature'.[38]

As an example of (1) Aquinas cites the case of the sun going back on its course or standing still (cf. Isaiah 38: 7 f.; Joshua 10: 12 ff.). Though he does not use such language, he seems to have in mind here what later writers call a violation of a universal law of nature.[39] As an example of (2) he instances the case of someone living after death, seeing after being blind, or walking after being paralysed.

It is a work of nature for an animal to live, to see, and to walk; but for it to live after death, to see after becoming blind, to walk after paralysis of the limbs, this nature cannot do—but God at times does such works miraculously.[40]

The idea here seems to be that some miracles are states or events which could exist in nature, but which would not exist unless produced miraculously. Finally, and by way of illustrating what he means by (3), Aquinas gives the example of someone being instantaneously cured of a disease, albeit that doctors might have been able to effect a cure given sufficient time. Here he seems to be saying that some miracles are quite ordinary or common states or processes, but ones brought about without the causes which usually bring them about.

Yet the differences in miracles which Aquinas notes are not, for him, of great significance since he believes that all miracles have one thing in common. And for him it is this which constitutes the miraculous as such. He thinks that miracles come about by virtue of the creative activity of God and nothing else.[41] The whole point

background to Aquinas with respect to the miraculous, see Benedicta Ward, *Miracles and the Medieval Mind* (London, 1982).

[38] *SG* 3. 101. 2 ff.
[39] Cf. Richard Swinburne (ed.), *Miracles* (New York, 1989), 3 f. and 75 ff.
[40] *SG* 3. 101. 3.
[41] Aquinas notes that 'the word miracle is derived from *mirari* (to be astonished)' (*De pot.* 6. 2), so he also holds that miracles have it in common that they cause wonder or astonishment. But he does not think that any event causing astonishment is *ipso facto*

about them is that nothing subject to God's providence, i.e. no cause other than God (no secondary cause), is at work in their occurrence. Only God is at work. And from this understanding of miracles, Aquinas derives two main theses.

The first is that miracles cannot be ascribed to anything other than God. A miracle , says Aquinas, is 'an event that happens outside the ordinary processes of the whole of created nature'.[42] As such, he asserts, miracles cannot by definition be produced by a created cause since, in doing whatever it does, such a cause would simply be working in accordance with what is part of created nature.

Whatever is completely confined under a certain order cannot work above that order. But every creature is established under the order which God has put in things. So, no creature can operate above this order; but that is what it means to work miracles.[43]

Some theologians have held that miracles can be brought about by, for example, angels. Such was the view of Pope Benedict XIV, who thought that something is a miracle if its production exceeds 'the power of visible and corporeal nature only'.[44] Aquinas, however, would disagree. As he writes:

If some event should occur outside the ordinary course of things with respect to any particular thing in nature, this would not be enough to make it a miracle—otherwise, someone throwing a stone up in the air would be working a miracle, since this is outside the ordinary course of the stone's nature. It is for this reason that a miracle is defined as an event that happens outside the ordinary processes of the *whole* of created nature. God, however, is the only one who can do this, since whatever an angel or any other created thing does by its own power takes place in accordance with the ordinary processes of nature and so is not miraculous. Thus God alone can work miracles.[45]

Or as he succinctly puts it elsewhere:

Since their abilities and activities are limited, all creatures are bound by the laws of nature, and a work exceeding the world in which they live cannot be

---

miraculous since astonishment, for him, is relative to knowledge and what one person finds astonishing may seem commonplace to another. Cf. *SG* 3. 101 as well as *De pot.* 6. 2.

[42] 1a. 110. 4.

[43] *SG* 3. 102. 2.

[44] *De servorum Dei beatificatione et beatorum canonizatione*, iv: *De miraculis* (1738). Cf. also Avicenna, *De anima*, IV. 4 and the reference to this in *SG* 3. 103. 2 and *De pot.* 6. 3.

[45] 1a. 110. 4.

produced by any power there. And if it comes about, then it is done immediately by God, such as raising the dead to life, giving sight to the blind, and the like.[46]

He notes the theory that angels and others (e.g. holy people) work miracles. His verdict, however, is that they can only be said to do so in the sense that God works miracles at their request.[47]

The second thesis which Aquinas draws out of his view of miracles is that the occurrence of a miracle is not to be thought of as a matter of God doing violence to the created order. To say that God can bring about what goes beyond the power of things in the universe (i.e. everything other than God) may seem to suggest that, were he to do this, creation would be intruded on or somehow interfered with or abrogated. But Aquinas does not think that this is so. For him, things in the universe (including events) are always the effect of God's will. So, if God miraculously brings about something in the created order, that is no more a violation of the created order than is the fact that this order exists in the first place. 'Whatever is done by God in created things is not contrary to nature, even though it may seem to be opposed to the proper order of a particular nature.'[48] God may raise the dead, which is not an action lying in the power of anything in the universe. But he would be doing the same sort of thing as he did in producing the universe from nothing. If there being something raised from the dead is contrary to nature, Aquinas would say, then so is there being a universe. And there being a universe, he would add, is not contrary to nature (it is a condition of there being nature), from which it would seem to follow that there being someone raised from the dead is not contrary to nature.

In effect, Aquinas does not think of miracles as occasions when God steps in where he does not exist already. It is often said that to believe in miracles is to believe in a God who can *intervene*.[49] The idea seems to be that a God capable of performing miracles must be one who observes a given scenario and then steps in to tinker with it (as I might step in to help someone whom I find to be in a difficult situation). But God, for Aquinas, can never intervene in his creation

---

[46] 1a2ae. 5. 6.
[47] 1a. 110. 4 ad. 1.
[48] *SG* 3. 100. 2.
[49] In criticizing certain modern writers in his book *The Divine Trinity* (London, 1985), David Brown makes much of the importance of God intervening.

in this sense. In his thinking, God, as Creator and sustainer, is always totally present to everything. And for this reason, he maintains, God is as present in what is not miraculous as he is in the miraculous. Miracles, for him, do not occur because of an extra added ingredient (i.e. God). They occur because something is *not* present (i.e. a secondary cause or a collection of secondary causes). That, he thinks, is why they can only be brought about by God.

Human Freedom

If God is the cause of all that happens, however, what are we to say of what we get up to? How do people and their actions fit into Aquinas's notion of divine providence? It is clear that, in his view, they must fit in somehow. But is it not also clear that they cannot really do this in view of his thinking as we have now seen it unfold? For would we not naturally say that people are capable of acting freely? And does it not seem obvious that they cannot do this in terms of Aquinas's teaching on providence? How can God eternally decree the course of the created order if it contains free individuals?

Aquinas frequently alludes to arguments suggesting that people cannot be free under God's providence. In *De malo*, 6, for instance, we find the three following arguments cited:

If change is initiated in the human will in a fixed way by God, it follows that human beings do not have free choice of their actions. Moreover, an action is forced when its originating principle is outside the subject, and the victim of force does not contribute anything to it. So if the originating principle of a choice which is made voluntarily is outside the subject—in God—then it seems that the will is changed by force and of necessity. So we do not have free choice of our actions. Moreover, it is impossible that a human will should not be in accordance with God's will: as Augustine says in the *Enchiridion*, either a human being does what God wills or God fulfils his will in that person. But God's will is changeless; so the human will is too. So all human choices spring from a fixed choice.[50]

A similar kind of argument constitutes the third objection to 1a. 83. 1:

What is *free is cause of itself*, as the Philosopher says (*Metaph*. i. 2). Therefore what is moved by another is not free. But God moves the will, for it is written

---

[50] I quote from *The Philosophy of Thomas Aquinas*, ed. Christopher Martin (London, 1988) 157. Altogether, in *De malo*, 6 Aquinas lists 24 objections to the thesis that human beings have a free choice of their actions.

(Prov. xxi. 1): *The heart of the king is in the hand of the Lord; whithersoever He will He shall turn it*; and (Phil. ii. 13): *It is God Who worketh in you both to will and to accomplish.* Therefore people do not have free-will.

Yet Aquinas insists that the reality of providence (which means the reality of God working in all things as first cause and sustainer) is not incompatible with human freedom.

To begin with, he says, people certainly have freedom. For one thing, the Bible holds that they do (in 1a. 83. 1 Aquinas cites Ecclesiasticus 15: 14 to this effect). For another, people, as rational agents, have it in them to choose between alternative courses of action (unlike inanimate objects or animals acting by instinct) and they also have it in them to act or refrain from acting. In fact, says Aquinas, human freedom is a prerequisite of moral thinking.

If there is nothing free in us, but the change which we desire comes about of necessity, then we lose deliberation, exhortation, command and punishment, and praise and blame, which are what moral philosophy is based on.[51]

Secondly, so Aquinas continues, human actions falling under providence can be free precisely because of what providence involves. In his view we are not free *in spite of* God, but *because of* God.

God does indeed change the will, however, in an unchanging manner, because of the manner of acting of God's change-initiating power, which cannot fail. But because of the nature of the will which is changed—which is such that it is related indifferently to different things—this does not lead to necessity, but leaves freedom untouched. In the same way divine providence works unfailingly in everything, but nevertheless effects come from contingent causes in a contingent manner, since God changes everything in a relative way, relative to the manner of existence of each thing . . . The will does contribute something when change is initiated in it by God: it is the will itself that acts, though the change is initiated by God. So though its change does come from outside as far as the first originating principle is concerned, it is nevertheless not a forced change.[52]

In other words, human freedom is compatible with providence because only by virtue of providence is there such a thing as human freedom. God, for Aquinas, really does act in everything. And since 'everything' includes human free actions, he concludes that God works in them as much as in anything else. But since they are free, he

---

[51] *De pot.* 6; 1a. 83. 1.
[52] *De malo*, 6.

adds, they cannot be thought of as unfree. He thinks that some created things do operate without freedom, for they do what they do because they are acted on by other created things which determine them to the course they follow. And God, he says, certainly acts in them. But not all things are determined in their course by the action on them of other created things, and people acting freely are a case in point. Aquinas therefore concludes that people acting freely fall under providence as free agents. But they are not free in the sense of being independent of God's causal operation, for without this they would not exist and would not be acting. They are free because God is making them free, because he has arranged that they function independently of the determining agency of other created things.

People are in charge of their acts, including those of willing and of not willing, because of the deliberative activity of reason, which can be turned to one side or the other. But that someone should deliberate or not deliberate, supposing that one were in charge of this too, would have to come about by a preceding deliberation. And since this may not proceed to infinity, one would finally have to reach the point at which a person's free decision is moved by some external principle superior to the human mind, namely by God, as Aristotle himself demonstrated. Thus the minds even of healthy people are not so much in charge of their acts as not to need to be moved by God.[53]

The same idea is expressed in Aquinas's commentary on Aristotle's *Peri hermeneias*:

If divine providence is, in its own right, the cause of everything that happens, or at least of everything good, it seems that everything happens of necessity . . . God's will cannot be thwarted: so it seems that whatever he wants to happen happens of necessity . . . [But] we have to notice a difference as regards the divine will. The divine will should be thought of as being outside the ordering of existent things. It is the cause which grounds every existent, and all the differences there are between them. One of the differences between existents is between those that are possible and those that are necessary. Hence necessity and contingency in things have their origin in the divine will, as does the distinction between them, which follows from a description of their proximate causes. God lays down necessary causes for the effects that he wants to be necessary, and he lays down causes that act contingently—i.e. that can fail of their effect—for the effects that he wants to be contingent. It is according to this characteristic of their causes that effects are said to be necessary or contingent, even though they all

---

[53] 1a2ae. 109. 3 ad. 1.

depend on the divine will, which transcends the ordering of necessity and contingency, as their first cause . . . The will of God cannot fail: but in spite of that, not all its effects are necessary; some are contingent.[54]

By 'necessary' here Aquinas means 'determined' or 'brought about by causes necessitating their effects'. By 'contingent' he means 'undetermined' or 'able to be or not to be'. His suggestion, therefore, is that God wills both what is determined and what is undetermined. Since he believes that each must derive from God's will, he locates them within the context of providence. But since he also believes that the determined and undetermined are genuinely different, he concludes that providence can effect what is undetermined as well as what is determined. And, on this basis, he holds that it can effect human free actions.

One may, of course, say that if my actions are ultimately caused by God then I do not act freely at all. Aquinas, however, would reply that my actions are free if nothing in the world is acting on me so as to make me perform them, not if God is not acting in me. According to him, what is incompatible with will is 'necessity of coercion' or the effect of violence, as when something acts on one and 'applies force to the point where one cannot act otherwise'.[55] But, he explains, it is not against will that one should be drawn to what one's nature needs for its fulfilment. This kind of necessity is, he thinks, essential to will, just as the being drawn of necessity to truth is needed for the intellect to be itself.

To quote McCabe again, Aquinas's position is that 'to be free means not to be under the influence of some other *creature*, it is to be independent of other *bits of the universe*; it is not and could not mean to be independent of God'.[56] For him, God does not interfere with created free agents to push them into action in a way that infringes their freedom. He does not act *on* them (as Aquinas thinks created things do when they cause others to act as determined by them). He makes them to be what they are, namely freely acting agents. In Aquinas's words:

Free-will is the cause of its own movement, because by their free-will people move themselves to act. But it does not of necessity belong to liberty that

---

[54] *In peri herm.* book 1, lectio 14.
[55] 1a. 82. 1.
[56] *God Matters* (London, 1987), 14.

what is free should be the first cause of itself, as neither for one thing to be the cause of another need it be the first cause. God, therefore, is the first cause, who moves causes both natural and voluntary. And just as by moving natural causes he does not prevent their acts being natural, so by moving voluntary causes he does not deprive their actions of being voluntary: but rather is he the cause of this very thing in them; for he operates in each thing according to its own nature.[57]

Prayer

For Aquinas, we may say, providence consists in God's voluntary governing of his creation. For him, God runs the world as he wills, and to hold that this is so is precisely what it means to believe in providence. But Aquinas also maintains that the way things go can accord with the will of people as well as with that of God. On this basis, and as we have seen, he can speak of human beings having freedom—the genuine power of acting voluntarily. But, on this basis too (and together with his views on human freedom), he can also find a place for prayer. For him, this is another aspect of God's providence—a very important aspect, and one which has to do with the day-to-day lives of Christians. People may believe in providence, but how are they to put their belief into practice apart from proclaiming that they have it? According to Aquinas, one answer is 'By prayer'. For by praying, he says, we presuppose the working of providence.

1. The Meaning of 'Prayer' for Aquinas

In modern Christian literature, the word 'prayer' seems to signify many different things. This, perhaps, is the reason why Christians today often find the whole notion of prayer a difficult one. They are encouraged by their pastors to pray. They are encouraged to pray by the New Testament. But they are frequently at a loss to know what it is that they are supposed to be doing when praying. And they are not much helped in their difficulties by the constantly growing number of books with titles like 'How to Pray'—titles which suggest that prayer is something difficult or mysterious, titles which also suggest that prayer is a kind of skill or art which needs to be learned and which, maybe, requires the mastering of a set of techniques.

---

[57] 1a. 83. 1 ad. 3.

The Latin word properly translated as 'prayer' is *oratio*. In classical Latin, *oratio* meant 'speech', but early Latin-speaking Christians used it in the sense of the classical term *precatio*, which meant 'petition'. And this usage survived well into the middle of the twelfth century, which is hardly surprising in view of the New Testament background. According to the Gospels, when Jesus taught his disciples how to pray, he gave them the 'Our Father', which is simply a string of requests or petitions.[58] And, when urging his disciples to pray, he told them to ask for things.[59]

By the time of Aquinas, however, the picture had become rather blurred, as it seems to be today. In 1 Thessalonians 5: 17 one is told to 'pray without ceasing'. And in 1 Timothy 2: 1 we read: 'I urge that supplications, prayers, intercessions, and thanksgiving be made for all men.' Texts such as these were taken by some medieval writers, and by some of their predecessors, to imply that prayer must be more than a matter of petition. Some held that petition should be thought of as a low-grade or elementary stage in prayer—as, for example, seems to have been the view of John Cassian (*c.*360–435), St Bernard of Clairvaux (1090–1153), and William of St Thierry (*c.*1085–1148).[60] According to St Bonaventure, prayer can be thought of in extremely general terms. 'Properly speaking', he says, 'prayer is an ascent to God in order to enjoy something or to obtain something or to pay some debt, but in a broader sense "prayer" is used to include any contemplative act related to God.'[61]

Traces of this confusion can be found in what Aquinas says about prayer in his *Commentary on the Sentences*, where there is a complicated and indecisive discussion of parts of prayer and kinds of prayer.[62] By the time he is writing the *Summa theologiae*, however, he has a definite and clear view to offer. In that work, prayer is simply petition, without qualification or decoration, and without any suggestion that petition is an inferior kind of prayer. It is asking for things from God. And, considered as such, it is, says Aquinas, some-

---

[58] Matt. 6: 7 ff.; Luke 11: 2 ff.

[59] Luke 11: 5 ff. and 18: 1 ff.

[60] For the history of the term *oratio*, and for its sense in the thought of Aquinas, see Simon Tugwell, OP, *Albert and Thomas: Selected Writings* (New York, 1988), 271 ff. and 'Prayer, Humpty Dumpty and Thomas Aquinas', in Brian Davies, OP (ed.), *Language, Meaning and God* (London, 1987).

[61] *Sent.* 4. 15. 4.

[62] *Sent.* 4. 15. 4. 3.

thing which falls within God's providence. Why? Because, in his
view, it is the way in which God wills to get certain things done.
Divine providence, he declares

does not merely arrange what effects are to occur; it also arranges the causes
of these effects and the relationships between them. And among other
causes, some things are caused by human acts. So human beings have to do
certain things, not so as to change God's plan by their acts, but in order to
bring about certain effects by their acts, according to the pattern planned by
God. The same thing applies also to natural causes. Similarly in the case of
prayer we do not pray in order to change God's plan, but in order to obtain
by our prayers those things which God planned to bring about by means of
prayers, in order, as Gregory says, that our prayers should entitle us to
receive what almighty God planned from all eternity to give us.[63]

2. *Aquinas on Prayer: Details*

The last quotation gives one the core of Aquinas's teaching on
prayer. But its sense needs to be explained, and, perhaps, the first
and most important thing to stress is that Aquinas thinks of prayer as
a thoroughly commonplace practice. Many accounts of prayer suggest
that it is essentially a matter of stopping what we normally do. In
terms of such accounts, prayer is a break from day-to-day life, a
stepping aside from one's ordinary activity, something special and
without parallel. For Aquinas, however, exactly the opposite is true.
On his account, it has nothing to do with techniques and skills. It is
not the preserve of a spiritual élite, whose members may be thought
of as 'experts' in prayer. It is an instance of something with which we
are perfectly acquainted quite apart from any religious concerns we
may have. And the something in question here is the practice of
trying to get what we need from people who are able to help us. If I
need money to buy a house, I will ask a bank for a loan, or something
like that. Well, says Aquinas, my praying is an instance of the same
kind of thing. It is, as he puts it, 'an act of our reason'.[64] More
precisely, it is an act of practical reason, i.e. a matter of recognizing
what we need and trying to acquire it in an intelligent way.

---

[63] 2a2ae. 83. 2. The reference to Gregory is to *Dialogues*, 1, 8. All quotations of
Aquinas dealing with prayer come from the translations of Simon Tugwell, OP in
Albert and Thomas, 363 ff.

[64] 2a2ae. 83. 1.

Prayer is an act of the reason, bringing the will's desire into relationship with him who is our superior, not subject to our control, namely God. So, Damascene's definition, 'Prayer is a petition made to God for things that are fitting,' displays the essential nature of prayer with the utmost accuracy.[65]

On this basis, therefore, Aquinas insists that we should pray for specific things, including what we need in order to live (i.e. temporal goods). It is, he says, 'lawful to ask in prayer for whatever it is lawful to desire'.[66] 'And it is lawful to desire temporal things . . . inasmuch as they serve to sustain our bodily life and play an instrumental role in our virtuous deeds.'[67]

Does it, however, make sense to conceive of prayer as a matter of asking for things from God? Critics of petitionary prayer have denied that it does for a number of reasons. They have said, for example, that the practice of petitionary prayer is inconsistent with belief in a God who is both omniscient and good. For, if God is omniscient, he knows what we want or need without us having to tell him. And, if he is good, he will give us what we want or need without being asked. As Origen voiced the argument centuries ago:

God knows all things before they come into being and there is nothing that becomes known to him from the fact of its beginning for the first time when it begins, as though it were not previously known. What need then is there to send up prayer to him who knows what we need even before we pray? For the heavenly Father knows what things we have need of before we ask him (*Matthew* 6: 8). And it is fitting that he, being Father and Maker of all, who loves all the things that are, and abhors nothing which he has made (*Wisdom* 11: 24), should order in safety all that has to do with each one, even without prayer, like a father provides for his little children, and does not wait for them to ask, either because they are quite unable to ask, or because through ignorance they often want to receive the opposite of what is of use and help to them. And we fall short of God more than those who are quite children fall short of the mind of those who begot them.[68]

It has also been held that the practice of petitionary prayer is improper since, if God is immutable, he cannot be changed by anything which we might say or do. Some authors have even complained that

---

[65] *Sent.* 4. 15. 4. 1. The reference to Damascene is to *De fide orthodoxa*, 68. 1.
[66] *Sent.* 4. 15. 4. 4. Cf. 2a2ae. 83. 6, where Aquinas says the same thing while (erroneously) ascribing his words to Augustine.
[67] 2a2ae. 83. 6.
[68] Origen, *Treatise on Prayer*, trans. E. J. Day (London, 1954), 94.

those who engage in petitionary prayer are subscribing to a form of
magic, not belief in God. Thus, for example, according to Hubert
Richards, petitionary prayer (which he often calls 'intercessory
prayer'), 'taken literally'

presupposes a God who is able to provide magically what we are unable to
provide for ourselves ... All intercessory prayer is, at one level, an attempt to
put pressure on God. It assumes that, given a formula which is liturgically or
psychologically appropriate, God can be bribed or blackmailed, manœuvred
or manipulated, coaxed, cajoled or controlled. And it is a God of this kind
that many people find they can no longer accept.[69]

Objections such as these do not, of course, apply to those who
think of prayer as not involving petition in the sense in which Aquinas
does—a sense which puts it on a level with everyday cases of asking
for things from those able to supply what is requested. But one can
easily see how the objections might be thought applicable to his view
of prayer. And he acknowledges the fact by raising the objections
himself, not in his earliest discussion of prayer, but in the *Summa
contra Gentiles* and the *Summa theologiae*.[70] Thus we read:

On the face of it, it is not appropriate to pray: (1) Prayer seems to be needed
to give information about what we want from the person we are asking for
something. But, as it says, 'Your Father knows that you need all these
things'. So it is not appropriate to pray to God. (2) Prayer is a way in which
we change the mind of the person to whom we are praying, so that he will
do what is being asked of him. But God's mind cannot be changed or deflected ... (3) It is more generous to give something without waiting to be
asked than it is to give something to someone who asks for it ... But God is
extremely generous. So it is apparently not appropriate that we should pray
to God.[71]

Yet, as we might expect, Aquinas does not find the objections
unanswerable. In praying, he replies, we are not trying to inform
God of anything. We are acknowledging our needs and the fact that
he can help us.

We do not have to present our prayers to God in order to disclose to him our
needs and desires, but in order to make ourselves realize that we need to
have recourse to his help in these matters ... By praying we offer God

---

[69] Hubert Richards, *What Happens When You Pray?* (London, 1980), 72 f.
[70] *SG* 3. 95 f. and 2a2ae. 83. 2.
[71] 2a2ae. 83. 2, objections.

reverence, inasmuch as we subject ourselves to him and profess, by praying, that we need him as the author of all that is good for us.[72]

Nor is it the case that prayer should be thought of as an attempt to effect a change in God. We aim to get by our prayers what he has planned. 'Our prayer is not designed to change God's plan; the purpose of prayer is to obtain by our entreaties what God has already planned.'[73]

Aquinas agrees that God gives much without being asked. But he also thinks that God wants to give us some things in response to our asking, so that we may be confident in going to him and so that we might recognize him as the source of all good.

God gives us many things out of sheer generosity. The reason why he wants to give us some things in response to our petition is that it is profitable for us to acquire a certain confidence in running to him and to recognize that he is the source of all that is good for us.[74]

Prayer, says Aquinas, is a means by which people are able to relate to God as to a friend. Friends, we find, aim to satisfy each other's needs. And they are able to do this because they can express their needs to each other. In the same way, so Aquinas suggests, people can express their needs to God, who can therefore bring it about, not just that certain goods come to pass, but that certain goods come to pass as desired by people.

It is part of friendship that people who love should wish the desire of those they love to be fulfilled, inasmuch as they want the good and the perfection of the ones they love. This is why it is said to be proper to friends that they want the same thing . . . God loves his creatures, and he loves each one the more, the more it shares in his own goodness, which is the first and primary object of his love. Therefore he wants the desires of his rational creatures to be fulfilled, because they share most perfectly of all creatures in the goodness of God. And his will is an accomplisher of things, because he is the cause of things by his will . . . So it belongs to the divine goodness to fulfil the desires of rational creatures which are put to him in prayer.[75]

One might reply that if the will of God is unchangeable, our prayers can make no difference to anything. But that, says Aquinas, would be a foolish objection.

[72] 2a2ae. 83. 2 ad. 1 and 2a2ae. 83. 4 ad. 1.
[73] 2a2ae. 83. 2 ad. 2.
[74] 2a2ae. 83. 2 ad. 3.
[75] *SG* 3. 95.

To claim that we should not pray in order to obtain anything from God, on the ground that the ordering of providence is immutable, is like saying that we should not walk in order to arrive at some place and that we should not eat in order to be fed, all of which is patently absurd.[76]

According to Aquinas, prayer can be thought of as causal in just the same sense as any other process in the world can be thought of as causal. The fact that God changelessly exists and works in everything does not mean that rain does not make things wet or that food does not nourish. By the same token, Aquinas reasons, the fact that God changelessly exists and works in everything does not mean that my prayer cannot be a cause of something coming about by virtue of God's will. If I do not pray for anything then nothing that occurs can be thought of as an answer to my prayer. But, Aquinas contends, if I pray for something, and if what I pray for occurs, its occurrence can be called an answer to my prayer. In other words, he thinks that, though nothing can cause God to will what he has not willed from eternity, God may will from eternity that things should come about as things prayed for by us. And he thinks that this is so because he also thinks that all that comes to pass does so in terms of providence.

According to Aquinas, then, providence governs all, but everything does not happen in accordance with natural necessity, and we need to allow for human freedom. Yet even human freedom falls within the scope of providence since God works in everything. He does not do so as an item in the world, as something acting to bring about change in a context which it inhabits itself. He does so as calling into being all the changing things we know or can comprehend.

That, of course, is what we have seen Aquinas saying from the beginning of Chapter 2. Now, however, it is time to see how he develops this teaching. As I have so far tried to expound it, his thinking consists of arguments and conclusions which, in his view, ought to be acceptable to anyone, whether Christian or not. Though it contains much teaching about God, it does not, for him, stand or fall as a body of doctrine because of what God has told us in the Christian revelation. In this sense, it is philosophy rather than theology. Yet Aquinas was a theologian as well as a philosopher. So what does he have to say about God when wearing what we might call his explicitly theological hat? And what does he have to say about matters other than God?

[76] *SG* 3. 96.

10

The Eternal Triangle

CHRISTIANITY takes its name from Christ. So one might naturally suppose that the heart of Christian doctrine should lie in Christology—as it seems to do in the New Testament. But Christology has a doctrinal background even in the New Testament, and, when it came to be formulated in creeds and symbols of faith, it was finally located in the context of the doctrine of the Trinity—the belief that God, though one, is also somehow three. For this reason one can say that the key Christian doctrine is that of the Trinity. At any rate, this is how Aquinas sees things. He thinks that Christian teaching is certainly about Christ. But he does not think that it is *just* about Christ or *primarily* about Christ. For him, the heart of Christian teaching is the doctrine of the Trinity, which is the first specifically Christian topic he turns to in the *Summa theologiae*. 'After discussing the unity of God's nature', he explains, 'it remains for us to discuss the trinity of persons in God.'[1] Historically speaking, Aquinas is one of the most important writers on the doctrine of the Trinity.

Aquinas and the Doctrine of the Trinity

For a classical statement of the doctrine of the Trinity we could refer to the creed promulgated by the First General Council of Constantinople (381), which reaffirms the teaching of the Council of Nicaea (325), and which adds that the Holy Spirit is 'the Lord and Giver of life who proceeds from the Father, who together with the Father and the Son is worshipped and glorified'.[2] For a more systematic statement, however, we can cite the so-called Creed of Athanasius, a document produced some time after the middle of the fifth century

---

[1] Introduction to 1a. 27.
[2] J. Neuner and J. Dupuis (eds.), *The Christian Faith in the Doctrinal Documents of the Catholic Church* (London, 1983), 9.

and commonly taken as a touchstone of Trinitarian orthodoxy. The relevant part of the text runs thus:

We worship one God in the Trinity and the Trinity in unity, without either confusing the persons or dividing the substance; for the person of the Father is one, the Son's is another, the Holy Spirit's another; but the Godhead of Father, Son and Holy Spirit is one, their glory equal, their majesty equally eternal. Such as the Father is, such is the Son, such also the Holy Spirit; uncreated is the Father, uncreated the Son, uncreated the Holy Spirit; infinite is the Father, infinite the Son, infinite the Holy Spirit; eternal is the Father, eternal the Son, eternal the Holy Spirit; yet, they are not three eternal beings but one eternal, just as they are not three uncreated beings or three infinite beings but one uncreated and one infinite. In the same way, almighty is the Father, almighty the Son, almighty the Holy Spirit; yet, they are not three almighty beings but one almighty. Thus, the Father is God, the Son is God, the Holy Spirit is God; yet, they are not three gods but one God. Thus, the Father is Lord, the Son is Lord, the Holy Spirit is Lord; yet they are not three lords but one Lord. For, as the Christian truth compels us to acknowledge each person distinctly as God and Lord, so too the Catholic religion forbids us to speak of three gods or lords. The Father has neither been made by anyone, nor is He created or begotten; the Son is from the Father alone, not made nor created but begotten; the Holy Spirit is from the Father and the Son, not made nor created nor begotten, but proceeding. So there is one Father, not three Fathers; one Son, not three Sons; one Holy Spirit, not three Holy Spirits. And in this Trinity there is no before or after, no greater or lesser, but all three persons are equally eternal with each other and fully equal.[3]

Here we are asked to accept that the Father and the Son and the Spirit are equally divine, though this does not mean that there are three Gods. The conclusion then drawn is that what is true of God is true of Father, Son, and Spirit. On the other hand, so it is said, the Father, Son, and Spirit are distinct in that what is true of each is not true of all. The Father is not created or begotten. The Son is begotten. The Spirit proceeds from the Father and the Son.

In other words: (1) God is Father, Son, and Spirit; (2) the Father is God; (3) the Son is God; (4) the Spirit is God; (5) the Father is not the Son or the Spirit; (6) the Son is not the Father or the Spirit; (7) the Spirit is not the Father or the Son; (8) there is one God, not three. Or, as Augustine writes:

---

[3] Ibid. 11 f.

Father and Son and Holy Spirit in the inseparable equality of one substance present a divine unity; and therefore there are not three Gods but one God; although indeed the Father has begotten the Son, and therefore he who is the Father is not the Son; and the Son is begotten by the Father, and therefore he who is the Son is not the Father; and the Holy Spirit is neither the Father nor the Son, but only the Spirit of the Father and of the Son, himself co-equal to the Father and the Son, and belonging to the threefold unity.[4]

This, says Augustine is the *initium fidei*. It is the starting point of faith.

Aquinas is of the same mind. His approach to the doctrine of the Trinity takes for granted the substance of texts like the Athanasian Creed. 'The teaching', he says, 'is this: although God is one and simple ... God is Father, God is Son, and God is Holy Spirit. And these three are not three gods, but are one God.'[5] He was certainly aware of deviations from orthodox teaching, and he alludes to such deviations. He refers, for example, to tritheism, according to which Father, Son, and Spirit are three individuals sharing a nature in the sense that Peter, Paul, and John are three individuals sharing a (human) nature.[6] But his own position is thoroughly orthodox. He accepts all of the eight propositions listed above concerning the persons of the Trinity. As a consequence of this, his treatment of the Trinity deals with three main topics. These are: (1) the relevance of philosophy to the doctrine, (2) the processions and relations involved in the Trinity, and (3) the persons of the Trinity taken individually.[7]

The Trinity and Philosophy

To start with, it is as well to be clear that Aquinas's notion of the Trinity runs entirely contrary to a supposition commonly found

---

[4] *De Trinitate*, 1. 4. 7.

[5] *Comp.* ch. 36.

[6] A famous medieval exponent of tritheism is normally taken to be Roscelin of Compiègne (d. *c.*1120), who was opposed by Anselm. See G. R. Evans, *Anselm* (London, 1989), ch. 5. Though he was accused of tritheism, however, there is room for debate as to whether Roscelin was a simple tritheist.

[7] The agenda here is not a creation of Aquinas, for writers earlier than he spoke of and explored the notion that there were processions and relations in God, this being something to their minds forced on them by biblical and credal teaching. They also spoke of the persons of the Trinity individually and collectively and a lot of what they say is taken up and developed by Aquinas.

among Christians. It is often said that the doctrine of the Trinity marks the point at which Christian teaching gets really incomprehensible. The idea seems to be that belief in the one, creating God is relatively clear and easy to understand, that our reason can cope with the notion of God as such, but that everything gets impossible when the Trinity enters the scene.[8] This, however, is not Aquinas's position. For him, as we have seen, our reason has, in a sense, already broken down as soon as we use the word 'God' (Chapters 3 and 4). He certainly believes that the Trinity is a mystery. But he does not think that it is a deeper mystery than God considered apart from the doctrine of the Trinity. For him, God is always as mysterious as anything can be. He is always beyond our understanding. We do not know what he is.

But there is a sense in which Aquinas does make a distinction between belief in God and belief in the truth that God is three. For, in his view, the doctrine of the Trinity cannot be proved to be true by means of philosophical argument. Since he holds that the existence of God can be defended in rational or philosophical terms, one might expect him to take a similar line when it comes to the reality of the Trinity. This, however, is just what he does not do. Some of his predecessors seem to teach that the doctrine of the Trinity can be argued for philosophically. A notable example (referred to by Aquinas in 1a. 32. 1) is Richard of St Victor (d. 1173), who argues that God is charity or love, and that there must therefore be in him a tending to another (implying duality in God) and a tendency to a third as one with whom the love between the first two can be shared.[9] A similar line of thinking occurs in chapter 7 of St Bonaventure's *Itinerarium mentis in Deum* (*The Soul's Journey into God*), and it has recently been defended by Richard Swinburne. According to Swinburne, love is worthwhile and 'the best love would share all that it had'. Therefore, 'there is overriding reason for a first God to create a second God and with him to create a third God.'

A God would see that for him too a best kind of action would be to share and to cooperate in sharing. Now a first God is the almighty principle of being; but for his choice there would be none other with whom to share.

---

[8] This line of thought seems to lie behind the familiar preacher's complaint that the worst day of the year to preach on is Trinity Sunday.

[9] *De Trinitate*, 3. 11. For the text of the work, see Gaston Salet, SJ, *Richard de Saint Victor: La Trinité* (Paris, 1959).

So the divine love of a first God G1 would be manifested first in creating another god G2, with whom to share his life, and the divine love of G1 or G2 would be manifested in creating another god G3, with whom G1 and G2 cooperatively could share their lives. G2 and G3 would then cooperate in keeping G1 in being, for but for their refraining from destroying him, there would be no G1. They would then cooperate further in backing the activities of each other in their respective spheres of activity.[10]

But Aquinas will have nothing to do with this kind of argument. 'The truth that God is three and one', he says, 'is altogether a matter of faith; and in no way can it be demonstratively proved.'[11] 'No one', he asserts, 'can know the trinity of persons by natural powers of reason.'[12]

Why not? Aquinas's reasons for his conclusion are not those of all medieval writers who agree with it in principle. Some, for example, thought that reason by itself cannot attain to a knowledge of the Trinity since it has been corrupted by the Fall of Adam. Such was the view attributed to Alexander of Hales (1186–1245), according to whom 'our mind fails in dealing with what most truly *is*' because of original sin.[13] For Aquinas, however, reason cannot show that God is the Trinity because it is intrinsically incapable of doing so regardless of original sin. And in saying why this is so he returns to his familiar theme—that our knowledge of God is derived from creatures, and that what we can grasp of him by reason comes from what we can deduce from them. As Peter Geach explains:

Since all the propositions of natural theology tell us only what is true of a being in virtue of his being God, they cannot serve to establish any distinction there might be between two Persons both of whom were God and the same God. Thus, so far as natural theology goes, the question whether many distinct Persons can be one and the same God is *demonstrably undecidable*, on Aquinas's view.[14]

Reason, says Aquinas, can indeed tell us that there is a God who is the source of the existence of things. But the creative power of God, and all that we can know of him by reason (the substance of 1a. 2 ff.

---

[10] Richard Swinburne, 'Could There be More Than One God?', *Faith and Philosophy*, 5 (1988).

[11] *Super De Trin.* 3. 4.

[12] 1a. 32. 1; cf. *Comp.* ch. 36 and *Super De Trin.* 1. 4.

[13] *Summa*, 1. 10. Note, though, that the *Summa Fratris Alexandri*, though attributed to Alexander, is not now thought to be his work.

[14] G. E. M. Anscombe and P. T. Geach, *Three Philosophers* (Oxford, 1973), 118 f.

and 1a. 44 ff. and parallels), belongs equally to Father, Son, and Spirit. For each of them is wholly divine. Reason can know of the existence of divinity, but not of any distinction within it.

Suppose we discovered what is evidently an indication of intelligent life on some planet. We have no direct access to the cause or causes of what we discover. All we can observe is that intelligence has been at work. Can we now number the alien inhabitants of the planet? Clearly not. There might be a dozen of them, all very active and highly efficient. There might be a million of them (slightly less active and individually less efficient). Or there might be just one very active, very efficient, very powerful alien. By the same token, Aquinas is arguing, we know that the world is created, but we are in no position by reason alone to fill in details of number. We can, however, know that divinity is not multipliable. So there cannot be two or more Gods.

It is impossible to come to the knowledge of the Trinity of divine persons through natural reason. For it has been shown already that through natural reason human beings can know God only from creatures; and they lead to the knowledge of God as effects do to their cause. Therefore by natural reason we can know of God only what characterizes him necessarily as the source of all beings . . . Now the creative power of God is shared by the whole Trinity; hence it goes with the unity of nature, not with the distinction of persons. Therefore through natural reason we can know what has to do with the unity of nature, but not with the distinction of persons.[15]

In short, Aquinas recognizes that philosophy can take us so far and no further. He thinks that philosophical argument can take us along the route we have seen him taking in Chapters 2 to 9. But he does not think that this route leads to the Trinity. We cannot prove the doctrine of the Trinity, and it is best for all concerned that we do not even try to do so.

Those who try to prove the trinity of persons by natural powers of reason detract from faith in two ways. First on the point of its dignity, for the object of faith is those invisible realities which are beyond the reach of human reason . . . Secondly, on the point of advantage in bringing others to faith. For when people want to support faith by unconvincing arguments, they become a laughing stock for the unbelievers, who think that we rely on such arguments and believe because of them.[16]

[15] 1a. 32. 1.
[16] 1a. 32. 1.

What Aquinas says here may be compared with the sentiments expressed in *SG* 1. 9, where the method and procedure of that work is explained. Is he out to demonstrate the philosophical cogency of religious truth in what follows? Yes, he replies: partly and insofar as it can be done. But there are truths of faith which cannot be demonstrated from any principle or premise available to anyone with sound habits of thinking and the like.

On the other hand, however, Aquinas also holds that philosophy can be of assistance even when it comes to the doctrine of the Trinity. I may not be able to prove the truth of a given assertion of mine, but I might well be able to show that someone arguing against me has committed a mistake and has not proved that I am wrong in what I say. I might also be able to show how what I believe coheres with other true beliefs, or with ones which we have reason to accept. And with these points in mind Aquinas maintains that, though the doctrine of the Trinity cannot be rationally demonstrated, it can still be rationally discussed.

This, in fact, is the position he adopts with regard to all those theological truths which he takes to be beyond the power of philosophy to demonstrate. That there are such truths is, he says, evident.

For the human intellect is not able to reach a comprehension of the divine substance through its natural power. For, according to its manner of knowing in the present life, the intellect depends on the sense for the origin of knowledge; and so those things that do not fall under the senses cannot be grasped by the human intellect except in so far as the knowledge of them is gathered from sensible things. Now, sensible things cannot lead the human intellect to the point of seeing in them the nature of the divine substance; for sensible things are effects that fall short of the power of their cause.[17]

We can articulate truths about God, and we can know that they are truths. But we cannot understand God as he is in himself. So, on some theological matters, we simply have to be taught. But this does not mean that we have to abandon our reflective or critical faculties. We can argue

on the basis of those truths held by revelation which an opponent admits, as when debating with heretics [*Sacra Doctrina*] appeals to received

[17] *SG* 1. 3. 13.

authoritative texts of Christian theology, and uses one article against those who reject another.[18]

And we can try 'to solve the difficulties against faith' which someone who holds no common ground of faith with the Christian may bring up. 'For since faith rests on unfailing truth, and the contrary of truth cannot really be demonstrated, it is clear that alleged proofs against faith are not demonstrations, but charges that can be refuted.'[19] Aquinas also allows for miracles, and for arguments which point in the direction of what is revealed. But he is quite explicit that these cannot demonstrate the truth of the propositions of faith such as the doctrine of the Trinity. They should, he says, be brought forward 'for the training and consolation of the faithful, and not with any idea of refuting adversaries.'[20]

In his view, this means that the primary task facing theologians writing about the Trinity is twofold. First, they must set forth the doctrine. Second, they must try to show that some sense can be made of it, or that arguments against its truth are answerable. And that, in effect, is what Aquinas himself does in writing about the Trinity. His procedure, we might say, is more or less the same as that of St Augustine, whose fifth-century treatise *De Trinitate* was the first really major, systematic, and powerfully influential theological statement of how we can think of God as three in one. Augustine starts from Scripture, for there, he thinks, the doctrine of the Trinity can be found as revelation on which to reflect. In reflecting on the doctrine, he then offers models, images, or analogies, so that his readers might get a glimmering of how it can be true. And that is what Aquinas does. The doctrine of the Trinity is not, for him, provable by philosophy. It is contained in Scripture and must be expounded with reference to that. Since, like Augustine, Aquinas thinks that there are analogies for aspects of the doctrine of the Trinity, he subsequently explores those.

You might put it by saying (1) that, though he thinks of God as incomprehensible, Aquinas still sees his task as one of trying to explain how we can reflect on what it is for God to be God, and (2) that, though he holds that the Trinity is mysterious, he also tries to explain how we can think of what it is for God to be Trinity. It is,

---

[18] 1a. 1. 8.
[19] 1a. 1. 8; cf. *SG* 1. 6 f.
[20] *SG* 1. 9.

however, also important to recognize that Aquinas never thinks of himself as offering a portrait of God, or a tourist guide to the highways and byways of divinity. He is exploring models and analogies which, in his view, will always fall short of the reality they are being used to talk about. In his discussion of the Trinity in the *Summa theologiae*, therefore, he can observe that

when we say things of God we should not understand them, to be like lowly creatures, namely bodies, but like the highest creatures, namely spiritual beings, although even the likeness taken from them falls short of an illustration of divine things.[21]

This means that the odds are on Aquinas agreeing with us should we complain that there are reasons for rejecting some model or analogy used by him when talking of the Trinity. As we shall see, his chief model when writing about the Son is that of what he calls 'the word in the heart' (*verbum cordis*), which he thinks of as something to be found in us. As we shall also see, his model for the Spirit is that of an upsurge of love, which, he believes, also occurs in us. But he does not intend us to suppose that these models, or others he employs in trying to think about the Trinity, are fully adequate. His treatment of the doctrine of the Trinity is, effectively, an attempt to steer a course between a bare assertion of the points of the doctrine as I summarized it above and the need to think about the Trinity in terms familiar to us so that we can appropriate the doctrine as something more than a bare formula, or as so much mumbo-jumbo.

Processions in the Trinity

Mention of divine processions could conjure up an image of something like a string of deities parading in a Caribbean carnival. To writers such as Aquinas, however, it would have seemed perfectly familiar and not at all ludicrous. For one thing, early Christian creeds and councils speak of the Spirit as 'proceeding'.[22] And the Bible contains passages which employ the language of procession with respect to what is divine. In John's Gospel, Jesus speaks of himself and the Spirit as proceeding from the Father. In chapter 8, for

---

[21] 1a. 27. 1.
[22] Henricus Denzinger and Adolfus Schönmetzer, *Enchiridion symbolorum definitionum et declarationum de rebus fidei et morum* (Freiburg, 1976), 150, 525, 800.

example, he says: 'If God were your Father, you would love me, for I proceeded and came forth from God',[23] while in chapter 15 we find: 'But when the Counsellor comes, whom I shall send to you from the Father, even the Spirit of truth, who proceeds from the Father, he will bear witness to me.'[24] St Paul, also, refers to the Son and the Spirit being *sent*.

But when the time had fully come, God sent forth his Son, born of woman, born under the law, to redeem those who were under the law, so that we might receive adoption as sons. And because you are sons, God has sent the Spirit of his Son into our hearts, crying 'Abba! Father!'[25]

The notion of sending is bound up with that of proceeding. When I send you a letter something proceeds from me to you. So what could be more natural than to think that the divine Trinity has something to do with proceeding? What could be more natural than to think of the Son and the Spirit proceeding?

But if Father, Son, and Spirit are equally divine, how can the Son or Spirit be spoken of as proceeding? In asking this question one might have two concerns in mind. Scripture speaks of the sending of the Son and Spirit with reference to events which come to pass in time. The Son is sent with the birth of Christ. And the sending of the Spirit is bound up with what happens in connection with the Incarnation. 'Jesus said to them again, "Peace be with you. As the Father has sent me, even so I send you." And when he had said this, he breathed on them, and said to them, "Receive the Holy Spirit".'[26] So one might wonder about the sending of the persons in historical terms. If God is immutable, however, then the sending of the Son and Spirit in history will reflect what is changelessly in God apart from the course of world events. In some sense there will be a coming forth of the Son and the Spirit in eternity, a procession in God apart from history. And one might also wonder what this can amount to.

Some theologians (Augustine is a notable example) turn to the question of procession in the Trinity by focusing on history, on the manifestation of God in time.[27] In the jargon familiar to theologians,

---

[23] John 8: 42.
[24] John 15: 26.
[25] Gal. 4: 4 ff.
[26] John 20: 21 f.
[27] For a succinct account of all this, see Edmund Hill, *The Mystery of the Trinity* (London, 1985).

they start with the 'economic' Trinity. And it is clear that Aquinas would have sympathy with their approach. In the first place, he derives the doctrine of the Trinity from the teaching of Jesus. 'Finally', he writes,

at the time of grace, the mystery of the Trinity was revealed by the Son of God himself, as is said [Matthew 16: 18], *Go therefore and make disciples of all nations, baptizing them in the name of the Father and of the Son and of the Holy Spirit.*[28]

In the second place, he thinks that the Trinity cannot be properly spoken of without allowing for the effects of the Incarnation. He says, for example, that the Trinity contains persons who are 'sent', and the sending in question here is something he understands in terms of the life of grace in the believer.[29]

But, in first turning to the doctrine of the Trinity, Aquinas's standard procedure, following that of earlier writers such as Peter Lombard, is to consider the Trinity as being what God changelessly is without respect to creatures (the so-called immanent Trinity). When he deals with the notion of processions and the Trinity, therefore, his first question is 'How in God himself can there be a coming forth?'

One thing he stresses (and we should not now be surprised to find him doing so) is that any talk of procession in God must be understood in a way that prevents us from attributing to him anything essentially creaturely.[30] On the other hand, however, he also thinks that we have to hand an analogy derived from creatures which we may invoke in trying to think of procession in God. Something can come from me because I make it or move it in a given direction. But it can also come from me without being distinct from me. For suppose I form a concept of something. My concept comes from me insofar as it is my concept (we can speak of conceiving ideas). But it is not something outside me and it is not something that can be sent as a physical object can be sent from one place to another. It is something that remains in me.

---

[28] 2a2ae. 174. 6.
[29] If in 'effects of the Incarnation' we include the teaching of the Church as it developed prior to Aquinas, we should note that this is also something to which Aquinas is extremely sensitive in his writings on the Trinity. These are full of references to patristic authors and they are thoroughly governed by creeds and councils.
[30] 1a. 27. 1.

Whenever anyone understands because of his very act of understanding, something comes forth within him, which is the concept of the known thing proceeding from his awareness of it. It is this concept which an utterance signifies; we call it 'the word in the heart' signified by the spoken word.[31]

And 'the word in the heart', says Aquinas, is a model for thinking of procession in the Trinity. More precisely, it is a model for thinking of the fact that the Father, from eternity, begets a Son.

If I form a concept of myself, there is similarity between me and my concept insofar as my concept of myself corresponds to what I am. So what I conceive of is in me (it is my concept), and yet distinct from me (I am not my concepts), while also being like me. By the same token, Aquinas suggests, the Son (or, in the language of the Gospel of John, the Word) can be thought of as like a concept in the mind of one conceiving of himself. In God's case this means that the Father brings forth the Son, who is like him insofar as he is properly understood, and who shares the divine nature since God and his understanding are the same.

The coming forth is like that in the mind's action . . . It reproduces specific resemblance, since what the intellect conceives is the likeness of what is understood; and it exists in the same nature, because to be and to understand are identical in God . . . [Hence] the Word comes forth as subsisting in the same nature, and is called 'begotten' and 'Son' in a strict sense.[32]

As Ceslaus Velecky observes:

St Thomas likens the procession of the Word in God to our act of self-awareness when the mind is both naturally and objectively identified with itself. So it is as if in thinking of himself that God begets God. He is pure intelligibility, and his act of understanding issuing in his Word is identical with his very being.[33]

There can be little doubt that it was his reading of the first chapter of John's Gospel which led Aquinas to this way of thinking.[34] He does not derive it from reflection on Aristotelian theories of mind, which feature in his account of divine procession. Hence, for example, he says that we can by philosophy know that God has knowledge, but

---

[31] 1a. 27. 1; cf. *De ver.* 4. 2 and *SG* 4. 11.
[32] 1a. 27. 2; cf. 1a. 34. 1.
[33] Appendix 5 to vol. vi of the Blackfriars edition of the *Summa theologiae*.
[34] Cf. Christopher Hughes, *On a Complex Theory of a Simple God* (Ithaca, NY, 1989), 192.

not how he has it.[35] Also worth noting is the commentary on Boethius's *De Trinitate*, 1. 4, where Aquinas observes:

In God, intellect and object of intellect are the same; and therefore, from the fact that he is intelligent, it need not be supposed that in him there is any concept really distinct from himself, as is the case with us; Trinity of persons, however, requires real distinction.

It is Scripture, too, which furnishes Aquinas with a development of this point, namely his teaching on the person of the Spirit.

As Aquinas explains, the Catholic faith also speaks of the Spirit proceeding,[36] and of the Spirit as distinct from the Son,[37] implying a second procession in God. So how are we to think of this? Is there another analogy to hand when it comes to the procession of the Spirit? Aquinas holds that there is, and that we can think of the procession of the Spirit with reference to the model of will or love. He says that, just as what is known can be in the knower by virtue of intellect, that which is willed or loved can be in the willer or knower. We can speak of a coming forth which is the act of intellect, and we can also speak of a coming forth which is an act of will or love. Aquinas therefore suggests that in God's case we can think of the Spirit as the coming forth of love from God. God knows what he brings forth as a concept (the Word) and he loves what he knows. This loving is a proceeding in God and, since all that is in God is God, it is divine.

In God procession corresponds only to an action which remains within the agent himself, not to one bent on something external. In the spiritual world the only actions of this kind are those of intellect and will. But the Word's procession corresponds to the action of the intellect. Now in us there is another spiritual process following the action of the will, namely the coming forth of love, whereby what is loved is in the lover, just as the thing expressed or actually understood in the conceiving of an idea is in the knower. For this reason besides the procession of the Word another procession is posited in God, namely the procession of Love.[38]

But the proceeding of the Spirit ought not, says Aquinas, to be called 'generation'. When *P* understands *X* there is a likeness between *P*

[35] *De pot.* 8. 1 ad. 12.
[36] John 15: 26.
[37] John 14: 16.
[38] 1a. 27. 3.

and *X*. But not so when *P* loves *X*. The procession of love is therefore
to be thought of in terms of motion towards. And 'spirit' is a proper
way of naming this motion since it bears the sense of living motion
and impulse, as when one says that people are impelled by love to do
something.[39]

Relations and the Trinity

The notion of procession inevitably implies relationship. For if one
thing proceeds from another, each is related to the other. And this
would seem to imply that there are genuine relations in the Trinity.
If, for example, the Son proceeds from the Father, then the Son is
related to the Father, and the Father is related to the Son. Or, as
Aquinas writes:

'Father' is named from fatherhood and 'son' from sonship. If then
fatherhood and sonship are not real relations in God, it follows that God is
not Father or Son in reality, but only because our minds conceive him so.[40]

On this basis, therefore, Aquinas asserts that the Trinity contains
relationship.

On the other hand, however, he also wants to steer clear of
tritheism. The position he adopts, therefore, is twofold. First, since
(by virtue of the doctrine of divine simplicity) all that is in God *is*
God, Father, Son, and Spirit share the undivided divine nature (i.e.
there are three who are God). Second, their being three is a
consequence of them being genuinely related to each other by virtue
of the processions.

When something springs from a principle which has the same nature, then
necessarily both that which issues and that from which it issues belong to
the same order; and so must have real relationships with each other. Since
processions in God are in the identical nature . . . the relations rising from
the divine processions must be real relations . . . While relation in created
things exists as an accident in a subject, in God a really existing relation has
the existence of the divine nature and is completely identical with
it . . . [so] . . . a real relation in God is in reality identical with nature and
differs only in our mind's understanding, inasmuch as relation implies a

---

[39] 1a. 27. 4.
[40] 1a. 28. 1.

reference to the correlative term, which is not implied by the term 'nature'. Therefore it is clear that in God relation and nature are existentially not two things but one and the same . . . By definition relation implies reference to another, according to which the two things stand in relative opposition to each other. Therefore, since in God there is a real relation . . . relative opposition must also really be there. Now by its very meaning such opposition implies distinction. Therefore there must be real distinction in God, not indeed when we consider the absolute reality of his nature, where there is sheer unity and simplicity, but when we think of him in terms of relation.[41]

In the end, therefore, Aquinas wants to say that it is by virtue of relations that the Trinity is the Trinity—that the three in the Trinity are constituted by the fact that in God there is procession implying relation.

An objector might reply that this reasoning makes Father, Son, and Spirit identical. For if the Son and the Father and the Spirit are identical with the divine nature, must not each be identical with each other? For Aquinas, however, we are here obliged to speak of distinction because we are obliged to speak of relation. The Son, as generated, must be distinct from the Father, even though he cannot be distinguished from the Father as if he were a thing of a different nature. And the same is true of the Spirit.[42] On the other hand, since God is entirely simple, Father, Son, and Spirit are to be identified with God's essence.[43] We must therefore say that they are God, not Gods,[44] and that all references to attributes and actions of God are references to attributes and actions of Father, Son, and Spirit.[45]

When something springs from a principle which has the same nature, then necessarily both that which issues and that from which it issues belongs to the same order; and so must have real relationships with each other. Since processions in God are in the identical nature . . . the relations rising from the divine processions must be real relations.[46]

In this sense, Aquinas argues, we can speak of there being three who are God. But this does not mean that there are three distinct Gods.

---

[41] 1a. 28. 1 ff.
[42] 1a. 28. 3 ad. 1.
[43] 1a. 39. 1 and 2; 42. 1.
[44] 1a. 39. 3.
[45] 1a. 39. 7.
[46] 1a. 28. 1.

The relations of which we speak in talking of the Trinity are, in reality, simply God himself.

While relation in created things exists as an accident in a subject, in God a really existing relation has the existence of the divine nature and is completely identical with it...[so]...a real relation in God is in reality identical with nature and differs only in our mind's understanding, inasmuch as relation implies a reference to the correlative term, which is not implied by the term 'nature'. Therefore it is clear that in God relation and nature are existentially not two things but one and the same.[47]

Here, we might add, Aquinas is treading very traditional ground, for the notion of relation as constituting distinction in the Trinity appears in the literature well before him. It is there, for example, in Augustine, according to whom:

Nothing is predicated of God as an accidental category since nothing in him can undergo change. Yet not every predicate belongs to the category of substance. For we use also 'relation', as when we speak of Father–Son or Son–Father. This is not accidental predication because the one has always been Father and the other Son... Hence although being Father and being Son are different, there is no difference of substance, for our predication refers to relation, not substance. However, relation is not used as an accidental category since there can be no change in God.[48]

The same teaching occurs in Boethius and Anselm. Boethius's conclusion was that 'the manifoldness of the Trinity is produced in the fact that it is predication of a relation'.[49] According to Anselm:

With respect to God the terms 'Father' and 'Son' express a relationship of opposition... Therefore, nothing prevents our saying that the two persons, Father and Son, are two things—provided it is understood what kind of things they are. For the Father and the Son are two things with respect to their relations, not their substance.[50]

'This therefore', Anselm argues elsewhere, 'is the only cause of plurality in God, namely that the names "Father", "Son" and "Holy Spirit" cannot all be predicated of one another.'[51]

For Aquinas, then, the Trinity is what it is by virtue of subsistent

[47] Ia. 23. 2.
[48] *De Trinitate*, 5. 5.
[49] *De Trinitate*, 6.
[50] *Epistola de Incarnatione Verbi*, trans. Jasper Hopkins and Herbert W. Richardson (New York, 1970), 13.
[51] *De processione Spiritus Sancti*, ch. 1.

relations. On this basis we can indeed speak of God as three persons. The 'persons' of the Trinity result from the fact that there is procession in God. And it is, of course, hardly surprising that Aquinas should say this. For 'person' is the word traditionally used in talking of distinction in the Trinity by those who subscribe to the doctrine of the Trinity in its orthodox form.[52] For the record, however, it is worth adding that there are grounds for supposing that, in common with some modern theologians,[53] Aquinas would have been willing, in principle, to dispense with speaking of distinction in the Trinity by means of the term 'person'. I say this for a number of reasons.

First, as we have seen, Aquinas is aware that 'person' is not used to refer to God in the Bible.[54] He also clearly thinks that one should ever be striving for new ways of expressing the truths of faith.[55] Taking these points together, we may well ascribe to him a prima-facie willingness to look beyond the word 'person' as a way of explaining how there is distinction in God.

Second, in ordinary discourse, to speak of a person is to speak of something sharing a nature with other things (i.e. other people). It is to speak of an individual member of a class. But Aquinas would deny that the divine persons are individual members of a class. He thinks that they are divine, and, as we have seen, he denies that divinity is a nature which can be exemplified by individual members of a class, as, for example, humanity is. In the sense that there can be three human persons, there cannot, for him, be three divine persons. In his writings on the Trinity, he accepts Boethius's definition of 'person' as 'an individual substance of rational nature'.[56] And he invokes this definition in what he says of the Trinity since, in his view, Father, Son, and Spirit are distinct in a way which can be indicated in terms of the models of understanding and love (implying intellect). But he also has views about God which, in a sense, seem to commit him to accepting that nothing divine can be an individual substance of

---

[52] Denzinger and Schönmetzer, *Enchiridion*, 75, 150, 800, 1330.
[53] Here I am thinking of authors such as Karl Barth and Karl Rahner. For Barth see *Church Dogmatics*, i (Edinburgh, 1975), 539. For Rahner see *The Trinity* (London, 1970), 109.
[54] 1a. 29. 3.
[55] See 1a. 29. 3 ad. 1.
[56] By 'substance' here Aquinas means 'subject', signifying subsistence. This is the notion of First Substance as found in Aristotle's *Categories*. For an account of this see Anscombe and Geach, *Three Philosophers*, 7. Cf. Aquinas, *In Meta.* book 5, lectio 10.

rational nature and that 'person', as Boethius defines it, might not be the only term to use in speaking of Father, Son, and Spirit. I am, of course, not trying to make it seem that Aquinas denies that the persons of the Trinity are individual or rational. He holds that they are distinct and therefore individual. They are also divine, and therefore rational. For there is intellect in God. But Aquinas denies that we can distinguish between *suppositum* and nature in God. So there is a sense in which he denies that anything divine can be an individual. And, insofar as 'rational' suggests 'undergoing processes of thought', his teaching that God is immutable is a denial that God is rational. For reasons such as these, it seems to me that he would have been happy to look beyond the notion of person as a way of expressing how God can be three in one.

The Persons Taken Individually

For Aquinas, then, all of the persons of the Trinity are identical with the divine nature, but they are also distinct since in God there is relationship constituted by procession. That, in a nutshell, is Aquinas's teaching on the Trinity. He does, however, have some further points to add about each of the divine persons and, before we turn to other matters, we will need to note what they are.

1. The Father

Over and above what I have already reported, Aquinas has two things to stress about the Father. The first is that the Father is the 'principle' of the Son and Spirit. The second is that, in the context of theologizing about the Trinity, the term 'Father' is a proper name standing for what can be thought of as the archetype of all fatherhood.

One might wonder why Aquinas thinks it important to labour the point that the Father should be spoken of by means of the word 'principle'. But the reason is quite an obvious one. He wants to deny that the Son and the Spirit are caused to exist by the Father and are therefore subordinate to him or dependent on him for their being. For him, all the persons of the Trinity are equally divine, and none of them can owe his existence to anything since divinity is not caused to be by anything. In speaking of what the Father is to the Son and

Spirit, therefore, we need, Aquinas adds, another term than 'cause', and may therefore use the word 'principle'. He thinks that if X causes Y there is disparity of power or perfection between X and Y. But this, he says, is not the case where X is a principle of Y for 'the word "principle" means simply that from which something proceeds'.[57] In his view, calling the Father the principle of the Son and Spirit allows us to preserve the notion of procession without ascribing any suggestion of dependence to what is divine.[58] At the same time, it allows us to express the thought that the Father is that from which the Son and the Spirit proceed, and not vice versa.

Even as among creatures we observe primary and secondary principles, so among the divine persons, while there is no first and second, there is a principle not from a principle, the Father, and a principle from a principle, the Son.[59]

With respect to the second point, Aquinas is saying that the term 'father' is applicable to God independently of the fact that God has created. Since the created order derives from God, says Aquinas, there is a sense in which God can be called 'father'. But, quite independently of creation, there is fatherhood in God himself by virtue of the fact that the Son and Spirit eternally proceed. Or, as Aquinas puts it: 'The term "fatherhood" applies to God first as connoting the relation of the one person to another, before it applies as connoting the relation of God to creatures.'[60] And this, for Aquinas, means that 'Father', although a common noun signifying a relation between two or more individuals, can, with respect to the Trinity, be treated as a proper name of one individual, i.e. of God the Father.[61]

2. The Son

We have already seen that Aquinas thinks of the Son on the analogy of the *verbum cordis*. The Son may be compared to a concept of himself formed by the Father. But it is also worth noting that, in

---

[57] 1a. 33. 1.
[58] For a recent and very different way of talking, cf. Swinburne, 'Could There be More Than One God?'
[59] 1a. 33. 4.
[60] 1a. 33. 3.
[61] 1a. 33. 2.

developing this notion, Aquinas arrives at the conclusion that, in knowing himself in the Son, the Father also knows creatures. Since the Son is generated as God knows himself and since, in knowing himself, God knows creatures (see Chapter 7), he finds creatures as he generates the Son. 'In knowing himself, God knows every creature . . . Because by the one act he understands both himself and all else, his single Word expresses not only the Father but creatures as well.'[62]

In other words, according to Aquinas, creatures are not a kind of afterthought from God's point of view. They are known by God as the Father brings forth the Son. For Aquinas, the Son of God is God as known to God. Since God is the Creator, the Son of God is known to God as Creator, and creatures are therefore in God simply because God is God. On this basis, of course, Aquinas is able to make sense of biblical language implying that the Son of God has a crucial role in the coming forth of creation.[63] He is also able to pick up the biblical teaching that the Son of God is the *image* of God.[64] Human beings, says Aquinas, are in God's image, but they fall short of it since they are not like God as God is like God. The Son, however, is fully like God and therefore God's image absolutely speaking, for he is literally divine.[65]

3. The Spirit

What Aquinas says about the Spirit is more or less what we would expect him to say given all the above. But there are two aspects of his teaching worth highlighting. The first concerns the notion that the Spirit proceeds from the Father and the Son. The second concerns the idea that the Spirit can be referred to as 'Love'.

1. By *c.*1013 the Niceno-Constantinopolitan Creed in its Western version said that the Spirit proceeds from the Father 'and from the Son' (*filioque*). But, though this teaching was championed by writers like Augustine,[66] it was disputed by Eastern Christians. On biblical grounds, and from a desire to rule out the suggestion that the Spirit is dependent for its being on the Father and the Son, they wanted to

---

[62] 1a. 34. 4.
[63] See Col. 1: 15 ff.
[64] See Col. 1: 15; Phil. 2: 6; Heb. 1: 3.
[65] 1a. 35. 2 ad. 3.
[66] See *De Trinitate*, 2. 4. 7.

say that the Spirit proceeded from the Father *through* the Son, not from the Father *and* the Son.[67] Controversy raged and the use of *filioque* in stating the doctrine of the Trinity became a major cause of the split between Western and Eastern Christians.[68]

In his account of the Holy Spirit, Aquinas shows that he wants to retain the Western doctrine of the Spirit as proceeding from the Father and the Son. But he evidently also wants to do something to effect a compromise with those who reject it. In his discussion of the Spirit in the *Summa theologiae*, he tries to bring East and West together by arguing that differences between them concerning the Spirit are more a matter of terminology than meaning.[69]

He cites numerous arguments for the conclusion that the Spirit does not proceed from the Father and the Son, but only from the Father. In his view, however, if the Spirit proceeds only from the Father, he would be indistinguishable from the Son, for the persons of the Trinity are distinguished only by relations. If the Spirit simply proceeds from the Father, says Aquinas, then he would only be that which proceeds from the Father, which is just what the Son is.[70] Aquinas therefore suggests that something must distinguish the Son and the Spirit and that this must be a relation other than that of proceeding from the Father.

Why? Because, he says, relations are a matter of origin in the Trinity. With respect to Son and Spirit, therefore, we have two options. Either the Son proceeds from the Spirit, or the Spirit proceeds from the Son. Since nobody wants to embrace the first of these options, says Aquinas, we must settle for the second one. And, since the Son proceeds from the Father, we can say that the Spirit proceeds from the Father and the Son.

So the Western tradition is upheld. But Aquinas also thinks that we can say that the Spirit proceeds from the Father *through* the Son. For the Spirit would not be if it were not for the Son, and the Son

---

[67] Cf. John 15: 26.

[68] The teaching that the Spirit proceeds from the Father and the Son was a major issue at the time of Aquinas, who was called to the Second Council of Lyons as an advisor on the matter. The Council was the culmination of proposals for reunion between East and West which began between Pope Urban IV and the Emperor Michael VIII, Paleologus.

[69] See also *De pot.* 10. 5.

[70] By the same token, so Aquinas adds, only his relation as begetter allows us to distinguish the Father as Father. If only the relation 'proceeding from the Father' identifies the Spirit, it will not serve to distinguish him from the Son.

would not be if it were not for the Father. A thing produced by a craftsman can come to be through the tool used to shape it, but it also comes to be through the man who wields it. In an analogous way, Aquinas suggests, the Spirit comes to be through the Son, since the Spirit exists by virtue of the Son. But the Son exists by virtue of the Father, and the Spirit therefore derives from both Father and Son.[71]

2. According to Aquinas 'the term "love" can be used of the divinity both essentially and personally. As personal it is a name proper to the Holy Spirit.'[72] In his writing on the Trinity, Augustine says that "love" is a term equally applicable to all the persons of the Trinity, which gives him some problems in distinguishing the procession of the Spirit.[73] Aquinas, however, argues that the Spirit alone is properly called 'Love', and he tries to explain why this is so and what it implies.

He repeats the point that the Son proceeds as concept known by God. He then argues that, when a knower loves what he knows, his will receives 'a kind of imprint' of 'the reality loved' and 'the object loved is present in the lover even as the object known is present in the knower'. So, when someone knows and loves himself, 'he is present to himself . . . as an object known in one knowing and as an object loved in one knowing'.[74] In the case of God, Aquinas adds, the Son is known and loved by the Father and the Spirit is the love which consequently arises.

On this account, the Spirit is the love of the Father for the Son. Also implied, however, is that the Spirit is the love of the Son for the Father. Since the Son is divine, he is all that the Father is. And, since the Father knows himself in knowing the Son, his knowledge of the Son is knowledge of what (*a*) is distinct from him and (*b*) has the love of the Father. So the Son loves as the Father loves. And, since the Spirit proceeds from Father and Son, and since the Father finds his creatures in knowing the Son, it follows that God loves his creatures through the Spirit. 'By the Holy Spirit, or Love proceeding', says Aquinas, 'Father and Son are loving both each other and us.'[75] As we shall see in later chapters, this thought is crucial to his whole conception of the significance of Christianity.

---

[71] 1a. 36. 3.
[72] 1a. 37. 1.
[73] *De Trinitate*, 9 and 15, and note especially 9. 12 and 15. 17.
[74] 1a. 37. 1.
[75] 1a. 37. 2.

Being Human

In the last chapter I was trying to indicate what Aquinas says about the Trinity considered in itself. In the jargon of modern theology, I was concerned with his teaching on the 'immanent Trinity'. But Aquinas also believes that the 'immanent Trinity' is the 'economic Trinity'.[1] For he thinks that God both acts in the world and is present in it.[2] That is why he holds that the Trinity matters to us. He does not see the doctrine of the Trinity as a complicated exercise in speculative celestial physics. He thinks of it as a wonderful truth which is full of implications for people. For he believes that the Trinity is 'economic' in and for humanity, and that its significance lies in the fact that we may come to share in its life.

Before we can appreciate why Aquinas thinks this, however, we will need to look further at his understanding of people. We have already seen something of what that amounts to, but the picture that has so far emerged still needs to be added to. Aquinas maintains that we share in the life of the Trinity as human beings, and to grasp the implications of that notion we must first know what he thinks human beings are.

Me and My Body

Aquinas obviously thinks of people as created, and as part of a world held in existence by God. Because he thinks of them as having

---

[1] This thesis that 'the immanent Trinity is the economic Trinity' is something of a commonplace in modern discussions of the Trinity. See John J. O'Donnell, SJ, *The Mystery of the Triune God* (London, 1988), 36 f. As readers of Aquinas will discover, however, it is not a new thesis.

[2] Aquinas believes in the Incarnation and the sending of the Spirit. So he says that we can speak, not just of processions in God, but also of sending or missions. The Son and the Spirit are sent. We are dealing here, says Aquinas, 'with a new way of being present somewhere' (1a. 43. 1). The Son comes to be present in a new way by virtue of the Incarnation. The Spirit comes to be present by virtue of the life of Christ and its

intellect and will, he also thinks of them as being in the image of God, to whom intellect and will can also be ascribed. But properly to grasp what Aquinas thinks people are, as well as to give his understanding a context, it will help if we bear in mind two major views representing opposite ends of the spectrum of opinion concerning the nature of people. The first is Dualism. The second is Physicalism.[3]

By 'Dualism' I mean the very influential theory classically expounded by Descartes in texts such as his *Meditations on First Philosophy* and still advocated by some philosophers. According to Descartes, people are composed of two distinct kinds of stuff: mental stuff and physical stuff, mind and body. These are connected and able to influence each other, but mind is radically distinct from body, and persons are identical with their minds, not their bodies. The real me is not my body; it is my mind, or, as Descartes sometimes says, my 'soul'.

My essence consists solely in the fact that I am a thinking thing. It is true that I may have (or, to anticipate, that I certainly have) a body that is very closely joined to me. But nevertheless, on the one hand I have a clear and distinct idea of myself, in so far as I am simply a thinking, non-extended thing; and on the other I have a clear and distinct idea of body, in so far as this is simply an extended non-thinking thing. And accordingly, it is certain that I am really distinct from my body and can exist without it.[4]

Physicalism is really just the opposite of Descartes's position. It holds that people are made up of one kind of stuff—matter or body—and that this includes all that we might call 'mind' or 'mental states and processes'. A version of Physicalism is the so-called 'Identity Theory', which holds that mind and body are identical in that mental events or states are nothing but brain processes under another name. According to the Identity Theory, persons are identical with a set of physical states or events just as lightning is identical

consequences. These missions are entirely temporal—they have to do with what has happened in the history of the world.

[3] Here I am merely sketching two opposing trends in philosophy of mind. For more comprehensive accounts see: John Perry (ed.), *Personal Identity* (Berkeley, Calif, 1975); Colin McGinn, *The Character of Mind* (Oxford, 1982); Paul M. Churchland, *Matter and Consciousness* (Cambridge, Mass., 1984); Peter Smith and O. R. Jones, *The Philosophy of Mind* (Cambridge, 1986).

[4] *The Philosophical Writings of Descartes*, trans. John. Cottingham, Robert Stoothoff, and Dugald Murdoch (Cambridge, 1985), ii. 54. For modern defences of Descartes's position see H. D. Lewis, *The Elusive Self* (London, 1982) and Richard Swinburne, *The Evolution of the Soul* (Oxford, 1986).

with electrical discharge, or just as the Morning Star is identical with the Evening Star.[5]

With these theories in mind, as good a way as any of describing Aquinas's position on what people amount to is to say that he adopts a position midway between the extremes of Dualism and Physicalism. He denies that people are essentially incorporeal. So he is not a Dualist. But neither does he think that people are nothing but collections of physical processes. So he is not a Physicalist either. For him, people are composite individuals.

Aquinas's teaching on the nature of the human person is close to that of Aristotle's *De anima*. Aristotle thought that people are not two things, mind and body, but complex unities both mental and physical. Those who think of people as made up of two things often speak of them as being composed of body plus soul. Aristotle, however, rejects this way of talking. For him, people are ensouled bodies. 'We can', he says, 'wholly dismiss as unnecessary the question whether the body and soul are one: it is as meaningless as to ask whether the wax and the shape given to it by the stamp are one.'[6] And such is Aquinas's position. He agrees that we can speak about people by means of the words 'soul' and 'body'. But he does not think of people as bodies plus souls. He holds that we are mental/physical units, where 'mental' and 'physical' are not simply reducible to each other. He says that a human being is 'a compound whose substance is both spiritual and corporeal'.[7] He thinks that to speak of us having souls is just to assert that we are substances of that kind.

In the Latin of Aquinas, the word translated as 'soul' is *anima*, which means 'that which animates' or 'that which gives life'. When he speaks of 'soul', therefore, Aquinas means something like 'principle of life'. 'Inquiry into the nature of the soul', he writes, 'presupposes an understanding of the soul as the root principle of life in living things within our experience.'[8] According to him, anything alive has a soul. And his view is that people are bodies of a certain kind, bodies with a certain kind of life (soul). Commenting on Aristotle, therefore, he explains:

[5] Cf. J. J. C. Smart ('Sensations and Brain Processes', *Philosophical Review*, 68 (1959): 'When I say that a sensation is a brain process . . . I am using "is" in the sense of strict identity. (Just as in the—in this case necessary—proposition "7 is identical with the smallest prime number greater than 5.")'
[6] *De anima*, 412^{b}6.
[7] Introduction to 1a. 75.   [8] 1a. 75. 1.

There had been much uncertainty about the way the soul and body are conjoined. Some had supposed a sort of medium connecting the two together by a sort of bond. But the difficulty can be set aside now that it has been shown that the soul is the form of the body. As Aristotle says, there is no more reason to ask whether soul and body make one thing than to ask the same about the wax and the impression sealed on it, or about any other matter and its form. For, as is shown in the Metaphysics, Book VIII, form is directly related to matter as the actuality of matter; once matter actually is it is informed ... Therefore, just as the body gets its being from the soul, as from its form, so too it makes a unity with this soul to which it is immediately related.[9]

The key words here are 'the soul is the form of the body'. By 'form', Aquinas means 'substantial form'. In the passage just quoted, therefore, he is saying that in the case of living things (in the case of things with souls) the principle of life (the soul) is what we get as we get the things with all their essential features or characteristics. The soul, for him, is the form of the body in the sense that living bodies of certain kinds have a principle of life.

So people, for Aquinas, are living things of a certain kind. But what kind of things are they? They are, says Aquinas, animals—living creatures of flesh and blood, things more like dogs and cats than sticks and stones. This means that much that is true of non-human animals is also true of people. They are, for instance, capable of physical movement. And they have biological characteristics. They have the capacity to grow and reproduce. They have the need and capacity to eat. These characteristics are not, for Aquinas, optional extras which people can take up and discard. They are essential elements in the make-up of a human being. And they are very much bound up with what is physical or material.

This line of thinking, of course, immediately sets Aquinas apart from writers like Descartes. Descartes maintains that I am my mind and that my body is something I *have* or something to which I am *connected*. For Aquinas, however, my body is not to be distinguished from me in this way.

For as it belongs to the very conception of 'this human being' that there should be this soul, flesh and bone, so it belongs to the very conception of 'human being' that there be soul, flesh and bone. For the substance of a species has to contain whatever belongs in general to every one of the individuals comprising that species.[10]

---

[9] *In De an.* 2. 1. 234.   [10] 1a. 75. 4.

At several points in his writings Aquinas directly refers to the thesis that people are essentially substances different from bodies on which they act (a view which he ascribes to Plato). But he rejects it quite strongly.

Plato and his followers asserted that the intellectual soul is not united to the body as form to matter, but only as mover to movable, for Plato said that the soul is in the body 'as a sailor in a ship'. Thus the union of soul and body would only be by contact of power . . . But this doctrine seems not to fit the facts.[11]

In Aquinas's view, if our souls moved our bodies as sailors move ships, our souls and our bodies would be distinct things and could not make up one thing distinct in its own right. We would be an amalgam or a collection of things rather than a unity. He adds that if we are souls using bodies, then we are essentially immaterial, which is not the case. We are 'sensible and natural realities' and cannot, therefore, be essentially immaterial.[12]

So Aquinas is clearly not a dualist. But nor is he what I have called a 'physicalist'. For, according to him, people (unlike other animals) have intellect (or understanding) and will, which means that they are rational animals able to comprehend, think, love, and choose. From what we have just seen, it will be evident that Aquinas takes the human body to be an essential element in human life. He thinks that being a human person is being a bodily animal. But he also holds that understanding and willing are not physical processes. And this leads him, without espousing Descartes's position, to speak of people as having both soul and body. It also leads him to hold that the soul can survive the death of the body.

Soul and Body

I say that Aquinas speaks of people as having both soul and body, and this might seem puzzling since I have also said that he does not believe that people are two distinct things: soul and body. But, though he denies that they are two distinct things, he still feels obliged to distinguish between what is true of people and what is true

---

[11] *SG* 2. 57.
[12] *SG* 2. 57. 3 ff.

of bodies. That is because he holds that the human soul cannot be something corporeal, though it must be something subsisting.

In arguing for the non-corporeal nature of the human soul, Aquinas begins by reminding us what *anima* means—i.e. 'that which makes living things live'. And, with that understanding in mind, he contends that soul cannot be something bodily. There must, he says, be some principle of life which distinguishes living things from non-living things, and this cannot be a body. Why not? Because, Aquinas continues, if it were a body it would follow that any material thing would be living, which is simply not the case. A body, therefore, is alive not just because it is a body. It is alive because of a principle of life which is not a body.

It is obvious that not every principle of vital activity is a soul. Otherwise the eye would be a soul, since it is a principle of sight; and so with the other organs of the soul. What we call the soul is the root principle of life. Now though something corporeal can be some sort of principle of life, as the heart is for animals, nevertheless a body cannot be the root principle of life. For it is obvious that to be the principle of life, or that which is alive, does not belong to any bodily thing from the mere fact of its being a body; otherwise every bodily thing would be alive or a life-source. Consequently any particular body that is alive, or even indeed a source of life, is so from being a body of such-and-such a kind. Now whatever is actually *such*, as distinct from *not-such*, has this from some principle which we call its actuating principle. Therefore a soul, as the primary principle of life, is not a body but that which actuates a body.[13]

In other words, the difference between, say, me and my pen is that I am not just a body. I am a living body. And that which makes me this cannot itself be a body since, if bodily things are alive just by being bodies, then all bodies would be alive, including my pen.

But why say that the human soul is something subsisting? The main point made by Aquinas in reply to this question is that the human animal has powers or functions which are not simply bodily, even though they depend on bodily ones. As we saw in Chapter 7, Aquinas maintains that knowledge comes about as the forms of things are received immaterially. When Fred has knowledge, there is more to Fred than what can be seen, touched, weighed, and so on. As Aquinas puts it, there is intellect or intellectual life, and it is by virtue of this that Fred is the kind of thing he is (a rational animal). Aquinas

---

[13] 1a. 75. 1.

calls this 'that by virtue of which Fred is the kind of thing he is' Fred's 'soul'. So he can say that Fred is bodily but also that Fred is (or has) both body and soul. The two cannot be torn apart in any way that would leave Fred intact. But they can be distinguished from each other, and the soul of Fred can therefore be thought of as something subsisting immaterially.

The principle of the act of understanding, which is called the human soul, must of necessity be some kind of incorporeal and subsistent principle. For it is obvious that the understanding of people enables them to know the natures of all bodily things. But what can in this way take in things must have nothing of their nature in its own, for the form that was in it by nature would obstruct knowledge of anything else. For example, we observe how the tongue of someone sick with fever and bitter infection cannot perceive anything sweet, for everything tastes sour. Accordingly, if the intellectual principle had in it the physical nature of any bodily thing, it would be unable to know all bodies. Each of them has its own determinate nature. Impossible, therefore, that the principle of understanding be something bodily. And in the same way it is impossible for it to understand through and in a bodily organ, for the determinate nature of that bodily organ would prevent knowledge of all bodies. Thus if you had a colour filter over the eye, and had a glass vessel of the same colour, it would not matter what you poured into the glass, it would always appear the same colour. The principle of understanding, therefore, which is called mind or intellect, has its own activity in which body takes no intrinsic part. But nothing can act of itself unless it subsists in its own right. For only what actually exists acts, and its manner of acting follows its manner of being. So it is that we do not say that heat heats, but that something hot heats. Consequently the human soul, which is called an intellect or mind, is something incorporeal and subsisting.[14]

Aquinas does not mean that the human soul is a distinct thing in its own right. His notion that it subsists does not entail that it is a complete and self-contained entity, as, for example, Descartes thought the soul to be. For Aquinas, my human soul subsists because I have an intellectual life which cannot be reduced to what is simply bodily. It does not subsist as something with its own life apart from me, any more than my left hand does, or my right eye. Both of these can be spoken of as things, but they are really parts of me. We do not say 'My left hand feels' or 'My right eye sees'; rather we say 'I feel with my left hand' and 'I see with my right eye'. And Aquinas thinks that something similar should be said about my soul. I have intellect

[14] 1a. 75. 2.

and will by my soul. But it is not my soul which understands and wills. I do.

We might add that there is a further significant aspect of Aquinas's thinking which distinguishes him from Descartes and the kind of dualism represented by him. According to Descartes (and to many of his philosophical successors) there is a problem when it comes to knowing the material world, but none when it comes to knowing the self. On his account, I know myself better than anything else. And I know myself as something non-bodily, as mind distinct from body, as a spiritual, non-material substance. This I do by introspection. The Cartesian view of persons typically lays stress on the importance of self-consciousness. According to Aquinas, however, there is no such thing as direct human self-knowledge, where the object known is something incorporeal. His view is that we come to knowledge of things as we encounter material objects and receive forms intentionally. And one of the things he takes this to mean is that we come to self-knowledge as (so to speak) we live a bodily life.

Since it is connatural for our intellect in the present life to look to material, sensible things, as said before, it follows that our intellect understands itself according as it is made actual by species abstracted from sensible realities by the light of the agent intellect.[15]

We come to know ourselves as we come to know about other things —by abstracting from sense experience. Or, in Aquinas's words: 'While the soul is joined to the body it understands by turning to sense images; it cannot even understand itself except in that it comes to be actually understanding through a species abstracted from sense images.'[16]

This, of course, entails that there will be considerable room for error when it comes to understanding what a person is. On Descartes's model, persons are directly present to themselves and there is no room for error concerning what they are. Just as I can look at a red patch and describe it accurately by gazing on it and describing what I see, so I can gaze on my (incorporeal) self and state what I see. For Aquinas, however, knowing what people are is the fruit of research. We have to learn what we are. 'Mere presence,' he

[15] Ia. 87. I.
[16] Ia. 98. 2.

writes, 'is not sufficient, and a diligent, subtle inquiry is needed. Many, for this reason, are simply ignorant of the soul's nature and many are positively mistaken about it.'[17]

Death and the Soul

Given all that, however, what happens when I die? To grasp Aquinas's thinking on this question, we will need to be clear on at least one thing. This is that he does not believe that human souls survive as complete human beings. He thinks that human beings are both bodily and non-bodily. He therefore concludes that the survival of them as nothing but body, or as nothing but what is not bodily, cannot be the survival of *them* properly speaking. To understand Aquinas on the survival of the human soul, we must forget about notions like that of people surviving their death as complete incorporeal persons, which is certainly the Cartesian view of survival after death, and which is also, perhaps, the most common view among non-philosophers. Aquinas's view is that Fred's soul can survive the death of Fred. But the soul of Fred when he has died is not itself Fred (i.e. Fred's soul, apart from Fred's body, is not Fred).

Yet why should we even say that Fred's soul can survive the death of Fred? At this point it is important to remember that Aquinas thinks of the human soul as 'the form of the body' and as something subsisting. For his argument is that, if that is what the human soul is, then the human soul is not something perishable. As we saw in Chapter 2, he thinks that for something (e.g. a cow) to perish is for the thing in question to lose its substantial form, to lose what makes it the kind of thing it is. Perishing, for Aquinas, is the loss of form, and form is that in terms of which we analyse perishing. He therefore concludes that it makes no sense to speak of form as such perishing. And if the form in question subsists, he reasons, it continues to exist as something subsistent. Not being a body capable of perishing (as the biological human organism is), and yet being subsistent, the human soul cannot perish. For Aquinas, that by virtue of which I understand and think is not the sort of thing which can die as bodies can die.[18] Of course, he is perfectly aware that people die and that

---

[17] 1a. 87. 1.
[18] See 1a. 75. 6.

their bodies perish. But he does not think that this entails that people are totally extinguished. It only entails the destruction of everything which belongs to them as animals. As we have seen, however, people, for Aquinas, are rational, understanding animals, and they are what they are by virtue of what is not material. This aspect of people must, he concludes, be capable of surviving the destruction of what is material. He does not think we can prove that the soul of Fred must survive Fred's death. In his view, whether or not Fred's soul survives the death of Fred will depend on whether God wills to keep it in being, and Aquinas does not think that we are in a position to prove that God must do that. For him, therefore, there is no 'proof of the immortality of the soul'. He holds that Fred's soul could, in principle, cease to exist at any time. But he also thinks that it is not the sort of thing of which it makes sense to say that it can perish as bodies can perish.

Yet, for Aquinas, neither is it the sort of thing which can survive as a human animal can survive. So the survival of Fred's soul is not the survival of the human being we call 'Fred'. Or, as Aquinas puts it, 'my soul is not I'.[19] People, for him, are very much part of the physical world. Take that world away and what you are left with is not a human person. You are not, for example, left with something able to know by means of sense experience. Nor are you left with something able to undergo the feelings or sensations that go with being bodily. On Aquinas's account, therefore, the human soul can only be said to survive as something purely intellectual, as the *locus* of thought and will.

Understanding through imagery is the proper operation of the soul so far as it has the body united to it. Once separated from the body it will have another mode of understanding, like that of other disembodied natures . . . It is said, *People are constituted in two substantial elements, the soul with its reasoning power, the flesh with its senses.* Therefore when the flesh dies the sense powers do not remain . . . Certain powers, namely understanding and will, are related to the soul taken on its own as their subject of inhesion, and powers of this kind have to remain in the soul after the death of the body. But some powers have the body–soul compound for subject; this is the case with all the powers of sensation and nutrition. Now when the subject goes the accident cannot stay. Hence when the compound corrupts such powers do not remain in actual existence. They survive in the soul in a virtual state only, as in their source or root. And so it is wrong to say, as some do, that

---

[19] *Super I ad Cor.* 15; cf. 1a. 77. 8.

these powers remain in the soul after the dissolution of the body. And it is much more wrong to say that the acts of these powers continue in the disembodied soul, because such powers have no activity except through a bodily organ.[20]

One implication of this teaching which Aquinas draws is that there is no joy or pain in the life of a surviving soul, where joy and pain involve physiological processes and states. 'A disembodied soul', he states, 'does not feel joy and sadness due to bodily desire, but due to intellectual desire, as with the angels.'[21]

Given all that, of course, one might naturally ask: 'Can I live after my death?' If my soul is not me, and if only my soul survives my death, then it would seem that I cannot really be said to survive my death. Aquinas, however, accepts this conclusion. He does not regard it as ruling out anything he wants to maintain. In his view, the existence of a human soul apart from what is bodily is unnatural. He also thinks that, if I die and only my soul survives, then I do not survive. For my soul is the soul of Brian Davies. And Brian Davies is a particular, perishable, bodily individual. Destroy my body, therefore, and Brian Davies ceases to exist.

On the other hand, however, not everyone who believes in human life after death wishes to conceive of it as survival of something incorporeal. And such is the case with biblical authors such as the evangelists and St Paul. In their scheme of things, life after death is not a matter of what we might call 'the immortality of the soul'. It is a matter of resurrection. And this is Aquinas's view as well. My soul is not me, he says. But he also believes that it shall be reunited with my body. And then, he thinks, I shall live again. When my soul is reunited with my body, he argues, I shall again be there as the person I am now. In fact, he adds, the soul naturally belongs with the body.

It belongs to the very essence of the soul to be united to a body, just as it belongs to a light body to float upwards. And just as a light body remains light when forcibly displaced, and thus retains its aptitude and tendency for the location proper to it, in the same way the human soul, remaining in its own existence after separation from the body, has a natural aptitude and a natural tendency to embodiment.[22]

---

[20] 1a. 75. 6 ad. 3 and 1a. 77. 8.
[21] 1a. 77. 8 ad. 5.
[22] 1a. 76. 1 ad. 6.

Aquinas does not think that human happiness consists in bodily life. He sees it as ultimately lying in the vision of God, which can be enjoyed without the body. 'There can', he says, 'be no complete and final happiness for us save in the vision of God.'[23] But he also holds that something is lacking with respect to happiness in disembodied souls, and that the lack here lies in the absence of the body.

So long as the soul enjoys God without its partner, its desire, though at rest with what it has, still longs for the body to enter in and share . . . Desire in a disembodied soul is wholly at rest on the part of the object loved, for it possesses what contents it. Yet not on the part of the subject desiring, for the good is not possessed in every manner that can be wished for. Hence when the body is reassumed happiness will grow, not in depth but in extent . . . Since it is natural for the soul to be united to the body how is it credible that the perfection of the one should exclude the perfection of the other? Let us declare, then, that happiness complete and entire requires the well-being of the body, both before and during its activity.[24]

In short, if human beings are to be happy after death as human beings, they will need to be raised from the dead in bodily form. They will need to be what Aquinas thinks people are now, i.e. human beings, not incorporeal substances. 'Therefore we believe according to our faith in the future resurrection of the dead.'[25] And this, Aquinas thinks, means that between what I am now, and what I am to be hereafter, there must be material continuity. Some philosophers speculating on the possibility of personal survival have settled for less than this. They have, for example, said that I can survive if there is some kind of psychological continuity between me now and me hereafter. Others, believing that for people to exist involves bodies existing, have said that I can live again if there is some body or other for me to 'inhabit' or for me to be identified with. For Aquinas, however, personal identity requires bodily continuity. For me to live again, he says, there must be a human body. But not just any old body will do if I am to live again.

Just as the same specific form ought to have the same specific matter, so the same numerical form ought to have the same numerical matter. The soul of an ox cannot be the soul of a horse's body, nor can the soul of this ox be the soul of any other ox. Therefore, since the rational soul that survives remains

---

[23] 1a2ae. 3. 8.
[24] 1a2ae. 5 ad. 4 and 5; 1a2ae. 6.
[25] *Super sym. apos.* 14; cf. *Comp.* ch. 162.

numerically the same, at the resurrection it must be reunited to numerically the same matter.[26]

How? Aquinas does not explain. He does not claim to know what processes must occur in the resurrection of an individual human being. And he does not think that there is any general scientific reason for holding that people survive their death. 'Since the human body substantially dissolves in death', he says, 'it cannot be restored to numerical identity by the action of nature.'[27] But he is absolutely clear that such numerical identity is needed if I am to live again, and, given his belief in the power of God, he finds no objection in principle to believing that it can be brought about.

Since all things, even the very least, are included under divine providence ... the matter composing this human body of ours, whatever form it may take after our death, evidently does not elude the power or the knowledge of God. Such matter remains numerically the same, in the sense that it exists under quantitative dimensions, by reason of which it can be said to be this particular matter, and is the principle of individuation. If then, this matter remains the same, and if the human body is again fashioned from it by divine power, and if also the rational soul which remains the same in its incorruptibility is united to the same body, the result is that identically the same man is restored to life.[28]

On this basis Aquinas firmly insists on the reality of Christ's resurrection. 'Whatever properties belong to the nature of a human body', he says, 'were totally present in Christ's risen body.'[29] And this, so he adds, means just what it says. It means, for example, that the risen Christ had flesh, bones, blood, 'and other similar elements [which] pertain to the nature of a human body'.[30] An objector with an awkward temperament might wonder about things which belong to us as bodily which one might not be too eager to think of as present in the resurrected Christ. Here Aquinas cites a passage from St Augustine:

Augustine says, *Perhaps given the presence of blood, a more bothersome adversary might press further in an embarrassing manner and state, If there was blood in* Christ's risen body, *why not also pituitary glands*, from which phlegm is

---

[26] *Comp.* ch. 153.
[27] *Comp.* ch. 154.
[28] Ibid.
[29] 3a. 54. 1.
[30] Ibid.

produced? *Why not also yellow bile* from the choleric parts of body, *and black bile* from the melancholic?[31]

But Aquinas is not to be deflected by this kind of objection. In addition to blood, he says, you can add to Christ's resurrected body whatever you like, 'provided that you avoid anything which implies corruption'.[32]

Desire and Action

For Aquinas, then, we are embodied souls. And one of the things this means for him is that we have emotions or, as he calls them, *passiones animae*. He does not think that people are just observers. He notes that they react to things around them. They are attracted or repelled by them. They delight in them or are saddened by them. They are frightened and angry because of them. And all of this is possible, says Aquinas, because people are bodily creatures. For him, emotion is chiefly a physical thing. It arises as our bodies meet other bodies and are affected by them. 'Emotion always involves some physiological modification.'[33]

But, as well as ascribing emotions to people, Aquinas wants to say that they are actors. They are not just affected by things at a bodily level. They are agents with desires, purposes, and goals. 'Of the actions a person performs', he writes, 'those alone are properly called human which are characteristically those of a human person.'[34] And he thinks that what marks characteristically human actions is that they are performed by virtue of mind and will. People have knowledge and they can choose in accordance with what they know.

To put it another way, people act through intellect and will. Intellect is that by virtue of which one recognizes what is true. Will, as we have seen, is a matter of being drawn to things insofar as one knows them and is attracted to them. So properly human action is a matter of moving voluntarily in the light of recognized ends or goals. To illustrate his point Aquinas distinguishes between human acts (*actiones humanae*) and acts of a human being (*actiones hominis*).[35] The

[31] 3a. 54. 4 ad. 2.
[32] Ibid.
[33] 1a2ae. 22. 3.
[34] 1a2ae. 1. 1.
[35] 1a2ae. 1. 1.

former are free acts proceeding from the will in view of an end apprehended by reason. They involve acting with a definite purpose of which one is aware and to which one is attracted—as when one picks up the telephone to make a call.

Acts are called human inasmuch as they proceed from deliberate willing. Now the object of will is the end and its good, and so it is clear that this is the determining principle of human acts as such.[36]

By contrast, 'acts of a human being' comprise unthinking bits of behaviour such as unthinkingly stroking one's cheek while talking.[37]

For Aquinas the mention of human action brings us to the realm of morality. Indeed, he uses the phrases *actiones humanae* (human actions) and *actus humani vel morales* (human or moral action) almost synonymously. He thinks that, since human actions are undertaken with a purpose, we can evaluate them with reference to their ends and the means employed to achieve them. We will be returning to questions of morality in the next chapter. But here, and in anticipation of what is to come, it is appropriate to note two final elements in Aquinas's treatment of human action. These are his contentions (1) that human actions can be voluntary, and (2) that people can have dispositions.

1. Voluntary Action

We have already seen something of the first contention. Human actions can be voluntary, says Aquinas, because people can act freely. But it is important to distinguish between what Aquinas says about voluntary behaviour and another view of the voluntary sometimes advanced. According to this second view, you need two things for the presence of the voluntary: (1) a mental, interior, invisible process called a volition and (2) a bodily action. Yet this is not how Aquinas sees things. For him, actions are voluntary if they come with a certain context of belief, initiative, and desire on the part of the agent. There is no need for agents to be doing anything over and above what they do with their bodies.

Suppose I am walking to work. As I walk I may have no particular thoughts at all (I may be half asleep), or my mind might be on

---

[36] 1a2ae. 1. 3.
[37] See 1a2ae. 1. 3 and 18. 9.

something quite different from walking (I may be ruminating on the affair I am having with my next-door neighbour). For Aquinas, however, none of this means that I cannot be walking voluntarily. I could, he thinks, be doing just that if I want to get to work, if nothing outside me forces me to do what I am doing, if I know what I am doing, and if I am doing it in order to get to work. Aquinas would say that if all this is true of me, I am walking to work voluntarily. And he would consequently hold that there can be voluntariness even without any action.

That over which we hold mastery is said to be voluntary. And we are the master with respect to acting or not, and to willing or not. Acting and willing are voluntary. So also is not acting and not willing ... Thus there can be voluntariness without an act, sometimes without an external act though with an internal act, as when a person wills not to act, sometimes, however, without even an internal act, as when he does not will to act.[38]

In other words, my will might be involved both (1) if I sit rigid in the chair and decide not to eat the strawberries and (2) if I sit in the chair and do not stop you eating the strawberries.

The fact that Aquinas does not identify voluntary behaviour with the occurrence of bodily behaviour linked to volitions or some mental action can be obscured for us since, in speaking of voluntary behaviour, he often uses the expression 'act of will' (*actus voluntatis*). But *actus* here does not mean 'act' in the sense of 'action done at some time'. It means 'act' as opposed to 'potency' (what could be but is not). For Aquinas, an act of will is what we have when we actually have the voluntary. He holds that all things seek what is good, but people do so in a special way. They have knowledge of what is good and can therefore choose it consciously as a good (unlike a plant, say, which seeks to be itself, and in this sense seeks its good, but does not set its good before itself as a goal to pursue consciously). This human choosing of the good is what Aquinas means by will. According to him, people can perceive what is good and be attracted to it and go for it. When this occurs there is voluntary action.

Whenever a thing so acts or is moved by an inner principle, namely as having some awareness of the end, then it holds within itself the principle of the activity, and not of the acting merely, but of the purposive acting as well ... Those things ... which have some grasp of what an end implies are said to

[38] 1a2ae. 6. 3.

move themselves, because within them lies the source, not only of acting, but also of acting with a purpose. And since on both counts the principle is internal to them, their acts and motions are termed voluntary.[39]

It might be objected that, if such is the case, then non-human animals act voluntarily. But Aquinas accepts this conclusion. On his account, non-human animals do act voluntarily. This is because, unlike stones, say, they have a source of movement inside themselves and can be said to have purposes. But Aquinas adds that we need to distinguish between aiming for a goal and aiming for what one can recognize explicitly as a goal to be achieved by such and such activity. Animals act for an end and have a measure of independence in their behaviour. But they lack the human faculty of reason for recognizing ends as ends. And they lack the ability to reflect on the way to bring about the ends which they desire. So people are capable of a more developed kind of voluntary action than animals.[40]

An implication of this position, one recognized by Aquinas, is that an action might not be voluntary if it is performed in ignorance. Suppose I give Fred a drink of poison while believing that I am giving him a refreshing cup of tea. Aquinas would agree that I am acting voluntarily in the sense that I am voluntarily giving Fred a cup of liquid to drink. But he would say that, in giving Fred this liquid, I am giving Fred poison, and I do not intend to do that even though I intend to give Fred liquid. So I am not voluntarily giving Fred poison. According to Aquinas, actions are subject to different descriptions. One and the same bodily movement might be describable both as giving Fred a drink and as poisoning Fred. How it should be described depends, for Aquinas, on the knowledge of the person whose action we are considering. If someone knows that he is giving Fred poison, and if his aim is to poison Fred, then he poisons Fred voluntarily. If he believes that he is giving Fred a cheering drink, and if his aim is to do just that, then he poisons Fred involuntarily. Notice, however, that Aquinas does not think that ignorance automatically renders what we do involuntary without qualification. For what if the ignorance is attributable to some earlier choice of mine? Suppose, for example, I choose to drive my car while drunk. And suppose that I then kill someone. My excuse might be, 'I did not know that anyone was there.' In Aquinas's view, however, even

[39] 1a2ae. 6. 1.
[40] See 1a2ae. 6. 2.

though I might speak truly here, my killing the person would not be entirely involuntary. For, in choosing to drive while drunk, I was choosing to do the sort of thing which might involve killing people.[41]

In general, Aquinas thinks of voluntary action as action for which the agent has a reason. It is action which is not forced on an agent by the activity of something other than the agent, action in which no violence is done to the agent.

> The violent is directly counter to the voluntary, as also indeed to the natural. For both voluntary and natural activity have this in common, that they well up from an intrinsic source, whereas violent activity is injected by an extrinsic source. Its effect is against the nature of unconscious things, and so likewise against the will of conscious things. That which is against nature is termed unnatural; that which is against will is termed involuntary. Therefore violence makes an act involuntary.[42]

So if my arm is pushed and I consequently hit someone, I do not hit the person voluntarily. I could only be said to hit people voluntarily if hitting them is something I want to do. 'When the will is moved to an object of desire by its own want', says Aquinas, 'its motion is not violent, but voluntary.'[43] This is so, he explains, even though it is true that I can voluntarily do what, in a sense, I do not want to do. Though inclined to carouse all night, I might have a sober evening because I have an early morning appointment the next day. Here, we might say, I do what I do not want to do. According to Aquinas, however, the truth of the matter is that I do something I generally would not want to do because I want something more.

An objector might reply that the more one wants to do something, the less responsible one is in doing it. For would we not say that, for example, someone carried along on a tide of passion is out of control and therefore acting involuntarily? Aquinas, however, takes exactly the opposite line. His view is that I am doing what I want when I am moved by passion. My action is voluntary, and the passion is precisely what makes it voluntary. Hence, for example, he denies that lust renders an action involuntary.

> Lust does not make an action involuntary, but rather the reverse. An object is called voluntary because the will is borne along towards it. By lust the will

---

[41] Cf. 1a2ae. 6. 8.
[42] 1a2ae. 6. 5.
[43] 1a2ae. 6. 4 ad. 2.

bears on the objects of desire. And so its effect is to make an act voluntary rather than involuntary.[44]

2. Dispositions

Concentrating on the picture that voluntary action involves behaviour plus volition can lead one to a very episodic view of human life. It can encourage us to think that, in understanding what people are about, we must forever concentrate on individual and discrete choices being made from moment to moment. Aquinas, however, has a more wide-ranging perspective from which to view human action. He thinks that there are patterns of action to which we tend as individuals, and that our tendencies can be affected or influenced by our past and by choices we make. We do not act in a historical vacuum. We act on the basis of *dispositions*.

What I am calling a 'disposition' Aquinas calls a *habitus*,[45] and, though *habitus* can be translated 'habit', it is better rendered by 'disposition'.[46] For a *habitus* is not a 'habit' in the modern sense. When we speak of people having a habit, we normally imply that they would find it hard not to act in a certain way. Hence, for example, we speak of someone having the habit of smoking. A habit, for us, is a kind of addiction. For Aquinas, however, a *habitus* puts one's activity more under one's control than it might otherwise be. In this sense, to

---

[44] 1a2ae. 6. 7; cf. 1a2ae. 6. 6. Aquinas also allows for the non-voluntary. I might set out to shoot Fred and my shooting him will be voluntary. I might set out to help Fred, but someone might force my hand on to a gun aimed at Fred and make me pull the trigger. In that case I will shoot Fred involuntarily. But another possibility is this: I might have every intention of shooting Fred, and would do so if I had the chance. Yet, mistaking Fred for something else I do not like (a lion, say), I might shoot him in ignorance of what I am actually doing. Here I do something in ignorance which I should have done had I not been in ignorance. Aquinas would say that in this case what I do is non-voluntary (1a2ae. 6. 8).

[45] There is an extended treatment of *habitus* in 1a2ae. 49 ff., which lacks a serious parallel in Aquinas's writings. In the course of these questions Aquinas writes as if he were basically expounding Aristotle, but his own treatment is original in that it develops what basically amount to suggestions in the text of Aristotle.

[46] For a defence of this translation see the Introduction to vol. xxii of the Blackfriars edition of the *Summa theologiae*. A possible objection to the translation is that some authors (e.g. Boethius in his commentary on the *Categories*) use *habitus* and *dispositio* with distinct meanings. I do not find the translation ideal, but I cannot think of a better one. Alternatives such as 'tendency' or 'inclination' are unsatisfactory since they suggest that, by *habitus*, Aquinas is thinking of what we will automatically do, while the truth is that, by and large, he thinks of a *habitus* as falling within the realm of the voluntary.

have a *habitus* is to be disposed to some activity or other—not because one tends to that activity on every possible occasion, but because one finds it natural, readily coped with, an obvious activity to engage in, and so on. In Aquinas's thinking, for example, fluency in a foreign language is a *habitus*. Someone who possesses it may refrain from displaying it for one reason or another. But, when speaking the language, such a person will do so easily and with a proficiency which many lack entirely. Or again, people who are naturally or instinctively generous would, for Aquinas, have a *habitus*. They would be generous without effort. There would be little or no question of 'going against the grain'.

As Anthony Kenny explains, a *habitus*, for Aquinas, is 'half-way between a capacity and an action, between pure potentiality and full actuality'.[47] Suppose you say that I can speak French. Your statement could be true even though I am not speaking French. But it will not be true just because it is possible for me to speak French in some abstract sense. 'Davies can speak French' does not entail that Davies is speaking French at the time the statement is made. On the other hand, however, it entails more than the suggestion that it is logically possible for Davies to speak French (as it is, perhaps, logically possible for a parrot to do so). It entails that Davies has a genuine ability which not everyone has. In this sense, 'Davies can speak French' ascribes to me an ability which endures over time and can, as things are, be exercised in actual definite bits of behaviour. In the thinking of Aquinas, it ascribes to me a *habitus* or disposition. 'A disposition', says Aquinas, quoting Aristotle, 'is a state which is either a good state or a bad state for its possessor either absolutely or relatively.'[48]

For Aquinas, therefore, our actions do not come out of the blue. They are voluntary and they spring from dispositions. And, as we shall see in the next chapter, this, he thinks, means that they are subject to moral evaluation.

[47] Introduction to vol. xxii of the Blackfriars edition of the *Summa theologiae*, xxi.
[48] 1a2ae. 49. 1. The reference is to Aristotle, *Metaphysics*, 5. 20. 1022^{b}10 ff.

12

How to be Happy

AQUINAS thinks of people as creatures with intellect and will, who are drawn to goals which attract them. For him, properly human action (*actiones humanae*), which he also calls 'moral action', is always a voluntary aiming for an end perceived as good. Since he thinks of goodness as perfective or fulfilling, this means that properly human action (or, as we may say, the moral life) is always a movement to what is fulfilling or perfecting of the agent whose movement it is. On Aquinas's account, people by nature desire or are attracted to what perfects and fulfils them, and in this fact lies the foundation of morality. 'Because in all things whatsoever there is an appetite for completion', he says, 'the final end to which each moves marks its own perfect and fulfilling good.'[1]

But what is it that perfects and fulfils human beings? What is really good for them? To put it at its simplest, Aquinas's answer is that we are perfect, fulfilled, and good when we are happy. But to describe his position like that is indeed to simplify. In this chapter, therefore, we shall note its content insofar as he is chiefly speaking of people independently of Christian revelation. In the next chapter we will begin to see how he develops it with an eye on Christianity. Once again, I stress that I am not implying a twofold system in Aquinas. He never thinks of people without thinking of them as creatures loved by God and destined for union with him by virtue of Christ. But he has things to say about human action which do not, in his view, stand or fall by virtue of the truth of Christianity. And it is these things which concern me in this chapter.

Happiness and God

In saying that human goodness lies in happiness, Aquinas does not mean that human fulfilment comes from doing whatever we happen

---

[1] 1a2ae. 1. 5.

to feel like at any particular moment. Happiness, for him, is not a
matter of 'whatever turns you on'. It is something to be understood
while bearing in mind that human life has a goal. It is an objective,
the nature of which might not be at all obvious from consulting our
feelings. In fact, says Aquinas, it is nothing less than God. 'Our
ultimate end', he explains, 'is uncreated good, namely God, who
alone can fill our will to the brim because of his infinite goodness.'[2]

One's first thought here might be that happiness can be gained
from something much less exalted. For we can surely be happy
without reference to God. We can have a good meal and be very
happy because of that. We can enjoy being with people we love. We
can listen to music and delight in the experience. And Aquinas, of
course, does not wish to suggest otherwise. He does not doubt the
value of food, company, music, and so on. But, as he sees it, human
actions are not just directed to this or that end or goal perceived as
good. Whether we realize it or not, they are also performed in pursuit
of an ultimate end or goal. 'Were there no ultimate end', he says,
'nothing would be desired, no activity would be finished, no desire
would come to rest.'[3] In his view, there cannot be endless ends, just
as there cannot be arguments which do not start with premises which
are basic, first, or ultimate. So there must, he thinks, be some final
good at which we aim, for otherwise we would be for ever aiming and
would never be satisfied or at rest. And nothing other than God can
lay claim to this title. He alone deserves to be called 'the final good at
which we aim'.

An objector might reply that our final good lies in material things.
For we do, after all, spend a lot of time trying to acquire them. And
they can certainly give us satisfaction. But, though Aquinas certainly
believes that material things are important and gratifying, he denies
that they are our final good. 'Things which fulfil our natural wants', he
argues (thinking of food, drink, clothes, shelter, transport, and so on),
'are sought for the sake of something else, namely the support of
human life, and so are subordinate to its ultimate end, not the end
itself.'[4] He also denies that human fulfilment lies in honours, fame,
and power. Honours, he argues, are paid to those who have already
achieved some kind of human fulfilment, so they cannot themselves

---

[2] 1a2ae. 3. 1.
[3] 1a2ae. 1. 4.
[4] 1a2ae. 2. 1.

be what human fulfilment ultimately consists in.[5] Nor can such
fulfilment lie in fame or power. Fame, like honour, belongs to those
who are independently fulfilled. It might even arise due to warped
human judgement, which often prizes what is less than truly good.[6]
As for power: Aquinas reasons that it is only a means to an end and
cannot, therefore, be the ultimate end for human beings. 'Because
power is held both for good and ill', one can even be powerful and
bad, from which it would seem to follow that power as such cannot
be ultimately fulfilling for people.[7]

No, says Aquinas. Nothing short of God can satisfy people
completely.

The object of the will, that is the human appetite, is the Good without
reserve, just as the object of the mind is the True without reserve. Clearly,
then, nothing can satisfy our will except such goodness, which is found, not
in anything created, but in God alone. Everything created is a derivative
good.[8]

Why? Aquinas's answer here depends on his view of people. As we
have seen, he thinks that everything naturally seeks its good. But the
good for a given thing will depend on what it is. What is good for a
kangaroo is not necessarily what is good for a mole. And so on for
other examples. With this point in mind, Aquinas maintains that to
see what fulfils people, which means to see what is good for them, we
have to consider what marks them out from other things in the world.
What is it that they are which other things are not? Aquinas thinks
that in noting the answer to this question we will see what really
fulfils them. And, in his view, the one thing that makes people
different from everything else in the world is the fact that they are
able to understand. The characteristic activity of people, he says, is
understanding. We are, by definition, intelligent animals. And from
this fact he concludes that our ultimate good must lie in us understanding, which, for him, means that we cannot be finally satisfied
until we have somehow understood the source and goal of all things,
i.e. God.

Final and perfect happiness can consist in nothing else than the vision of the
divine essence. To make this clear, two points must be observed. First, that

[5] 1a2ae. 2. 2.
[6] 1a2ae. 2. 3.
[7] 1a2ae. 2. 4.
[8] 1a2ae. 2. 8.

people are not perfectly happy so long as something remains for them to desire and seek: secondly, that the perfection of any power is determined by the nature of its object . . . [Now] the intellect attains perfection in so far as it knows the essence of a thing . . . [and] . . . for perfect happiness the intellect needs to reach the very essence of the first cause.[9]

For Aquinas, then, human happiness, properly speaking, is the vision of God. It is the cleaving to God as the mind's all-fulfilling object. This, of course, means that his view of moral action is hardly a secular one. His interpreters have sometimes suggested otherwise on the ground that what he says on this topic is an endorsement of Aristotle, and the suggestion is not entirely silly. His views on moral action are, in general, similar to those of Aristotle, who also speaks of a goal of human action which is perfective and fulfilling. He calls it *eudaemonia*, which is best translated as 'flourishing', but which is often translated as 'happiness'.[10] Yet, while Aristotle concentrates on *eudaemonia* as the ultimate goal for people, Aquinas thinks in terms of *beatitudo*, for which there is no strict equivalent in Aristotle. Aristotle's teaching on human action makes no mention of God (as Aquinas understands the word 'God'), while *beatitudo* involves knowing and enjoying (loving) God. 'Complete happiness (*beatitudo*)', Aquinas writes, 'requires the mind to come through to the essence itself of the first cause. And so it will have its fulfilment by union with God as its object.'[11]

The ultimate perfection of rational or intellectual beings is twofold. In the first place, the perfection they can reach through natural capacities, for this can be called bliss (*beatitudo*) or happiness (*felicitas*) in a sense: thus Aristotle identified our ultimate joy with his highest contemplative activity, that is to say with such knowledge as is possible to the human mind, in this life . . . But beyond this happiness there is yet another, to which we look forward in the future, the joy of seeing God 'as he is'.[12]

---

[9] 1a2ae. 3. 3.

[10] An excellent introduction to Aristotle's moral thinking is J. O. Urmson, *Aristotle's Ethics* (Oxford, 1988). I have pointed out that happiness, for Aquinas, is not simply equivalent to feeling happy, as we tend to understand that expression. In a similar way, as Urmson observes, 'happiness' is a misleading translation of Aristotle's *eudaemonia* since, according to Aristotle, 'to say that somebody is *eudaemon* is the very same thing as to say that he is living a life worth living' and 'is emphatically not to say, as might be the case when one describes somebody as happy, that he is, at the time of speaking, feeling on top of the world, or any other way' (11 f.).

[11] 1a2ae. 3. 8.

[12] 1a. 62. 1.

Happiness and Need

As the last quotation also shows, however, Aquinas does not want to deny that there are things or activities which are objectively good for people before they achieve the vision of God in love. For him, there is a relative or imperfect happiness which people 'can reach through natural capacities', and in pursuing this idea he follows Aristotle quite closely.[13] Both authors believe that people in this life are good insofar as they do what is perfective or fulfilling from a human point of view. And both of them construe 'perfective' and 'fulfilling' in this context to mean 'needful to humans *qua* humans'. The idea here is that there is such a thing as what we might grandly call 'the human project'. According to Aristotle and Aquinas, human beings are things of a particular kind. Considered as such, they have particular needs which they must satisfy in order to function to the extent of their capacities. Reason can perceive these needs and, insofar as people act in the light of reason so as to satisfy them, they act well and are good. Insofar as their reason is impaired, insofar as they neglect these needs, they are diminished or thwarted and, therefore, bad in some respect. Insofar as they function to the extent of their capacities, they are living the best life possible this side of the grave and, in this sense, are happy.

Now when we speak of 'good' and 'evil' in human acts we take the 'reasonable' as our standard of reference; as Dionysius remarks, *our good is to live according to reason and our evil is to live outside it*. For to each thing that is good which is in keeping with its form, and that is evil which is out of keeping with its form . . . Acts indeed are termed 'human' or 'moral' in so far as they issue from reason.[14]

What Aquinas is saying here is that human goodness lies in acting in harmony with what people are by nature insofar as reason can discern this. Our primary moral imperative, you might say, is to recognize what we are and to act accordingly.

---

[13] As Georg Wieland says, 'The theological distinction between perfect and imperfect happiness goes back to William of Auxerre, but it was Thomas who was the first to make it fruitful by treating the concept of happiness in the *Nicomachean Ethics* as a paradigm of imperfect happiness.' See 'Happiness: The Perfection of Man', in Norman Kretzmann, Anthony Kenny, and Jan Pinborg (eds.), *The Cambridge History of Later Medieval Philosophy* (Cambridge, 1982), 679.

[14] 1a2ae. 18. 5.

But this, of course, raises the question 'What actually is perfective or fulfilling for people in this life?' What needs does reason reveal us to have? In the course of his writings Aquinas mentions a number of things as needed for living well. He says, for instance, that to flourish in this world we need food, health, sleep, and friends. We also need to be able to exercise our minds in the contemplation of truth. More generally, however, Aquinas holds that to be good as human beings we need to be skilled at practical reasoning.

Practical Reasoning

I do not mean that he thinks that only clever people can be moral, or that acting morally always involves going through a complicated process of argumentation. He does not believe that human goodness can only be found in those with a university degree or the equivalent. For him, we may say, it is not simply an intellectual or cerebral matter. But he does hold that our judgements concerning properly human actions can be arrived at rationally, and that their logic can be displayed. He does not regard morality as a subjective matter or as nothing but a question of taste, as some philosophers have done. He would not, for instance, have agreed with Hume, who speaks of moral approval and disapproval as springing from 'sentiment' (i.e. feelings and emotions) rather than reason (i.e. our capacity to judge of truth and falsity).[15] Nor would he have endorsed anything like the Emotivist Theory of ethics, which was very influential in the early twentieth century and which saw moral utterances as expressing attitudes and as analogous to exclamations like 'Boo!' and 'Hooray!'[16] Aquinas believes that morality is something with respect to which there are questions of truth and falsity at stake. He thinks that we can reason about it.

According to him, reason is not to be thought of as divisible into parts. But it can, he says, be thought of as working in two ways—

---

[15] David Hume, *Enquiries Concerning Human Understanding and Concerning the Principles of Morals*, ed. L. A. Selby-Bigge (3rd edn., Oxford, 1975) 294.

[16] See J. O. Urmson, *The Emotive Theory of Ethics* (London, 1968). The Emotive Theory is especially associated with C. K. Ogden and I. A. Richards (*The Meaning of Meaning* (London, 1923)) and C. L. Stevenson (*Ethics and Language* (New Haven, Conn., 1944)). See also A. J. Ayer, *Language, Truth and Logic* (1st edn., 1936; 2nd edn., London, 1946).

namely theoretically (or speculatively) and practically (in a way concerned with action). He also holds that there is a parallel between 'speculative reasoning' (*ratio speculativa*) and practical reasoning, or reasoning about moral matters (*ratio operativa/ratio practica*). In speculative reasoning, he thinks, we proceed from premisses known to be true without argument to conclusions which follow from them. The same, he says, is also the case with practical reasoning, which for him is embodied in what he calls the 'practical syllogism' (*syllogismus operativus*).

1. Synderesis

For Aquinas, practical reasoning starts with general principles immediately recognized by the intellect as true. An example he gives is, 'Good is to be done and evil avoided.' These principles are grasped by virtue of what he calls 'synderesis', which he thinks of as a disposition. According to him, knowledge of fundamental moral principles, like all knowledge, arises as a result of sense experience. So he does not think of it as innate, if that is taken to mean that people are just born knowing fundamental moral principles. But, for him, *synderesis* is more than a bare capacity. To say that people can understand and assent to the first principles of morality is to say more than that it is logically possible for them to do so, or that they can do so from time to time if they so choose. It is to say that they have a natural tendency to do so at any time. As Timothy Potts explains, according to Aquinas, *synderesis* 'is a natural disposition of the human mind by which we apprehend the·basic principles of behaviour, parallel to that by which we apprehend the basic principles of theoretical disciplines, and in both cases these principles are apprehended without inquiry'.[17] Or, as Aquinas himself writes:

Just as there is a natural disposition of the human mind by which it apprehends the principles of theoretical disciplines, which we call the understanding of principles, so too it has a natural disposition concerned with the basic principles of behaviour... This disposition relates to *synderesis*... We may therefore conclude that '*synderesis*' either names a natural disposition, without qualification, comparable to the disposition by which theoretical principles are apprehended, or names the potentiality of reason endowed with such a disposition.[18]

[17] Kretzmann, Kenny, and Pinborg, *Cambridge History*, 700.
[18] *De ver.* 16. 1.

And, for Aquinas, *synderesis* is infallible. Why? Not because, as some philosophers have urged, people have an ability to recognize that they know basic moral principles by having a look inside themselves and considering their state of mind. Aquinas does not think of *synderesis* as a kind of self-guaranteeing awareness which one can identify as knowledge simply in the having of it. His view is that if *synderesis* is not infallible, then there could be no body of knowledge. To quote Potts again, his argument is that 'the whole edifice of knowledge whether theoretical or practical, rests upon basic principles, so that, if we could be wrong about these, nothing would be certain'.[19] In Aquinas's words:

Nature, in all its works, aims at what is good and at the maintenance of whatever comes about through the working of nature. Hence, in all the works of nature, its first principles are always permanent and unchangeable and conserve right order, because first principles must endure ... For there could be no stability or certainty in what results from the first principles, unless the first principles were solidly established. Anything which is variable goes back, accordingly, to some first fixed thing. So it is, also, that every particular apprehension comes from some absolutely certain apprehension about which there can be no mistake. This is apprehension of basic general principles, by reference to which all particular apprehensions are tested and in virtue of which everything true wins approval but everything false is rejected. If any mistake could occur about these, then there could be no certainty in the entire subsequent apprehension. Hence, in order that there can be some rightness in human deeds, there must be some enduring principle which has unchangeable rightness and by reference to which all deeds are tested, such that this enduring principle resists everything evil and gives assent to everything good. This is what *synderesis* is, whose job it is to murmur back in reply to evil and to turn us towards what is good. Hence, it is to be admitted that it cannot do wrong.[20]

So the mind, says Aquinas, can directly grasp certain general moral principles. But these principles need to be applied as we find ourselves in concrete circumstances. Aquinas therefore recognizes a stage in practical reasoning to which he gives the name 'conscience' (*conscientia*).

---

[19] Timothy Potts, *Conscience in Medieval Philosophy*, (Cambridge, 1980), 48.
[20] *De ver.* 16. 2.

2. Conscience

The most famous philosophical account of conscience is probably that of Joseph Butler (1692–1752). According to him:

There is a superior principle of reflection or conscience in everyone, which distinguishes between the internal principles of our heart, as well as our external actions: which passes judgment upon ourselves and them; pronounces determinately some actions to be in themselves just, right, good; others to be in themselves evil, wrong, unjust.[21]

As D. J. O'Connor observes, conscience, on this account, is 'intuitive and authoritative'. 'It distinguishes right from wrong without argument and directs us to the one and away from the other. It serves to detect moral values as our senses detect sensory differences and has, for that reason, often been referred to as a "moral sense".'[22] But this is not how Aquinas thinks of conscience. For him it is nothing like a 'moral sense' picking out right and wrong as a torch might light up some objects. It is a process of reasoning.

First, he says, we start with principles grasped by virtue of *synderesis*. Then we add judgements about what sort of actions we are thinking about on any given occasion. We might, for example, judge that such and such an act is a case of theft. Finally, we draw a conclusion concerning the goodness or badness of the act in question. This drawing of the conclusion is what Aquinas means by 'conscience' (*conscientia*). For him, therefore, conscience consists of applying general principles to the case in hand and with recognition of what kind of action we are dealing with. The work of conscience is to use principles grasped by *synderesis* to determine what is to be done, or whether what we have done is right or wrong.

Reason directs human action with two types of knowledge, general knowledge and knowledge of particulars. In deciding to act, the mind constructs a syllogism the conclusion of which is a judgment or a choice. Actions exist in individual situations. Hence, the conclusion of this practical syllogism is singular. We cannot conclude to a particular application of a general premise unless the situation fits the general definition, e.g. to avoid par-

---

[21] *Fifteen Sermons*, quoted from D. D. Raphael (ed.), *British Moralists 1650–1800* (Oxford, 1969), i. 351.

[22] D. J. O'Connor, *Aquinas and Natural Law*, in W. D. Hudson (ed.), *New Studies in Ethics*, i. (London, 1974), 121.

ricide someone would have to know not only that it was wrong but also that the intended victim was that person's father. Ignorance of either of these truths would be the cause of an act of parricide; one would be ignorance of a general principle by which reason is directed, the other would be ignorance of a particular circumstance.[23]

In other words, first one recognizes (by *synderesis*) that murdering one's father is bad. Second one recognizes that some action is a case of murdering one's father. Finally, by conscience one concludes that this action is bad.[24]

In terms of Aquinas's thinking, however, conscience is not a moral virtue. It is simply the judgement we may come to on a piece of our behaviour in the light of various rational considerations. It is a matter of thinking (in the sense of reflecting and judging) rather than willing (i.e. wanting), and it might therefore fail to result in good action (just as a clever person can be a bad person). According to Aquinas, one can by conscience judge that such and such an action is evil, and still do it. He also thinks that by conscience one can even be led to do what is objectively wrong, even though one does not wish to do wrong, and even though one may wish to do nothing but right. Conscience, for Aquinas, is not infallible. It is a process of reasoning, and, like any such process, it can result in mistaken conclusions if its premisses are false or if it fails to be valid.

I have argued that *conscientia* is no other than the application of knowledge to some special actualization. Mistakes can occur in two ways in this application: first, because what is applied contains a mistake; second, because it is not applied properly. In the same way, mistakes in reasoning can occur in two ways: either because some false [premise] is used, or because one does not reason correctly.[25]

Even though he insists on this point, however, Aquinas also maintains that one ought to do what, by conscience, one believes one ought to do, even if what conscience tells one to do is objectively wrong. 'We should', he declares, 'state quite simply that every act of will against reason, whether in the right or in the wrong, is always bad.'[26] By this he does not mean that it is bad to act unreasonably

---

[23] 1a2ae. 76. 1.
[24] Note, however, that Aquinas does not think that when we make moral judgements on given occasions we are necessarily going through a process of reasoning which takes time. His view is that if we are really good we might decide rightly in a kind of instinctive way and then be hard pressed to spell out our reasoning.
[25] *De ver.* 17. 2.   [26] 1a2ae. 19. 5.

(though he believes this). He means that if one's reason tells one that such and such ought to be done, then one should do it, whether or not a more informed perspective would show that it should not be done. He means that a mistaken conscience is binding. He even goes so far as to say that should one's reason tell one to deny Christ, then that is what one should actually do, even though to do so is to do something bad.[27]

3. *Acting Morally*

From this last point it should be clear that Aquinas is not of the opinion that goodness in action is simply determined by what we might call a 'good intention', i.e. the belief that one is doing what is right. Nor does he think, as, for example, Peter Abelard famously did, that the actions we perform are morally neutral or indifferent and 'are called good or evil only on account of the intention of their agent'.[28] For Abelard, though an action is not right just because one believes it to be so, merit and praise accrue to people for their intentions, not for their actions. Aquinas's position, however, is more complex.

To begin with, he seems to concede that hard and fast rules are none too easily available as yardsticks against which to measure the rightness or wrongness of particular actions in precise situations. He is clear enough that certain kinds of action are always wrong or evil in kind—killing the innocent, for example. But he also thinks that error is possible in practical reasoning and that moral agents must, in the end, make up their own minds and decide what to do.

Since discourse on moral matters even in their universal aspects is subject to uncertainty and variation it is all the more uncertain if one wishes to descend to bringing doctrine to bear on individual cases in specific detail, for this cannot be dealt with by either art or precedent. Therefore judgement concerning individual cases must be left to the prudence of each person.[29]

Without wishing to deny this point, however, Aquinas also affirms that every action we actually perform is either morally good or morally bad in that anything we do either helps us to our ultimate

---

[27] 1a2ae. 19. 5.
[28] *Peter Abelard's Ethics*, ed. D. E. Luscombe (Oxford, 1971), xxxii; cf. 53.
[29] *In Eth.* 2. 2.

good or hinders us from achieving it. To be sure, he concedes, we can speak of there being types of action which are morally neutral: plucking a blade of grass, for instance.[30] But in day-to-day life we must choose particular actions, not types of actions considered in the abstract. And these, he says, are never morally neutral.

Since it is the office of reason to control, if an act issuing from deliberate reason is not shaped by due purpose it will be against reason, and will have the character of evil, while if it is so shaped it will accord with reasonable order and have the character of good. A human act is bound to be one or the other, that is either having or not having this direction towards a fitting end.[31]

So we need to consider what is required for an action to be good. And intention, for Aquinas, is only one necessary factor. It is, he insists, certainly necessary. For an action to be good, he thinks, it must be one in which one is willing a good end. But, he also holds that, though I must aim at what is good in order for my action to be good (i.e. though good intention is a *necessary* condition of an action being morally good), my action need not be good just because I aim at what is good (i.e. good intention is not a *sufficient* condition of an action being morally good). For my action to be good, says Aquinas, it must be a good kind of thing to do, and it must be done in appropriate circumstances.

Suppose I give Fred some food. That, we might say, is a good kind of thing to do. But suppose I do it because I want to gain his confidence in order to gain access to his house and rob him. Then, Aquinas would say, I do not have a good intention and my action is not good.

Or again, suppose I read the *Summa theologiae* with care and a desire to learn. That, too, might be regarded as a good thing to do, and it seems that I do it with a good intention. But what if I am doing it while someone is dying of hunger beside me and begging me for food which I can easily provide? Then, Aquinas would hold, my action is not good because of the circumstances in which it is performed.

Aristotle says that *virtuous people act as they ought and when they ought, and so forth according to other circumstances* [*Ethics*, 2. 3. 1104ᵇ26]. And so con-

---

[30] 1a2ae. 18. 8.
[31] 1a2ae. 18. 9.

trariwise vicious people act according to their vice when they ought not and where they ought not and so forth in other circumstances. Therefore by their circumstances human actions are good or bad.[32]

Virtues

In this sense, then, Aquinas holds that we can be properly guided in our actions by reason. By *synderesis* we can know general moral principles, and we can apply them to cases at hand. But Aquinas does not believe that the use of reason alone is sufficient to ensure that people are truly good or that they live a truly moral life. For that, he says, we need virtues.

1. Virtues in General

In the *Summa theologiae* Aquinas turns directly to the topic of virtue in 1a2ae. 55 ff., where he says that any virtue (*virtus*) is 'a good quality of mind by which one lives righteously, of which no one can make bad use'.[33] The definition by itself may not seem very illuminating, but it is easy to indicate what Aquinas is driving at. For him, virtues are what, in the last chapter, I called 'dispositions'. They are abilities, tendencies, or capacities which make it easy for us to do certain things or to behave in certain ways. But they are not just any old kind of disposition. For Aquinas, there can be bad dispositions leading us to act in ways which do not perfect us or help us to states of well-being of which we are capable as human beings. Virtues, by contrast, are good dispositions. They are abilities, tendencies, or capacities which help us to act in ways which contribute to our flourishing, or to our functioning to our best advantage, so that our needs as people are satisfied. 'Virtue', says Aquinas, 'is a *habitus* which is always for good.'[34] It 'is a *habitus* by which a person acts well'.[35]

Another way he makes the point is to say that virtue is a certain perfection of a power and therefore an 'operative *habitus*'. For him,

---

[32] 1a2ae. 18. 3.
[33] 1a2ae. 55. 4.
[34] 1a2ae. 55. 4.
[35] 1a2ae. 56. 3.

people can be said to have various powers or faculties since they are things of a certain kind functioning in certain characteristic ways.[36] In particular, and in distinction to other animals, they have the powers of understanding and willing (or appetite), which Aquinas calls 'intellectual powers' and which, in his view, can be trained so as to work well rather than badly. Insofar as these intellectual powers are aided by dispositions (*habitus*) leading them to work to the advantage of the human agent, then, he says, virtue is present. So virtue is present when understanding and will operate under the influence of good dispositions so as to enable someone to bring about what is really perfective of that person.

Virtue denotes a determinate perfection of a power ... Now there are some powers which according to their very natures are set towards their acts, such as inborn active powers ... The rational powers, proper to people, however, are not determined to one act, but in themselves are poised before many. It is through habits (*per habitus*) that they are set towards acts ... Human virtues, therefore, are habits (*habitus sunt*).[37]

One might put it by saying that virtues, for Aquinas, are learned responses by which we naturally act well. Some people, he notes, are congenitally predisposed to certain good ways of behaving.

There are some rudimentary appetitive dispositions which are natural to individuals on account of their bodies. Some people, for instance, are disposed by their bodily constitution to chastity, others to mildness of temper, and so on.[38]

In general, however, people, for Aquinas, need acquired dispositions in order to be good. And it is of such dispositions that he is thinking when he speaks about virtues.

Aquinas distinguishes between three kinds of virtues, of which only two need concern us for the moment. These are 'intellectual virtues' and 'moral virtues'. The first have to do with recognizing what is good. The second have to do with tending to what is recognized as good (with appetite).

2. *Intellectual Virtues*

Under the heading of 'intellectual virtues', Aquinas acknowledges three virtues of what he calls 'speculative intellect', and two virtues

---

[36] See 1a. 77 ff.
[37] 1a2ae. 55. 1; cf. 1a2ae. 55. 2.   [38] 1a2ae. 51. 1.

of 'practical intellect'. By 'speculative intellect' he means the mind as understanding at a purely theoretical level, and, under this heading, he distinguishes between 'understanding' (*intellectus*), 'science' (*scientia*), and 'wisdom' (*sapientia*). By 'practical intellect' he means the mind as understanding with a view to action. Under this heading he distinguishes between 'art' (*ars*) and 'prudence' (*prudentia*). 'Understanding' is a matter of grasping basic principles of reasoning. 'Science' is a matter of good reasoning using these principles to arrive at truth regarding different kinds of things in the world. 'Wisdom' is a matter of good reasoning concerning God. 'Art' is correct reason about things to be made. 'Prudence' is correct reason about things to be done and aims at the good of the agent.[39]

Strictly speaking, says Aquinas, there is a sense in which some intellectual virtues are not really virtues. Someone with wisdom, science, and understanding, for instance, need not actually do anything, while, according to Aquinas, a *habitus* 'may be called a virtue for two reasons: first, because it gives the capability of functioning well; secondly, because together with this, it effectively ensures a right performance'.[40] In other words, someone with a virtue is not just *able to act* well. Such a person actually *does act* well.

Yet, Aquinas argues, we can still speak of virtue with respect to dispositions of speculative intellect since 'they make us capable of a good activity, namely to consider the truth, which is a good work for the intellect'.[41] And we can certainly, he adds, think of prudence as being more than something intellectual. Prudence is 'right reason about things to be done' and, on that account, it is intellectual.[42] But its presence in people means that they are actually drawn to right ends of action. It involves the engagement of the will and is not just a judgement for the will to obey if the one who has will has intelligence enough to recognize the judgement. Considered as such, it is absolutely indispensable for human well-being.

One way of bringing out what Aquinas is getting at here is to stress that prudence, for him, is different from cunning. In theoretical reasoning, he says, one can argue well without reaching a true conclusion and without even being concerned to reach one. One might

---

[39] 1a2ae. 57. 2 ff.
[40] 1a2ae. 57. 1.
[41] Ibid.
[42] 1a2ae. 57. 4; cf. 2a2ae. 47. 1.

validly argue from false premises to a false conclusion, and one might do so deliberately (e.g. to hoodwink someone). The same, he thinks, is true with respect to practical reasoning. For one can reason well with warped goals and without aiming at what is really good. Just as valid but non-knowledge-producing reasoning can exist in theoretical reasoning, says Aquinas, so cogent but non-good-attaining reasoning (i.e. cunning) can exist in practical reasoning. For the good to be attained, therefore, something more than mere cleverness is needed. Prudence is required.

Prudence is a virtue of the utmost necessity for human life. To live well means acting well. In order to perform an act well, it is not merely what people do that matters, but also how they do it, namely that they act from right choice and not merely from impulse or passion. Since, however, choice is about means to an end, rightness of choice necessarily involves two factors, namely a due end and something suitably ordained to that due end . . . For people to be rightly adapted to what fits their due end, however, they need a *habitus* in their reason; because counsel and choice, which are about things ordained to an end, are acts of reason. Consequently, an intellectual virtue is needed in their reason to complement it and make it well adjusted to these things. This virtue is prudence. And this, in consequence, is necessary for a good life.[43]

Prudence is important since it is the virtue which actually disposes us to think well about what to do. It is the developed disposition to deliberate well, to decide well, and to execute actions well. For this reason, Aquinas also lists it among what he calls 'moral virtues'.[44]

3. Moral Virtues

In speaking of moral virtues Aquinas says that they are named from the Latin word *mos* where that means 'a natural or quasi-natural

---

[43] 1a2ae. 57. 5.

[44] In 'Aquinas on Good Sense' (*New Blackfriars*, 67 (1986)) Herbert McCabe interestingly suggests that Aquinas's *prudentia* is very much what Jane Austen means by 'good sense'. By way of illustration he writes: 'Elizabeth Bennett is shown as having and growing in good sense, in contrast both to the silliness of her younger sisters, who think of nothing beyond present pleasures and, on the other hand, to the pedantry of her elder sister Mary, who thinks that book learning is enough. She also stands in contrast to her witty and perceptive but almost purely voyeuristic father, who uses his intelligence to survey a life in which he refuses to become involved. Finally, there is a contrast with her friend Charlotte, who succumbs to worldly wisdom and marries the dreadful Mr Collins for "prudential" reasons. All these people are presented as *morally* inferior (and thus ultimately unhappy) because they lack good sense' (419 f.).

inclination to do some particular action'.[45] So he is thinking about dispositions which lead one to act well, and not of those which might enable one to act well only if one chooses to.

For people to act well, it is requisite that not only their reason be well disposed through a *habitus* of intellectual virtue, but also that their appetite be well disposed through a *habitus* of moral virtue.[46]

That is to say, knowledge is not enough to make people fully virtuous or good as people. As I mentioned above, it is not Aquinas's view that you are good just because you are clever or quick witted. You may have doctorates from Oxford and Yale, but you might not be good. You also have to act in the light of what you know, which means that you must be engaged at the level of will as well as intellect, that you must actually pursue or be drawn to what you see to be good— which, for Aquinas, is where prudence comes in again.

As we have seen, prudence, as he understands it, is more than a matter of knowledge. 'The worth of prudence', he explains, 'consists not in thought merely, but in its application to action' and is therefore practical as well as theoretical.[47] In this sense, therefore, it is a moral virtue as well as an intellectual one.

The role of prudence is to charge our conduct with right reason, and this cannot be done without rightful desire. And so prudence has the nature of virtue, not only that which the other intellectual virtues possess, but also that possessed by the moral virtues, among which it is counted.[48]

Or as Aquinas writes in another place:

Prudence means more than practical knowledge. That has to do with making a general judgement about what to do, as when one sees that fornication is bad or that it is wrong to steal and so on. Even where this knowledge exists, the judgement of reason can be intercepted in a particular action so that it does not judge properly. So prudence is equally a matter of virtue because with knowledge alone someone may sin against virtue.[49]

Indeed, Aquinas maintains, prudence is at work whenever the other virtues are. For virtue, in general, helps us to act well and prudence

[45] 1a2ae. 58. 1.
[46] 1a2ae. 58. 2.
[47] 2a2ae. 47. 1 ad. 3.
[48] 2a2ae. 47. 4.
[49] *De virt.* 6 ad. 1.

is displayed by actually acting well. 'Nobody can be virtuous without possessing prudence . . . The other virtues can never be true virtues unless their seeking is prudently conducted.'[50] Aquinas does not want to say that somebody who lacks some intellectual virtues cannot be morally good. He thinks that a person can be morally good without wisdom, science, and art. But he does not think that anyone can be morally good without choosing well in action. And choosing well, for him, depends on acting in accordance with prudence.

People may be virtuous without their reason being vigorous as to everything, but merely as to those things which have to be done virtuously. And to this extent all virtuous people use reason soundly. Hence even those who seem to be simple, by their lack of worldly shrewdness, can be prudent.[51]

As for other moral virtues, Aquinas maintains that the major, principle (or, as he puts it, 'cardinal') ones are justice, temperance, and courage. People live in society with others, so they need to deal rightly with others. They therefore need justice, which Aquinas defines as 'the *habitus* whereby a person with a lasting and constant will renders to each his due'.[52] People are also subject to physical desires (for food, drink, and sex) as well as to fear of danger or death. They therefore, Aquinas adds, need temperance or fortitude. Their desires must be governed by a *habitus* inclining them to suitable moderation (hence temperance) and their fear must be governed by an ability to stand up to danger and to act effectively in the face of it (hence fortitude).[53]

Natural Law

Although Aquinas has much more to say on the topic of 'relative happiness' or goodness as we can achieve it in this life, we have now seen the substance of his teaching on the matter. So far, however, I have said nothing of what, for many, is the most important feature of his moral thinking, namely his concept of natural law. That is largely because it adds very little to what I have already expounded. To

---

[50] 2a2ae. 47. 14.
[51] 1a2ae. 58. 4 ad. 2.
[52] 2a2ae. 58. 1.
[53] Aquinas discusses temperance at length in 2a2ae. 141 ff. He deals with fortitude in 2a2ae. 23.

complete the picture, however, we had better look at it briefly before moving on.

The notion of natural law has a long history stretching back to authors of Greek and Roman times, authors such as Aristotle, Cicero, and Augustine.[54] It also has a long and complicated background in the work of ancient and medieval legal writers.[55] But its content, as Aquinas develops it, is fundamentally simple and amounts to the view that, by using our reason and reflecting on our nature as people, we can come to formulate general principles of action. As Ralph McInerny observes:

This for Thomas is the peculiar mark of the human agent, that he puts his mind to what he does and consciously directs himself to the goods he recognizes as fulfilling of him ... From the nature of the human agent so considered we can formulate great ungainsayable truths about the human good. Such truths are implicit in any particular decision; their articulation is of value since they suggest that, despite the contingency and continuous alteration of the circumstances in which we act, despite the historical changes which make one century so different from another, there are absolutes of human action: some goods which will ever be constitutive of the human moral ideal, some kinds of action which are always destructive of the human good. This is the conviction that Thomas develops in his theory of natural law.[56]

For Aquinas, natural law is grounded on principles grasped by means of *synderesis*. Using these principles, and noting what is perfective and fulfilling of people in general, we can, he thinks, lay down guide-lines for human behaviour.

The precepts of natural law are to human conduct what the first principles of thought are to demonstration ... Every agent acts on account of an end, and to be an end carries the meaning of to be good. Consequently the first principle for the practical reason is based on the meaning of good, namely that it is what all things seek after. And so this is the first command of law, 'that good is to be sought and done, evil to be avoided'; all other commands of natural law are based on this. Accordingly, then, natural-law commands

---

[54] For an account of Aquinas's predecessors *vis-à-vis* natural law see Patrick M. Farrell, OP, 'Sources of St. Thomas' Concept of Natural Law', *Thomist*, 20 (July 1967). See also 'Natural Morality and Natural Law' by D. E. Luscombe, in Kretzmann, Kenny, and Pinborg, *Cambridge History*.

[55] See Luscombe, 'Natural Morality and Natural Law'.

[56] Ralph McInerny, *Ethica Thomistica* (Washington, DC, 1982), 124.

extend to all doing or avoiding of things recognized by the practical reason of itself as being human goods.[57]

Having respected principles acquired by *synderesis*, we can proceed to note in what our perfection lies and, on that basis, we can formulate precepts concerning our behaviour.

The order in which commands of the law of nature are ranged corresponds to that of our natural tendencies. Here there are three stages. There is in people, first, a tendency towards the good of the nature they have in common with all substances; each has an appetite to preserve its own natural being. Natural law here plays a corresponding part, and is engaged at this stage to maintain and defend the elementary requirements of human life. Secondly, there is in people a bent towards things which accord with their nature considered more specifically, that is in terms of what they have in common with other animals; correspondingly those matters are said to be of natural law which nature teaches all animals, for instance the coupling of male and female, the bringing up of the young, and so forth. Thirdly, there is in people an appetite for the good of their nature as rational, and this is proper to them, for instance, that they should know truths about God and about living in society. Correspondingly whatever this involves is a matter of natural law, for instance that people should shun ignorance, not offend others with whom they ought to live in civility, and other such related requirements.[58]

The idea here is that human beings are fulfilled or made happy in ways which can be seen by noting what they are (including how they act and what they are drawn to) and that practical reason can therefore be used to indicate how, in general, they should behave.

For Aquinas, then, natural law is what reason tells us to do or to avoid in order to function well as people. It is not, he explains, a detailed list of instructions for acting in the multitude of different circumstances in which people might find themselves. It is not a table of rules for acting in every situation. It is a framework within which people can make particular choices on particular occasions in particular circumstances. And for this reason it needs to be supplemented by sound practical reasoning, the working of conscience, and by what Aquinas calls 'human law', i.e. institutional legislation ('laws of the land') designed to promote the well-being of people in concrete societies.

---

[57] 1a2ae. 94. 2.
[58] 1a2ae. 94. 2.

Law is a kind of dictate of the practical reason. Now the processes of the theoretic and practical reasons are parallel; both, as we have held, start from certain principles and come to certain conclusions. Accordingly we say this, that just as from indemonstrable principles that are instinctively recognized the theoretic reason draws the conclusions of the various sciences not imparted by nature but discovered by reasoned effort, so also from natural law precepts as from common and indemonstrable principles the human reason comes down to making more specific arrangements. Now these particular arrangements human reason arrives at are called 'human laws', provided they fulfil the essential conditions of law already stated.[59]

The back-reference here is to 1a2ae. 90. 4 where Aquinas concludes that 'Law is nought else than an ordinance of reason for the common good made by the authority who has care of the community and promulgated.' So his argument is that from natural law we can derive laws governing society, laws which aim at the good of society and which are promulgated somehow. This, in turn, means that, according to Aquinas, human law derives from natural law.

Does natural law derive from anything? Is there a law which is in any sense 'above' it or superior to it? If we are thinking in terms of a code or list of precepts, Aquinas's answer is 'No'. But in one sense his answer is 'Yes', because natural law, for him, falls under, or is grounded on, what he calls 'Eternal Law', which is nothing less than God himself.

As we saw in Chapter 5, in his scheme of things, the natures of created things derive from God and their goodness is what he intends for them. With this point in mind, he holds that all creatures are ruled or governed by what is in God, and therefore by what is God (on the now familiar principle that everything in God is God). And in this sense, he suggests, we can speak of them as governed by Eternal Law, for God himself is eternal.

Law is nothing but a dictate of practical reason issued by a sovereign who governs a complete community. Granted that the world is ruled by divine Providence ... it is evident that the whole community of the universe is governed by God's mind. Therefore the ruling idea of things which exists in God as the effective sovereign of them all has the nature of law. Then since God's mind does not conceive in time, but has an eternal concept ... it follows that this law should be called eternal ... Through his wisdom God is the founder of the universe of things, and ... in relation to them he is like an

---

[59] 1a2ae. 91. 3.

artist with regard to the things he makes ... [Also] he is the governor of all acts and motions to be found in each and every creature. And so, as being the principle through which the universe is created, divine wisdom means art, or exemplar, or idea, and likewise it also means law, as moving all things to their due ends. Accordingly the Eternal Law is nothing other than the exemplar of divine wisdom as directing the motions and acts of everything.[60]

In other words, since our world is God's world, all things are subject to him and to his will. As ruler of the universe, God governs all things, and the plan by which he does so is a kind of law, though not one conceived in time. It is, furthermore, a law which everything obeys simply by existing and being as God wills.

However, Aquinas adds, there is a sense in which rational agents with freedom can participate in God's will for them in a way that non-rational things cannot. And here, once again, he refers to natural law.

Since all things are regulated and measured by Eternal Law ... it is evident that all somehow share in it, in that their tendencies to their own proper acts and ends are from its impression. Among them intelligent creatures are ranked under divine Providence the more nobly because they take part in Providence by their own providing for themselves and others. Thus they join in and make their own the Eternal Reason through which they have their natural aptitudes for their due activity and purpose. Now this sharing in the Eternal Law by intelligent creatures is what we call 'natural law'.[61]

Since people act as voluntary agents, Aquinas is saying, they are subject to God as creatures able to seek their good by moral activity.[62] This, in turn, means that there is a sense in which they share in God's governance of things. For they can will that for themselves and not just have it imposed on them. They, so to speak, can share in God's planning.

---

[60] 1a2ae. 91. 1 and 91. 3.

[61] 1a2ae. 91. 2.

[62] Can one construct a genuinely Thomistic account of natural law without reference to God? In *Natural Law and Natural Rights* (Oxford, 1980), John Finnis suggests that one can. But, as Alasdair MacIntyre observes, religion is a moral virtue for Aquinas since it is part of justice. And Aquinas, as we have seen, holds that the true goal for human beings is nothing less than God. 'It follows that human beings who fail to discover what their true good and happiness consist in will be perpetually balked and frustrated ... Subtract the goodness of God, as it is understood in the *Prima Pars*, from Aquinas's account, and what is left is not Aristotle, but a radically truncated version of the *Nicomachean Ethics* ...' (*Whose Justice? Which Rationality?* (London, 1988), 192 f.). One may be able to construct a theory of natural law analogous to Aquinas's without mentioning God. But it will not be a genuinely Thomistic theory.

As we have seen, though, Aquinas does not think that the final good for people is something which they can attain to in this life. For him, complete human happiness lies in the vision of God. So it now seems appropriate to start considering how he thinks that this is reached.

13

How to be Holy

At the beginning of Chapter 11 I said that Aquinas thinks of the Trinity as something in whose life we may come to share. The Trinity has dropped out of my account of Aquinas's teaching since then, but we can now begin to connect what he says about people in general with his teaching concerning the Trinity. More precisely, we can now start to see why belief in the Trinity is, for him, more than what I earlier called 'a complicated bit of speculative celestial physics'. To put it very simply, his position is that the Trinity makes us divine since God, who is Father, Son, and Holy Spirit, brings us to the final or ultimate good or end of rational creatures, which is nothing less than God himself. For Aquinas, the Trinity is not just a fact from eternity, so to speak. It is the means of human redemption and deification. It is God in love with us making us his friends.

The Human End and Human Nature

To appreciate what Aquinas intends by that suggestion we can start with his claim that God is the means by which we can be better than we are when considered as merely human. As we have seen, he thinks that people can attain a limited and partial happiness simply by being human. We can link up with Aristotle in the quest for human excellence, and we can fulfil ourselves to some degree by means of acquired moral virtues. As we have also seen, however, Aquinas does not think that this will give us perfect happiness. For that, he says, we need *beatitudo*, or a union of mind and will with God.

The ultimate happiness of people lies in their highest activity, which is the exercise of their minds. If therefore the created mind were never able to see the essence of God, either it would never attain happiness or its happiness would consist in something other than God.[1]

---

[1] Ia. 12. 1.

Is there any guarantee of such union coming about? In Aquinas's view, philosophy can tell us that God exists, that the world has a maker and sustainer. It can also tell us something about human life in general, about what makes people different from other things, about their basic human needs and so on. But that is as far as it can go. And from this, says Aquinas, it follows that we will not get directly to God unless he, so to speak, reaches out to us.

It is impossible that any created mind should see the essence of God by its own natural powers . . . Only to the divine intellect is it connatural to know subsistent existence itself. This is beyond the scope of any created understanding, for no creature *is* its existence, it has a share in existence. Hence no created mind can see the essence of God unless he by grace joins himself to that mind as something intelligible to it.[2]

When this occurs, says Aquinas, human beings become more than merely human. He does not, of course, think that they stop being human. They do not turn into things of another kind. But knowledge of God's essence is, for Aquinas, a special form of God's presence. In this sense, it is a deification of the knower.

It is not surprising that Aquinas should speak in such terms, for the language of deification is found in the New Testament. The author of 1 John looks to the culmination of salvation history by observing: 'Beloved, we are God's children now; it does not yet appear what we shall be, but we shall be like him, for we shall see him as he is.'[3] In similar vein, the author of 2 Peter writes:

His divine power has granted to us all things that pertain to life and godliness, through the knowledge of him who called us to his own glory and excellence, by which he has granted to us his precious and very great promises, that through these you may escape from the corruption that is in the world because of passion, and become partakers of the divine nature.[4]

The notion of deification is also very much present in patristic writers, in authors such as Irenaeus (*c.*130–*c.*200), Athanasius (*c.*296–373), Basil the Great (*c.*330–79), Gregory of Nazianzus (329–89), Gregory of Nyssa (*c.*330–*c.*395), and Cyril of Alexandria (d. 444). It is a notable feature of St Augustine's thinking as well.[5]

---

[2] 1a. 12. 5.
[3] 1 John 3: 2.
[4] 2 Pet. 1: 3 f.
[5] See Patricia Wilson-Kastner, 'Grace as Participation in the Divine Life in the Theology of Augustine of Hippo', *Augustinian Studies*, 7 (1978).

Though these sources are undoubtedly an influence on him, however, Aquinas also has his own reasons for speaking as he does about
people and the result of them being one with God.

Here we need to remember his teaching that understanding occurs
in people as the forms of things are received immaterially in the
mind—that to know what a thing is means having what it takes to be
the thing, without actually being the thing itself. This, says Aquinas,
is just as much the case when the object of knowledge is God as it is
when the object is something else. In this life, he thinks, we do not
have a direct knowledge of God as an object of sensory experience,
so there is nothing we can call 'knowledge of God' which compares,
for example, with our knowledge of horses. There is no form of God
existing in matter which is raised to a level of meaning by its reception immaterially in the mind. With direct knowledge of God by
grace, however, there is, says Aquinas, something like this. God, for
him, is pure form, for he is wholly immaterial. And, in knowing him
directly, we are, says Aquinas, informed with his form. In the vision
of God the actual life by which our minds are what they will have
become is divinity pure and simple. In Aquinas's view, to enjoy the
vision of God is to be made like God.

When a created intellect sees the essence of God, that very divine essence
becomes the form through which the intellect understands. Hence there
must be some disposition given to the understanding beyond its own nature
so that it can be raised to such sublimity. Since, as we have shown, the
natural power of the intellect is not sufficient to see the essence of God, this
power of understanding must come to it by divine grace. This increase in the
power of understanding we call 'illumination' of the mind, as we also speak
of the intelligible form as 'light'. This is the light that is spoken of in the
Apocalypse, The brightness of God will illuminate her, i.e. the community of the
blessed enjoying the vision of God. By this light we are made deiform, that is,
like to God, as is said by John, *When he shall appear we shall be like to him, and
we shall see him just as he is.*[6]

So, we are drawn to the vision of God, which means becoming like
God. But we cannot become like God unless he raises us up beyond
what is merely natural to us. In that case, however, an obvious
question arises. Is it God's will to raise us up in this way? Aquinas's
answer is 'Yes', and this is why he thinks that the Trinity is significant to us. For, in his view, we derive the doctrine of the Trinity

---

[6] 1a. 12. 5. The references are to Rev. 21: 23 and 1 John 3: 2.

from what has come to pass in history. And what has come to pass there is the action of God drawing us to himself in the strongest possible sense. There is, observes Aquinas, 'a general love, by which *God loves all things that are*, as *Wisdom* says; by this he bestows natural being on created things'. But there is also

a special love, by which he draws the rational creature above its natural condition to have a part in the divine goodness. And it is by this love that he is said to love someone simply speaking; because by this love God simply speaking wills for the creature that eternal good which is himself.[7]

This conclusion of Aquinas can be quickly stated. But it is one which he develops at great length by treating of various distinguishable topics, and we will not fully understand it until we have seen what he says about them. We can, however, start to see something of what it involves by noting what he thinks about the course of human history. For he sees God's raising up of people to union with him as part of a long story which can be distinguished into definite phases or stages.

The Start of the Human Race

In Chapter 5 we saw how Aquinas thinks that human beings can be said to be in the image of God since they have the power of knowing and loving. But, following St Augustine, he also holds that people can image God in a deeper sense. For he holds that it is possible, not just to know and love in general, but to know and love God. And he suggests that when people do this they image God by reflecting his life as three in one. For the Trinity is God bringing forth God, knowing God, and loving what is divine.[8]

In people there exists the image of God, both as regards the divine nature and as regards the trinity of persons ... The divine persons, as above stated, are distinguished from each other according to the procession of the word from the speaker, and the procession of love from both. Moreover, the word of God is born of God by the knowledge of himself; and love proceeds from God according as he loves himself ... Hence we refer the divine image in

---

[7] 1a2ae. 110. 1.

[8] The special relationship between Aquinas and Augustine on the image of God in man is documented in D. Juvenal Merriell, *To the Image of the Trinity: A Study in the Development of Aquinas' Teaching* (Toronto, 1990).

people to the verbal concept born in the knowledge of God, and to the love
derived therefrom. Thus, the image of God is found in the soul according as
the soul turns to God, or possesses a nature that enables it to turn to God.[9]

According to Aquinas, the special goal for human beings, the
reason why they were created, is to image God in knowing and loving
him. And people, he thinks, were first created with the image of God
intact in them. Here he refers to the biblical story of Adam. On his
account, Adam knew and loved God, and everything in his life
contributed to him doing this in peace and harmony with the whole
created order. Adam, says Aquinas, did not see God's essence. He
did not enjoy the beatific vision.[10] But he was physically and intellectually mature, as befits the father of the human race, and his
reason and actions were graced.[11] Furthermore, he was immortal 'by
virtue of a supernatural force given by God to the soul, whereby it
was enabled to preserve the body from all corruption so long as it
remained itself subject to God'.[12] In this sense, Adam lived the life of
God, 'his reason being subject to God, the lower powers to reason,
and the body to the soul'.[13] The Bible teaches that Adam was created
in Paradise. Aquinas interprets this to mean that he lived in a state
where God 'might himself work in people and keep them by sanctifying them'.[14] In Paradise, he says, Adam, in a sense, possessed all the
virtues, for 'the virtues are nothing but those perfections whereby
reason is directed to God and the inferior powers regulated according to the dictate of reason'.[15]

Yet, as the Bible also teaches, Adam fell by virtue of sin. Quoting
Augustine, Aquinas defines sin as 'a word, deed, or desire contrary to
the eternal law'.[16] He also says that the sin of Adam affected the
whole human race. Here he picks up St Paul's declaration that 'sin
came into the world through one man and death through sin'.[17]

---

[9] 1a. 93. 6 and 8.

[10] 1a. 94. 1.

[11] 1a. 95. 1 ff.

[12] 1a. 97. 1.

[13] 1a. 95. 1.

[14] 1a. 102. 3.

[15] 1a. 95. 3.

[16] 1a2ae. 71. 6.

[17] Rom. 5: 12. Notice that you do not, as is often mistakenly supposed, have to
believe in all the details of the biblical story of Adam in order to conclude that sin had
a beginning. As Richard Swinburne writes: 'At some stage in the history of the world,
there appeared the first creature with hominoid body who had some understanding of

Again under the influence of Augustine, he argues that these words cannot be taken simply to mean that Adam gave us an example of sin, as Pelagius taught in the early fifth century. Nor is their meaning exhausted by reading them as saying that people after Adam suffered from the penalty following his sin.[18] They also mean that Adam's descendants inherited the guilt of what Christians call 'original sin'.

According to the Catholic faith we are bound to hold that the first sin of the first human being is transmitted to his descendants, by way of origin. For this reason children are taken to be baptized soon after their birth, to show that they have to be washed from some uncleanness. The contrary is part of the Pelagian heresy, as is clear from Augustine in many of his books.[19]

How is this possible? How can the first sin lead to guilt in people later than Adam? Some theologians have maintained that there can be no serious question of guilt being passed from person to person. For them, therefore, these questions do not arise.[20] Whatever the rights and the wrongs of the matter, however, Aquinas is clear that original sin involves guilt. For him, the questions are pressing, and he therefore attempts to deal with them.

He starts by recognizing that some attempts to deal with them fall short. He denies, for example, that guilt can be inherited because the soul is passed to a child from its father, who might therefore pass on an infected soul if his own soul is infected. He also denies that guilt can be inherited from parent to child in reproduction on the ground that guilt can be transmitted from parents to children like bodily defects. Guilt, he observes, presupposes the occurrence of voluntary activity, which is absent in the case of what is passed on genetically. I may look like my parents, but I do not look like them because I have willingly done something to bring this about.

---

the difference between the morally obligatory, the morally permissible (i.e. right), and the morally wrong; and an ability freely to choose the morally right. So much is obvious; since on modern evolutionary views, as well as on all views held in Christian tradition, once upon a time there were no such creatures and now there are some, there must have been a first one. It seems reasonable to consider such a creature the first man; and we may follow biblical tradition and call him "Adam".' (*Responsibility and Atonement* (Oxford, 1989), 141.)

[18] Aquinas does, however, believe that people after Adam suffered from the penalty following his sin, for he takes death and bodily defects to be the playing out in time of the punishment due to Adam's sin. See 2a2ae. 85. 5.

[19] Ibid.

[20] For a reasoned critique of the notion of original guilt, see Swinburne, *Responsibility and Atonement*, 144 ff.

Granted that some bodily defects are transmitted by the way of origin from parent to child, and granted that even some defects of the soul are transmitted in consequence, on account of a defect in the bodily habit, as in the case of idiots begetting idiots; nevertheless, the fact of having a defect by way of origin seems to exclude the notion of guilt, which is essentially something voluntary.[21]

The solution Aquinas therefore adopts is to say that the guilt of original sin is not a matter of individual responsibility. It is guilt which follows from the fact that the will of Adam runs through his successors. In political thinking, he says, people belonging to a state are considered to be members of one body, and all of them together are deemed to be one person. In the same way, he adds, Adam's descendants can be regarded as one body with Adam as their head or soul. On this basis they are implicated in Adam's sin as the limbs of human beings are involved in the will by virtue of which they act voluntarily.[22] As Timothy McDermott puts it:

Thomas decides that in fact inheritance cannot be reconciled with *individual* responsibility, and that individually Adam's progeny are not guilty of any inherited sin; it can only be reconciled with a solidary responsibility dependent on a conception of men as all having one will in certain respects. The one will which Thomas identifies is the will of Adam reproducing a faulty nature, a will which runs through reproduced humanity, Thomas believes, like the will of a murderer runs through his whole body. So that the hand of the murderer justly dies along with his head and his heart, not because the hand itself willed the murder, but because the hand was a tool one-with-the-head, one-with-the-will in the willing doing of it. In the same way, Thomas seems to regard our very being in the world without the intended integrity of our nature as a way of being a tool of Adam's sin.[23]

Aquinas is convinced that the human race inherited from Adam a kind of sickness tinged with guilt. The occurrence of the first sin incurred guilt and punishment for Adam, who lost that grace by which his intellect and will latched on to God before he sinned. As a result of this, people descended from Adam were born with a degree of guilt and, in their lives, became prone to sin and less and less inclined to God by intellect and will. In Paradise, says Aquinas,

---

[21] Ibid.
[22] 1a2ae. 81. 1.
[23] *St Thomas Aquinas, Summa Theologiae: A Concise Translation*, ed. Timothy McDermott (London, 1989), 223.

Adam was at one with God because God helped him to be such. If the rightness of his intellect and will were a natural endowment rather than a matter of grace, it would, Aquinas reasons, have remained after he sinned.[24] This, in turn, suggests to him that, if human beings are to acquire the original state of rectitude in which Adam stood, grace is necessary again. God must step in and elevate them.

The Old Law

Aquinas holds that the elevation of people to union with God is the chief purpose and effect of the Incarnation of Christ. So he thinks of Christ as standing at the beginning of the time in which the image of God created in Adam is restored in his descendants. But he also thinks that God was taking steps to lead people to him prior to this time. For, so he says, between Adam and Christ came 'the Old Law', by which he means the Torah, the commands and injunctions found in the early books of the Old Testament. And his view is that these were given by God for two main purposes.

In the first place, he says, the Old Law was given to help human beings at a time when they were unable to apply the precepts of natural law as they needed to be applied in particular circumstances. For Aquinas, the Old Law was not identical with natural law as that can be derived from human reason. But it was partly continuous with what reason can discover about how we should act, because some of its commandments specified what should be done in the light of natural law. And, says Aquinas, considered as such, it was needed after the fall of Adam since people then were prone to sin and liable to fail in correctly applying the dictates of reason with respect to behaviour. Aquinas agrees that 'human reason could not go astray in the abstract, as to the universal principles of the natural law'. But he also maintains that 'through being habituated to sin it became obscured in the point of things to be done in detail' and that

with regard to the other moral precepts, which are like conclusions drawn from the universal principles of the natural law, the reason of many people went astray, to the extent of judging to be lawful things that are evil in themselves.[25]

----

[24] 1a. 95. 1.   [25] 1a2ae. 99. 2 ad. 2.

Because this is so, says Aquinas, the Old Law was given to help people live properly with each other and with God. The purpose of any law, he argues, lies 'in establishing friendship, either between people, or between people and God'.[26] And that was also the purpose of the Old Law. By giving instructions on how to behave in accordance with natural law, it was designed to lead people to be closer to each other and, thus, to be closer to God. The Old Law, says Aquinas, was given 'as a help which was most needed at the time when the natural law began to be obscured on account of the exuberance of sin'.[27] It was there to assist when 'the dictate of the natural law' was 'darkened by habitual sinning'.[28]

But Aquinas goes on to affirm that the purpose of the Old Law was wider than this. It 'showed forth the precepts of the natural law'. But it also 'added certain precepts of its own'.[29] In fact, says Aquinas, it added two further kinds of precepts: ritual and judicial ones. Here he has in mind Old Testament cultic regulations and rules governing details of life in Jewish society. Neither of these can be derived directly from rational reflection about how to behave, he says. He is clear that reason tells us that we should aim to be at one with God, for it tells us to seek our happiness, which lies ultimately in God. He also holds that reason leads us to see that justice should be pursued. But he denies that we can deduce details of divine worship (i.e. what to do liturgically and the like) from rational reflection about human action and ends appropriate to it. He also thinks that reason does not specify what counts as just and unjust behaviour in concrete circumstances. So he concludes that the Old Law contained ritual or ceremonial precepts together with judicial precepts aimed to provide a framework in which God could be fittingly worshipped in society by people governed by ways of dealing with each other on a day-to-day basis.

It belongs to the divine law to direct people to one another and to God. Now each of these belongs in the abstract to the dictates of the natural law, to which dictates the moral precepts are to be referred. Yet each of them has to be determined by divine or human law, because naturally known principles are universal, both in speculative and in practical matters. Accordingly, just as the determination of the universal principle about divine worship is

[26] Ibid.
[27] 1a. 98. 6.
[28] 1a. 98. 6 ad. 1.
[29] 1a2ae. 98. 5.

effected by the ceremonial precepts, so the determination of the general precepts of that justice which is to be observed among people is effected by judicial precepts.[30]

Notice, however, that, in speaking as he does about ritual and judicial precepts, Aquinas has a definite historical situation in mind. For he sees the Old Law as given, not to all human beings, but to the Jews. In his scheme of things, Jesus Christ is the definitive cause of human salvation and the primary means by which people become one with God. He therefore holds that, since Christ had to be born as a member of some human society or other, the society from which he came needed to be established and set working by laws designed to make of that society a fitting context for the coming of Christ. 'The Old Law . . . was given to the Jewish people, that it might receive a prerogative of holiness, in reverence for Christ, who was to be born of that people.'[31] That, in turns, means that many of its precepts had binding force only on the Jews and only for a time. Where the Old Law explicitly enjoins what natural law requires, it is binding on all and forever. But its ritual and judicial precepts were not, Aquinas holds, binding on everyone even in Old Testament times. And they are not binding now. Indeed, so he argues, the Old Law can be regarded as severely limited. It was only imperfectly good.

Why? Because it came before Christ and was concerned with the limited goal of preparing a single people from which he would be born. 'The end of the divine law', says Aquinas, 'is to bring people to that end which is everlasting happiness.'[32] And this, he adds, 'cannot be done save by the Holy Spirit'.[33] The precepts of the Old Law accord with reason and are good. But they cannot by themselves bring people to their final end. So Aquinas concludes that the Old Law is lacking. 'There is', he holds, 'imperfect goodness when a thing is of some assistance in attaining the end, but is not sufficient for the realization thereof.'[34] And, since the Old Law is merely a stage to the end of final human happiness, its goodness is imperfect.

But why, one may ask, should this be so? Just why is the Old Law so inefficacious? To appreciate Aquinas's response to these questions

[30] 1a2ae. 99. 4.
[31] 1a2ae. 98. 5.
[32] 1a2ae. 98. 1.
[33] Ibid.
[34] Ibid.

we must now move on to what he says about what he calls 'the New Law', or 'the Law of the Gospel'. For, in his view, the failure of the Old Law only properly emerges when we contrast it with that.

The New Law

At this point it will help if we remember something I noted in Chapter 10, where we found Aquinas teaching that persons of the Trinity are 'sent'. Though I did not labour the fact earlier, it is now important to stress that the sending (or 'mission') of these persons is central to Aquinas's understanding of God and his activity in history. He holds that divine persons are sent because the Son and the Spirit have actually become present in the world in a way which goes beyond the presence there which each of them has simply by being divine. The Son, he says, was sent with the conception of Christ. After the death of Christ, the Spirit was sent as a power causing grace in those who believed in him. And, for Aquinas, it is the sending of the Son and the Spirit which marks the transition to the New Law. 'The New Law', he states, 'consists chiefly in the grace of the Holy Spirit, which is shown forth by faith working through love . . . People became receivers of this grace through God's Son made human, whose humanity grace filled first, and thence flowed forth to us.'[35]

Aquinas's understanding of faith and the effects of the Incarnation will concern us in later chapters. For the moment, however, the point to grasp is that, in his view, the sending of Christ and the Spirit brought us closer to God than anything in the Old Law. The Old and New Law, he says, 'have the same end, namely, the subjection of people to God; and there is but one God of the New and of the Old Testament'.[36] So he is clear that the Old Law was good. He also allows that there were those under the Old Law who benefited from the giving of the New Law and were, as he puts it, 'justified by faith in the passion of Christ as we ourselves are'.[37] Nevertheless, even with these allowances made, Aquinas still maintains that the Old Law was lacking. It was, he says, 'like a pedagogue of children, as the

---

[35] 1a2ae. 108. 1.
[36] 1a2ae. 107. 1.
[37] 3a. 62. 6.

Apostle says, whereas the New Law is the law of perfection, since it is the law of charity'.[38]

Here Aquinas takes his lead from the biblical tradition which distinguishes between the law of God as a written thing and the law of God as something interior. The prophet Jeremiah writes:

Behold, the days are coming, says the Lord, when I will make a new covenant with the house of Israel and the house of Judah, not like the covenant which I made with their fathers when I took them by the hand to bring them out of the land of Egypt, my covenant which they broke . . . But this is the covenant which I will make with the house of Israel, after those days, says the Lord: I will put my law within them, and I will write it upon their hearts; and I will be their God, and they shall be my people.[39]

In the New Testament, this passage is quoted by the author of the letter to the Hebrews, and for Aquinas it signifies that with the coming of Christ and the Spirit people are able to love with God's love and not simply to obey him. As he understands it, the Old Law was a written law obeyed, if it was obeyed, out of fear or desire for reward. The New Law, by contrast, 'is instilled in our hearts', and it has its effect 'not only by indicating to us what we should do, but also by helping us to accomplish it'.[40] According to Aquinas, therefore, the New Law is the actual coming about in people of a loving response to God himself. In this sense, he says, people subject to it can be thought of as having genuine virtue.

Those who are possessed of virtue are inclined to do virtuous deeds through love of virtue, not on account of some extrinsic punishment or reward. Hence the New Law which derives its pre-eminence from the spiritual grace instilled into our hearts, is called the *Law of love*.[41]

On this account, the text of the New Law, which Aquinas identifies with injunctions in the New Testament, is secondary. First and foremost, the New Law is a reality in people. It is God acting in

---

[38] Ibid. 'The Apostle', of course, is St Paul. Aquinas has in mind Gal. 3: 24 f.: 'The law was our custodian (*paidagogos*) until Christ came, that we might be justified by faith. But now that faith has come, we are no longer under a custodian.' A *paidagogos* was a slave who accompanied children to school and guided them. But *paidagogos* became *paedagogus* in the Vulgate, which Aquinas would have read as meaning 'teacher'. He would not have seen the Old Law as a 'custodian'. He would have seen it as informing people and guiding them into truth.

[39] Jer. 31: 31 ff.

[40] 1a2ae. 106. 1 and 1a2ae. 106. 1 ad. 2.

[41] 1a2ae. 107. 1 ad. 2.

them so as to make them more than what they can be as human beings exercising their human faculties after the fall of Adam. Or, as Aquinas also insists, it is the work of grace leading to beatitude.

Grace

1. The General Account

The word 'grace' has appeared several times so far in this chapter, and the general sense it bears for Aquinas should be evident.[42] The New Testament speaks about *charis*, translated into Latin as *gratia*, and then into English as 'grace', though lacking any exact Old Testament equivalent. In Hellenistic Greek it has the sense of 'favour', and in the New Testament it is frequently used to refer to God's free giving, especially in the work of Christ and the Gospel. Broadly speaking, this is how Aquinas conceives of it. By 'grace' he means 'God's action in us leading us to union with him'.

But why should he think that grace is so important when it comes to the New Law? How does he fill out the details of the general picture just noted? The core of his position is given in 1a2ae. 112. 1.

No being can act beyond the limits of its specific nature, since the cause must always be of a higher potency than its effect. Now the gift of grace surpasses every capacity of created nature, since it is nothing other than a certain participation in the divine nature, which surpasses every other nature.

Grace and the New Law go together for Aquinas since, in his thinking, the New Law involves people sharing God's nature. Because doing this is not something open to human natural abilities, it can only, says Aquinas, be brought about by God's assistance. As we read later in the article just cited:

For just as it is impossible for anything to make fiery but fire alone, so it is necessary that God alone should make godlike, by communicating a share in his divine nature by participation and assimilation.

[42] The picture of Aquinas on grace which I am attempting to convey reflects his mature position as presented in texts like the *Summa theologiae*. But Aquinas's thinking about grace, especially concerning terminology, underwent development from his earliest writings on the subject in the *Commentary on the Sentences* to his latest writings. For a brief account of the development which occurred, see Alister E. McGrath, *Iustitia Dei: A History of the Christian Doctrine of Justification: The Beginnings to the Reformation* (Cambridge, 1986), 100 ff.

Even with this explanation given, however, there is more to add if the reader is to get an adequate picture of Aquinas's concept of grace. And we can begin with the substance of 1a2ae. 62, where the first question raised is 'Are there any theological virtues?', and where the answer given is 'Yes'.

2. *Theological Virtues*

By 'theological virtues' Aquinas means virtues which take us beyond what we need in order to flourish in the basic, human way for which virtues such as justice, temperance, and courage equip us. In his view, the cardinal virtues are indeed necessary to us, for without them we will not be as good as we can be in this world. But he also thinks that in this world we cannot be as good as we can be. His view is that our happiness lies in God himself, not in anything we can possess here and now. So he concludes that we have need of another kind of virtue. We need whatever it takes to possess God. We need theological virtues.

A person is perfected by virtue towards those actions by which he or she is directed towards happiness . . . Yet our happiness or felicity is twofold . . . One is proportionate to human nature, and this we can reach through our own resources. The other, a happiness surpassing our nature, we can attain only by the power of God, by a kind of participation of the Godhead; thus it is written that by Christ we are made *partakers of the divine nature*. Because such happiness goes beyond the reach of human nature, the inborn resources by which we are able to act well according to our capacity are not adequate to direct us to it. And so, to be sent to this supernatural happiness, we have to be divinely endowed with some additional sources of activity; their role is like that of our native capabilities which direct us, not, of course, without God's help, to our connatural end. Such sources of action are called theological virtues.[43]

The complete and final end for human beings, Aquinas is saying, is at once both necessary and impossible for them. Left to my own devices (insofar as any creature can be said to be that), I can strive to acquire certain moral and intellectual virtues and thus gain a limited happiness or fulfilment. If I am to become deiform, however, if I am

---

[43] 1a2ae. 62. 1. The reference to Scripture here is to 2 Pet. 1: 4, where Aquinas's notion that the end for humanity is to become deiform finds its clearest biblical statement.

to enjoy the vision of God, I need assistance from God which goes beyond what he provides in making and sustaining me *qua* human being. 'Our reason and will by nature go out to God in that he is the cause and the end of nature ... Yet this is not enough for them to reach out to him as the object of supernatural happiness.'[44] For beatitude (*beatitudo*), I need virtues which are, so to speak, divine rather than human. 'Not as though God were virtuous by means of them, but because through them we are made virtuous by God and unto God.'[45] Aquinas thinks that grace is at work when people come to be virtuous in this way. That is what he means by 'grace' primarily. For him it is the work of God in human beings raising them above their human nature to the point where they become sharers in the divine nature.

3. From Adam to Christ

Aquinas develops this account by starting with Adam. We saw above that Adam, for Aquinas, lived at one with God. As we also saw, however, Aquinas does not teach that Adam enjoyed the beatific vision before his fall. In this respect, he thinks of Adam in Paradise as being in the situation of all human beings in this life. But he goes on to say that there is a difference between Adam in Paradise and Adam's descendants. In his view, Adam, as we might put it, was more fully human than his heirs. On Aquinas's account, Adam was at one with God because his human faculties were working in the best possible way. He conceives of Adam as exercising his reason in a way unfettered by interference whether internal or external. For him, Adam was simply humanity as it is meant to be.

Adam in a state of perfect nature, could, by his natural power, do the good natural to him without the addition of any gratuitous gift ... Now to love God above all things is natural to humanity and to every nature ... Hence, in the state of perfect nature Adam referred the love of himself and of all other things to the love of God as to its end; and thus he loved God more than himself and above all things.[46]

Aquinas holds that all goodness and activity derive from God. So he does not think of Adam as being independent of God. The exercise

---

[44] Ia2ae. 62. 1 ad. 3.
[45] Ia2ae. 62. 1 ad. 2.
[46] Ia2ae. 109. 3.

of Adam's reason and his acting as he did are, for Aquinas, always attributable to God as first cause and sustainer of his creatures. But he also holds that Adam was united to God in a way explicable from a knowledge of his nature. His living as he did in 'the state of perfect nature' was not miraculous. It does not, in Aquinas's view, call for special explanation. It is what we should expect given a knowledge of what human beings are essentially and in the absence of factors causing them to fail. 'In the state of integrity', says Aquinas, 'human nature by its natural endowments could wish and do the good proportionate to its nature.'[47]

For Aquinas, then, Adam before his fall was naturally at one with God. But this, so he argues, was not enough for final happiness. He therefore insists that Adam needed grace even in Paradise, and that his descendants needed it even more. For they inherited guilt, and even their ability to develop acquired virtue was damaged as a consequence of Adam's sin. 'In the state of corrupt nature', says Aquinas, 'people fall short of what they could do by their nature, so that they are unable to fulfil it by their own natural powers.'[48] They can do a lot, but they cannot do all the good natural to their nature 'so as to fall short in nothing.'[49] They therefore need grace for two reasons.

In the state of perfect nature humanity needs a gratuitous strength added to natural strength for one reason, viz. in order to do and wish supernatural good; but for two reasons in the state of corrupt nature, viz. in order to be healed, and furthermore in order to carry out works of supernatural virtue.[50]

All in all, then, you might say that Aquinas paints a somewhat grim picture of human beings after the sin of Adam. They are guilty by virtue of Adam's sin, and they even lack the natural virtue possessed by Adam in Paradise. They are stained, and they fail to be even what

---

[47] 1a2ae. 109. 2.

[48] 1a2ae. 109. 2.

[49] Ibid. Notice that Aquinas does not maintain that human beings after the fall of Adam are wholly corrupt and incapable of good. Thus, though he would agree with Luther that 'Original sin is the privation or lack of original righteousness', he would reject Luther's teaching that 'it is a total lack of uprightness and of the power of all the faculties both of body and soul and of the whole inner and outer man. On top of this, it is a propensity toward evil. It is a nausea toward the good, a loathing of light and wisdom, and a delight in error and darkness, a flight from and an abomination of all good works, a pursuit of evil . . .' (*Commentary on Romans*, 5. 12).

[50] Ibid. 50. 22.

they can be by nature. Considered as human, they are flawed. On top of this, without grace they lack the means to become like God by means of the theological virtues. Yet, though this picture seems to give little hope for humanity, it is not, says Aquinas, the only one to paint, for grace has indeed been given in full measure. By the life, death, and resurrection of Christ, he teaches, the guilt of original sin is removed in those who have faith in Christ. And the love of God has been poured into the heart of Christ's faithful, who are recipients of grace because of Christ and because of the work of the Spirit and the Church. For Aquinas, in other words, the human race has been restored to its pristine state, and that state has been added to.

As I said above, however, these are matters to consider in detail later. For the remainder of this chapter, and as background to what follows, I simply wish to highlight two aspects of Aquinas's teaching on grace. These concern the cause of grace and the kinds of grace which Aquinas thinks there are.

The Cause and Kinds of Grace

1. The Cause of Grace

The point to emphasize under this heading is one which has already been mentioned. But it needs to be emphasized lest the reader should misunderstand Aquinas's teaching by confusing it with a different one which has surfaced in different forms in the history of Christian theology and which is still commonly adopted. Here I am thinking of the view that grace is merely a help for us to do what we finally do on our own.[51] And the point which needs to be stressed is that this is emphatically not Aquinas's position. His line is that grace is wholly the work of God.

The view of grace which I am contrasting with that of Aquinas springs from an understanding of human freedom which sees it as something permitted by God but not caused by him. In terms of this understanding, if God is responsible for what I do in any other sense than simply allowing it, then I do not act freely. With this notion in

---

[51] One classical exponent of the view now in question was Louis de Molina (1563–1600), who propounded it in his *Concordia liberi arbitrii cum gratiae donis, divina praescientia, praedestinatione et reprobatione* (1588).

mind, people have argued that grace must be thought of merely as something which helps me to act well, where my acting well is my doing, not God's, and where grace can be compared to favourable circumstances in which things are made easier for me. Just as you might assist me in studying for an exam by giving me a quiet room and some free time, so God, it has been said, can aid us in drawing close to him by doing something analogous. And this is what grace is. But the drawing close to God, though he wills it somehow, is my doing, not his.

As we have seen, however, Aquinas does not think of human freedom as a case of God leaving us alone to get on with things. For him, my actions are caused by God without ceasing to be free. And this, he says, is the case when grace is present. In his view, grace is the result of God's action in me drawing me to himself. It is not just a help to my acting on my own. It is what there is when I am wholly the end product of what God is doing. And, for this reason, Aquinas insists that *only* God is the cause of grace. He accepts that I can achieve some good without grace. 'Without grace', he writes, 'people of themselves can know good.'[52] 'Even in the state of corrupted nature', he adds, 'human nature . . . can, by virtue of its natural endowments, work some particular good.'[53] But he is equally insistent that 'for the knowledge of any truth whatever people need divine help, that the intellect may be moved by God to its act'.[54] He also firmly maintains that people 'need the help of God as first mover to do or wish any good whatsoever'.[55] And grace, so he thinks, is entirely and only brought about by God.

The gift of grace surpasses every capability of created nature, since it is nothing short of a partaking of the divine nature, which exceeds every other nature. And thus it is impossible that any creature should cause grace. For it is as necessary that God alone should deify, bestowing a partaking of the divine nature, as it is impossible that anything save fire should enkindle.[56]

We, of course, would say that fire can be produced by something other than fire—by electricity, for instance. In spite of the dated illustration, however, Aquinas's point is clear and, one may argue,

---

[52] 1a2ae. 109. 1.
[53] 1a2ae. 109. 2.
[54] 1a2ae. 109. 1.
[55] 1a2ae. 109. 2.
[56] 1a2ae. 112. 1.

correct. Given the limits of human nature, only what is divine can
impart divine life to human beings. As Cornelius Ernst puts it,
expressing the contents of 1a2ae. 109. 1:

> God's creative purpose establishes a finite order, the order of Nature, within
> which action can be perfect within the limitations of this order, though always
> in dependence on the ultimate source of all activity, God as First Mover. But
> by that same creative purpose there exist in the order of Nature creatures
> who are ordained to an end which transcends their own powers as part of
> nature: to reach that end they need assistance from God which, being a gift
> over and above the gift of their created nature, is called grace.[57]

If receiving divine life is receiving grace, it follows that only God can
impart grace. It will also follow that people can do nothing to ensure
or prepare for the giving of grace, which is what Aquinas also argues.
Even to prepare ourselves for grace, he says, we need grace.

> Since then God is the primary mover absolutely, it is by his motion that all
> things are turned to him in that general tendency to the good by which every-
> thing tends towards likeness to God in its proper mode. And so Dionysius
> says that God turns all things to himself. But he turns just people to himself
> as to a special end, to which they tend and to which they desire to cling as
> their own good . . . And so it is only by way of God's converting them that
> people are turned to God. But to prepare oneself for grace is a kind of
> turning to God . . . And so it is clear that people cannot prepare themselves to
> receive the light of grace except by the gratuitous assistance of God moving
> them within.[58]

Yes, Aquinas asserts, people are free when they turn to God. So they
can be enjoined to turn to God. 'But the free decision can only be
turned to God when God turns it to himself.'[59] 'People can do
nothing unless they are moved by God . . . And so, when people are
said to do what is within them, this is said to be in their power in so
far as they are moved by God.'[60] Hence *John* 15: 5: 'Without me you
can do nothing.'

2. Kinds of Grace

For Aquinas, therefore, grace is God's doing, not ours. And it is
essentially nothing but that. 'When people are said to have the grace

---

[57] *The Gospel of Grace*, vol. xxx of the Blackfriars edition of the *Summa theologiae*,
71.
[58] 1a2ae. 109. 6.
[59] 1a2ae. 109. 6 ad. 1.   [60] 1a2ae. 109. 6 ad. 2.

of God', he writes, 'there is signified something bestowed on them by God.'[61] In the history of theology, however, there have been numerous attempts to divide and subdivide over grace in itself, attempts to classify grace under different aspects. Thus one finds reference to, for example, 'created grace', 'uncreated grace', 'habitual grace', 'actual grace', 'sufficient grace', and 'efficacious grace'. In view of this one might wonder how Aquinas thinks of distinctions with respect to grace.

The first thing to note is that, though he speaks of the division of grace, he does not mean to imply that there are different graces as, for instance, there are different species of mammals. Grace, for him, is always the same thing, however we think of it. But, like many of his predecessors and successors, he believes that we can think of it in different ways. In the *Summa theologiae*, and under the heading 'Of the Division of Grace', he actually lists six ways in which we can think of it.

(a) Sanctifying Grace and Grace Freely Bestowed

To begin with, he says, we can think of it as (1) 'sanctifying' (*gratia gratum faciens*), and (2) 'freely bestowed' (*gratia gratis data*). Here he is distinguishing between (a) God drawing someone to himself directly, and (b) his giving a gift to someone who thereby helps someone else to be drawn to God, albeit that the second person is drawn to God by God's action and not just the action of a human being. In the first case, Aquinas is thinking of grace as we can speak of it being present in someone conformed to God's image. In the second, and influenced by 1 Corinthians 12, as well as by his conviction that secondary causes can be real causes, he is thinking of God as enabling someone to teach, prophesy, or work miracles in a way that surpasses that person's natural abilities and deserts while, at the same time, helping another to become united to God.

The order of things consists in the fact that some things are brought back to God by others . . . Since therefore grace is ordained to the bringing back of people to God, this takes place in a definite order, namely, the bringing back to God of some by others. Accordingly, grace is of two kinds. Firstly, there is grace by which people are united to God, and this is called sanctifying grace. Secondly, there is the grace by which one person cooperates with another so

---

[61] 1a2ae. 110. 1.

that the other might be brought back to God. Now this kind of gift is called freely bestowed grace, because it is granted to people beyond the capacity of their nature and beyond their personal merit; it is not called sanctifying, however, because it is not given so that individual people might themselves be justified by it but rather so that they might cooperate in the justification of someone else.[62]

On this account, someone with 'sanctifying grace' is made holy. But the same does not necessarily hold when someone has 'grace freely bestowed', though a person with such grace might indeed be holy and have 'sanctifying grace'. A wicked man might utter moral truths and thereby lead another to a life of virtue. In the same way, so Aquinas thinks, someone not drawn to share in the life of God might yet lead another to that life.

(b) Operating Grace and Co-operating Grace

Aquinas's second division is between (3) 'operating (*gratia operans*) and (4) 'co-operating' grace (*gratia co-operans*), and it is one which is sometimes misunderstood. To suggest that there is both operating grace and co-operating grace could be taken to mean that sometimes grace is what God does ('operating grace', grace in which *God* is at work) and sometimes it is what we do in falling into line with that— where *we* are the initiators in what comes to pass (where we, on our own or independently of God, co-operate with him). An analogy would be a situation in which a political leader established a regime in which people could subsequently work with him to perpetuate it. But this is not at all what Aquinas has in mind in speaking of operating grace and co-operating grace. God, for him, is the first mover and cause of all goodness. He is also the only cause of grace. In speaking of 'co-operating grace', therefore, Aquinas could never be thinking of people falling into line with what God is doing in terms of the above analogy. Indeed, he does not even think that the co-operation involved in co-operating grace is co-operation on the part of the one who has grace. For him, co-operative grace is a matter of God co-operating with us, or, as he puts it, quoting Augustine: 'God by co-operating with us, perfects what he began by operating in us, since he who perfects by co-operation with such as are willing, begins by operating that they may will.'[63]

---

[62] 1a2ae. 111. 1.

[63] 1a2ae. 111. 2. The reference is to Augustine's *De gratia et libero arbitrio*, 17.

In developing this idea Aquinas first concentrates on particular occurrences in us, and particular actions, rather than on dispositions to act in certain ways. These, he says, can themselves be divided into two. To begin with, there are movements of the will whereby we are drawn to good without actually doing anything with our bodies ('the interior act of the will'). The repentant recognition that one has sinned, this being distinct from physical tokens of repentance, would be a case in point. Then there are particular bodily movements which one might perform in the light of such recognition ('the exterior act . . . commanded by the will'). The first, says Aquinas, is simply a case of us being moved by God and may therefore be designated an effect of operative grace. The second, he holds, involves us as moving as well as God. So here we can speak of God co-operating with us.

First, there is the interior act of the will, and with regard to this act the will is a thing moved, and God is the mover; and especially when the will, which hitherto willed evil, begins to will good. And hence, inasmuch as God moves the human mind to this act, we speak of operating grace. But there is another, exterior act; and since it is commanded by the will . . . the operation of this act is attributed to the will. And because God assists us in this act, both by strengthening our will interiorly so as to attain to the act, and by granting outwardly the capability of operating, it is with respect to this that we speak of co-operating grace.[64]

With this distinction made, Aquinas then turns to dispositions. We can, he says, think of people as graced when we are thinking, not of some particular action of theirs, but of the fact that they are disposed to act in a way proper to those who have received the New Law. And here, once again, we can distinguish between God operating and God co-operating. He operates in so far as he confers the disposition in the first place. He co-operates insofar as we do things as those who have the disposition.

If grace is taken for the habitual gift, then again there is a double effect of grace . . . Habitual grace, inasmuch as it heals and justifies the soul, or makes it pleasing to God, is called operating grace; but inasmuch as it is the principle of meritorious works, which spring from the free will, it is called co-operating grace.[65]

Notice that in all of this Aquinas is clearly conceiving of grace as something which makes a definite, historical difference in people. He

---

[64] 1a2ae. 111. 2.   [65] Ibid.

does not regard it merely as a matter of God being well disposed to us. He thinks of it as actually making us better. That, of course, is why he can speak of grace by focusing on the idea that we become deiform. By grace, he thinks, we are not just loved by God. We become lovable in the way that God is lovable—a principle much to the foreground in Aquinas's treatment of his last two divisions of grace: (5) 'prevenient grace' (*gratia praeveniens*) and (6) 'subsequent grace' (*gratia subsequens*).

(c) Prevenient Grace and Subsequent Grace

According to Aquinas:

There are five effects of grace in us: firstly, the healing of the soul; secondly, willing the good; thirdly, the efficacious performance of the good willed; fourthly, perseverance in the good; fifthly, the attainment of glory.[66]

Hence the point of saying that, for him, grace improves us. And it is with reference to these effects that he also thinks that, though grace in itself is simple and indivisible, it can be further broken down. For he reasons that in terms of these effects we can speak of it as 'leading to' (being prevenient) and as 'following on' (being subsequent).[67]

Thus, for example, performing the good which is willed follows, as a matter of fact, upon the soul being healed. So we can speak of the grace involved in the soul being healed as leading to that involved in performing the good which is willed. And so on for the other ways in which effects of grace can be thought of in terms of leading to and following on.

Grace, inasmuch as it causes the first effect in us, is called prevenient with respect to the second, and inasmuch as it causes the second, it is called subsequent with respect to the first effect. And as one effect is posterior to this effect and prior to that, so may grace be called prevenient and subsequent on account of the same effect viewed relatively to divers others.[68]

In Chapter 4 we saw how Aquinas thinks the simple and changeless creator can be spoken of in tenses in a way which appears to attribute

---

[66] 1a2ae. 111. 3.
[67] 'Leading to' and 'following on' are expressions suggested by Timothy McDermott's rendition of *gratia praeveniens* and *gratia subsequens*. See *St Thomas Aquinas, Summa Theologiae: A Concise Translation*, 315.
[68] 1a2ae. 111. 3.

accidents and change to him without really doing so. In his division of grace into 'prevenient' and 'subsequent' he is employing a similar logical strategy. Our tensed statements about God are true, not because God changes, but because things in the created order change. In the same way, so Aquinas holds, the division of grace into that which leads to and that which follows on is legitimate because we can live lives of grace in which there is a before and after.

In these ways, then, Aquinas is the successor and predecessor of those who have attempted to classify grace—though he never maintains that grace is anything other than God's action leading people to him. Even with all that we have noted in this chapter behind us, however, there is more to add concerning the way in which Aquinas develops his account of what it is for people to be holy. As I said above, his teaching on grace centres on the notion of theological virtues. In the next chapter, therefore, we shall turn to what he says about them.

14

The Heart of Grace

ARISTOTLE speaks of virtues as dispositions which make people good and cause them to function well. In 1 Corinthians 13, and elsewhere, St Paul speaks in a similar way about faith, hope, and love.[1] With these points in mind, and following the practice of his day, Aquinas asserts that the theological virtues are faith, hope, and charity.[2] These, he says, are the means by which we come to God by grace as opposed to nature. Their presence is what chiefly allows us to say that, in the time of the New Law, people have become sharers in the divine nature. For Aquinas, they are the heart of the life of grace. In this chapter, therefore, we will explore what he says about them in some detail. The discussion, I hope, will help the reader to see how it is that much of his thought as covered in earlier chapters comes to a kind of culmination when he turns to what, for him, is clearly the most important aspect of our lives.

Faith

1. What Faith is

In much day-to-day discourse, and in much that is written, 'faith' is what you have when you believe in the existence of God. For many people, 'religious belief', 'religious faith', and 'belief in God's existence' can all be used interchangeably. But this is not how it is with Aquinas. He thinks of faith as the virtue of wanting and attaining God, the ultimate good, as he has revealed himself to us in the person of Christ. To put it another way, it is a divinely given disposition by which we begin to share in God's understanding of himself as Father, Son, and Spirit. For Aquinas, belief in the exist-

---

[1] 1 Cor. 13: 13; cf. 1 Thess. 1: 3; Gal. 5: 5 f.; Col. 1: 4 f.
[2] In 1 Corinthians the term which I have rendered by 'love' is *agape*. In the Latin New Testament this word was translated by *caritas*.

ence of God does not constitute faith and is not, strictly speaking, even a part of faith. It is part of the *preambula fidei*, the preambles of faith, or what faith presupposes.[3]

In general, Aquinas takes faith to be something which distinguishes Christians from others who acknowledge the existence of God. More precisely, it has to do with the teaching of Christian creeds, with 'the articles of faith', as he calls them. 'Those realities are properly matters of faith', he explains, 'the vision of which will be our blessedness in eternal life and the help of which will bring us there.'[4] As he also puts it, those who have faith believe the substance of the Niceno-Constantinopolitan creed, which in his view either explicitly or implicitly contains what is important in the teaching of all other councils. 'The doctrine of the Catholic Faith', he says, 'was sufficiently laid down by the Council of Nicaea: wherefore in the subsequent councils the fathers had no mind to make any additions.'[5] For Aquinas, though not for all his contemporaries, this, in turn, means that there are fourteen articles of faith. 'The first basis for classifying the articles of faith', he writes, 'is that some refer to the majesty of the Godhead, some to the mystery of Christ's humanity, *the mystery of godliness*.'[6] He continues:

With regard to God's majesty there are three points singled out for our belief. First, the oneness of the Godhead; the first article refers to this. The second is the Trinity of persons; there are three articles on this, corresponding to the three persons. Third to be proposed are the works proper to divinity. The first of these relates to the being of nature; on this we have the article about creation. The second work relates to the being of grace; on this we have under the one article all that concerns our sanctification. The third work relates to the being of glory; on this we have another article, namely about the resurrection of the body and life everlasting. In all, then, there are seven articles about the divinity. Seven articles are also set forth about Christ's humanity: the first on his incarnation and conception by the Holy Spirit; the second on his birth of a virgin; the third on his passion, death and burial; the fourth, on his descent into hell; the fifth on his resurrection; the sixth on his ascension; the seventh on his coming again to judge. In all there are fourteen articles.[7]

---

[3] 1a. 2. 2 ad. 1.
[4] 2a2ae. 1. 8.
[5] *De pot.* 10. 4 ad. 13.
[6] 2a2ae. 1. 8.
[7] Ibid.

What all this boils down to is that those with Christian faith believe in one God, the Creator, who is Father, Son, and Spirit. They also believe that the Son was born a man, of a virgin, that he died for us, was raised from the dead, and will come again as judge of human beings whose final salvation consists in their bodily resurrection from death for life with him.

2. *Faith and Propositions*

Because he thinks in these terms, it will be evident that Aquinas's view of faith can be described as propositional. Some theologians, both medieval and modern, have been critical of such an approach. To take a modern author, according, for example, to John Coventry, SJ:

Faith is primarily in Christ, and not in doctrines; in God presenting himself for recognition as a person, and not in any series of doctrinal statements or propositions, which we are asked to believe . . . Faith is the correlative of revelation. Those who believed when confronted with Christ's life, death and resurrection, were those who recognized that it was God who confronted them. This is faith . . . not a process of argument resulting in a conclusion; not the acceptance of a proposition; but religious experience, sometimes sudden and overwhelming, to which you may well respond by saying 'depart from me for I am a sinful man, O Lord'.[8]

But Aquinas would clearly resist this way of talking. His view is that we can say what people with faith believe. He holds that faith has a statable content, that, as he puts it, 'from the perspective of the one believing . . . the object of faith is something composite in the form of a proposition'.[9] Those with Christian faith believe *that* God is three in one, *that* Christ is God, and so on. This, in Aquinas's view, is why Christians have creeds and why preaching is important.[10] It is also why he thinks that those with faith can be expected to articulate it, or confess it, in words.[11]

It would, however, be wrong to think that, in saying all this, he means that faith is a dry or, as we might put it, a *merely* propositional or cerebral matter. He has often been taken to favour such a con-

[8] *The Theology of Faith* (Cork, 1968), 9 ff.
[9] 2a2ae. I. 2.
[10] See 2a2ae. I. 6 and 6. I.
[11] 2a2ae. 3. I.

clusion, but he does not, in fact, do so. He denies, for example, that one needs to be educated and articulated in order to have faith. He says that simple people stand by their Christian teachers and are not obliged to be intellectuals. What is required is that they assent to the articles of faith.

> The uneducated are not cross-examined in the subtleties of faith except when there is a suspicion that they have been corrupted by heretics...[and]...should they err innocently in such matters, the simple are not held to blame, so long as it is clear that they do not obstinately cling to wrong doctrine.[12]

More at the centre of his thinking, however, is the idea that faith is our beginning to share in God's life. Far from being nothing but a matter of propositions, it is union with God himself. Or, as Aquinas also explains, its formal object is God, and 'from the perspective of the reality believed in...the object of faith is something non-composite, i.e. the very reality about which one has faith'.[13] In terms of this account, faith is indeed propositional. But if one were to say, in accordance with an objection mentioned by Aquinas himself, that 'the Creed sets forth realities, not propositions', then he would agree. The Creed, he observes, 'expresses the things of faith as they are the term of the believer's act. Such an act does not have a proposition as its term, but a reality.'[14] For him, faith is believing God himself since the truths of faith are revealed by God. He also thinks that to believe God revealing himself is to share in what God knows, albeit imperfectly. As he puts it in one place: 'God is the end of faith in that he is the unique good, who by his eminence transcends the capacities of human beings, but by his liberality offers his own very good to be shared in.'[15]

3. Faith and Knowledge

Yet, though Aquinas is quite clear that by faith we share in God's own very good, he is also convinced that the sharing involved here is imperfect. For he holds that, though faith embraces what God knows, it is not a matter of knowledge when considered from the viewpoint

---

[12] 2a2ae. 2. 6 ad. 2.
[13] 2a2ae. 1. 2.
[14] 2a2ae. 1. 2 obj. 2 and ad. 2.
[15] *Sent.* 3. 23. 2. 1.

of the one who has it. Employing a very influential definition of Hugh of St Victor (d. 1142), he says that it is 'mid-way between science and opinion'.[16] It is not, he thinks, a matter of seeing or understanding. 'That a knowledge be without clarity or vision indicates its imperfection', he suggests. And with this point in mind, he concludes that 'to be imperfect as knowledge is of the very essence of faith'.[17]

When Aquinas speaks of 'science', 'seeing', or 'understanding' in this context, he is again talking the language of Aristotle, for whom there is a big difference between knowledge and belief. According to Aristotle, we have knowledge when we clearly see that some truth or other must be so, whether on the basis of argument or directly and without argument. We have knowledge, for instance, when we see that a valid deductive argument is valid, or when we grasp a logical truth like 'No squares are triangles'. In other cases, says Aristotle, we have belief or opinion. What we believe or opine may indeed be the case. We may believe or opine that-p, and it may well be that-p. But Aristotle does not think that we therefore know that-p. For him, knowing is getting our minds around truth, not just taking it that such and such is the case. And this is how Aquinas thinks. Since he also thinks that the truths of faith are not provable, since he thinks that they have to be revealed and believed, he therefore concludes that faith and knowledge differ. In faith, he says, we believe, but we do not know. 'Things are said to be seen', he argues, 'when they themselves cause the mind or the senses to know them. Clearly, then, no belief or opinion can have as object things seen, whether by sense or by intellect.'[18] Or, as he also explains:

Any science is possessed by virtue of principles known immediately and therefore seen. Whatever, then, is an object of a science is in some sense seen. Since it is impossible that the same thing be seen and believed by the same person . . . it is also impossible that the same thing be an object of science and belief for the same person . . . Matters set before the whole human community for belief . . . are in no instance the object of any science, and these are the object of faith pure and simple. In these terms faith and science are not about the same object.[19]

[16] Hugh of St Victor writes: 'Faith is a form of mental certitude about distant realities that is greater than opinion and less than science' (*Fides est certitudo quaedam animi de rebus absentibus supra opinionem et infra scientiam constituta*). See *De sacramentis*, I. 10. 2.
[17] 1a2ae. 67. 3.
[18] 2a2ae. 1. 4.
[19] 2a2ae. 1. 5.

For Aquinas, the articles of faith tell us about what we cannot demonstrate. With respect to them, we are like people who believe or opine that this, that, or the other is true.

And yet, so Aquinas quickly adds, there is a difference. Belief or opinion is usually accompanied by doubt or a lack of conviction. But Aquinas maintains that faith in the Christian sense is a matter of certitude, certainty, and commitment. He thinks that those with faith hold fast to what they profess. They do not embrace it as a kind of hypothesis or tentatively held theory. Hence his remark that faith is midway between science and opinion. Science (*scientia*) is had by those who clearly see that such and such must be the case. It therefore goes with conviction. Opinion is different. That implies a lack of vision and a consequent hesitance in assent. Well, says Aquinas, faith is partly like science and partly like opinion. Like those with opinion, those with faith do not see. But, like those with science, they are settled in their assent.

The act of believing is firmly attached to one alternative and in this respect the believer is in the same state of mind as one who has science or understanding. Yet the believer's knowledge is not completed by a clear vision, and in this respect he is like one having a doubt, a suspicion, or an opinion.[20]

To indicate what Aquinas is driving at here, an analogy might help. So consider the case of someone with no medical knowledge to speak of (the case with most of us), who falls ill and goes to a doctor for a check up (as many of us must from time to time). Suppose the doctor concludes that the patient is suffering from kidney stones. And suppose that the doctor explains this to the patient. Also suppose that the patient believes the doctor, is quite convinced by the diagnosis, and explains to others, 'I have kidney stones.' In our example, the doctor is skilled and the diagnosis is correct. So the patient has a true belief and is, in this sense, at one with the doctor. In the loose way in which we often use the verb 'to know', we might even say that the patient now knows that the problem is kidney stones, for the doctor has shared his knowledge to this effect.[21] On the other hand, however, there is an obvious sense in which the patient does not know as

---

[20] 2a2ae. 2. 1.

[21] I speak here of a 'loose' way of using 'to know'. But it has been argued that 'to know' is the proper verb to use in talking of the situation I now have in mind. See Michael Welbourne, *The Community of Knowledge* (Aberdeen, 1986).

the doctor knows. The doctor's knowledge springs from an understanding of medicine which the patient does not have. In a perfectly obvious sense, the doctor knows what is going on while the patient does not.

Aquinas's view of faith is that it is something like what the patient has in the example just envisaged. He sees the articles of faith as truths about God which are taught by him and believed by Christians. In this sense, he thinks, to have faith in them is to share God's knowledge of himself and, therefore, to anticipate in a manner the vision of God. But he also thinks that those with faith, rather like our patient, do not understand what it is that makes the articles of faith true. In this sense, he holds, they are in the dark. They have the truth, and they can say what the truth is. They have their equivalents to 'I have kidney stones'. But they do not understand what they are saying. They do not have the fullness of the vision of God and are still, as Aquinas says, *in via* (on the way) rather than *in patria* (at home).

4. Coming to Faith

In that case, however, one might wonder why those with faith come to have it. What makes someone into a Christian? What, in Aquinas's view, turns Saul of Tarsus into Paul the Apostle? The answer which Aquinas would give is that Christians are what they are because they love God and he loves them. He thinks that those with faith are attracted to God as Christian preaching proclaims him to be. And he thinks that they are attracted in this way because God makes them so. His view is that God, in time, has spoken to us, and that some people can hear him and be drawn to him in the light of what he has said.

In some recent discussions of Aquinas a different picture of his thinking has been presented. For it has been suggested that, in his view, faith, at least for some, is a matter of being convinced by evidence. The idea is that those with faith, or at least some of them, are rationally convinced of the truths stated in the classical Christian creeds, and that this is enough to give them what Aquinas means by 'faith'. They are like a judge who is forced to admit that X murdered Y because the facts cannot be otherwise interpreted or because the balance of probability comes down in its favour.[22] But this reading of Aquinas needs to be contested.

---

[22] For this reading of Aquinas, see: John Hick, *Faith and Knowledge* (Ithaca, NY, 1966), 20 f.; Terence Penelhum, 'The Analysis of Faith in St Thomas Aquinas',

In its support we can note that Aquinas does not deny that believers accept the articles of faith with what they take to be reason. He clearly does not think that people embrace Christianity in a vacuum. They do so because they are taught, and because they respect their teachers and believe them. Insofar as they go beyond this, they may, says Aquinas, believe in the articles of faith because something seems to point in their favour. Matters of faith, he declares, 'are indeed seen by the one who believes: he would not believe unless he saw that they are worthy of belief on the basis of evident signs or something of the sort'.[23] And he certainly thinks that there are 'evident signs or something of the sort' which tell in favour of the truths of Christian revelation. He thinks that the Gospels are credible testimonies of events which occurred, so he holds that the reported miracles of Jesus bear witness to his status. In the *Summa contra Gentiles*, he appeals to the fact that people have embraced the Christian religion in the face of adverse circumstances. In his commentary on the Apostles' Creed, he adds that, if you think these circumstances none too impressive as grounds for believing in Christianity, you might reckon with the fact that it is somewhat miraculous that people can be brought to believe without a miracle.

It is a fact that all the world cultivated idols, as the very history of the pagans shows. But how were all of them converted to Christ, both the wise and the rich, both the powerful and the multitude, by the preaching of simple people who were both poor and few in number, preaching poverty and flight from delights? Either this fact is miraculous, or not. If it is miraculous, I have made my point. If it is not miraculous, I say that there cannot be a greater miracle than that the world should be converted without miracles. No need to search any further.[24]

In general, so we may say, Aquinas does not think that those with faith must lack reason for believing as they do.

But he does not think that reasons given by believers can ever be regarded as demonstrating that the articles of Christian faith are true. This is clear from what he says in general, but it is nicely highlighted by what he says of the apostle Thomas, who appears at the end of the Gospel of John and is reported as saying that he will not believe that

---

[23] 2a2ae. 1. 4 ad. 2.
[24] *Super sym. apos.* 1.

Jesus is risen until he has seen him and felt his wounds. Someone who thinks that believing Christ to be God might be an inevitable and unavoidable rational reaction to seeing the risen Christ, as Thomas came to do, might maintain that seeing Christ as Thomas did would be quite enough to show one that Christ is certainly God. But Aquinas argues the other way. He says: 'Thomas *saw one thing and believed something else. He saw a man; he believed him to be God and bore witness to this, saying, "My Lord and my God"*.'[25] In common with all medieval theologians, therefore, he concludes that the proper definition of faith is that given in Hebrews 11: 1: 'Faith is the substance of things to be hoped for, the evidence of things that appear not.' Or, to put it more properly definitionally, says Aquinas: 'Faith is that habit of mind whereby eternal life begins in us and which brings the mind to assent to things that appear not.'[26] For him, faith is a kind of middle state between knowing and merely opining.

Among acts of the intellect, some include a firm assent without pondering—thus when people think about what they know scientifically or intuitively; thinking of that kind reaches a finished term. Other mental acts are marked by a pondering that is inconclusive, lacking firm assent, either because the act leans towards neither of the alternatives—the case with doubt; or because it leans to one alternative, but only tentatively—the case with suspicion; or because it decides for the one side but with fear of the opposite—the case with opinion. The act of believing, however, is firmly attached to one alternative and in this respect the believer is in the same state of mind as one who has science or understanding. Yet the believer's knowledge is not completed by clear vision, and in this respect a believer is like one having a doubt, a suspicion, or an opinion.[27]

Given what we have now seen of Aquinas's thinking, we should not be unduly surprised by this conclusion. But we might still wonder about the difference between Christian believers and others. If those with faith have not shared God's knowledge of himself by virtue of their intelligence, how have they managed to get where they are? Here Aquinas has a twofold answer.

To begin with, he observes, people come to faith because they are given revelation, because God tells us about himself.

The things of faith surpass our understanding and so become part of our knowledge only because God reveals them. For some, the prophets and

---

[25] 2a2ae. 1. 4 ad. 1.
[26] 2a2ae. 4. 1.
[27] 2a2ae. 2. 1.

Apostles for example, this revelation comes from God immediately; for others, the things of faith are proposed by God's sending preachers of the faith: *How shall they preach unless they be sent?*[28]

In Aquinas's view, God has directly taught some people about himself and thereby made public what people cannot discover by means of their reasoning or intellect. He thinks that God has taught us about himself through the words of Christ, 'the first and chief teacher of the faith' (*fidei primus et principalis Doctor*), who knows divine truth without benefit of revelation because he is himself divine. Aquinas also thinks that the teaching of Christ has been handed on, which is how later generations come to receive it.

Yet he does not suppose that merely being told the content of Christian faith is enough to guarantee that one will come to have faith in it. 'One person believes and another does not, when both have seen the same miracle, heard the same preaching.'[29] Something else is required, therefore, and this, Aquinas explains, is God acting directly on us to cause us to love the reality set forth as the object of faith. Faith, he says, is wrought in us by God.

Since in assenting to the things of faith people are raised above their own nature, they have this assent from a supernatural source influencing them; this source is God. The assent of faith, which is its principal act, therefore, has as its cause God, moving us inwardly through grace.[30]

For Aquinas, faith is entirely a matter of gift. It has no natural explanation and derives from God who brings it about in a person. As he sometimes asserts, faith is an 'infused virtue'.

5. *Faith and Love*

On the other hand, however, there is a sense in which Aquinas does think that faith in a person can be explained in terms which we can understand. For, as he sees it, faith can be viewed as a kind of love. It is a case of believing because we are drawn to what we believe.

Consider Mary who loves John. He tells her that he loves her too. And she believes him. She is terribly drawn to him. Let us now suppose that Paul tells Mary that John is unfaithful to her. She may

---

[28] 2a2ae. 6. 1. The reference is to Rom. 10: 15.
[29] Ibid.
[30] Ibid.

have no reason at all to think that John is actually unfaithful, apart from the fact that Paul has said so. She might therefore disbelieve the report. On the other hand, however, she might not feel able to say that she knows that John is really faithful. She might admit that, so far as anything she could cite as evidence goes, there is the possibility of him being unfaithful. Yet she does not believe in his infidelity. Not for a moment. She believes that he loves her.

How are we to account for this? Aquinas would say that here we must say that Mary sticks by John because she loves him. John could be unfaithful as far as the evidence available to Mary goes. So Mary is not forced to agree that John loves her. She cannot help accepting that there are no square triangles. But she does not, in the same sense, have to accept that John loves her. As Aquinas would say, she does not *know* that John loves her. On the other hand, she does not know that he does not love her. She simply stands by her conviction that John does love her. So, as Aquinas would argue, Mary sticks by John because she loves him. She believes what he says, not because she has evidence which forces her to accept his declarations, but because she is drawn to him.

And thus it is, Aquinas thinks, with those who have faith. They are drawn to what the articles of faith proclaim. Or, as Aquinas puts it, the assent to the articles of faith comes about by virtue of the will. Since reason cannot by itself settle or reveal as luminously clear the truth of the articles of faith, 'the mind of the one believing settles upon the one side of a question not in virtue of his reason but in virtue of his will'. Or, as we read in the *De veritate*:

Sometimes, the mind . . . is determined through the will, which chooses assent to one determined side, and precisely from a motive that is sufficient to move the will, but insufficient to move the intellect, e.g. that it appears good or appropriate to assent to the one alternative. Such is the condition of one who believes . . . This is the way we are moved to believe what is preached to us, namely in that we are promised, if we believe, the reward of eternal life; by such a reward the will is moved to assent to what is proposed, although the mind is not moved by anything understood.[31]

This is not to say that faith, for Aquinas, is nothing but wishful thinking, or that it is a conscious or deliberate leap in the dark. Such an interpretation of his thinking would be assuming a separation between intellect and will that is foreign to him. He holds that will

[31] *De ver.* 14. 1.

and intellect are always connected or bound up with each other, if only because we can choose to shut our eyes even in the presence of truth which would convince us should we care to stare it in the face.[32] He also holds that every choosing follows upon a perceiving, for he thinks that the will moves to what is thought to be good. In the case of faith, however, he maintains that there is nothing forcing us to assent to what is proposed. We must be drawn to assenting. In this sense, will plays a greater role than intellect when it comes to faith, even though the articles of faith have intellectual content. For Aquinas, faith is what you have when it seems good to you to embrace what is taught by the content of Christian teaching as God reveals it. And you have it because God gives it to you, not just in the sense that he can be said to have given you anything you have, but in the sense that nothing you can do with your natural human powers can result in you having it.

Hope

Like any other virtue, hope is a virtue in Aquinas's view because it leads us to our good. Alluding to Aristotle's *Ethics*, 2. 6. 1106ª15, he says that 'in anything virtue is what makes its possessor good and its activity sound'.[33] Since 'every human act coming up to reason or to God is by that very fact good', and since hope 'reaches God', it follows that hope is a virtue.[34] It reaches God since hope is for what only God can provide.

The emphasis here falls on 'what only God can provide'. When he speaks of hope, Aquinas is not thinking of general optimism, or a looking forward to what one has rational grounds for expecting to occur in this world. He has his mind on union with God as it follows from the action of God in Christ and the sending of the Spirit. For him, therefore, it entirely depends on the possession of faith. 'Faith', he explains, 'gives rise to hope', and its object is 'eternal beatitude' and 'the divine assistance . . . both of which are made manifest to us by faith, whereby we know that we can attain to eternal life and that the divine help lies open to us for this very purpose'.[35] Specifically,

---

[32] See 1a2ae. 17. 1 and 1a. 81. 3.
[33] 2a2ae. 17. 1, in which Aquinas is alluding to Aristotle's *Ethics*, 2. 6. 1106ª15.
[34] Ibid.
[35] 2a2ae. 17. 7.

hope is for life eternal, 'consisting in the joyful possession of God himself'.[36]

This is simply to say that we should hope for nothing less from God than his very self; his goodness, by which he confers good upon creaturely things, is nothing less than his own being. And so the proper and principal object of hope is indeed eternal blessedness.[37]

Considered from this point of view, hope would seem to be a rather private thing. It would seem to be a case of hoping for something for oneself. And that, in fact, is how Aquinas sees it first and foremost. In thinking of hope, altruistic people, at least, might be expected to give a great deal of weight to things to be hoped for on the part of other people. They might even add that it is better to hope for what could befall others than it is to hope for what can befall oneself. Aquinas, on the other hand, is concerned with hope as a virtue, and virtues, for him, are primarily of benefit to those who possess them. In his view, too, hope is concerned with what is not to hand but can be, so it must be distinguished from concern for others since it reaches out beyond any union of love on which such concern is based.[38] From this perspective, he therefore holds that the object of hope is essentially 'always something arduous and pertaining to the person who hopes'.[39] Hope, he maintains, 'regards directly one's own good, and not that which pertains to another'.[40]

In spite of teaching this, however, Aquinas also allows for hope on behalf of others. At the end of the day it is not his view that hope is entirely a private affair. For what if there is, in fact, a union of love between one person and another? Then, says Aquinas, one may hope for the final good of others just as one hopes for this for oneself.

If, however, we presuppose a union of love with another . . . one can desire and hope in the other's behalf quite as in one's own. On this basis, namely because of the union of love, it is possible to hope for eternal happiness for another. And just as there is but one virtue of charity whereby we love God, self, neighbour, so there is but one virtue of hope expressing our aspirations for ourselves and for others.[41]

---

[36] 2a2ae. 17. 2.
[37] Ibid.
[38] 2a2ae. 17. 3.
[39] Ibid.
[40] Ibid.
[41] Ibid.

For Aquinas, then, hope is part and parcel of the Christian life. This, in turn, means that he is unequivocally harsh when considering the possibility of its opposite, despair, which, in his view, is at odds with proper belief concerning God. He agrees that one may despair without entirely renouncing the content of Christian faith. For him, despair, like hope, is an affective matter and can, therefore, be distinguished from intellectual assent. One may believe in God's gift of beatitude and be drawn to it in confidence. But one may also find that, just as one can sin while believing that what one does is sinful, one's confidence in God can be shaken in particular circumstances, even though one's beliefs about God are true. Nevertheless, Aquinas is clear that despair is thoroughly out of place in the life of grace, not only because it leads people away from good works and into sin, but also, and more fundamentally, because it contradicts the Gospel if translated into terms of belief.

The mind's true appraisal about God acknowledges that he grants pardon to sinners and brings people to salvation . . . Contrariwise, false opinion envisions God as denying pardon to the repentant sinner, or as not converting sinners to himself through justifying grace. And so the act of hope, squaring with true judgement, is praiseworthy and virtuous; while the opposite attitude, which is despair, reflecting as it does a false view of God, is vicious and sinful.[42]

This is not, Aquinas adds, to say that everyone should presume on eternal life. If despair conflicts with true belief, the same, he thinks, is true of presumption. For beatitude is a matter of union with God and there are barriers to that.

Just as it is false that God does not pardon the repentant, or that he does not turn sinners to repentance, so it is false that he grants forgiveness to those who persevere in their sins, and that he gives glory to those who cease from good works. And it is to this estimate that the movement of presumption is conformed.[43]

For Aquinas, though, it still remains true that, in the light of the New Law, despair should give way to hope. That, he believes, is a consequence of faith and a cause of our beatitude.

Notice however, that he does not regard it as essential to beatitude. On the contrary. He says that hope has no place in the final end of

---

[42] 2a2ae. 20. 1.
[43] 2a2ae. 21. 2.

people. And he says the same of faith. In the beatific vision, he holds, there is neither faith nor hope. Faith is unnecessary because God will then be known directly.[44] And hope is redundant since what is hoped for will have come to pass. 'Thus hope will pass away in heaven, just as faith will, and so neither of them is found in the blessed.'[45] What is found, however, is charity, the theological virtue which, in Aquinas's thinking, surpasses all others and unites us with God because it is what he essentially is.

Charity

1. Charity in General

In order to appreciate how Aquinas thinks about charity it will help if we start by forgetting about the notion of charity as essentially a matter of kindness between people. The sense of 'charity', where that is taken to designate the third theological virtue, is not, for him, first and foremost that which we usually have in mind when we speak of people giving money 'out of charity' and the like. As we shall see in a moment, he certainly thinks that doing good to others is part of what charity involves. But what engrosses him to begin with is the idea that charity is a participation or a sharing in what God is from eternity in himself and apart from creation.

Here we need to refer once again to the way in which he thinks about the Trinity. As we saw in Chapter 10, he maintains that the Holy Spirit is the coming forth from God of love. God knows what he brings forth as a concept (the Word), and he loves what he knows. This loving is a proceeding in God and, since all that is in God is God, it is divine. It is the love of the Father for the Son. It is also the love of the Son for the Father. This means that love is in God from eternity because God, as we may put it, loves God from eternity. And the thing to note now is that this loving of God by God, this divine loving which is not to be distinguished from God, is what Aquinas takes charity to be. In his view, by charity we share in what God is from eternity insofar as we love God in the way that God loves God. For him, charity in people is the image of what the Holy Spirit is.

---

[44] See 1a2ae. 67. 3.
[45] 2a2ae. 18. 2.; cf. also 1a2ae. 67. 4.

Indeed, it is the presence of the Holy Spirit because it is caused by the Holy Spirit. 'God's love has been poured into our hearts through the Holy Spirit which has been given to us', says St Paul.[46] Aquinas takes this to mean that the Christian virtue of charity is the effect in us of the Holy Spirit, who thereby produces in us what love is in God.

> The divine essence itself is charity even as it is wisdom and goodness. Now we are said to be good with the goodness which is God, and wise with the wisdom which is God, because the very qualities which make us formally so are participations in the divine goodness and wisdom.[47]

2. Charity as Friendship

A characteristic way in which Aquinas develops this idea is to say that charity is a matter of *amicitia* between human beings and God. The term *amicitia* is normally translated as 'friendship'. One might quarrel with the translation, but for present purposes I shall let it stand. It is questionable since 'friendship' now can mean little more than 'cordial relationships', with the suggestion of a companionship of some sort or other, while *amicitia* suggests something much deeper—a serious love and bonding. Let us, however, take 'friendship' to mean just this. Given what we have seen of Aquinas's profound sense of the difference between creature and Creator, one might expect him to take quite a different line from the one he does. For 'friendship' (even in the sense of *amicitia* as just expounded) suggests equality of some kind. We speak of people being friends with (or being in love with) each other, but not with their furniture or their pets. In John 15: 15, however, Jesus declares, 'No longer will I call you servants but my friends', and Aquinas takes this kind of saying as a way of defining what the Christian life of grace is about. In the *Summa theologiae*, indeed, the first question raised in the treatise on charity (2a2ae. 23 ff.) is 'Whether charity is friendship (*amicitia*)?' The answer given begins with John 15: 15 and concludes with the words 'it is evident that charity is the friendship (*amicitia*) of people for God'.[48]

Why? Aquinas's thinking here depends on two assumptions, both

---

[46] Rom. 5: 5.
[47] 2a2ae. 23. 2 ad. 1.
[48] 2a2ae. 23. 1.

of which can be found in Aristotle.[49] The first is that friendship involves loving another for his or her own sake and not for anything else. The second is that it involves a working together towards a common goal. Given these assumptions, we can, says Aquinas, speak of charity as *amicitia* because with charity there arises a love of God for himself, a love which is essential to God's being as well as present in the person with charity. People with charity, he thinks, have a kind of project in common with God. Both love God for God's own sake and as an end in itself.

According to the philosopher, not every love has the characteristic of *amicitia*, but that love which is together with benevolence, when we love someone so as to wish good to him. If, however, we do not wish good to what we love, but wish good for ourselves ... it is love not of *amicitia*, but of a kind of concupiscence ... Yet neither does well-wishing suffice for *amicitia*, for a certain mutual love is requisite, since *amicitia* is between friend and friend: and this well-wishing is founded on some kind of communication. Accordingly, since there is communication between people and God, inasmuch as he communicates his happiness to us, some kind of *amicitia* must needs be based on this same communication, of which it is written: *God is faithful: by whom you are called into the fellowship of his son.* The love which is based on this communication is charity: wherefore it is evident that charity is the *amicitia* of people for God.[50]

On this basis Aquinas can go on to cite a definition of charity from Augustine. 'Charity I call a movement of the soul towards enjoying God for his own sake.'[51]

This 'God for his own sake' motif is especially worth noting, for it lies behind what we have already found Aquinas saying about the New Law or the Law of the Gospel. Central to his thinking on this is the Old Testament promise of a law 'instilled within our hearts'. He suggests that the fulfilment of this promise comes by grace which, insofar as its effect is charity, leads us not just to obey God, but to want him for the goodness that he is, as opposed, for example, to wanting him for personal gain or in fear of punishment. For Aquinas, God's own love is in no way a product of need in him. He does not love because there is something which he lacks and can get if he does

---

[49] Note, however, that Aquinas is stretching Aristotle's notion of friendship in speaking of it as something existing between people and God. For Aristotle friendship is only to be found among virtuous people.

[50] 2a2ae. 23. 1. The biblical reference is to 1 Cor. 1: 9.

[51] 2a2ae. 23. 2; *De doctrina Christiana*, 3. 10.

so. We saw all this in Chapter 8. In terms of Aquinas's thinking, God's love is simply a matter of him being drawn to himself as the perfect or ultimate good. And that, so Aquinas also thinks, is what is at issue when it comes to the love that is charity. Those with charity, he says, are drawn to God purely and simply for the goodness that God is. The New Law 'is the law of perfection, since it is the law of charity'.[52] This, in turn, means that those with charity aim for God as God aims for himself in willing himself. They are attracted to God, not as a means to an end, but as an end in itself, not as something extrinsic, but as something interior because it is loved for what it is.

Those who as yet are not endowed with virtuous habits are directed to the performance of virtuous acts by reason of some outward cause: for instance, by the threat of punishment, or the promise of some extrinsic rewards, such as honour, riches, or the like. Hence the Old Law, which was given to people who were imperfect, that is, who had not yet received spiritual grace, was called the *law of fear*, inasmuch as it induced people to observe its commandments by threatening them with penalties; and is spoken of as containing temporal promises. On the other hand, those who are possessed of virtue are inclined to do virtuous deeds through love of virtue, not on account of some extrinsic punishment or reward. Hence the New Law, which derives its pre-eminence from the spiritual grace instilled into our hearts, is called the *law of love*: and it is described as containing spiritual and eternal promises, which are the objects of the virtues, chiefly of charity. Accordingly such persons are inclined of themselves to those objects, not as to something foreign, but as to something of their own . . . Hence the New Law, which is the law of love, is said to restrain the will.[53]

That is why Aquinas thinks that, while faith and hope will pass away, charity cannot. 'Faith and hope', he says, 'attain to God according as from him comes knowledge of truth or possession of good, but charity attains God himself so as to rest in him without looking for any gain.'[54]

3. The Source of Charity

This attaining to God of which Aquinas speaks is in his view, of course, only produced by God. That is because it is a matter of grace. But it is worth spelling out why he thinks charity is a matter of grace.

---

[52] 1a2ae. 107. 1.
[53] Ibid.
[54] 2a2ae. 23. 6.

For does it not seem sensible to suppose that one can love God for himself without special help from God? And would it not seem reasonable to say that there must have been those who did this even before the time of the New Law, which Aquinas identifies as the era of grace?

With regard to the second question here, Aquinas does, in fact, allow that charity was in evidence before the coming of Christ. 'There were some in the state of the Old Testament', he says, 'who having charity and the grace of the Holy Spirit, looked chiefly to spiritual and eternal promises: and in this respect they belonged to the New Law.'[55] His meaning here seems to be that certain people before Christ (e.g. Abraham and Moses) had a kind of incipient faith in Christ as he was to come in something like the way in which certain scientists of the past might be said to have had faith in the scientific community which now exists. Thinking counterfactually, one might reasonably say, 'Were Newton alive today he would be proud of his scientific heirs.' By the same token, Aquinas seems to think that the faith of the Church is continuous with, and therefore somehow anticipated by, that of Old Testament saints. And, for him, this means that these individuals benefited from what was to come.

Be that as it may, though, Aquinas also holds that time makes a difference and that the Holy Spirit was not sent into the world until well after people like Abraham and Moses. He quotes John 7: 39: 'As yet the Spirit had not been given because Jesus was not glorified.' Though he allows for there being charity in people before Christ, he does not think of this as anything brought about by the Old Law. 'Although the Old Law contained precepts of charity', he explains, 'nevertheless it did not confer the Holy Spirit by whom charity is spread abroad in our hearts.'[56] In his view, therefore, people in the time of the Old Law were unable to have charity without the work of grace as effected in the time of the New Law. This, of course, means that, in Aquinas's judgement, all charity in people is the work of grace.

Why should this be so? Why does charity depend on grace? Aquinas's answer is that charity depends on grace for the same reason that any other effect of grace does—because it cannot be produced by anything less than God. That, in turn, is because those

---

[55] 1a2ae. 107. 1 ad. 2.
[56] Ibid. Aquinas is here quoting Rom. 5: 5.

with charity are godlike. We saw in Chapter 4 how Aquinas believes
that the reality in an effect reflects the nature of its cause, and that
created effects ultimately owe their reality to what is in God. With
this principle in mind, he subsequently reasons that, where an effect
shares the nature of divinity, it must derive from God alone. His
conclusion, therefore, is that, since charity is a sharing in God's
nature, only God can bring it about. Two people can produce a baby,
so we can adequately account for babies with reference to people and
without reference to God—though Aquinas, of course, would say
that people can only procreate because God is at work as Creator,
sustainer, and first mover. With charity, however, we are, so Aquinas
thinks, dealing with what cannot have a human explanation since it is
not a natural product of human activity. It is God's life of love
projected into history. It must, therefore, be caused by God alone.

Charity is an *amicitia* of people for God, founded upon the fellowship of
everlasting happiness. Now this fellowship is in respect, not of natural, but of
gratuitous gifts . . . So charity surpasses our natural faculties. Now that which
surpasses the faculty of nature cannot be natural or acquired by natural
powers since a natural effect does not transcend its cause. Therefore charity
can be in us neither naturally, nor through acquisition by the natural powers,
but by the infusion of the Holy Spirit, who is the love of the Father and the
Son, and the participation of whom in us is created charity.[57]

4. The Object of Charity

All of this sounds fairly exalted, of course. And that is clearly how
Aquinas intends it to sound. He believes that charity is a matter of
possessing God. He thinks that it makes us more like God than
anything else. But he does not mean to imply that it is other worldly
or extraordinary. He never says that people cease to be people when
they have charity. Nor does he suppose that they have reached the
end of their road. He thinks of charity as something which can and
does grow. Why? Because God cannot be loved by us to the degree
that he is lovable. Only he can love himself to that degree. And in this
life a person's whole heart cannot be always actually intent on God
because of 'the weakness of the human condition'.[58] Aquinas also
thinks that even with the natural virtues, and even with faith, hope,

---

[57] 2a2ae. 24. 2.
[58] 2a2ae. 24. 4 and 10.

and charity, people need something more. They require a kind of ongoing tutelage. In Edward D. O'Connor's words, he holds that:

As an actor who has not fully mastered his part must rely on a prompter to help him, so people, given a participation in the divine life by grace, are so little at home there that they must be assisted by the promptings of the Holy Spirit, to which the Gifts make them docile. Thomas compares our situation to that of an apprentice physician who cannot function on his own, but only under the guidance of a master physician.[59]

The 'Gifts' in question here are the 'Gifts of the Holy Spirit', which Aquinas, invoking Isaiah 11: 2 f., identifies as wisdom, understanding, counsel, knowledge, piety, fortitude, and fear of the Lord.[60]

But there is yet another reason for saying that charity, in Aquinas's view, is not entirely other worldly. And this lies in the fact that he thinks of charity as a sharing by us in time of the life that belongs to God. He maintains that the primary object of charity is God. In charity, it is God we love first. But he also holds that the good of everything derives from God and reflects him. So consistency would seem to demand that he should think that those with charity will love whatever is good as well as loving the source of goodness which is God himself. And this is a point which he takes well enough. 'There can be no true virtue without charity', he says.[61] This is because 'true virtue is directed to our principal good'. Insofar as in acting we aim at what is really good, even when aiming at particular goods we require charity if the particular goods aimed at are true, not just apparent, goods.[62] So 'charity directs the acts of all the other virtues to our final end', and it may therefore be called 'the form of the virtues'.[63] It can, says Aquinas, be compared to a mother. A mother conceives

---

[59] Edward D. O'Connor, CSC, *The Gifts of the Spirit*, vol. xiv of the Blackfriars edition of the *Summa theologiae* (London, 1974), xvi. Cf. 1a2ae. 68. 2.

[60] There is some development in Aquinas's teaching on the gifts: one can trace differences between his treatment of them in the *Commentary on Isaiah* and the *Commentary on the Sentences*, his treatment in the *prima secundae*, and his treatment in the *secunda secundae*. Differences include (1) ways of classifying the gifts, (2) a shift from talking of the gifts as making people act in a superhuman mode to talking of them as making people docile to the prompting (*instinctus*) of the Spirit, (3) the development of an analogy between the gifts and the moral virtues (the latter make one amenable to the movement of reason, the former make the faculties amenable to the movement of the Spirit), and (4) reinterpretation of the gifts of knowledge, wisdom, understanding, and counsel. On all this see O'Connor, *The Gifts of the Spirit*.

[61] 2a2ae. 23. 7.

[62] Ibid.

[63] 2a2ae. 23. 8.

from another. Charity brings to conception all aiming at true good since it is desire of Goodness itself. It is the desire for God. 'Since a mother is one who conceives in herself from another, charity is called the mother of the other virtues, because from desire of the ultimate end it conceives their acts by charging them with life.'[64]

In day-to-day life, this means that charity can be said to have many objects. It extends, for example, to our neighbour.

The light in which we must love our neighbours is God, for what we ought to love in them is that they be in God. Hence it is clear that it is specifically the same act which loves God and loves neighbour. And on this account charity extends not merely to the love of God, but also to the love of neighbour.[65]

For Aquinas, too, charity includes self-love. It sounds odd, he admits, to speak of *amicitia* with oneself. And charity is a matter of *amicitia*. But Aquinas thinks that being friends with God means loving what belongs to him and what he has willed. And that includes ourselves.[66] It even includes our bodies.

Our bodily nature, far from issuing from an evil principle, as the Manichees imagine, is from God. We can therefore use it for God's service ... Accordingly, with the same love of charity by which we love God, we ought also to love our body.[67]

As Timothy McDermott writes:

Thomas refuses to condemn self-love, and indeed believes that true *amicitia* for God involves us in loving his whole creation in an ordered and truthful way. For him even our natural love of life is love of the world as God has made it, with its natural order in which the one loving also has a place and must be loved as everything else is loved. So his conception of natural love is at once more selfless and his conception of charity more self-ful than spiritual writers sometimes allow. Natural love already loves God above all things since in the natural order of things that is where God ranks; and in charity we love our friend's world because we love him, and that means loving ourselves and our fellows as ourselves, and not only as *we* love ourselves but as *he* does.[68]

---

[64] 2a2ae. 23. 8 ad. 3.
[65] 2a2ae. 25. 1.
[66] 2a2ae. 25. 4.
[67] 2a2ae. 25. 5.
[68] *St Thomas Aquinas, Summa Theologiae: A Concise Translation* (London, 1989), 327.

One might add that the insistence on the goodness of the material world implied by all of this is typical of Aquinas. In 1a. 65. 2 he asks whether material creatures come from God. He replies:

> Certain heretics take the position that these visible things have not been created by a good God, but by an evil principle . . . Their position, however, is completely untenable . . . Material creatures are by nature good.

The point is carried forward in the next article, where Aquinas rejects the view that 'material creatures were not at first intended by God, but were made as a punishment for the sin of spiritual creatures'. Among other things he does in replying to this suggestion, he cites Genesis 2: 10: 'God saw that it was good.'

For Aquinas, however, people are not just part of a good world. They belong to a world which has been redeemed by Christ. As Aquinas sees it, God has not only looked at his world. He has entered it. And, by doing so, he has drawn us to himself. So it is to this aspect of Aquinas's teaching that we now turn.

15

God Incarnate

The Oxford Dictionary of the Christian Church tells us that Christology is 'the study of the Person of Christ, and in particular of the union in Him of the Divine and human natures'. Not everyone would agree with this definition. And we cannot say whether or not Aquinas would have agreed with it, for he lived before the time when 'Christology' was a word to be listed in dictionaries. But we might well surmise that he would at least sympathize with it were he alive today. That is because Christology, in the sense now in question, is his chief concern when he talks about Christ directly. It is also an area of inquiry in which he draws heavily on what he has to say before he turns to the subject of Christ. His 'Christology' is indebted to his teaching on God considered as Creator and Trinity. It is also bound up with what he thinks about human beings and their natural and supernatural happiness. For he conceives of Christ as the definitive means by which creatures who have come from God return to their source. And he takes him to be the point at which divinity and humanity come closest to each other. For Aquinas's Christ is both truly human and truly divine.

The General Nature of Aquinas's Christology

Sticking with the definition of 'Christology' just cited, it is fair to say that many Christologies, both ancient and modern, fight shy of, or even deny, the assertion that Christ is both human and divine.[1] Aquinas, on the other hand, is uncompromisingly orthodox in his teaching about Christ. By this I mean that he accepts without qualifi-

---

[1] As he would admit himself, a clear case would be the Christology presented by Maurice Wiles in *The Remaking of Christian Doctrine* (London, 1974), *Working Papers in Doctrine* (London, 1976), and *Faith and the Mystery of God* (London, 1982). For a brief account of ancient and modern Christologies, see John Macquarrie, *Jesus Christ in Modern Thought* (London, 1990).

cation the doctrine of the Incarnation laid down by the Council of Chalcedon.[2] He holds that Christ is one logical subject of whom divine and human attributes can be truly predicated without equivocation. In calling Christ human and divine there is, for him, no question of metaphor, myth, symbol, or anything else which might be taken to imply that Christ is not both what God is by nature and what people are by nature. Nor is there any question of belief in Christ's humanity and divinity being just an expression of human values, as, for example, Albrecht Ritschl (1822–89) is credited with teaching.

He does not adopt this view as a conclusion of argument or reasoning based on premises the truth of which are evident to us. He starts with it. Everything he has to say about Christ is an attempt to explore the sense and significance of what he takes to be the teaching of Chalcedon. For him, therefore, belief in Christ's humanity and divinity is on a par with belief in the doctrine of the Trinity. It is a matter of faith. As we saw in the previous chapter, his view is that 'Thomas *saw one thing and believed something else. He saw a man; he believed him to be God and bore witness to this, saying, "My Lord and my God"*.'[3] Some theologians have held that the doctrine of the Incarnation should be seen as a conclusion arrived at by Christians in the light of the resurrection and/or their experience as members of the Church. The general idea here is that the doctrine makes the best sense of events or experiences following the death of Christ. But, though one can certainly attribute to Aquinas the suggestion that this is somehow the case, his presiding view is that belief in the Incarnation stems from the teaching of Christ. The author of the letter to the Hebrews speaks of Christ as 'the pioneer and perfector of our faith'.[4] Among other things, Aquinas takes this to mean that the divinity of Christ was taught by Christ himself. 'Our faith', he observes, 'rests on the first truth. And therefore Christ is the pioneer of our faith by reason of his divine knowledge, which is absolutely one.'[5] Christ, he says, was 'the first and original teacher of the faith'.[6] With this point in mind, he denies that Christ had faith. His

---

[2] He seems to have been the first scholastic of the high Middle Ages to quote the texts of Chalcedon and other early Councils. Cf. James Weisheipl, *Friar Thomas d'Aquino* (Washington, DC, 1983), 164 f.

[3] 2a2ae. 1. 4 ad. 1.

[4] Heb. 12: 2.

[5] 3a. 11. 6 ad. 2.

[6] 3a. 7. 7.

position is that, in teaching his own divinity, Christ was speaking from knowledge.

> The field of faith is divine reality that is hidden from sight . . . Now, a virtue, like any other habit, takes its character from its field of action. Hence, where divine reality is not hidden from sight there is no point in faith. But from the moment of conception Christ had the full vision of the very being of God . . . Therefore he could not have had faith.[7]

The belief that Christ enjoyed the beatific vision from his conception is not much favoured in modern theological writings on Christ. But, as we shall presently see, Aquinas has his reasons for accepting it. At this point, however, an implication of what we have just noted needs to be drawn out. This is the fact that, as I mentioned in Chapter 14, Aquinas presumes that the New Testament gives us a substantially accurate account of the life and teaching of Christ. Following the course taken by biblical criticism since the nineteenth century, many theologians now decline to base the doctrine of the Incarnation on the teaching of Christ. Some of them doubt that we have access to that teaching. Others think that we cannot reasonably say that it directly asserted or clearly implied that Christ is divine. But neither position is shared by Aquinas. Christ is presented in the New Testament as laying claim to divinity and as acting as God was supposed to act. Though Aquinas does not argue for the accuracy of the New Testament records (this was simply not an issue among theologians in his day), he presumes that the picture they convey is substantially correct. Hence, for example, in dismissing the claim that Christ was never angry, sad, or hungry, he observes that, if this claim is true, 'the reliability of the Gospel account would perish. What is prophetically announced in figurative speech is one thing; what is described in historical terms by the Evangelists in a literal sense is another.'[8] So he subsequently maintains that the doctrine of the Incarnation derives from Christ himself. One imagines that, were he alive today, as well as repeating his point about the reliability of the Gospel account, he would be saying that it must have done so in order to qualify as what he means by an article of faith. He believes that the content of faith is truth which exceeds the reach of human knowledge and which must be taught by God if it is to be anything more than unwarranted speculation.

[7] 3a. 7. 3.
[8] 3a. 5. 3.

It should now, therefore, be clear where Aquinas begins in his treatment of the Incarnation. The next thing to note is that he proceeds by dealing with issues of two kinds. To start with, he considers what can be said to elucidate the claim that Christ is truly both divine and human, i.e. what is involved in Christ being God Incarnate. In the light of his answer to this question, he then reflects on what is achieved by virtue of the Incarnation, i.e. what the effects of the Incarnation are. For the remainder of this chapter we shall follow him on the first topic. We shall see how he thinks about the second topic in Chapter 16.

The Union of Divinity and Humanity

Given that Aquinas starts with the doctrine of the Incarnation as stated by Chalcedon, we need to remember how that Council formulated the doctrine.[9] It will therefore be convenient to have its declaration before us. The relevant part of the text runs thus:

Following the saintly fathers, we all with one voice teach the confession of one and the same Son, our Lord Jesus Christ: the same perfect in divinity and perfect in humanity, the same truly God and truly human, of a rational soul and a body; consubstantial (*homoousios*) with the Father as regards his divinity, and the same consubstantial with us as regards his humanity; like us in all respects except for sin; begotten before the ages from the Father as regards his divinity, and in the last days the same for us and for our salvation from Mary, the virgin God-bearer (*theotokos*), as regards his humanity; one and the same Christ, Son, Lord, only-begotten, acknowledged in two natures which undergo no confusion, no change, no division, no separation; at no point was the difference between the natures taken away through the union, but rather the property of both natures is preserved and comes together into a single person (*prosopon*) and a single subsistent being; he is not parted or divided into two persons; but is one and the same only-begotten Son, God, Word, Lord Jesus Christ, just as the prophets taught from the beginning.[10]

---

[9] I should, of course, stress that lying behind Aquinas's theology of the Incarnation are several important treatments of the topic coming from medieval authors earlier than him. Space and my current purposes prevent me from going into details concerning these treatments, but valuable material can be found in Walter H. Principle, *The Theology of the Hypostatic Union in the Early Thirteenth Century*, 4 vols. (Toronto, 1963–75).

[10] *Decrees of the Ecumenical Councils*, ed. Norman P. Tanner (London, 1990), i. 86.

In saying that Christ is *homoousios* with the Father, Chalcedon is asserting that he and the Father are both God. We can put the point by saying that, according to Chalcedon, sentences with 'Christ' as subject can be rewritten with 'God' as subject.

In saying that Christ is one person begotten of the Father, Chalcedon is asserting that he and the Father are two as well as one—that the Father is not the Son, and the Son is not the Father, even though both are God, and even though this does not mean that there are two Gods.

To say that Christ must be acknowledged in two natures is to say that one may truly affirm of Christ what is properly affirmed of God and of human beings.

All of this means that Chalcedon maintains that to call Christ God is to affirm that he is one subject with two natures. And this is the position which Aquinas wants to defend.

There are alternatives to such a position. One might, for example, hold that to speak of Christ as God is to take him to have a single nature which is both human and divine. One might think that humanity and divinity are united in Christ because he has the nature of 'godmanhood'. In terms of this theory, commonly known as 'monophysitism', one should conceive of the union of divinity and humanity in Christ as being effected only by virtue of one nature, which Aquinas, citing Boethius, thinks of as constituting the essence of a thing, that which gives something form through specific difference.[11]

But Aquinas does not agree with the theory. We may speak of a unity based on one nature when, for example, a collection of things of one kind come together to form a collection—as when a pile of stones is made up from individual stones. But Aquinas does not think that the unity of humanity and divinity in Christ is like this. If it were, he argues, Christ would be divine and human only accidentally. For stones which make a pile are just as much stones when the pile is broken up. He would also fail to be a genuine subject having a definite nature, for a pile of stones is not a natural unit.[12]

Another way in which a unity might be based on one nature is when two distinct substances mix to form a new one, as when a

---

[11] 2a. 2. 1. Monophysitism comes in different versions. Its original proponent is often said to be Eutyches (d. 454), to whom Aquinas refers in 3a. 2. 6. and 3a. 18. 1.
[12] 3a. 2. 1.

compound results from elements coming together. So can we suppose that the unity of divinity and humanity in Christ is like what occurs when that takes place? Once again, Aquinas replies in the negative. For one thing, he says, to be divine is to be changeless. So there can be no question of divinity mixing with something to result in a new nature. And if the union of divinity and humanity in Christ were like that of a compound, then Christ would be neither divine nor human. For a compound of elements X and Y is neither X nor Y. It is something different again. In any case, so Aquinas suggests, divinity cannot mix with humanity leaving humanity present. It would swallow humanity up as wine swallows up a drop of water.[13]

Another possibility which Aquinas considers is that Christ is human and divine as people can be said to be single things even though they are constituted of body and soul. My body and my soul are both human, and they unite to form an individual. So might it not be like this with the union of divinity and humanity? But Aquinas is also unhappy with this suggestion. He says that the union of divinity and humanity in Christ cannot be like this since humanity and divinity are complete in themselves and since the human body and the human soul are not describable in the same way. He also denies that divine and human nature can come together to make a whole as the parts of a body do, for divinity is not made up of quantitative parts. It might be replied that the divinity and humanity of Christ are related as form is to matter when something has both form and matter. But Aquinas denies that as well. The divine nature, he says, cannot be the form of anything, certainly not something material. And if the divine nature were the form of something material, it could be shared by many individuals and there could be many Christs. But there cannot be many Christs (where 'Christ' is a proper name) any more than there can be many instances of Brian Davies.[14]

For these reasons Aquinas concludes that Chalcedon was right to speak of divinity and humanity coming together in Christ in one person and not in one nature. But what does this conclusion mean for him? It will help, I think, if we cast the reply to this question in logical terms. For him, Christ is one person. And, in saying that, he means that 'Christ' is a proper name, that 'in all singular statements which we make with "Christ" as subject he to whom we refer is the same'.[15] To put it another way, in terms of Aquinas's thinking:

---

[13] Ibid.
[14] Ibid.
[15] C. J. F. Williams, 'A Programme for Christology', *Religious Studies*, 3 (1968), 522.

The general rule governing affirmative statements about Christ may be put as follows. Given the mystery of the Incarnation, and taking note of the fact that affirmative statements assert identity between what the Subject stands for and what the Predicate stands for, we may make about Christ any affirmative statement the Subject and Predicate of which stand for the unique person of Christ (or any statement which may be reduced to this form).[16]

Take, for example, 'Christ went walking and Christ went running'. Aquinas thinks that, if Christ is one person, we can read this statement as saying that a subject went walking and a subject went running, and it was the same subject who walked and ran. This subject we call 'Christ'. By the same token, Aquinas also thinks that to say that humanity and divinity come together in Christ in one person is to say that one subject can be truly spoken of as we speak of a man, and that the same subject can be truly spoken of as we speak of God. We can say of a man that he has a body since 'human nature includes a true body'. So we can say of Christ that he has a body.[17] We can say of God that he is omniscient and omnipotent. So we can also say of Christ that he is omniscient and omnipotent.

The Word of God ... from all eternity had complete being in *hypostasis* or person, but human nature came to be his in time, not as assumed into a single *esse* as this pertains to nature (as a body is assumed to the *esse* of the soul), but to the single *esse* as this pertains to *hypostasis* or person. And thus the joining of human nature to the Son of God is not in the manner of an accident.[18]

For all practical purposes, *hypostasis* and 'person' are equivalent here. They signify what Aquinas has in mind when he uses the word *suppositum* in the sense of 'subject' or 'individual'. The only difference between them is that 'person', for Aquinas, adds to *hypostasis* the notion of being rational, as Boethius teaches.[19] In his view, therefore, the Incarnation occurred since it came to pass that the second person of the Trinity (the Son, the Word) acquired a nature other than his divine nature, the result being not two things but one thing, or, as Aquinas puts it, one *esse*. This, in turn, means that with Christ we have one subject of whom we may truly predicate 'is human' and 'is divine'.

Once again, there are other positions which might be adopted.

---

[16] Appendix 1 to vol. 1 of the Blackfriars edition of the *Summa theologiae*, 218 f.
[17] 3a. 5. 1.
[18] 3a. 2. 6 ad. 2.
[19] *De duabus naturis*, 3.

One might, for example, say that in the Incarnation there is a divine subject (*hypostasis*) and a human subject (*hypostasis*), as is often said to be the view of Nestorius (d. *c*.451) and Theodore of Mopsuestia (*c*.350–428).[20] But Aquinas thinks that this view does not allow us to speak of Christ really being God Incarnate. If there are two individuals involved in Christ being divine, 'it would follow that those things relating to his human condition . . . would be verified by someone other than the Word'.[21] In other words, statements like 'Christ was born', 'Christ suffered', and 'Christ died' would be true because something other than a divine person was born, suffered, and died, which Aquinas regards as incompatible with orthodoxy, as, indeed, it is.

For him, then, divinity and humanity are united in Christ because one subject, the Word, has two distinct natures. And he takes this to mean that what belongs essentially to God and to human beings must belong to Christ. It follows, for example, that Christ is omniscient, omnipotent, and all good. It also follows that Christ is a composite of body and soul. A human being is body and soul, he says. So Christ is body and soul. The main thing that distinguishes him from other people is that while they are subjects having only a human nature, he, being God, is a subject with two natures. In him, says Aquinas, soul and body 'are united in such a way as to be conjoined to another and higher principle which subsists in the nature composed of body and soul'.[22]

In speaking of the union or conjunction involved here, Aquinas puts things by saying that Christ's human nature was assumed by a divine person. For him, of course, the second person of the Trinity, the Word, is eternal. So it would have been true to say 'The Word exists' before the birth of Christ. It would not, however, then have been true to say 'Christ exists', for Christ had not been born. With these points in mind, Aquinas concludes that we may speak of the Incarnation as a matter of it coming about in time that a human nature, involving the existence of a human being, came to be assumed by a divine person. The term 'assumed' is required, he thinks, in order not to deny the eternal being of God the Son.[23] As we may

---

[20] There is, however, much divergence of opinion concerning what precisely these theologians did teach.

[21] 3a. 2. 3

[22] 3a. 2. 5 ad. 1

[23] 3a. 3. 1 ff.

put it, 'since the person of the Word pre-exists, Christ's created human nature does not constitute his person but rather joins it'.[24]

Notice, however, that Aquinas does not want to say such things as 'The Son of God assumed a person' or 'The Son of God assumed a man'. In his view, to say that the Son of God assumed a person would be tantamount to saying that after the birth of Christ there were two individuals constituting the union of divinity and humanity in Christ.[25] And to say that the Son of God assumed a man is erroneous for the same reason. 'It is not precise to say that the Son of God assumed a man', he observes, 'given the truth of the matter that in Christ there is one *suppositum* and one person.'[26] What we have to say is that a man who was God was born. This means that with Christ we have one human subject who is also a divine subject, that divinity and humanity are united in one being. And on this basis Aquinas maintains that we may say such things as 'God is a man', 'A man is God', 'Christ is the Lord', and 'God was made (became) a man'.[27] Since there is but one subject involved in the Incarnation, however, and since that subject is divine as well as human, we cannot say such things as 'A man was made God', or 'Christ is a creature' or 'Christ began to be'. If a man was made God, then the Incarnation involves two subjects each of them pre-existing the union of divinity and humanity. If Christ is a creature, then he is not divine. Nor is he divine if he began to be. What began to be with the Incarnation, Aquinas thinks, is the union of what is united in one subject. And that occurred when a human being whom we call 'Christ' was conceived. It occurred when the changeless Son of God (God the Son, the Word, the second person of the Trinity) took to himself a changeable human nature conceived by the Virgin Mary.

Might it have occurred differently? The question is not much asked by modern theologians.[28] For the record, though, and because

---

[24] Romanus Cessario, OP, *The Godly Image: Christ and Salvation in Catholic Thought from Anselm to Aquinas* (Petersham, Mass., 1990), 135.

[25] 3a. 4. 2.

[26] 3a. 4. 3.

[27] 3a. 16. 1 ff.

[28] For a modern author finding the question worth asking, however, see Macquarrie, *Jesus Christ in Modern Thought*, 170: 'Now that we are much more conscious than was Thomas both of the variety of revelations or so called revelations that have come through saviour-figures on this planet, and of the possibility that there are in the universe other personal races of beings who stand in need of a knowledge of God, the notion of a plurality of incarnations ... cannot be dismissed without

it throws light on what he thinks the Incarnation to be, we ought to note that Aquinas considers it and replies affirmatively. He does not think that the union could have come about without there being a union in a subject of distinct natures. To agree to that would undermine his whole position on the Incarnation. But he does think it possible for a person other than the Son to have become incarnate. The Father or the Holy Spirit, he says, could each have taken to themselves a human nature (i.e. each could have been incarnate in different human beings). Alternatively, all three could have done so (i.e. all three could have been incarnate in one human being). Nor, Aquinas also suggests, is there any inherent impossibility in the Son becoming incarnate a second time.[29]

These, however, are just possibilities in Aquinas's view. In the jargon of modern philosophy, he only thinks that there are 'possible worlds' in which they obtain.'[30] For him, their possibility follows from it being true that each divine person is fully divine, and from the fact that *suppositum* and nature are not distinct in God. He says that the Incarnation of the Word is the incarnation of an undivided divine nature. So the whole of the Godhead exists in Christ, and there is nothing to stop what constitutes divinity (i.e. the Trinity of persons) existing in him or in any other human being who is united to divinity by person (or 'hypostatically'). But Aquinas does not believe that any such incarnation has actually occurred (that it is part of the 'actual world'), for this conclusion does not belong to the content of faith. He even thinks that we can say why it is especially appropriate that only the Son should assume a human nature. He holds, for example, that this is so in the light of some points which we noted in Chapter 10.

There we saw that the Son, for him, may be thought of as the Father's concept of himself in whom the Father knows himself. In knowing himself in the Son, says Aquinas, the Father also knows his creatures, and 'his single Word expresses not only the Father but creatures as well.'[31] This suggests to Aquinas that the Son may be

---

consideration.' See also, Thomas V. Morris, *The Logic of God Incarnate* (Ithaca, NY, 1986). 7.

[29] 3a. 3. 1.

[30] I am not implying that Aquinas agrees that there are possible worlds in the sense intended by many modern philosophers. He emphatically does not. As I say in the text, I am here merely invoking jargon.

[31] 1a. 34. 4.

compared to what a craftsman has in mind in conceiving of what he makes, and that he is therefore the exemplar or model for all creation, which may, in this sense, be said to resemble him. Since like goes with like, he adds, it is therefore appropriate for the Son to become joined to what is created.[32] This is also appropriate, Aquinas goes on to say, since the Son of God incarnate was the means by which humanity was saved from the effects of the sin of Adam. Here he thinks of Christ's saving role as a kind of mending or repairing. He then reasons that, as a craftsman repairs damage in something he has made according to the idea (or blueprint) of the thing in him, so it is fitting that God repairs humanity by means of the Son, who is the exemplar or model of humanity.[33] Since, he also thinks that those saved by Christ can be called heirs of Christ and sons of God,[34] he adds that it is also appropriate that the Son become incarnate so that Christians may 'share by adoption in a likeness to his sonship'.[35]

A further reason can be taken from the purpose of the union, the accomplishment of the predestination of those who are preordained for a heavenly inheritance. To this sons alone have a right: 'If sons heirs also'. Appropriately, then, through him who is Son by nature we share by adoption in a likeness to his sonship: 'Those whom he foreknew he predestined to share the image of his Son.'[36]

What was Christ Like?

In general, then, Aquinas regards the Incarnation as a literal uniting of God and humanity by which humanity is conformed to the image of the eternal Son of God, who is himself God. But what does he think this implies for the existence of Christ as a human being? What does he think Christ was like?

We have already seen that he takes him to be what all human beings are insofar as they are body and soul. One might object to saying such things as that Christ had a real body, for one might think that this would detract from his dignity. But Aquinas insists that 'human nature includes a true body' and that if Christ did not have a

---

[32] 3a. 3. 8.
[33] Ibid.
[34] See Rom. 12: 14 ff.
[35] 3a. 3. 8.
[36] Ibid.

genuine body he would not have undergone real death and 'the
events narrated [sc. in the Gospels] would not be factual, but a kind
of pretence'. This, in turn, means that Christ had a human mind
or intellect. 'There would not be true human flesh were it not
completed by a human, i.e. rational soul. Therefore if Christ had a
soul without a mind, he would not have taken true human flesh, but
animal flesh, since our soul differs from that of a brute animal only by
the mind.'[37]

We have also seen that Aquinas thinks of Christ as conceived, as
born, and as subject to suffering and death. He takes such conclusions to be implications of holding that Christ has a human nature.
As we may put it, his view is that 'where a statement of the form "All
people have flesh and blood" is true there is a corresponding true
statement of the form "Christ has flesh and blood". Generalizations
about people have implications for Christ . . . To talk about "nature"
in connection with Christ is to talk about a particular type of common
noun which can enter into true statements of which Christ is the
subject.'[38]

But Aquinas certainly does not think that Christ is just like everybody else. We can express this by saying that Aquinas distinguishes
between an 'individual essence' and a 'kind essence', and between
properties which are universal to members of a natural kind and
properties which are essential. He holds that Christ is fully human,
but it does not follow for him that Christ is therefore exactly and only
like every other human being.[39] He believes that there are things
which set him apart from other people, and we now need to follow
him as he tries to say what these are, starting with his teaching
concerning the grace of Christ.

1. The Grace of Christ in General

The fundamental principle guiding Aquinas's thinking on this topic is
that, because Christ is a divine subject, the fullness of the divine
life is present in him, and he therefore has all that could ever be
considered to be the effect of grace. The soul of Christ, he argues, is

---

[37] 3a. 5. 4.

[38] Williams, 'A Programme for Christology', 522.

[39] Cf. Thomas V. Morris, 'The Metaphysics of God Incarnate', in Ronald J.
Feenstra and Cornelius Plantinga, Jr. (eds.), *Trinity, Incarnation and Atonement* (Notre
Dame, 1989), 155 ff.

'joined more closely to God than any other spiritual creature'.[40] Since 'the closer a subject is to the cause which is acting upon it, the more will it be affected by it', it follows, says Aquinas, that Christ's soul thus 'receives the maximum outpouring of [God's] grace'.[41] This, in turn, means that, if we consider grace as a disposition by which one embraces God by intellect and will, Christ has grace because 'he had to know and love God in the most intimate possible way'.[42] We should note that, as background to this teaching, Aquinas maintains that Christ had a human will distinct from the divine will. He does not think of Christ's actions as being directed only by the will of the Son, as if Christ were a kind of puppet. Since Christ is fully human, says Aquinas, his actions proceed both from a divine will and from a human will, albeit one totally in line with the divine will, and albeit one assumed by a divine person.[43]

In saying all this, Aquinas, of course, is thinking of Christ with respect to his human nature. It seems absurd to suggest that the second person of the Trinity, considered simply as such and without reference to the Incarnation, either needs grace or gets it. And Aquinas would agree that the suggestion is truly absurd. But he does not think that Christ is just the second person of the Trinity. He takes him to be the Word made flesh—the flesh here being something created.[44] He therefore points out that since 'the soul of Christ is not intrinsically divine' it has 'to be made divine by the kind of sharing that comes with grace'.[45] Aquinas accepts that the coming to pass of the Incarnation is not effected by grace of this kind, for 'a nature does not have existence in its appropriate complete substance through the medium of any disposition'.[46] It is not our dispositions which make us to exist as the subjects we are, and the same goes for Christ. But Aquinas insists that we must think of him as graced in his human nature because his soul is united to the Word of God and because it is precisely the work of grace for a human soul to be raised to this level. From the beginning, Aquinas therefore con-

---

[40] 3a. 7. 9.
[41] Ibid.
[42] 3a. 7. 1.
[43] See 3a. 18. 1.
[44] Cf. 3a. 2. 7, where Aquinas maintains that the union involved in the Incarnation is something created because it began in time.
[45] 3a. 7. 1 ad. 1.
[46] 3a. 2. 10.

cludes, Christ's human nature was 'conjoined to the divine person
and his soul was filled with the gifts of grace'.[47]

The grace of union is not natural to Christ in his humanity, as though caused
by the principles of human nature. Thus it need not belong to all people. Yet
it is natural to him in his human nature, because of the singular character of
his birth, i.e. he was conceived by the Holy Spirit in such a way as to be the
natural Son of God and of what is human. It is natural to him as well in his
divine nature in so far as that nature is the active principle of this grace. And
this is attributed to the whole Trinity.[48]

A position which Aquinas draws from this reasoning is that Christ
possessed the gifts of the Holy Spirit.[49] He concedes that the gifts
help the virtues and that the virtues are fully developed in Christ. So
he admits that they are not given to Christ in order to improve him.
But he thinks that, no matter how well developed the virtues are in a
human being, the gifts are required for fuller perfection and must
therefore be present in one in whom is found the fullness of grace.
For this reason, he explains, we may even attribute 'fear of the Lord'
to Christ. He did not fear separation from God by sin. Nor did he fear
punishment due to sin. Christ, for Aquinas, is without sin.[50] But 'his
soul was moved, under the impulse of the Holy Spirit, to a sense of
reverence for God' and 'as human, Christ had a deeper sense of
reverence for God than anyone else'.[51]

Another conclusion drawn by Aquinas from his teaching that
Christ has the fullness of grace is that in him were to be found the
effects of 'grace freely bestowed' (*gratia gratis data*). As we have seen,
these are special charisms given to people so that others might be led
to the fullness of the New Law. And they can, he holds, be ascribed
to Christ when we recall that he is the supreme preacher, 'the first
and most authoritative doctor of the faith'. 'It is clear', he argues,
'that Christ had all the charisms in a surpassing degree, as befits the
first and original teacher of the faith.' He had, for example, the gift of
prophecy.[52]

With all this in mind, one might wonder what to make of the

---

[47] 3a. 2. 12.
[48] 3a. 2. 12 ad. 3.
[49] 3a. 7. 5.
[50] See especially 3a. 15. 1 f.
[51] 3a. 7. 6.
[52] 3a. 7. 8.

biblical texts which have classically been thought of as pulling in a different direction. The Gospels record that Christ was baptized and that Christ was tempted by the devil.[53] Must it not therefore follow, for example, that Christ was both sinful and susceptible to sin? Aquinas, however, argues differently. He denies that Christ's baptism cleansed him from any stain. It was the water of Christ's baptism that was cleansed and thereby made holy and suitable for the baptism of others.[54] Christ was not a sinner, says Aquinas, but he took on the nature of sinful humanity, and when he was baptized this too was plunged in water and purified.[55] As for Christ's temptation, the problem for Aquinas here is not so much 'How could Christ be tempted?' as 'How could the devil have been bothered to waste his time tempting Christ?' He agrees that, since Christ had genuine human needs, he was offered something genuinely desirable to him when tempted by the devil. But his suggestion is that the story of Christ's temptation basically records something which happened for our benefit. It occurred, he says, to strengthen us against temptations, to warn us that even the holiest is vulnerable to temptation, to teach us how to overcome temptation, and to give us confidence in Christ's mercy.[56]

On the other hand, however, there are effects of grace which Aquinas does not think of as coming about in Christ. He holds that virtue can be brought about by grace, so he judges that Christ, by grace, had virtues. 'Since, then, grace was at its very best in Christ', he says, 'it gave rise to virtues which perfected each of the faculties of the soul and all its activities. In this way Christ had all the virtues.'[57] But, as I noted above, he does not think it makes sense to assert that Christ had faith. He also denies that Christ had hope. In strong contrast to those who think that Christ was only a particularly good human being, Aquinas does not believe that all virtues able to perfect us belonged to Christ in his life on earth. Faith and hope are good for us, he says. But Christ was faithless and hopeless.

[53] See Luke 3: 21 f. and 4: 1 ff., together with parallel passages in Mark and Matthew.

[54] 3a. 39. 1.

[55] Ibid.

[56] 3a. 41. 1. Aquinas's last point here is intended to draw on Heb. 4: 15. In reply to the question 'How could the devil have been bothered to waste his time tempting Christ?' he makes the familiar patristic move of holding that the devil did not really know what he was dealing with.

[57] 3a. 7. 2.

Why? For much the same reason, says Aquinas, as leads to the teaching that we do not have faith or hope in the beatific vision. Faith is unnecessary to Christ because he sees the essence of God. And he does not need hope, considered as a theological virtue, because it involves looking forward in the confidence of faith to union with God, while Christ was already united with God and could not, therefore, look forward to being so.

> The main assurance of the virtue of hope is about the prospect of enjoying God ... Christ enjoyed the full possession of God. Hence he had not the virtue of hope.

Aquinas never denies the merit of faith. But he does not think it required in the absence of certain limitations, among which he includes not being already in possession of the knowledge of God's essence. He also insists that hope is a fine thing. But he cannot see how it really has place in one who is already perfectly united to God. He will only accept that Christ can be thought of as hoping for what he did not possess. He says, for example, that he could hope for the immortality and glory of his body. He also says that Christ could hope for the building up of his Church, though Aquinas sees this as more a case of Christ wishing to communicate his fulfilment to *others* than of him hoping for what fulfils *him*.

2. *The Grace of Christ as Head of the Church*

This idea that from Christ comes fulfilment for his Church, however, plays a particularly important role in Aquinas's overall account of Christ's grace. For he thinks that all grace derives from Christ as the Son of God in whom the fullness of grace is present. Here he has in mind texts such as John 1: 16 f.: 'And from his fullness we have all received, grace upon grace. For the law was given through Moses; grace and truth came through Jesus Christ.' Influenced by such texts, and by others referring to Christ as the head of the body which is the Christian Church,[58] medieval theologians spoke of Christ's 'capital grace' ('grace as head'). Often, however, they tended to conceive of it as simply a matter of grace present in him. Aquinas, by contrast, sees the grace of Christ as something flowing from him into others.

He does so, in fact, before he singles out the grace of Christ as

---

[58] Cf. Col. 1: 18.

head of the Church for separate consideration. In arguing that Christ
had grace as disposition, for instance, he also observes that Christ
must have had grace 'to such an extent that it would overflow to
others' because he was the mediator between God and human
beings.[59] Then again, part of his case when arguing that Christ had
the fullness of grace is that grace is passed on from Christ to others
and the cause of grace in someone must derive from what has grace
in fullness.[60] But the most detailed treatment of Christ's grace as
head comes in 3a. 8, where these arguments are fleshed out.

We need to be clear, of course, that Aquinas does not believe that,
for instance, grace is like a fluid which pours out of Christ to affect
people as water can do when a tank is filled beyond its capacity.
Among other things, an image like that would fail to allow for the
conviction Aquinas has that those with grace are free in what they are
and do.[61] But he does think that grace comes only from God, as we
saw in Chapter 13. And, since he holds that Christ is divine, he
naturally holds that all grace comes from him, for divinity is shared
by all the divine persons. Since Christ is a definite, historical figure,
since the Trinity is 'economical' as well as 'immanent', Aquinas also
maintains that all grace may be said to come from Christ considered
as such. In his view, it is not the case that the eternal God remains
apart from his creation, handing out grace in the role of a distant
divinity with a soft spot for human beings. He holds that God is also
a man, and that grace derives from him on that basis. And, since
Christ is the founder of the Church, he puts this by saying that there
is such a thing as the grace of Christ as head of the Church.

Aquinas thinks of the effects of this grace as including the redemption of humanity by virtue of Christ's life and work. So his
teaching on this subject must wait until the next chapter. For the
moment I only want to note how he thinks of Christ's 'capital' grace
in general terms. To what I have already said, therefore, it largely
only remains to be explained that he thinks of it on analogy with the
human body. As he writes in the *De veritate*, 'Christ and the Church
are taken as one person.'[62] Christ as the head of the Church, he says
(here echoing St Paul), may be compared with the head of a man in
relation to his body. For example, so he argues, the head of a man is

---

[59] 3a. 7. 1.
[60] 3a. 7. 9.
[61] See 1a2ae. 110. 2.
[62] *De ver.* 29. 7.

higher than his body and is crucial when it comes to him seeing and hearing. By virtue of his head, a man also has power over the rest of his body. In the same way, Christ is higher than everyone else, for he is first in grace. And it is through him that the Church receives grace and is acted on by God in grace.[63] He is head of all people because his very existence is geared to them. He is even, so Aquinas suggests, the head of people who pre-date him in time. For before the time of Christ there were those who effectively looked forward to him, and these too can be thought of as part of the Church which is Christ's body.

The body of the Church is made up of people from the beginning to the end of the world ... People can be classed as members of the mystical body because of their potentiality, and not merely when they are actually in it.[64]

3. The Knowledge of Christ

When he says that Christ possesses the fullness of grace, Aquinas is partly concerned to give full weight to the idea that the human nature of Christ is as perfect as it is possible for such a nature to be because it is joined most intimately to God. He has no doubt that Christ shares the perfection of God. For he thinks of Christ as God. But he also thinks of him as human, and this leads him to say that Christ is also perfect insofar as a human being is capable of being so. 'The human nature assumed by the Word of God', he says, 'ought not to be in any way imperfect.'[65]

This principle, we now need to note, governs much that Aquinas writes as he goes on to consider what else we may say about Christ as a human being.[66] He invokes it, for instance, in considering Christ's knowledge. Since God is omniscient, he says, it follows that the person of the Son is omniscient, and that Christ is therefore omniscient. 'Christ', he reasons, 'knew everything by divine know-

---

[63] 3a. 8. 1 f.
[64] 3a. 8. 3.
[65] 3a. 9. 3.
[66] In this respect, Aquinas's line of thinking may be compared with that of the 20th-century theologian Karl Rahner. According to Rahner, 'Christology may be studied as self-transcending anthropology, and anthropology as deficient Christology' (*Theological Investigations*, i (London, 1961), 164 n. 1). I take this to mean that 'christology shows us in Christ what humanity can be, when brought to the fullness of its possibilities, and at the same time shows us how our everyday humanity falls short of its archetype in Jesus Christ' (Macquarrie, *Jesus Christ in Modern Thought*, 306).

ledge, through an uncreated operation which is the divine essence itself; for God's act of understanding is his very substance.'[67] But what of the Son considered as human? Here Aquinas repeatedly argues that, insofar as knowledge is open to people, and insofar as it perfects them, it is open to Christ in his human nature. For he is perfect as a human being.

To begin with, therefore, he holds that Christ was able to know, as all human beings know, by means of an agent intellect and possible intellect (cf. Chapters 7 and 13). 'The Son of God', he writes, 'assumed an integral human nature; he assumed not only a body but a soul; a soul capable not only of sense knowledge but of thought.'[68] The operation of the agent intellect ('drawing out intelligible species from images') is, says Aquinas, 'a natural human activity'. So 'it seems proper to attribute it to Christ'.[69] In the *Commentary on the Sentences* Aquinas denies that a properly functioning agent intellect exists in Christ.[70] But this is not his final verdict. By the time he writes the *Summa theologiae* he has come to take more seriously the implications of holding that Christ has a truly human nature. So there he concedes that he was wrong in what he previously wrote. If Christ was truly human, it follows, he argues against himself, that he must have had knowledge as other people do, and that 'he knew everything that can possibly be known by the exercise of active intellect.'[71]

But just to put things this way will not, he adds, be quite enough if we want to maintain that Christ is perfect as a human being. For we need to consider, not just what is involved in people knowing, but also the content of their knowledge. And with this point in mind he suggests that Christ's knowledge must extend to whatever can be known by people. If someone can be said to have knowledge of a certain kind, then, so Aquinas reasons, Christ can be said to have such knowledge, for otherwise he would be less perfect than someone else. If, for example, people can be said to have a knowledge of God's essence, then Christ can be said to have this.[72] Aquinas accepts that the soul of Christ does not comprehend the divine essence.[73]

[67] 3a. 9. 1 ad. 1.
[68] 3a. 9. 1.
[69] 3a. 12. 2.
[70] *Sent.* 3. 14. 3. 5 ad. 3, 3. 18, 3 ad. 5.
[71] 3a. 12. 1.
[72] 3a. 9. 1.
[73] 3a. 10. 1.

Drawing on what he says in the *prima pars*,[74] he notes that 'it is impossible for a creature to fully comprehend the divine essence'. So he concedes that 'the soul of Christ has no full comprehension of the divine essence'.[75] In this connection he also invokes a principle which he quotes from St John Damascene (*c.*675–*c.*749): 'The uncreated remains uncreated and the created remains within the confines of the created.'[76] But he goes on to observe that one may see God's essence without comprehending him. And he argues that, if the Word in his human nature had not enjoyed the beatific vision, he would have been less perfect than any beatified human being. On this basis, therefore, he ascribes the beatific vision to Christ from the moment of his conception. In his view, Christ in his earthly life can be thought of as both a 'pilgrim' and a 'beholder' (*simul viator et comprehensor*).

People are called pilgrims because they are proceeding towards beatitude; they are called beholders because they have already obtained it . . . Before his passion Christ, in his mind, saw God perfectly. And so he had beatitude in all that belongs specifically to the soul. But in other respects he lacked beatitude, because his soul could still suffer, and his body was liable to pain and death . . . So, he was a beholder, having the beatitude characteristic of the soul, and at the same time a pilgrim, proceeding towards beatitude in the areas in which he still lacked it.[77]

As for Christ's knowledge of other things, Aquinas goes on to say that we must also ascribe to him whatever can be known by people apart from the essence of God.

The human nature assumed by the Word of God ought not to be in any way imperfect. But everything that is in potentiality is imperfect, until reduced to actuality. Now the passive intellect of people is in potentiality to all intelligible objects . . . Christ, therefore, has to be credited with infused knowledge: intelligible species covering everything to which the passive intellect is in potency have been imprinted by the Word of God on the soul of Christ.[78]

In other words, although his sense experience was limited, Christ must have known all that people can come to know by means of the agent and possible intellect. And, since his sense experience was limited, this must mean that knowledge was given to him directly by

[74] 1a. 12. 7.
[75] 3a. 10. 1.
[76] Ibid. The principle from Damascene can be found in his *De fide orthodoxa*, III, 3.
[77] 3a. 15. 10; cf. 3a. 11. 2.
[78] 3a. 9. 3.

God (it was 'infused') and was always there to be drawn on (it was 'habitual' or dispositional).

The normal way for the human soul to receive knowledge is in the form of habits. And therefore it must be said that the infused knowledge of the soul of Christ was habitual, and that he could use it whenever he wished.[79]

It does not follow from this that Christ was constantly drawing on his knowledge of all that people can know. Aquinas is not thinking of him as being in a changeless state of omniscience. But we must, he holds, think of Christ as able to spell out what he knows if he wishes, and we can do so without detracting from his perfection.

A habit is actuated at the command of the will... Although it does not actually reach out to everything it is not frustrated, provided it can actually reach out to what suits a given place and time. And therefore a habit is not futile even when everything that falls within its range is not actualized.[80]

One might wonder how Aquinas can say this kind of thing since he has also asserted that Christ, like the rest of us, has knowledge by means of experience and the operation of his agent intellect. In fact, however, he seems happy to remind us that the infused knowledge of Christ goes hand in hand with knowledge he acquires as other people do. He says, for example:

Just as by infused knowledge the soul of Christ knew everything to which the passive intellect is in potency in any way whatever, so by acquired knowledge he knew everything that can possibly be known by the exercise of active intellect.[81]

To this one might reply that Christ did not experience everything, while the knowledge we acquire is got by experience. One might also observe that not all the objects of sensation were presented to the bodily senses of Christ. Aquinas, however, acticipates these objections. And he answers them by arguing that, though Christ was immediately, and without experience, given the grace of knowing all that we can know by experience, it does not follow that he cannot have had the wherewithal to know by experience. He argues, for example, that, since we can reason from effects to causes, we may hold that 'although Christ did not experience everything, he was able

---

[79] 3a. 11. 5.
[80] 3a. 11. 5 ad. 2.
[81] 3a. 12. 1.

to know everything as a result of what he did experience'. From those
objects which were presented to Christ's senses, says Aquinas, he
could come to know other things.[82] This conclusion, in turn, leads
him to hold that Christ can be said to have grown in his knowledge
by experience. Given the operation of an agent intellect in him, he
suggests, we may conclude that 'Christ did not know everything from
the beginning'.[83]

4. The Power and the Weakness of Christ

It should be obvious from what we have seen in this chapter that
Aquinas is very much concerned to deny that the Incarnation involves
a swamping or obliteration of human existence. Though he rigidly
insists that Christ is God, and though he takes this to mean that
Christ is not like other men, he constantly strives to allow for the fact
that Christ was a man with a real human nature. So far, however, I
have said little about how he deals with the question of the ways in
which human weakness enters into the Incarnation. Now, therefore,
it needs to be noted that, in his view, we must not only ascribe such
weakness to Christ. We must also suppose that it was quite extensive.

For example, says Aquinas, the human nature of Christ is not
omnipotent. Why? Because it is created and because it does not
belong to any created nature to be omnipotent. It belongs to the
divine nature.[84] Christ can only be called omnipotent because the
union of the Incarnation involves one subject, who is omnipotent
because he is divine. And it follows from this, says Aquinas, that the
soul of Christ cannot have created itself,[85] and that Christ's human
nature depends on God for its existence. 'Just as God alone can
create', he argues, 'so he alone can reduce creatures to nothingness;
and he alone can conserve them in being, preventing them from
dissolving into nothingness.'[86]

On this basis Aquinas is also prepared to add that Christ did not
have unlimited power over his body. He could not, for instance,
directly will himself to be nourished and well. Though we can do a
lot to promote our physical health, we cannot make ourselves healthy

---

[82] 3a. 12. 1.
[83] 3a. 12. 2 ad. 1.
[84] 3a. 13. 1.
[85] 3a. 13. 1 ad. 2.
[86] 3a. 13. 2.

by fiat. And thus it was with Christ. What goes on in the physical realm apart from what can be willed by us is, Aquinas observes, 'subject only to God, who is the author of nature'. So Christ only had power over everything by virtue of the grace of union, and the power involved here belongs to the Word rather than to Christ's human, created soul.[87] Bearing in mind the miracle stories in the Gospels, Aquinas concedes that Christ willed events to come about miraculously. But this, he explains, was a matter of him willing things 'to be done by the divine power', for miracles, 'were things Christ could not do by his own [human] power, but only as an instrument of the divinity'.[88]

Aquinas can therefore be thoroughly clear that we can happily believe the Gospels when they say that Christ experienced pain and the like. With an eye on Christ's uniqueness, he accepts that the Word of God could have miraculously preserved Christ from suffering. He also thinks that the death of Christ was not an inevitable punishment due to sin inherited from Adam. In Aquinas's view, Christ embraced his sufferings willingly. So they can always be viewed as voluntary.[89] But he sees no objection to holding that Christ genuinely suffered and died. He actually sees it as appropriate that this should be so. For one thing, so he reasons, if Christ had not endured physical pain, he would not have seemed human to people, and faith in the Incarnation would have been thwarted. For another, his bearing of pain gives us an example of patience.[90]

Yet Aquinas wants to say that the human nature of Christ serves purposes other than this. He does not regard faith in the Incarnation as simply a matter of believing that God became human. He sees the Incarnation as the climax of God's self-revelation begun in the creation of the world. For him it is a matter of God's eternal Son uniting himself to creation and raising it up to the likeness of its cause. He also holds that, because of the Incarnation, the human race is made right before God, saved from its sins, and brought to the Father, from whom it derives in the first place. Now that we have seen what he thinks the Incarnation involves for Christ, therefore, we can move on to what he thinks it involves for us.

---

[87] 3a. 13. 3.
[88] 3a. 13. 4.
[89] 3a. 14. 2.
[90] 3a. 14. 1.

16

The Life and Work of Christ

ACCORDING to 1 Timothy 1: 15: 'Christ Jesus came into the world in order to save sinners.' And Aquinas, of course, accepts this. 'The work of the Incarnation', he says, 'was directed chiefly to the restoration of the human race through the removal of sin.'[1] According to him, God became incarnate so that sinners might be brought back to God. But how can the Incarnation lead to this effect? How can the fact that Christ was God do anything to bring us anything we might think of as salvation? In this chapter we shall be chiefly looking at ways in which Aquinas answers these questions. In Chapter 17 we shall carry his thinking forward in order to apply it to the day-to-day lives of those who find their salvation in God incarnate in Christ.

The General Picture

To begin with, we can start with what he says of the passage in Isaiah in which we read: 'For to us a child is born, to us a son is given, and the government will be upon his shoulder.'[2] Aquinas's Latin Bible (the Vulgate) translates 'to us . . . is given' as *datus est nobis*, and 'upon his shoulder' as *super humerum eius*. Treating what 'is given' to us as Christ (the standard Christian reading, of course), he subsequently comments:

Noting the phrase *datus est nobis*, it can be said that Christ is given to us first as a brother [S. of S. 8: 1]; . . . second as a teacher [Joel 2: 23] . . . third, as a watchman [Ezek. 3]; . . . fourth, as a defender [Isa. 19: 20]; . . . fifth, as a shepherd [Ezek. 34: 23]; . . . sixth, as an example for our activities [John 13: 15]; . . . seventh, as food for wayfarers [John 6: 52]; . . . eighth, as a price of redemption [Matt. 20: 28]; . . . ninth, as a price of remuneration [Rev. 2: 17].

---

[1] 3a. 1. 5.
[2] Isa. 9: 6.

Similarly it should be observed concerning the words *super humerum eius* that God placed upon the shoulders of Christ first sins, as upon one who satisfies [Isa. 53: 6]; ... second a key, as upon a priest [Isa. 22: 2]; ... third, principality, as upon a conqueror [Isa. 9: 6]; ... fourth, glory, as upon one who triumphs [Isa. 22: 24].[3]

The quotation here may seem to lack excitement, for there are no rhetorical flourishes, and the whole thing reads like a list. But the list is important, and its existence serves to tell one a lot about Aquinas's approach to the life and work of Christ. In just a few lines, he is maintaining that Christ is our brother, watchman, teacher, defender, shepherd, example, food, and means of redemption. He is also telling us that Christ satisfies for sin, that he is our priest, and that he is our ruler and champion.

At the outset, then, we may note a significant fact about the way in which Aquinas conceives of Christ and the achievement of the Incarnation. This is that, unlike some Christian writers, he does not think' that we rightly express the truth about Christ by focusing on only one concept or image. 'Characteristically, he finds a place for all sorts of insights where others have been hypnotised by one model or another.'[4] He has a whole range of ways for drawing out the purpose of the Incarnation. He thinks of the life and work of Christ as being significant for various reasons and as having a number of effects.

Just to say this, however, will do little to explain how Aquinas actually does view the life and work of Christ as being for us. To take matters further, therefore, we can turn to what he says about the fittingness of the Incarnation. His treatment of this topic leads him to make several points characteristic of him and is as good a point of entry into the details of his thinking on the life and work of Christ as any other which may be suggested.

Sin and the Incarnation

Presiding over the discussion is the quotation from 1 Timothy cited above: 'Christ Jesus came into the world in order to save sinners.' In the twelfth century, Rupert of Deutz (*c.*1075–1129/30) held that

---

[3] *Super Isaiam*, 9. 1. 1.
[4] Herbert McCabe, OP, *God Matters* (London, 1987), p. 99.

God would have become incarnate even if people had not sinned.[5] The same view was taught by Grosseteste, and by later Franciscan thinkers including John Duns Scotus (*c*.1265–1308).[6] But it is not Aquinas's view. Or, at any rate, it is not his final view. In the *Commentary on the Sentences* he concedes that the Incarnation might have taken place even if people had never sinned.[7] And, even in later works, he has no difficulty in entertaining the notion of an incarnation in a world without sin. 'Even had sin not existed', he writes, 'God could have become incarnate.'[8] He also declares that 'the actual union of natures in the person of Christ falls under the eternal predestination of God'.[9] So he does not take the Incarnation to be a kind of afterthought on God's part. For him, God is one who eternally and changelessly wills to become incarnate. But, true to his theistic agnosticism, Aquinas's mature verdict in the *Summa theologiae* is that we do not have sufficient knowledge of God's will to be confident in holding that reason can assert that the Incarnation was inevitable. His view is that we must rely on revelation to tell us why God became incarnate. And he thinks that revelation tells us that the reason lies in sin. 'Everywhere in sacred Scripture', he observes, 'the sin of the first man is given as the reason for the Incarnation.'[10]

Does this mean that our union with God cannot be brought about without the Incarnation? Before the time of Aquinas, the most important and influential treatment of this question was St Anselm's *Cur Deus homo?*, where the conclusion reached was that the human race can only be united to God by virtue of one who is both divine and human. In Anselm's view, human beings were created for happiness with God lying beyond this life, but there is an obstacle to them receiving this happiness. All people have sinned, and a state of disorder has therefore been set up between them and God which

---

[5] He does so in his treatise *De gloria et honore Filii hominis*. Rupert of Deutz was the first theologian clearly to articulate the question 'Would the Incarnation have occurred if people had not sinned?'

[6] Grosseteste's position can be found in his treatise *De cessatione legalium*, in a sermon, *Exiit edictum*, and in parts of the *Haexemeron*. For Scotus's position see *Reportata Parisiensia*, book 3, d. 7, q. 4. For an account of other medieval authors considering the reasons for the Incarnation, see Peter Raedts, *Richard Rufus of Cornwall and the Tradition of Oxford Theology* (Oxford, 1987), ch. 9.

[7] *Sent.* 3. 1. 1. 3.

[8] 3a. 1. 3.

[9] 3a. 24. 1.

[10] 3a. 1. 3.

cannot be rectified simply by God forgiving them.[11] Anselm defines sin as 'nothing else than not to render God his due', and, on this basis, he argues that recompense or compensation must be paid in order for God's purpose in creating people to be fulfilled. He also argues that what is paid must be greater than everything other than God, and that the person to pay it must be greater than everything other than God, from which, he thinks, it follows that only God can pay it. At the same time, however, it is people who ought to make the payment, for it is they who have sinned. Thus, says Anselm, it is necessary for one who is both God and human (*deus homo*) to pay what is owed, and, in this sense, the Incarnation was required for people to reach their final goal.[12]

There is a great deal in common between this account and that of Aquinas. But Aquinas denies that the Incarnation was necessary for the restoration of humanity, if 'necessary' means that people could not have been restored without it. We can, he says, speak of something as necessary for an end to be achieved 'when the goal is simply unattainable without it, e.g. food for sustaining human life'. With this sense of necessity in mind, he adds, 'the Incarnation was not necessary for the restoration of human nature, since by his infinite power God had many other ways to accomplish this end'.[13] Here Aquinas invokes Augustine. 'Let us point out that other ways were not wanting to God, whose power rules everything without exception.'[14]

Yet Augustine goes on to say that, assuming the Incarnation to be given, 'there was no other course more fitting for healing our wretchedness'.[15] And Aquinas agrees with this too. We may also call a thing necessary, he says, 'when it is required for a better and more expeditious attainment of the goal, e.g. a horse for a journey'.[16] In this sense, he argues, the Incarnation 'was needed for the restoration

---

[11] *Cur Deus homo?* 1. 11.

[12] Ibid. 2. 6. For a breakdown of Anselm's argument, see David Brown, 'Necessary and Fitting Reasons in Theology', in William J. Abraham and Steven W. Holtzer (eds.), *The Rationality of Religious Belief* (Oxford, 1987). See also G. R. Evans, *Anselm* (London, 1989), ch. 7 and R. W. Southern, *Saint Anselm: A Portrait in a Landscape* (Cambridge, 1990), ch. 9.

[13] 3a. 1. 2.

[14] *De Trinitate*, 13. 10. This passage is cited again by Aquinas in 3a. 46. 2, though there the issue is the necessity of the passion of Christ rather than that of the Incarnation.

[15] Ibid.

[16] 3a. 1. 2.

of human nature'. It was, he thinks, a specially fitting way of restoring humanity.

Why? One answer he gives is that the Incarnation shows us God's goodness. We have already seen that Aquinas denies that the goodness of God entails that God must go out of himself and create. But he does think that goodness in things is caused by God and that it reveals (or 'communicates') something of what God is. He therefore reasons that the Incarnation may be taken as revealing God's goodness in a special way. It is, he observes, 'appropriate for the highest good to communicate itself to the creature in the highest way possible'.[17] Given that Christ is God, he adds, we may look to him especially as an outpouring and reflection of God's goodness. Nothing in creation can reveal God more than God incarnate.

Another point made by Aquinas is that the Incarnation gives us proper warrant for believing the content of faith. For faith is a matter of believing God, and, by virtue of the Incarnation, God has spoken to us in person. Here again Aquinas draws on Augustine. 'In order that people might journey more trustfully toward the truth', he writes, 'the Truth itself, the son of God, having assumed human nature, established and founded faith.'[18] He also suggests that, because of the Incarnation, we have the best possible guide for our behaviour together with grounds for hope and charity. For, in the person of Christ, God himself serves as an example to us and shows us how much he loves us.

But Aquinas has more to say than this about how the Incarnation is a specially fitting way of restoring humanity. For he also holds that it was a proper, and indeed necessary, means for delivering people from sin and estrangement from God because it was a matter of 'satisfaction' (*satisfactio*). The goal of the Incarnation, he explains, is 'our furtherance in good'. And it occurred 'in order to free us from the thraldom of sin . . . by Christ satisfying for us'.[19]

Satisfaction

1. From the Bible to Aquinas

What does this mean? The roots of the idea lie in the Bible. One of the most prominent and influential teachings in the New Testament

---

[17] 3a. 1. 1.
[18] *The City of God*, 11. 2.
[19] 3a. 1. 2.

is that people subject to sin are restored to a right relationship with God by virtue of Christ's suffering and death. New Testament authors tend to state this as a fact. They do not explain how the operation works.[20] Sometimes, however, they describe the role of Christ by means of language influenced by the Old Testament notion of acts of atonement ('at-one-ment'/'bringing together'), by which people do what is needed on their part for sin to be forgiven by God. Thus, for example, the author of 1 John calls Christ "the expiation (*hilasmos*) for our sins', and St Paul asserts that he is 'a means of expiation' (*hilasterion*).[21] In Hebrews 9, Old Testament images connected with atonement abound with reference to Christ's death. The general idea seems to be that this was the definitive means by which people are reconciled to God, a means which supersedes the Old Testament sacrificial system.

In the Middle Ages there were differing interpretations of these texts. Abelard, for instance, argued, or has been thought of as arguing, that they are best understood as teaching us that God has forgiven our sins and provided us with an inspiring token of his love.

It seems to us that we are justified in the blood of Christ and reconciled to God in this: that through the singular grace manifested to us in that his son took our nature and that teaching us both by word and example he persevered even unto death, Jesus bound us closer to himself by love, so that, fired by so great a benefit of divine grace, true charity would no longer be afraid to endure anything for his sake.[22]

Abelard seems to hold that, if God wills to forgive sin, the sin is forgiven and that is the end of it. He also seems to hold that God has willed to redeem humanity. It appears, therefore, that he believes that the death of Christ is not strictly necessary as a means of forgiving sin or reconciling people with God. Rather, it is God loving us in human form and drawing us to himself as we recognize the extent of his love. As one commentator explains, for Abelard,

Jesus was not the Man of Sorrows carrying the burden of our guilt or the victim offered up to the Father as a recompense for our sins, so much as the divine Logos made manifest to the world, incarnate because he would reveal to mankind the path of righteousness.[23]

---

[20] 1 Cor. 15: 3; Rom. 5: 6 ff.
[21] 1 John 2: 2; Rom. 3: 25. Scholars vary in their translation of *hilasterion*. Some prefer 'propitiation' to 'expiation'. Cf. John Ziesler, *Paul's Letter to the Romans* (London, 1989), 112 ff.
[22] *Epis. ad Romanos*, II. 3.
[23] J. G. Sikes, *Peter Abailard* (Cambridge, 1932), 208.

Much more widespread than Abelard's view, however, was the one classically associated with Anselm, for whom the death of Christ brings us to God because it is a matter of 'satisfaction' (*satisfactio*).

The word 'satisfaction' was a key-term in Roman law. As F. W. Dillistone explains, it was

a word bearing the fundamental idea that wherever the harmonious ordered working of the whole society has been disturbed by a failure to comply with its essential laws ... an adequate reparation must be offered not only in the sense of doing now what was originally commanded but also of offering now an extra which can be accepted as sufficient payment for the delinquency.[24]

For Anselm, 'satisfaction' sums up the significance of Christ's death since, in his view, the death of Christ made amends required to offset the consequences of sin. We have seen how he denies that sin can be simply forgiven by God. He thinks that compensation has to be made, and here he has in mind a giving back of what is not owed. That is to say, the compensation must be a matter of satisfaction. 'Every one who sins,' he argues, 'ought to pay back the honor of which he has robbed God; and this is the satisfaction which every sinner owes to God.'[25] And, for Anselm, the satisfaction owed here is provided by the death of Christ.

Why? To begin with Anselm suggests that, because satisfaction involves paying more than what is owed, it is necessary that the one who makes it 'somehow gives up himself, or something of his, which he does not owe as a debtor'.[26] He then goes on to argue that Christ can satisfy for the sin of human beings by dying since sin deserves death and since Christ was sinless.

Is it not proper that, since what is human has departed from God as far as possible in sin, that which is human should make to God the greatest possible satisfaction? ... Now nothing can be more severe or difficult for a human being to do for God's honor, than to suffer death voluntarily when not bound by obligation ... Therefore, the one who wishes to make atonement for human sin should be one who can die by choosing to do so.[27]

According to Anselm, Christ made perfect satisfaction for sin, and thereby made it possible for others to turn to God and enter into the

---

[24] F.W. Dillistone, *The Christian Understanding of Atonement* (Welwyn, 1968), 188.
[25] *Cur Deus homo?* 1. 11.
[26] Ibid. 2. 11.
[27] Ibid.

destiny originally intended for them, by going to his death without constraint and out of love for others.

2. *Aquinas on Satisfaction*

When Aquinas declares that we are freed from sin 'by Christ satisfying for us' he comes very close to Anselm's position. For one thing, he believes in that in certain circumstances there is a need for satisfaction. He thinks that people who sin produce a kind of disharmony between themselves and God which needs to be erased if proper relationships with God are to be established again. How is it to be erased? Aquinas is clear that the sinner must refrain from sin. But he does not think that things are made right between sinners and God simply because sinners stop sinning. 'If someone is parted from another', he observes, 'that person is not reunited to the other as soon as the movement ceases; the person needs to draw nigh to the other and to return by a contrary movement.'[28] On this basis, therefore, Aquinas maintains that repentance is in order. He also thinks that sinners must do something to make up for what they have done in sinning. His view is that sin deserves punishment since it transgresses the order of divine justice. So compensation must be paid.

A sinful act makes people punishable in that they violate the order of divine justice. They return to that order only by some punitive restitution that restores the balance of justice, in this way, namely, that those who by acting against a divine commandment, have indulged their own will beyond what was right, should, according to the order of divine justice, either voluntarily or by constraint be subjected to something not to their liking.[29]

One might say that God can merely forgive a person who has sinned. And Aquinas would agree. But he would add that forgiveness without compensation does not do enough to meet the requirements of justice. If you wrong me, I may forgive you and act as if nothing has happened. But even my forgiveness cannot abolish the fact that something has happened and that you are, in a sense, indebted to me. By the same token, so Aquinas thinks, for the consequences of sin to be properly dealt with the sinner must take on some form

---

[28] 1a2ae. 86. 2.
[29] 1a2ae. 87. 6.

of penance to atone for the sin, or must patiently bear with one imposed by God.[30] In other words, sinners must acknowledge the need for satisfaction, which Aquinas also sees as having a remedial or healing effect. As he says in his commentary on the *Sentences*:

Satisfaction can be defined in two ways. One way is with respect to past faults, which it heals (*curat*) by recompense; thus it is said that satisfaction is a recompense for injury according to justice's measure. This is also expressed in Anselm's definition that satisfaction gives to God an honour due him, due because of a fault committed. Satisfaction can also be defined with regard to future faults, from which one is preserved (*praeservat*) by satisfaction.[31]

In general, then, Aquinas is at one with Anselm in his view that sin requires satisfaction. He also agrees with another element in Anselm's position. Anselm presupposes that it is possible for satisfaction to be made by someone other than the person who has sinned, and Aquinas shares Anselm's presupposition here. He does not think that one person can satisfy for another where the satisfaction is thought of as only remedial. He accepts that satisfaction can have a healing effect in the sense that one who makes it behaves in a proper way and may be improved by doing so. But, since my improvement is a fact about me, not you, he denies that, if you make satisfaction on my behalf, it follows that you improve as well. On the other hand, he allows that you may take on yourself the punishment due to me for my sin. In Galatians 6: 2, St Paul writes: 'Bear one another's burdens, and so fulfil the law of Christ.' With this injunction in mind, Aquinas holds that, just as it is possible in law for people to pay fines on behalf of each other, so it is possible for people to take on themselves the penalty of other people's sin. He writes:

Satisfactory punishment has a twofold purpose, viz. to pay the debt, and to serve as a remedy for the avoidance of sin. Accordingly, as a remedy against future sin, the satisfaction of one does not profit another, for the flesh of one

---

[30] Ibid.

[31] *Sent.* 4. 15. 1. In the *Sentences* treatment of satisfaction, Aquinas is drawing on two influential definitions of 'satisfaction', one from the *Liber ecclesiasticorum dogmaticum*, 54 (thought by Aquinas's contemporaries to be by Augustine, but actually produced by Gennadius of Marseille (*c*.470)), the other from Anselm's *Cur Deus homo?* The first definition runs: 'Satisfaction is to uproot the causes of sins and to give no opening to their suggestions' (*Satisfactio est peccatorum causas excidere et eorum suggestionibus aditum non indulgere*). The second definition is: 'Satisfaction consists in giving God due honor' (*Satisfactio est honorem Deo impendere*).

person is not tamed by another's fast; nor does one person acquire the habit of well-doing through the actions of another, except accidentally . . . On the other hand, as regards the payment of the debt, someone can satisfy for another, provided that the person in question is in a state of charity.[32]

Elsewhere Aquinas makes the point by saying that 'in some cases those who are different in their purely penal obligations remain one in will, through their union in love.'[33]

From all of this, it should be evident how the thinking of Anselm and Aquinas overlaps on the question of satisfaction. Not surprisingly, therefore, it also overlaps when it comes to satisfaction and the Incarnation. For with the Incarnation directly in mind Aquinas offers what one might readily be forgiven for reading as a paraphrase of Anselm's *Cur Deus homo?* argument.

Justice demands satisfaction for sin. But God cannot render satisfaction, just as he cannot merit. Such a service pertains to one who is subject to another. Thus God was not in a position to satisfy for the sin of the whole of human nature; and a mere human being was unable to do so . . . Hence divine Wisdom judged it fitting that God should become human, so that thus one and the same person would be able both to restore the human race and to offer satisfaction.[34]

'A mere human being', Aquinas observes at one point, 'could not have satisfied for the whole human race, and God was not bound to satisfy; hence it was fitting for Jesus Christ to be both God and human.'[35]

People effectively make satisfaction for an offence when they offer to the one who has been offended something accepted as matching or outweighing the former offence. Christ, suffering in a loving and obedient spirit, offered more to God than was demanded in recompense for all the sins of the human race, because first the love which led him to suffer was a great love; secondly, the life he laid down in atonement was of great dignity, since it was the life of God and of a man; and thirdly, his suffering was all-embracing and his pain so great.[36]

A sin committed against God, says Aquinas, 'has a kind of infinity from the infinity of the divine majesty'.[37] For proper satisfaction of

---

[32] *Sent.* 4. 20. 2.
[33] 1a2ae. 87. 7.
[34] *Comp.* ch. 200.
[35] 3a. 1. 2.
[36] 3a. 48. 2.
[37] 3a. 1. 2 ad. 2.

sin, therefore, 'it was necessary that the act of the one satisfying should have an infinite efficacy, as being of God and of what is human'.[38]

Although one person can satisfy for another . . . that person cannot satisfy for the whole race because the act of one mere human individual is not equal in value to the good of the whole race. But the action of Christ, being that of one both divine and human, had a dignity that made it worth as much as the good of the entire human race, and so it could satisfy for others.[39]

Aquinas also holds that the fact that Christ is without sin means that he can satisfy for sin properly. Commenting on the phrase 'through the redemption which is in Christ Jesus' in Romans 3: 23, he suggests:

It is as if someone, having committed some fault, became indebted to the king and was obliged to pay a fine. Someone else who paid the fine for this person would be said to have redeemed the person. Such a debt was owed by the whole human race because of the sin of the first parents. So it was that no other one apart from Christ was able to satisfy for the sin of the whole human race since he alone was free of every sin.[40]

On this basis, Aquinas is able to say that Christ was both a priest and a victim, and that his work bore the character of sacrifice. Christ is a priest since he mediates between people and God and since 'the characteristic function of a priest is to act as mediator between God and his people'. He communicates to people the things of God and somehow makes reparation for sin.[41] Christ was simultaneously priest and victim, Aquinas goes on to say, since his priestly work was achieved by his offering of himself as a sacrifice (i.e. as something 'placed before God with the purpose of raising the human spirit to him').[42]

Yet Aquinas's teaching on the satisfaction of Christ is not quite that of Anselm. For, unlike Anselm, Aquinas does not think that God can only unite people to himself by means of satisfaction. Anselm does seem to think this. At any rate, he does not entertain the notion of it not being so. But the emphasis with Aquinas is different. As

---

[38] Ibid.
[39] *De ver.* 29. 7.
[40] *Super ad Rom.* 3. 1.
[41] 3a. 22. 1.
[42] 3a. 22. 2.

Romanus Cessario states, in his thinking satisfaction 'is not some-thing God requires of man, or even of Jesus, as a condition for accomplishing his saving plan. Rather it is the means whereby God in very fact accomplishes his plan to bring all men and women into loving union with himself.'[43]

We have already seen that Aquinas explicitly holds that people can be brought to God without satisfaction since we have noted him maintaining that 'God in his infinite power could have restored human nature in many other ways' than by becoming incarnate. Or as he says in another place: 'Simply and absolutely speaking, God could have freed us otherwise than by Christ's passion, for *nothing is impossible with God*.'[44] Now we need to note that he also maintains both that God can pardon sin without exacting any penalty and that there are important senses in which the passion of Christ was un-necessary. 'If God had wanted to free people from sin without any satisfaction at all', he writes, 'he would not have been acting against justice.'

God has no one above him, for he is himself the supreme and common good of the entire universe. If then he forgives sin, which is a crime in that it is committed against him, he violates no one's rights. People who waive satisfaction and forgive an offence done to themselves act mercifully, not unjustly.[45]

As for Christ's passion, says Aquinas, this was not necessary in the sense that it was something 'which of its nature cannot be otherwise', i.e. it was not logically necessary.[46] Nor was it necessary in the sense of being forced on God or Christ by an agent apart from them. 'It was not necessary for Christ to suffer from necessity of compulsion, either on God's part, who ruled that Christ should suffer, or on Christ's part, who suffered voluntarily.'[47]

With respect to satisfaction and Christ, Aquinas's position is that satisfaction by Christ is necessary only in two senses. The first is a purely logical one. Given that God has ordained that people be brought to God by satisfaction through Christ, and given that God

---

[43] Romanus Cessario, OP, *The Godly Image: Christ and Salvation in Catholic Thought from Anselm to Aquinas* (Petersham, Mass., 1990), xviii.
[44] 3a. 46. 2.
[45] 3a. 46. 2 ad. 3.
[46] 3a. 46. 1.
[47] Ibid.

knows how people are to be brought to God, then satisfaction by Christ is necessary.

Since it is impossible for God's foreknowledge to be deceived and his will and ordinance to be frustrated, then, supposing God's foreknowledge and ordinance regarding Christ's passion, it was not possible at the same time for Christ not to suffer and for people to be delivered otherwise than by Christ's passion.[48]

Secondly, so Aquinas argues, satisfaction through Christ is necessary in the sense that it is a means of bringing people to God in a way that accords with God's justice and mercy.

That people should be delivered by Christ's passion was in keeping with both his mercy and his justice. With his justice, because by his passion Christ made satisfaction for the sin of the human race; and with his mercy, for since no single human being could alone satisfy for the sin of all human nature ... God gave people his son to satisfy for them ... And this came of more copious mercy than if he had forgiven sins without satisfaction.[49]

Aquinas thinks that God could have acted only out of mercy. But he also thinks that in Christ's passion God was acting both out of mercy and out of justice. He admits that people could have been brought to God without the Incarnation and, therefore, without Christ suffering. But he is governed by the recognition that the Incarnation and the death of Christ have, in fact, occurred. And he thinks it is good that this should be so. His line is that, where an offence against God is at issue, full satisfaction is possible, and that God has actually laid this on. Given the desirability of full (or, as Aquinas calls it, 'condign') satisfaction, his conclusion, then, is that everything possible has been done to set matters right between people and God. 'It was', he explains, 'more fitting that we should be delivered by Christ's passion than simply by God's good will.'[50]

Merit

According to the theology of Aquinas, then, the death of Christ delivers us from the punishment due to sin. But Aquinas believes that it also does more than this. For he wants to say that people are

[48] 3a. 46. 2.
[49] 3a. 46. 1 ad. 3.
[50] 3a. 46. 3.

given grace because of Christ's death and because of his whole life as God incarnate. By itself, he thinks, the satisfaction made by Christ is of limited worth, for a person may hear of it and still remain in sin. 'Christ's satisfaction', he argues, 'brings about its effect in us in so far as we are incorporated into him as members are into the head. But members should be conformed to their head.'[51] His judgement, therefore, is that something more is required for Christ's satisfaction to be effective. And the something in question is grace.

To understand Aquinas's thinking here we need to remember what we saw in the last chapter concerning his teaching on the grace of Christ as head of the Church. According to him, Christ has the fullness of grace and is therefore the source of grace for those who rally to him. As he writes in the *Compendium of Theology*:

Since the man Christ possessed supreme fullness of grace, as being the only begotten of the Father, grace overflowed from him to others, so that the son of God, made human, might make people gods and sons and daughters of God, according to the Apostle's words in *Galatians* 4: 4: 'God sent his son, made of a woman, made under the law, that he might redeem them who were under the law: that we might receive the adoption of sons.'[52]

On this basis Aquinas holds that the grace present in Christ is shared with members of the Church. In his view, those who are members of the Church have, in St Paul's phrase, 'put on Christ' and are 'members' of his body. This means that they can be considered as one with Christ and as therefore sharing in the grace which belongs to him.

Grace was in Christ . . . not simply as in an individual human being, but as in the Head of the whole Church, to whom all are united as members to the head, forming a single mystic person. In consequence, the merit of Christ extends to others in so far as they are his members. In somewhat similar fashion in individual human beings the action of the head belongs in some measure to all their bodily members.[53]

The idea here is that, because of the Incarnation, the relationship between Christ and his father is one which also exists between Christians and God. 'Christ and the Church are in a sense one person. On the basis of that unity, he speaks in the name of the

[51] 3a. 49. 3 ad. 3.
[52] *Comp.* ch. 214.
[53] 3a. 19. 4.

Church in the words of the Psalm (21: 1): 'O God, my God, look upon me.'[54] Like St Paul (on whose teaching he is clearly drawing at this point), Aquinas teaches that, just as all people can be said to be 'in Adam', so members of Christ's Church can be said to be 'in Christ'.[55] And, so he holds, being in Christ means being the recipient of grace.

Adam's sin is communicated to others only through bodily generation. In similar fashion Christ's merit is communicated to others only through the spiritual regeneration of baptism, by which we are incorporated into Christ. 'As many of you have been baptized in Christ, have put on Christ' [Gal. 3: 27]. Now that it should be given to us to be regenerated in Christ is itself a gift of grace. Our salvation is, then, from the grace of God.[56]

Being in Christ, says Aquinas, means standing in relation to God as Christ stands. Insofar as he stands as one who is graced, so do those who are in him. And insofar as his life is one which deserves (or merits) acceptance by God or the outpouring of grace, so is that of those who are in him.

There is the same relation between Christ's deeds for himself and his members, as there is between me and what I do in the state of grace. Now it is clear that if I in the state of grace suffer for justice's sake, I by that very fact, merit salvation for myself...Therefore Christ by his passion merited salvation not only for himself, but for all who are his members, as well.[57]

In fact, so Aquinas adds, 'Christ merited eternal salvation for us from the moment of his conception.' The only reason why his passion is important in this connection is because 'on our part there were certain obstacles which prevented us from enjoying the result of his previously acquired merits. In order to remove these obstacles, then, it was necessary for Christ to suffer.'[58] In Aquinas's view, our sharing in Christ's merit depends on him making satisfaction, which means that it is tied in with his suffering and death.[59]

---

[54] *De ver.* 29. 7.
[55] Cf. 1 Cor. 15: 21. For a brief account of Paul on 'in Adam' and 'in Christ' see Morna D. Hooker, *Pauline Pieces* (London, 1979), ch. 3.
[56] 3a. 19. 4 ad. 3.
[57] 3a. 48. 1.
[58] 3a. 48. 1 ad. 2.
[59] He also thinks that by dying, Christ showed how much God loves us, which thereby stirs us to love in return, and which gives us 'an example of obedience, humility, constancy, justice, and the other virtues displayed in the passion, which are requisite for human salvation' (3a. 46. 3).

Justification

As he goes on to develop this account Aquinas observes that
Christians receive justification by virtue of Christ's grace. 'By his
passion', he explains, 'Christ merited for us the grace of justification
and the glory of beatitude.'[60] Christ, he says, was obedient to his
father even to death. Commenting on this notion, he goes on to
suggest that 'it was altogether fitting that Christ should suffer out of
obedience'. And the first reason he gives for saying so is that 'his
obedience was in keeping with our justification (*justificatio*)'.[61]

To understand what this means it is important to recognize that
Aquinas taught about justification long before the subject became a
matter of controversy during the period of the Reformation and
afterwards. So it would be quite wrong to read what he says about it
as, for example, a polemic directed against views on justification such
as those of Martin Luther (1483–1546). What Aquinas considers
under the heading 'Justification' was in his day traditionally dealt with
in treatments of Penance, and he himself deals with it in connection
with that in Book 4, d. 17 of the *Commentary on the Sentences*. In the
Summa theologiae, his account of justification is part of a wider
discussion of grace in general. Hence he speaks in the Prologue to
1a2ae of how we must next consider 'the effects of grace' and 'firstly
the justification of the unrighteous, which is the effect of operative
grace'. 'The justification of the unrighteous as a whole', he says,
'consists by way of origin and source in the infusion of grace.'[62]

What does this last statement mean? The answer is effectively
given in Aquinas's explanation of what is required for justification.
According to this:

Four requirements for the justification of the unrighteous may be listed:
namely, the infusion of grace; a movement of free choice directed towards
God by faith; a movement of free choice directed towards sin; and the
forgiveness of sin.[63]

In Aquinas's thinking, justification occurs as, under the influence of
grace, one moves towards God with faith in Christ. Justification, he
says, is a 'kind of rightness of order in people's own interior

---

[60] Ibid.
[61] 3a. 47. 2.
[62] 1a2ae. 113. 7.
[63] 1a2ae. 113. 6.

disposition, namely when what is highest in people is subject to God and the lower powers of their souls are subject to what is highest in them, their reason'.[64] In other words, it is what you have when sinners repent and change direction. Or, as Aquinas also wants to say, it is what you have when God forgives sin.

Some people hold that, when God forgives sin, he goes through a process of some kind. This is because they think of God's forgiveness by assimilating it to that of human beings. When I forgive you, I have to go through a process. I have to learn of your offence against me. Then I have to decide to ignore it. With that behind me, I must next do something to put my decision into effect—albeit that this may largely mean me *not* doing something (e.g. not being angry with you). And such, so it has been thought, is how it must be with God. But it should now almost go without saying that Aquinas could never agree with this suggestion—unless it is taken as a metaphor or image of some kind. Since he believes in God's immutability, he cannot accept that God's act of forgiveness involves him in going through a process of any kind. For him, therefore, to say that God has forgiven us is equivalent to saying that we have changed direction and turned to him.

An offence is only forgiven someone when the mind of the offended party is reconciled to the offender. And so sin is said to be forgiven us when God is reconciled to us. Now this reconciliation and peace consists in the love with which God loves us. But God's love, as far as the divine act is concerned, is eternal and immutable; but as to the effect which it impresses on us, it is sometimes interrupted, namely when we sometimes fall away from it and sometimes regain it. Now the effect of divine love in us which is removed by sin is the grace by which someone becomes worthy of eternal life, from which people are excluded by mortal sin. And therefore the forgiveness of sin would not be intelligible unless there were present an infusion of grace.[65]

Though God cannot change, we can. And, when we change by moving towards him, that is because he is drawing us to himself in love, and has therefore forgiven our offence against him. As one of Aquinas's modern commentators observes: 'When God forgives our sin, he is not changing *his* mind about us; he is changing *our* mind

---

[64] 1a2ae. 113. 1.
[65] 1a2ae. 113. 3.

about him . . . Our sorrow for sin just *is* the forgiveness of God working within us.'[66]

For Aquinas, then, justification is a matter of God making us more godly. That is why he discusses it in the context of a treatment of grace in the *Summa theologiae*. And, for him, it is an effect of the Incarnation since, in his view, the Incarnation is all about God making us more godly through Christ. Aquinas believes that, in the life and death of Christ, God is doing nothing but making his love present in the world. He sees Christ's life and death as divinity incarnate cancelling the barriers between people and God and calling us to accept that these barriers really have been cancelled. That is why he can say that we are justified by means of Christ.

Notice, however, that in reaching this conclusion, Aquinas is not merely saying that God has deemed people to be at one with him. For some Christian authors, influenced by texts like Romans 3: 28, to say that someone is justified by God does not imply that the person in question is necessarily better than he or she would be if unjustified. It is to say that one has been accepted by God, or acquitted by him, or declared to be right or innocent in his eyes. This seems to have been Luther's understanding of justification.[67] One can also find it in Calvin's declaration that the saved 'receive justice, but such as the people of God can obtain in this life. It is possessed only by imputation, because our Lord in his mercy considers them just and innocent.'[68] Aquinas, however, thinks of justification as making a difference to people. Because it involves the work of grace, it must also, so he thinks, involve a moving away from sin. In this respect, his teaching on justification is in line with typical medieval accounts considered as contrasting with typically Reformation ones. For, as Alister McGrath explains:

[66] Herbert McCabe, OP, *Hope* (London, 1987), 17 f.

[67] 'It is clear that, as the soul needs only the Word of God for its life and righteousness, so it is justified by faith alone and not by any works; for if it could be justified by anything else, it would not need the Word, and consequently would not need faith' (*The Freedom of a Christian*: see *Martin Luther: Selections from His Writings*, ed. John Dillenberger (New York, 1961), 55. Again: 'So the Christian who is consecrated by his faith does good works, but the works do not make him holier or more Christian, for that is the work of faith alone. And if a man were not first a believer and a Christian, all his works would amount to nothing and would be truly wicked and damnable sins' (ibid. 69).

[68] *Institutes of the Christian Religion*, edition reprinted under the direction of A. Lefranc (Paris, 1911), 548.

The characteristic medieval understanding of the nature of justification may be summarised thus: justification refers not merely to the beginning of the Christian life, but also to its continuation and ultimate perfection, in which the Christian is made righteous in the sight of God and the sight of men through a fundamental change in his nature, and not merely his status. In effect, the distinction between justification (understood as an external pronouncement of God) and sanctification (understood as the subsequent process of inner renewal), characteristic of the Reformation period, is excluded from the outset. This fundamental difference concerning the *nature* of justification remains one of the best *differentiae* between the doctrines of justification associated with the medieval and Reformation periods.[69]

Yet Aquinas is at least in accord with the typically Reformation insistence that justification is a gift of God and not something earned. This, or course, is because of the way in which he thinks of it as an effect of grace. As we saw in Chapter 13, he denies that people can do anything to ensure or prepare for the giving of grace.[70] As he puts it:

If we speak of grace in the sense of the assistance of God moving us towards the good, no preparation as it were anticipating the divine assistance is required on our part; rather, whatever preparation there might be in us derives from the assistance of God moving the soul towards the good. In this sense, that good movement of free choice itself, by which someone prepares to receive the gift of grace, is the action of a free choice moved by God ... The principal agent is God moving the free choice; and in this sense it is said that *our will is prepared by God*, and *our steps are directed by the Lord*.[71]

In his view, therefore, justification is in no way a consequence of 'works'. He certainly does not think that we get to God by confronting him with a righteousness that obliges him to reward us. He thinks that we are justified by God on the basis of sheer liberality. For him, our repentance, and what follows that in the way we behave (our 'works'), are the projection into history of God's eternal love making and sustaining goodness where there is no prior claim

---

[69] Alister E. McGrath, *Iustitia Dei: A History of the Christian Doctrine of Justification: The Beginnings to the Reformation* (Cambridge, 1986), 41.

[70] Notice, however, that there are grounds for attributing to Aquinas some development of thinking on this issue. In the *Commentary on the Sentences* he speaks of people being moved to receive grace by secondary causes such as other people or illness. In later works, the emphasis falls on God as moving one to the graced life. See McGrath, *Iustitia Dei*, 82.

[71] 1a2ae. 112. 2. Aquinas is alluding here to Prov. 8: 35 in the Vulgate translation, and Ps. 36: 23.

obliging him to do so. Luther attacked Aquinas by saying that he taught that we become righteous, not by faith, but by doing righteous acts. He thought that Aquinas belittled the role of grace. But, as Denis R. Janz makes clear, Luther's understanding of Aquinas was decidedly deficient on this aspect of his teaching.

For Thomas, human beings are not justified by their acts if 'justification' means what it sometimes means for Luther, i.e., the forgiveness of sins. This first step and *sine qua non* presupposition for progress towards one's final end, the *initium fidei*, is 'from God moving inwardly through grace'. On the other hand, if 'justification' refers to the entire process by which one reaches the final goal, then human actions are of course part of the process. As Thomas puts it in his commentary on Romans, justification is *sola gratia sine operibus precedentibus*, but not *sola gratia sine operibus subsequentibus*. Or, as he says in the *Summa Theologiae*, the grace of God does not presuppose goodness in human beings but creates it. In view of all this, it is a misunderstanding or at least an oversimplification to say as Luther does that for Thomas, one is justified through one's good acts.[72]

The Resurrection and Ascension of Christ

For Aquinas, then, the life and death of Christ is the centre of God's going out of himself to share with people the life he lives from eternity. By taking human nature on himself, God the Son calls us to accept divine forgiveness in union with himself and his grace. He also provides evidence of God's love for sinners, encouragement for those who doubt it, and grace to accept and be transformed by it. But Aquinas does not think that the saving or restoring work of Christ ends with his death. In his view, it continues with the resurrection and ascension of Christ, and, from that point on, it continues in the life of the Church.

1. The Resurrection

We need to be quite clear that Aquinas takes the resurrection of Christ to be something entirely new. The Gospels and the Old Testament record how people other than Christ were raised from the dead. For Aquinas, however, the resurrection of Christ was another

---

[72] Denis R. Janz, *Luther on Thomas Aquinas* (Stuttgart, 1989), 57.

thing again. 'We find', he observes, 'that many people rose from the dead, such as Lazarus, the son of the widow, and the daughter of the synagogue ruler. The resurrection of Christ differs from the resurrection of those and others.'[73]

Why? Chiefly, so Aquinas thinks, because the divinity of Christ meant that his resurrection, like his death, was something under his own control and, as a consequence, something able to bring about for others what it constituted in reality itself. The death of Christ was the point at which his obedience to his father reached a climax. For Aquinas, it was also the point at which the members of his Church were most united to God, for, with him as their head and with them as his body, they 'share in his passion by faith, love, and the sacraments of faith'.[74] In the same way, so Aquinas goes on to say, those with faith in Christ are with him in his resurrection, and they therefore gain what he does from it. The resurrection of Christ, Aquinas maintains, was 'the model and cause of our own resurrection'.[75]

With respect to the notion of the resurrection of Christ as a 'model' of ours, Aquinas says more or less what one would expect him to say given his grounding in Scripture. According to St Paul, 'Christ has been raised from the dead, the first fruits of those who have fallen asleep.'[76] Paul thinks of Christ's resurrection as being an indication of what Christians can expect. And that is how Aquinas conceives of it. 'Christ is the pattern of our resurrection', he writes, 'in that Christ assumed flesh, and also rose embodied in the flesh.'[77] 'We see in his exaltation', he explains, 'what is proposed to us to hope for through him.'[78]

In triumph over death, which resulted from our first parent's sin, Christ was the first of all people to rise to immortal life. Thus, as life first became mortal through Adam's sin, immortal life made its first appearance in Christ through the atonement for sin he offered. Others, it is true, raised up either by Christ or by the prophets, had returned to life before him; yet they had to die a second time. But 'Christ being raised from the dead will never die again' [Rom. 6: 9]. As he was the first to escape the necessity of dying, he

---

[73] *Super sym. apos.* 8.
[74] 3a. 49. 5.
[75] 3a. 54. 2.
[76] 1 Cor. 15: 20.
[77] *Super I ad Thess.* 4. 2. 95.
[78] *Comp.* ch. 236.

is called 'the first born of the dead' [Rev. 1: 5] and 'the first fruits of those who have fallen asleep' [1 Cor. 15: 20].[79]

Making a connection between Christ dying and people dying to sin, Aquinas can also pursue the notion of Christ's resurrection as a model so as to indicate how people can imitate it in their lives. Just as Christ rose from the dead, he says, so we should rise from the death of the soul which constitutes sin. Just as Christ rose quickly ('on the third day'), so we should be quick to seek the things of God. Just as Christ died once and for all, so we should die to sin once and for all. Just as he rose to a glorious life, so we should rise from death to sin to a 'life of justice, which renews the soul and leads it on to the life of glory'.[80]

But Aquinas, as I have noted, does not just think of Christ's resurrection in terms of it being a model. St Paul declares that 'as by a man came death, by a man has come also the resurrection of the dead'.[81] Influenced by this teaching, Aquinas understands the resurrection of Christ to have a causal effect. 'As Christ destroyed our death by his death', he says, 'so he restored our life by his resurrection.'[82] He does not mean that we can only be raised from the dead because Christ has been raised. Nor does he think of the resurrection of Christ as if it were a physical process inexorably leading to other physical processes. His idea is that God has willed for us to be finally restored to him in a particular way, namely through the Incarnation and the work of Christ. For him, Christ's human nature is an 'instrument' of his divinity. It is the tool by which he operates as God in the created realm. This means for him that, since our resurrection comes as we share in Christ's victory over death, his resurrection is a cause of our own. He agrees that 'the justice of God is the first cause of our resurrection'. So he accepts that 'there was no obligation that Christ's resurrection be the cause of our own. God could have used other means for our liberation.'[83] But he also maintains that all that Christ accomplished for us is accomplished by God through the power of Christ's divinity. Since our resurrection is brought about by God who was acting in Christ

---

[79] *Comp.* ch. 236.
[80] *Super sym. apos.* 8.
[81] 1 Cor. 15: 21.
[82] *Comp.* ch. 239.
[83] 3a. 56. 1 ad. 2.

to save us, he therefore concludes that what comes to Christ in his resurrection comes to us by virtue of this as we are raised in his wake.

> The Word of God is a life-giving principle ... Therefore to the Word is attributed the immortal life bestowed on the human body united to his person, and so through him resurrection is worked in all others ... The resurrection of Christ is not, strictly speaking, the meritorious cause of our resurrection. It is the efficient and exemplar cause. The efficient causality is through the humanity of Christ in which the resurrection took place and which is like an instrument acting in the power of divinity. Therefore, just as all the other things which Christ in his humanity accomplished or suffered for us are saving acts through the power of his divinity, so too is his resurrection the efficient cause of ours through the same divine power whose proper effect is to raise the dead to life.[84]

In other words, just as any saving action performed by Christ can be causally attributed to his human nature working with divine power, so can our resurrection. That is because our resurrection comes about by divine power which, in the wake of the Incarnation, is exercised by one who is human as well as divine. Or, as Aquinas writes in his commentary on 1 Thessalonians:

> The things done by Christ's humanity were done not only by the power of his human nature, but also by virtue of his divinity united in him. Just as his touch cured the leper as an instrument of his divinity, so also Christ's resurrection is the cause of our resurrection, not merely because it was a body that arose, but a body united to the Word of life.[85]

For Aquinas, so we may say, the resurrection of Christ is not just something which happens to follow his life and death. Nor is it just a reward for Christ. It is a way in which God teaches us about the significance of Christ in general. And what Aquinas thinks he is teaching us is that God loves the human race enough to become a man and to lead us back to him on that basis.

2. The Ascension

This theme of 'a body united to the Word of life' is also at work in what Aquinas says of Christ's ascension.[86] 'The presence of his

---

[84] 3a. 56. 1, corpus and ad. 3.
[85] *Super I ad Thess.* 4. 2. 95.
[86] *Luke* 24: 51; *John* 20: 17; *Acts* 1: 9.

human nature in heaven', he writes, 'is itself an intercession for us, for God, who exalted the human nature in Christ, will also show mercy towards those for whose sake this nature was assumed.'[87] In Aquinas's view, influenced this time by the letter to the Hebrews, the work of Christ as mediator between people and God is not something over and done with as his earthly life ends.[88] Since Christ continues to live, he continues to be the means by which God brings people to himself, though now without threat to his body.

To some extent, and as with his treatment of the resurrection of Christ, Aquinas thinks that what is going on here is best understood in terms of what can come about in us as we learn of Christ's ascension.

By the ascension, our minds are lifted up to Christ because . . . his ascension fosters, first faith, secondly, hope, thirdly, charity. Fourthly, our reverence for him is increased, since we no longer deem him an earthly man, but the God of heaven.[89]

But Aquinas also wants to say that the ascension of Christ has what we might call an 'objective' (*ex parte ipsius*) rather than a 'subjective' (*ex parte nostra*) consequence. Here he draws on the Old Testament custom by which the high priest entered the sanctuary of the Jerusalem temple to represent the people in the presence of God. Christ, he says, has gone before us to do just that in his role as priest. And, since Christ is divine, the upshot is that we continue to be drawn to God by one like ourselves. Through his ascension, Aquinas argues, Christ 'initiated as our head what we as his members share in union with him'.[90]

Another way of putting this would be to say that Christ as head of the Church is God's human instrument for leading us back to the source of our being. The trouble, however, is that the ascension of Christ is something past, and we live in the present. Whatever may be said about the work of God incarnate, it remains that an era is definitely over with the ascension of Christ. As Aquinas makes the point, now Christ is not a *viator* (wayfarer) but a *comprehensor* (possessor) only.[91] And this raises a practical problem. For how do

---

[87] 3a. 57. 6.
[88] See especially Heb. 7.
[89] 3a. 57. 6.
[90] 3a. 57. 6 ad. 2.
[91] *Comp.* ch. 237.

people living after the death of Christ come to benefit from his life on earth and from the life he lives now? To some extent, we have already begun to see how Aquinas would answer this question. But now we shall follow him as he goes on to deal with it in more detail.

17

Signs and Wonders

THOSE who have made a study of the twentieth-century theologian Rudolf Bultmann (1884–1976) will know that he is famous for attacking what he calls the tendency 'to objectify' (*objektivieren*). In Bultmann's view, it is wrong to think of Christian faith as a system of beliefs or theses, or as a world-view (*Weltanschauung*) which can be singled out and presented to the mind in a theoretical, academic, or detached manner. According to Bultmann, faith is a matter of personal engagement between the believer and the word of God. And theology is an expression of such engagement.

It would be wrong to say that on this matter Bultmann is merely echoing Aquinas. Their thinking is clearly very different, and there is little reason to believe that Bultmann was influenced by Aquinas. But Aquinas would certainly agree that articulating the content of faith, or expressing assent to it, is merely a first stage as far as Christians are concerned. In his view, to proclaim the Christian creeds is to tell what God has done in history. And, since he believes that God in history has united himself to humanity in order to raise it to a share in his life, he takes it for granted that Christian faith has implications for what we do or how we behave. As we noted in Chapter 14, though he thinks of faith as propositional, he does not conceive of it as a *merely* propositional or cerebral affair. He thinks of it as a virtue by which our lives are improved or enhanced. In his view, receiving the word of God is not just a matter of getting to know something. It is a matter of coming to live a more intense life—the life of God himself. For Aquinas, therefore, we need to consider what it means to live our lives in faith. Christian doctrine is not, for him, nothing but a list of truths about God. It is a summons to respond to God. It is a summons to a way of life. We have already seen something of how he conceives of the Christian response to this summons. In essence, his view of the matter is contained in his teaching on faith, hope, and charity. But he has other things to say about the details of the Christian life, and, to round off this survey of his thinking, we

need to turn to some of these. In this chapter, therefore, we shall
look at what he has to say about sacraments. There are other things
we could look at, but space is limited. In any case, the choice made
here is determined by Aquinas himself. For he believes that it is by
means of the sacraments that faith, hope, and charity are perfected.
By means of the sacraments, he holds, we live in Christ and he lives
in us.

Sacraments

1. Background

It would be fair to say that modern Roman Catholic teaching on the
sacraments basically derives from the Council of Trent (1545–63).
According to Trent, there are seven sacraments, each of them
celebrated by means of rites (baptism, confirmation, eucharist,
penance, last anointing, holy orders, and matrimony).[1] These are 'the
sacraments of the new law', distinct from 'the sacraments of the old
law'. And they were 'all instituted by our lord Jesus Christ'. They are
'necessary for salvation', and through them 'people obtain the grace
of justification'. Each time they are celebrated they 'contain the grace
which they signify'. 'Through the sacramental action itself', they
confer grace on 'those who place no obstacle in the way'.[2]

Early Christian writings, however, provide no systematic attempts
to explain what the essence of a sacrament is. Such attempts date
only from the twelfth century. The English word 'sacrament' comes
from the Latin word *sacramentum*, which originally meant a 'promise'
or an 'oath' by which one publicly entered into service or took on
responsibility or privilege. With this sense in mind, and from the time
of Tertullian (c.100–65), *sacramentum* came to be used by Christians
as a way of referring to Christian rites of initiation. But it was also
the word used by Latin Christians to translate certain occurrences in
the New Testament of the Greek term *mysterion*. On this basis it
came, in addition, to refer to anything in the world which showed

---

[1] Someone who knows nothing about Catholic teaching on the sacraments might
start by consulting Roderick Strange, *The Catholic Faith* (Oxford, 1986), ch. 8.

[2] *Decrees of the Ecumenical Councils*, ed. Norman P. Tanner, SJ (London, 1990), ii.
684 ff.

forth or signified the hidden mysteries of God (e.g. Scripture, prayers, the Incarnation, the passion of Christ). It also came to refer especially to the rites involved in Christian baptism and the celebration of the eucharist.[3]

With the writings of St Augustine, however, the picture begins to change. In common with many of his predecessors, Augustine uses *sacramentum* in a variety of senses. For him, almost anything can count as a *sacramentum*. But he also asks what it means to use the word *sacramentum* in speaking about Christian rites. And what he has to say on the subject proved to be enormously influential. As Liam Walsh, OP puts it: 'It was Augustine who brought the full catholic tradition to light and, in doing so, gave *sacramentum* technical refinements that have remained with it ever since.'[4] We will certainly not understand Aquinas's place in the history of thinking about sacraments if we do not have some idea of the position adopted by Augustine. For much of what he says derives directly from that.

According to Augustine, a sacrament is always a 'sign' (*signum*) of some sacred 'thing' (*res*). By 'sign' here Augustine means something visible (e.g. the materials used and the procedure followed in celebrating a Christian rite, including the words spoken). And he thinks of this as an image or reflection of the sacred 'thing' considered as something invisible.[5] A *sacramentum*, says Augustine, is a 'sacred sign'.[6] For him, therefore, it has the character of a divine revelation. It shows forth and, indeed, brings about what is not, in the physical sense, able to be seen. Hence, for example, the *sacramentum* of baptism (involving water and so on) shows forth and brings about the fact that those who are baptized are cleansed from sin. Insofar as the baptism is a matter of someone being totally immersed in water, it shows forth and brings about the fact that, as St Paul asserts, those who are baptised are buried with Christ and rise to new life.[7]

Also, so Augustine holds, with sacraments comes grace or sanctification. For Augustine, sacraments are signs of Christ, who instituted

---

[3] For a brief, modern account of early uses of *sacramentum*, see Liam Walsh, OP, *The Sacraments of Initiation* (London, 1988), 21 ff. See also Jaroslav Pelikan, *The Growth of Medieval Theology (600–1300)*, iii: *The Christian Tradition* (Chicago, 1978), 204 ff.

[4] Walsh, *The Sacraments of Initiation*, 28.

[5] Augustine's notion of 'sign' can be found, for example, in book 2 of his *De doctrina Christiana* and in his *De magistro*.

[6] *City of God*, 10. 5.

[7] Rom. 6: 3–4.

them and delivered them to the Church to administer. Considered as such, they are means by which the purpose of the Incarnation (i.e. the salvation and redemption of human beings) is achieved in the lives of believers. They can be thought of as the work of Christ himself, acting through the ministers of the sacraments and sanctifying the faithful. With this point in mind, Augustine rejected the position of the followers of Donatus (the Donatists), who held that people receiving sacraments at the hands of unworthy ministers fail to benefit from them. In Augustine's judgement, a sacrament can have an effect by 'sealing' independently of the worthiness of the minister.[8] This allows him to argue against rebaptizing converts from other churches. For Augustine, the sacrament of baptism seals or marks a person as belonging to, as consecrated to, Christ. And it does so once and for all.[9]

Theologians between Augustine and Aquinas added to what Augustine taught about sacraments. A particularly influential definition of *sacramentum* came, for example, from Hugh of St Victor. According to him,

A sacrament is a physical or material element admitted to the perception of the external senses, representing a reality beyond itself in virtue of having been instituted as a sign of it and containing within itself some invisible and spiritual grace in virtue of having been consecrated.[10]

Sacramental thinking between Augustine and Aquinas was also deeply affected by Peter Lombard, who emphasized the idea that sacraments have a causal effect (i.e. that something really gets done because sacraments are celebrated), and who held that there are precisely seven sacraments—a doctrine which prevailed and was accepted by the Church, though Augustine does not explicitly defend

---

[8] The 'seal' language is used by St Paul (2 Cor. 1: 22; Eph. 1: 13 ff; 4: 30) and by Eastern and Western Christians concerned with Christian initiation.

[9] Cf. P. Pourrat, *Theology of the Sacraments* (St Louis, 2nd edn., 1914), 23: 'In its most restricted meaning, the Augustinian sacrament is a sacred sign which calls forth the idea of a religious thing, of which it is the image; that sign is a material element; with that sign is connected the spiritual gift which is signified and is destined to sanctify man; the efficient cause of a sacrament, viz., that which makes the material element the sign of a spiritual reality, and joins to that element the gift of the spiritual reality thus signified, is the formula of blessing used by the minister; finally the institutor of the Sacraments is Jesus Christ. Thus we have the four essential ideas of St. Augustine's definition; not all of them are peculiar to the holy Doctor; some are borrowed from previous authors, especially from St. Ambrose.'

[10] *De sacramentis*, 1. 9. 2.

it.[11] Sometimes, too, there emerged definitions of *sacramentum* which coflicted with Augustine's notion of sacraments as signs. St Isidore of Seville (560–636), for instance, held that *sacramentum* derives from *secretum* ('secret', 'mystery') and laid stress on the idea that sacraments are 'sacred secrets', material things veiling some mystery.

But Augustine's conception was the one which lasted, and it dominates Aquinas's discussion of sacraments. In fact, it is the first thing cited by him when he turns to the issue of sacraments in the *Summa theologiae*. The opening article of his question headed 'What is a sacrament?' asks whether sacraments fall under the general category of signs. In dealing with objections, Aquinas's initial move is to quote from Augustine's *City of God*. 'The visible sacrifice is the sacrament, i.e. the sacred sign, of the invisible sacrifice.'[12] 'When we speak of the sacraments', says Aquinas, 'we have in mind one specific connection with the sacred, namely that of a sign. And it is on these grounds that we assign sacraments to the general category of signs.'[13]

2. Aquinas on Sacraments in General

But what does Aquinas mean by speaking of sacraments as signs? You might say that the question cannot be answered until we know what Aquinas counts as a sacrament. But even knowing the answer to that question does not give us an answer to the original question. Aquinas, like Peter Lombard, holds that there are seven sacraments, all of which are celebrated by rites. For him, the sacraments are those eventually listed by the Council of Trent: baptism, confirmation, penance, eucharist, ordination to priesthood, matrimony, and the rites given to the dying (extreme unction). But what makes these rites *signs* and, therefore, on Aquinas's account, *sacraments*?

His teaching about sacraments has a complex background in scripture and theology. It is also very detailed. But it is important to stress that there is a great simplicity in what he has to say about sacraments,

---

[11] For Lombard, see *Sentences*, 4. 2. 1. Writers earlier than Lombard spoke of the number of sacraments as seven, but it was his defence of seven sacraments that proved decisive. The teaching that there are seven sacraments was promulgated by the Second Council of Basle—Ferrara–Florence–Rome (1431–45) in its Bull of union with the Armenians as well as by the Council of Trent. See *Decrees of the Ecumenical Councils*, i. 534 ff.

[12] 3a. 60. 1.

[13] Ibid.

at least in his mature writings on them. As David Bourke writes, speaking of the account of sacraments in the *Summa theologiae*:

If there is one key idea which lies at the very roots of St Thomas's treatise as a whole it is the idea that the new life of the redemption wrought by God in the incarnate Word is communicated to man through created media, physical things, or acts combined with words.[14]

According to Aquinas, the Incarnation is the means by which God definitively draws people to himself by virtue of what is created. This drawing of people to God is not over and done with after the death, resurrection, and ascension of Christ. It continues in what the Church does by means of ritual. By means of the sacraments people directly share in what was going on in the Incarnation. These rites are ways in which people who live after Christ live as though they were Christ's contemporaries. As Bourke again writes, what Aquinas wants to say is that:

The sacraments as a whole are designed to instill, sustain, intensify, or disseminate the 'newness of life' achieved by Christ in his Resurrection, and to restore it when it has been diminished or weakened in the individual's soul. Thereby mankind is bound together in a visible union of which Christ is the head, and consecrated in him to the Church's life of worship, again expressed in visible and sacramental forms.[15]

To bring out the thrust of Aquinas's thinking here we may contrast what he says about sacraments with what can be found in the work of Hugh of St Victor. In much modern parlance, the adjective 'sacramental' means nothing more than 'revelatory' or 'indicative of spiritual reality', or something like that. On this basis people speak of there being a 'sacramental view of the world', meaning 'a view of the world which sees it as showing us something about God or a realm beyond that of sense experience'. And Hugh of St Victor speaks in a somewhat similar way. As we saw above, he maintains that:

A sacrament is a physical or material element admitted to the perception of the external senses, representing a reality beyond itself in virtue of the similitude it bears to it, actually pointing to that reality in virtue of having been instituted as a sign of it and containing within itself some invisible and spiritual grace in virtue of having been consecrated.

---

[14] Introduction to vol. lvi of the Blackfriars edition of the *Summa theologiae*, xx.
[15] David Bourke, in vol. lvi of the Blackfriars edition of the *Summa theologiae*, xxii.

For Aquinas, however, this is only part of the truth. In his view, a sacrament is not just something standing as a sign of what cannot be seen by the physical eye (though he certainly thinks that it *is* a sign of what cannot be seen by the physical eye). It is also a process by which something is actually effected. Hence, for example, speaking of the water of baptism he declares that this, by itself, is *not* a sacrament. It is *part* of the sacrament of baptism. And it is this only because it is applied to someone who is thereby incorporated into the Church and sealed for Christ. 'The term "sacrament"', he explains, 'signifies the reality which sanctifies [and this means] that it should signify the effect produced.'[16] His view is that in the sacraments God shows us what he does and does what he shows us.[17] A sacrament, for Aquinas, is 'a sign of a sacred reality inasmuch as it has the property of sanctifying people'.[18] Thus, for example, in the case of baptism:

A person is incorporated into the passion and death of Christ through baptism: *If we have died with Christ, we believe that we shall also live with him*. It is clear from this that to every one baptized the passion of Christ is communicated for his healing just as if he himself had suffered and died.[19]

Alluding to Hugh of St Victor, Aquinas notes the opinion that the water of baptism is, by itself, a sacrament. But he rejects it. 'The perfection of the sacrament', he insists, 'is not in the water by itself but in the application of the water to someone—the act of washing.'[20] On this basis he is able to insist that sacraments are genuine causes of grace. They are this, he says, not because the materials used in the sacraments have, in themselves, power to cause grace, but because the materials used in the sacraments are things used by God in bringing grace about. They are, as he puts it, 'instrumental causes' of grace.

It is necessary to say that the sacraments of the New Law do cause grace in some way. For it is manifest that through the sacraments of the New Law people are incorporated into Christ... Now people are not made members of Christ except through grace... There are two kinds of efficient causes, principal and instrumental. The principal cause produces its effect in virtue of its form, to which that effect is assimilated, as fire warms in virtue of its

---

[16] 3a. 60. 3 ad. 2.
[17] Cf. Herbert McCabe, OP, *The Teaching of the Catholic Church* (London, 1985).
[18] 3a. 60. 2.
[19] Ibid.
[20] 3a. 66. 1.

own heat. Now it belongs to God alone to produce grace in this way as its principal cause. For grace is nothing else than a certain shared similitude to the divine nature ... An instrumental cause, on the other hand, acts not in virtue of its own form, but solely in virtue of the impetus imparted to it by the principal agent. Hence the effect has a likeness not to the instrument, but rather to the principal agent, as a bed does not resemble the axe which carves it but rather the design in the mind of the carpenter. And this is the way in which the sacraments of the New Law cause grace. For it is by divine institution that they are conferred upon us for the precise purpose of causing grace in and through them.[21]

In this connection it is important to note that in Aquinas's teaching Christ is the first sacrament, the primary sign and cause of God's life in us. In his thinking, Christ was not just a revelation or a sign of God. He was God. He was quite literally divine. And his physical life and death are actual means by which God brings to completion his work of creation. By means of Christ's life and death, says Aquinas, people are actually brought to share in God's life. And, so he wants to add, the same can be said of the sacraments. Christ, he teaches, is effective in the life of the Church considered as sacramental. Just like the life, death, and resurrection of Christ, the sacraments of the Church are physical signs and genuine causes of grace. They are symbols which make real what they symbolize. Through them we are united to God even in this life. Through them we have been made partakers of the divine nature. As Liam Walsh observes:

[Aquinas] wants to see the sacraments as the ultimate, historical realization of the whole process of God's work of creation and self-giving and the moral response in which humans receive that gift ... In the theology of St Thomas, when one has fully understood what the sacraments are there is nothing more that needs to be thought about except the resurrection![22]

Or, as Timothy McDermott effectively puts it, for Aquinas:

The rituals are tools the cutting edge of which is their symbolic representation of Christ's sacrifice, tools actually being wielded in history by Christ (through his institution of the church ministry of those sacraments) to incorporate men into his own life. The sacraments are visible historical gestures of Christ in the present world. They are the outward bodily tools of the life of unity with God, just as kisses and embraces are the outward bodily tools of love between human beings.[23]

---

[21] 3a. 62. 1.
[22] Walsh, *The Sacraments of Initiation*, 33 f.
[23] *St Thomas Aquinas, Summa Theologiae: A Concise Translation*, (London, 1989), 543 f.

With this thinking in mind, Aquinas is at pains to stress that there is a difference between grace in general and the grace of the sacraments in particular.

Grace perfects the essence of the soul in virtue of the fact that this participates, by way of a kind of likeness, in the divine being. And just as it is from the essence of the soul that its powers flow, so too it is from grace that there flow into the powers of the soul certain perfections called the virtues and the Gifts, by which those powers are perfected so as to achieve a further fulfilment in the acts proper to them. Now the sacraments are designed to achieve certain special effects which are necessary in the Christian life. Thus baptism is designed to achieve a certain kind of spiritual regeneration by which people die to all kinds of vice and become members of Christ. And this effect is in fact something special over and above the acts appropriate to the powers of the soul. And the same is true of the other sacraments.[24]

In Aquinas's view, the grace which Christians acquire by properly celebrating the sacraments is not just the dispositional wherewithal to live well. It is the actual appropriation of the effects of Christ's specific work—not just virtue or good living in general, but that which Christ uniquely came to bring. It should therefore come as no surprise to the reader to be told that, for Aquinas, sacraments essentially belong to the Christian's life rather than to the lives of those who know nothing of Christ or who have no faith in him. Aquinas allows that, in a sense, there were sacraments before the time of Christ. He calls them 'sacraments of the Old Law', and he identifies them with the rituals legislated for in the Old Testament, together with the objects and people involved in them. Commenting on Aquinas's theology of sacraments, Karl Rahner observes that a 'significant effect of Aquinas' presentation is to suggest that we should view the sacraments within the totality of the history of religion in general as well as within the universal history of salvation, the central point of which is Christ himself'. This, Rahner goes on to say, 'naturally suggests the idea that in other places too and at other periods within the history of religion, i.e. outside the New Testament revelation, analogates to the Christian sacraments may be discovered'.[25] And Aquinas, so we may note, agrees. The sacraments of the Old Law are, he says, 'certain sensible signs of invisible things by which people are sanctified'.[26] They were 'predictions of the coming

---

[24] 3a. 62. 2.
[25] Karl Rahner, SJ, 'Introductory Observations on Thomas Aquinas' Theology of the Sacraments in General', in *Theological Investigations*, xiv (London, 1976), 155.
[26] 3a. 61. 3.

of Christ', 'visible signs which people could use to attest their faith in the future coming of the Saviour'.[27]

Some of the things pertaining to the Old Testament had the force of signs pointing to the holiness of Christ inasmuch as he is holy in himself. Others, however, had the force of signs pointing to his holiness inasmuch as we are sanctified by it. In this sense the immolation of the passover lamb signified the immolation of Christ, by which we have been sanctified. And it is proper to call such things as these latter the sacraments of the Old Law.[28]

For Aquinas, however, the important sacraments are 'the sacraments of the New Law', by which he means the Christian sacraments. Why? Because, so he thinks, these cause grace while the sacraments of the Old Law did not. The sacraments of the Old Law, he argues, pre-dated the death of Christ by which justifying grace comes, and they were signs representing faith in Christ only in the sense that they anticipated what was to come. They looked forward to something which was not yet. The sacraments of the New Law, on the other hand, signify something actually present.[29] The sacraments of the Old Law 'fulfilled the function of prefiguring grace' while those of the New Law 'are appropriate as manifestations of a grace that is already present'.[30]

The sacraments of the Old Law differ from those of the New in that they have no sanctifying power intrinsically present in them in virtue of their real continuity with the previously existing humanity of Christ and the Passion. Nevertheless they were real sacraments in that they were physical signs prefiguring Christ as Redeemer, which people could use to protest their faith in him, and so eventually receive the fruits of his Redemption.[31]

In Aquinas's thinking, therefore, history makes a difference and the person and work of Christ are crucial to what is going on in sacraments considered as part of the life of the Church. 'As a sign', he explains, 'a sacrament has a threefold function. It is at once commemorative of that which has gone before, namely the Passion of Christ, and demonstrative of that which is brought about in us through the Passion of Christ, and prognostic, i.e. a foretelling of

[27] Ibid.
[28] 3a. 60. 2 ad. 2.
[29] 3a. 62. 6; cf. also 3a. 60. 2.
[30] 3a. 61. 4 ad. 3.
[31] David Bourke, in vol. lvi of the Blackfriars edition of the *Summa Theologiae*, 70 f.

future glory.'[32] Since the passion of Christ was effective in delivering from sin, and since 'through his Passion he also inaugurated the rites of the Christian religion by *offering himself as an oblation and sacrifice to God* ... it is manifest that in a special way the sacraments of the Church derive their power from the Passion of Christ, and that it is through the reception of the sacraments that the power flowing from this becomes, in a certain way, conjoined to us'.[33]

But Aquinas also holds that the Incarnation plays a determining role in the nature of sacraments since only because of Christ are we able to say what is to count as a sacrament. The aspect of Aquinas's teaching which I have in mind here is his conclusion that we can only give the name 'sacrament' to a particular ritual because it has been instituted by Christ as a means of human sanctification. One might wish to argue that any object or ritual can be a means of grace. One might also wish to maintain that some human authority (e.g. religious leaders) can determine whether an object or ritual can be a means of grace. But this is not Aquinas's view. His line is that things in nature do not by themselves have intrinsic power to sanctify (he does not view sacraments in magical terms). He also thinks that the occurrence of sanctification cannot be determined by any human decision. Whether a physical process involving physical objects is actually a means by which people are taken up into God's plan to lead them to himself depends, he thinks, on whether God is actually leading people to himself by that physical process or those physical objects. And whether or not he is doing that, says Aquinas, is ultimately to be gleaned only from what, in the person of Christ, he tells us about his activity.

In the question of the use of the sacraments two factors can be taken into consideration, namely divine worship and human sanctification. The first of these involves human activity in relation to God. The second, on the contrary, involves divine activity in relation to us. Now it is not for one person to decide how another shall use what is under the latter's power and authority. All that person can decide is how to apply what is under his or her own power. Since, therefore, human sanctification lies under the power of God who sanctifies, it is not for us to decide of our own judgement which materials are to be chosen for us to be sanctified by. This rather is something which should be determined by divine institution ... It is not in

---

[32] 3a. 60. 3.
[33] 3a. 62. 5.

virtue of any power naturally instilled into them, but only by divine institution, that such sensible things [as are used in celebrating the sacraments] are ordered to our sanctification.[34]

'Sensible things have of their very nature a certain aptitude to signify spiritual effects', Aquinas writes.[35] 'Nevertheless', he continues, 'it is by divine institution that a special determination is imparted to this aptitude restricting it to one special significance.'[36] He thinks it important to stress that in celebrating the sacraments we certainly use what we might call 'natural symbols'—i.e. words, objects, and rituals which one can easily (or naturally) think of as imaging or reflecting what is going on when sacraments are celebrated. Washing with water in baptism, for instance, is, so he would say, a natural symbol of spiritual cleansing, not a procedure having no obvious connection with such cleansing.[37] He thinks that sacraments are sacred signs because they are first of all ordinary and intelligible human signs or symbols. But the final and indispensable warrant for celebrating the sacraments as we do, he concludes, lies in the fact that they are instituted by Christ. The Church over time may decide that this, that, or the other form of ritual is to be used when sacraments are celebrated; so differences determined by people may be found in the way sacraments are celebrated at different times and in different places.

But those things which belong to a given sacrament of necessity are instituted by Christ himself who is both divine and human. And while it is true that not all of them are handed down in Scripture, still the Church possesses them from the family tradition of the Apostles.[38]

3. Why Sacraments?

But why should it be thought that sacraments are needed at all? What particular purpose do they serve? And why should they have been instituted in the first place? As we have seen, Aquinas holds that sacraments are means by which Christians receive grace. But he does not think that grace cannot be received without sacraments. So it is

[34] 3a. 60. 5, corpus and ad. 2.
[35] 3a. 64. 2 ad. 2.
[36] Ibid.
[37] 3a. 66. 3.
[38] 3a. 64. 2 ad. 2.

not his view that sacraments are necessary conditions of grace. Nor does he think that salvation is impossible without them. For him, salvation is effected by the life, death, and resurrection of Christ. As he says in one place: 'The Passion of Christ is the sufficient cause of the salvation of human beings.'[39] Why, then, should he think of the sacraments as in any sense necessary?

The short answer is that he believes that the work of Christ needs to be made effective over time and in the day-to-day lives of Christians. In his view, the sacraments are the visible expressions of an ongoing relationship of love between Christians and the God who loves them—expressions which actually constitute a life of love between Christians and God. As Timothy McDermott explains, Aquinas's position is that 'each sacrament is a moment in my human life on this earth, a moment which develops the identification of my individual life with the saving life of Christ, and so at the same time marks my individual life as a continuation of that saving life'.[40]

If I fall in love with you, then you are secure in my love at the point when I can truly say 'I love you'. But a relationship of love is not a static thing to be frozen in a moment of time and established by fiat. For love to develop between me and you, my declaration of love is not enough. You have to be in love with me. And your love for me will be shown in what you do day in and day out. If our love for each other is genuine, it will make a difference to our lives. And, among other things, it will be shown by how we express it in physical terms. We will declare our love for each other. And we will make love. But we will also do other things. We will talk to each other in certain ways. We will eat together. We will give each other presents. We will celebrate our anniversaries. And so on.

Well, so Aquinas thinks, it is much the same between Christians and God. Their life of love with each other is also something with a physical history. To begin with, there is Christ. He was a physical, historical individual. And the story of his life is the final revelation and expression in history of God's love for us. But there are also the physical, historical lives of Christians to be reckoned with—the lives of those who come after Christ. How are they to live out their vocation as objects of God's love as revealed in Christ? According to Aquinas, and assuming that they love God as revealed in the Word

[39] 3a. 61. 1 ad. 3.
[40] McDermott, *St Thomas Aquinas*, 543.

Incarnate, they do so in much the same way as anybody lives out a life of love with one who loves them. They do things comparable with declaring love, making love, talking, eating together, giving each other presents, and celebrating anniversaries. They express their love in concrete, physical terms which signify their love and which also count as the embodiment of their love and, therefore, the living out of it. And it is for this reason that Aquinas thinks that the sacraments are so important. In his view, Christians cannot think of God as distant or remote. For them he must be always present. And his revelation of himself in Christ is something to be received, acted on, and lived out by Christians in physical, bodily, everyday behaviour. Christians are those who do things which truly constitute a history of love between them and God. As surely as the history of love between people includes declaring love, making love, talking together, eating together, giving presents, and celebrating anniversaries, so, says Aquinas, the history of love between Christians and God includes engaging in those things which the Church calls 'sacraments'. For him, these are a natural and obvious means by which Christians can be, and continue to be, what they believe themselves to be as Christians. They are means by which Christians join themselves to and benefit from what God was doing in the life, death, and resurrection of God the Word Incarnate. They 'constitute certain sensible signs of invisible things by which people are sanctified'.[41]

Hence it is that, when he turns directly to the question 'Are the sacraments necessary for the salvation of human beings?', Aquinas's answer is affirmative on three counts. First, he says, people are helped by them in a way appropriate to their manner of knowing, since human beings achieve knowledge of spiritual and intelligible things through their 'experience of physical and sensible realities'.

It is characteristic of divine providence that it provides for each being in a manner corresponding to its own particular way of functioning. Hence it is appropriate that in bestowing certain aids to salvation upon us the divine wisdom should make use of certain physical and sensible signs called the sacraments.[42]

Second, so Aquinas continues, people are engrossed in physical things and needs to be helped by means of them.

---

[41] 3a. 61. 3.
[42] 3a. 61. 1.

For if they were to be confronted with spiritual realities pure and unalloyed their minds, absorbed as they are in physical things, would be incapable of accepting them.[43]

Finally, he adds, people are prone in their activity to be involved with physical things. Sacraments allow us to continue with our predilection in this respect and therefore make things easier for us. You might almost put it by saying that, in Aquinas's view, sacraments are fun.

The third reason is taken from the fact that in our activities we are particularly prone to involve ourselves with physical things. Lest, therefore, it should be too hard for us totally to dispense with physical actions, we were given certain physical practices to observe in the sacraments. The purpose of these was to enable us to exercise our powers in salutary ways, and so to avoid the superstitious practices of demon worship or any of the harmful activities consisting of sinful deeds.[44]

Basically, then, Aquinas thinks of sacraments as helpful to human beings considered as what he takes them to be, i.e. things of flesh and blood. They lead people to God by using the raw materials of human interest. As Aquinas himself writes: 'Through the sacraments, therefore, sensible things are used to instruct people in a manner appropriate to their nature.'[45] Or as he puts it in another place:

It is connatural to people to arrive at a knowledge of intelligible realities through sensible ones, and a sign is something through which a person arrives at knowledge of some further thing beyond itself. Moreover the sacred realities signified by the sacraments are certain spiritual and intelligible goods by which we are sanctified. And the consequence of this fact is that the function of the sacrament as signifying is implemented by means of some sensible realities.[46]

For Aquinas, as we have seen, our knowledge takes its rise from the senses. For him, therefore, sacraments can be viewed as means designed to show forth what our new life in Christ amounts to. They can also be viewed as means designed to help us understand it. And for this reason he insists that sacraments are not just to be identified with reference to physical objects and processes. Since we are intellectual animals using language, he thinks that they also involve words

---

[43] Ibid.
[44] Ibid.
[45] Ibid.
[46] 3a. 60. 4.

which express, and are understood to express, the work effected by the physical objects and processes.

The sacraments can be considered from the aspect of human beings who are sanctified by them. As they are made up of soul and body, the sacramental medicine is made to correspond to this. For the visible materials in it touch the body, while the word in it is accepted in faith by the soul ... Hence in order that the communication of meaning through the sacraments might achieve its full perfection it was necessary to give precision to the meaning that sensible materials have the power to convey as signs by adding certain words to them.[47]

Sacraments, for Aquinas, are anything but mumbo-jumbo. They are meant to engage us at the levels which mean most to us—i.e. the physical and the intellectual. They signify what is going on between Christians and God. And they effect what they signify. We should also note that, in Aquinas's view, they do all this for Christians considered as a group or society, not just considered as so many individuals. For Aquinas, the sacraments, with their ritual and physical elements, bring people to God as a body or collection. They knit people together with each other as well as with God. They are, as Aquinas significantly calls them, 'the sacraments of the Church' (*ecclesiae sacramenta*).[48] Hence it is that, even before Aquinas gives the reasons noted above for sacraments being necessary, he quotes from St Augustine to say: 'It is impossible to unite people within a religion of any name, whether true or false, unless they are kept together by means of some system of symbols or sacraments in which they all share.'[49] 'It is necessary', he continues, 'for human salvation that people should be united in the name of the one true religion. Therefore the sacraments are necessary for the salvation of people.'[50]

But what does Aquinas have to say in dealing with particular sacraments rather than sacraments in general? In the *Summa theologiae* he has separate discussions of baptism (3a. 66 ff.) and confirmation (3a. 72). He also has a discussion of penance (3a. 84 ff.), a discussion which was unfinished at his death. There can, however, be little

---

[47] 3a. 60. 6.
[48] See Introduction to 3a. 60. 'Now that we have completed our consideration of the mysteries of the Incarnate Word, our next field of investigation is the sacraments of the Church.'
[49] The quotation from Augustine is from *Contra Faustum*, 19. 11.
[50] 3a. 61. 1.

doubt that the most original and influential detailed treatment of a sacrament in the *Summa theologiae* is that in which Aquinas writes about the eucharist. He is often thought of as the eucharistic theologian *par excellence* of the Catholic Church, and he clearly holds that the eucharist is enormously important in the lives of Christians because he speaks of it as being the sacrament which crowns all the others and to which they are ordered. So, to illustrate how Aquinas's mind works when he turns to one sacrament in particular, it seems fair to follow him in what he has to say about the eucharist.

The Crowning Sacrament: The Eucharist

1. The Significance of the Eucharist

It is often said that Aquinas has no developed theology of the Church (ecclesiology). And that, in a sense, is true. For he wrote no sustained treatise on the Church as such, no *De Ecclesia*. On the other hand, however, and as authors like Yves Congar have shown,[51] a distinct ecclesiology can be discerned from what he writes in different places. And a lot of it can be found in what he has to say about the eucharist. This, he says, points to 'the unity of the Church, into which people are drawn together through this sacrament'.[52] It is 'the sacrament of the Church's unity'.[53]

First and foremost, Aquinas thinks of the eucharist as that to which the lives of all Christians are directed—i.e. the state of being united together as those who are joined to God by means of God himself (the life of grace). He therefore asserts that the eucharist 'constitutes the *goal and consummation of all the sacraments*, as Dionysius tells us'.[54] For him, it is 'the summit of the spiritual life and all the sacraments are ordered to it'.[55] Hence, he asserts, baptism takes its point from the eucharist (*per baptismum ordinatur homo ad eucharistiam*).[56] As we have seen, Aquinas maintains that a new phase of human history

---

[51] See Yves Congar, *Thomas d'Aquin: Sa vision de théologie et de l'Église* (London, 1984).
[52] 3a. 73. 4.
[53] 3a. 73. 2. In this connection Aquinas cites 1 Cor. 10: 17 ('Because there is one bread, we who are many are one body, for we all partake of the one bread').
[54] 3a. 63. 6.
[55] 3a. 73. 3.
[56] Ibid.

came with the Incarnation. In the person of the Word Incarnate, he holds, God came to share himself with creatures of flesh and blood. In the celebration of the eucharist, he goes on to say, this effect of the Incarnation is spread out in time in a definitive sense. He holds that, by means of the eucharist, God Incarnate continues to live at one with human beings who are, therefore, living at one with him on condition that they want to do that. In this sense, the eucharist contains the source (the life of God) of its effect (the life of grace). It is 'the union of Christ with his members'[57] and the ultimate sign of what people are meant to be. By it, says Aquinas, they are 'brought to spiritual perfection in being closely united to Christ who suffered for us'.[58] So it is also that by which people *are* what they are meant to be.

The effect of this sacrament should be looked at first and foremost from what the sacrament holds, and this is Christ. Just as by coming visibly into the world he brought the life of grace into it, according to John, *Grace and truth came through Jesus Christ*, so by coming to people sacramentally he causes the life of grace ... This sacrament signifies three things. It looks back to the past: in this sense it commemorates the passion of the Lord ... In regard to the present, there is another thing to which it points. This is the unity of the Church into which people are drawn together through this sacrament ... It has a third significance with regard to the future. It prefigures that enjoyment of God which will be ours in heaven ... Through this sacrament *we take to ourselves the godhead of the Son.*[59]

In the eucharist, says Aquinas, Christ is truly present and truly received. And his death is represented. So all the benefits involved in the Incarnation (considered as such and also with respect to the passion) carry over into the eucharist. Citing St Augustine in the *secunda pars*, Aquinas explains that a sacrifice is 'Any work done in order that we may cleave to God in holy companionship'.[60] For this reason, so he goes on to say in the *tertia pars*, the celebration of the eucharist is simply the sacrifice of Christ. 'The celebration of this sacrament is a definite image representing Christ's passion, which is his true sacrifice ... [and] ... by this sacrament we are made sharers in the fruit of the Lord's passion.'[61] In other words, in celebrating

---

[57] 3a. 79. 5.
[58] 3a. 73. 3 ad. 3.
[59] 3a. 79. 1 and 3a. 73. 4. The first quotation is from John 1: 17. The second comes from John Damascene, *De fide orthodoxa*, 4. 13.
[60] 2a2ae. 85. 1 ff.; cf. *City of God*, 10. 28.
[61] 3a. 83. 1.

the sacrament of the eucharist the Church shares in all that we can mean by 'Christ's priesthood'.

From all of this it would, of course, seem to follow that the eucharist should be thought of as a typical or regular part of Christian life, not something to be celebrated only on rare occasions and only by a special group of people. And, though some Christians would disagree with him, this is what Aquinas believes. In the early Middle Ages the eucharist came to be somewhat removed from the lives of ordinary people. It became a kind of clerical preserve—a development augmented by such things as the rise of chantries and mass chapels and the moving of church altars against the rear wall of the apse separated from the congregation.[62] For Aquinas, however, the eucharist is the sign of what makes the Church the Church. It is also the reality which constitutes the Church as the Church, and it is the ordinary means of growing in grace. It is, he says 'our spiritual food', 'our spiritual refreshment'.[63] So, in an age when reception of the eucharist by the many was not common, we find him recommending daily communion or, at least, speaking of this as an ideal. 'Augustine says, *This is our daily bread: take it daily that it may profit you daily* ... It is profitable to receive daily so as to gather its fruits daily.'[64] Daily communication by the laity was so uncommon in the Middle Ages that the Fourth Lateran Council had to decree that the faithful must receive communion at least once a year.[65] One modern author suggests that even until the Reformation the basic popular eucharistic doctrine of the Middle Ages was not 'Take and eat' and 'Take and drink', but 'Gaze on the Host and find your salvation in the gazing'.[66] Aquinas, on the other hand, thinks of the eucharist as something which Christians will inevitably and regularly be drawn to receive. It is 'food' which is 'required that a person may be kept alive'.[67] It is not, he says, necessary for salvation, for someone can be saved simply by baptism. It is not 'needed for basic Christian living'.[68] But it is, he adds, 'the natural culmination to baptism'. And it is necessary if the

---

[62] See Joseph M. Powers, *Eucharistic Theology* (London, 1968), 24 ff.

[63] 3a. 73. 1 corpus and ad. 1; also 3a. 79. 1.

[64] 3a. 80. 10.

[65] *Decrees of the Ecumenical Councils*, i. 245. For some discussion of medieval eucharistic practice, see Gary Macy, *The Theologies of the Eucharist in the Early Scholastic Period* (Oxford, 1984), 93 ff. and 119 ff.

[66] Powers, *Eucharistic Theology*, p. 31.

[67] 3a. 73. 1.

[68] 3a. 73. 3.

life of Christians, begun at baptism, is to be brought to its culmination.[69] And, even though he thinks that one can be saved just by
being baptized, he also maintains that one should desire to participate
in the celebration of the eucharist given the chance. 'A person cannot
be saved', he writes, 'without the desire of receiving this sacrament.
Now a desire would be pointless unless it could be fulfilled when the
opportunity presents itself.'[70]

2. The Presence of Christ in the Eucharist

But what is one receiving when one receives the sacrament of the
eucharist? Aquinas obviously thinks that those who receive the
eucharist receive grace. Since he holds that the eucharist makes its
receivers sharers in the effect of Christ's passion, he also speaks of it
as having the power to forgive sin. 'The power is there', he writes,
'of forgiving any sin whatever from Christ's Passion.'[71] Perhaps most
famously of all, however, Aquinas insists that to receive the sacrament of the eucharist is to receive Christ himself. He is emphatic
that Christ is truly present in the eucharist. 'Christ', he asserts, 'is
sacramentally contained in the eucharist.'[72] 'The real body of Christ
and his blood are in this sacrament.'[73] 'The reality of this sacrament',
he says, 'demands that the very body of Christ exist in it.'[74] And
when Aquinas uses the phrase 'the body of Christ' in this context he
seems to be thinking in very literal terms. In his own words: 'We have
under this sacrament—under the appearance of the bread—not only
the flesh, but the whole body of Christ, that is, the bones and nerves
and all the rest.'[75]

Various Christian theologians both before and after Aquinas have
taught, or have been thought to have taught, that Christ is present in
the eucharist only in the sense that the bread and wine used for the
eucharistic celebration stand as symbols of the body and blood of
Christ. Berengarius of Tours (c.1040–80) was believed to have done
this in the eleventh century, and he is interpreted as doing so by

---

[69] Ibid.
[70] 3a. 80. 11.
[71] 3a. 79. 3.
[72] 3a. 73. 5.
[73] 3a. 75. 1.
[74] 3a. 75. 2.
[75] 3a. 76. 1 ad. 2.

Aquinas.[76] A symbolic interpretation of the eucharistic presence is also, of course, commonly associated with certain Reformation leaders, notably Ulrich Zwingli (1484–1531).[77] But Aquinas can in no way be associated with the opinion that Christ is only symbolically present in the eucharist. 'The complete substance of the bread', he writes, 'is converted into the complete substance of Christ's body, and the complete substance of the wine into the complete substance of Christ's blood.'[78] And the change involved here, he adds, 'can be called by a name proper to itself—"transubstantiation"'.[79]

The change involved in the eucharist is not, Aquinas agrees, a natural change, for in natural change you have a change of form, while in the eucharist you have bread and wine changed wholly into something else. The eucharistic change is, for Aquinas, miraculous. In the eucharist, he says, God, not being limited in the range of his action, is

able to bring about not merely a changing of form, so that different forms follow one after another in the same subject, but the changing of the whole being of a thing, so that the complete substance of this is changed into the complete substance of that . . . Hence this change is not a formal change, but a substantial one. It does not belong to the natural kinds of change, and it can be called by a name proper to itself—'transubstantiation'.[80]

Aquinas thinks that what goes on in the change of the bread and wine can, in fact, be compared both to creation and to ordinary change. It is like creation since there is no subject being modified. It is like ordinary change since first there is one thing, then another, and since after the change there appears to be a continuation of something (the accidents).

At this point it is important to stress that Aquinas does not rely on rational or philosophical argument as a means of establishing that Christ is present in the eucharist. He uses philosophical arguments in trying to give an account of the celebration of the eucharist. But belief in the literal or non-symbolic eucharistic presence of Christ is not, for him, something grounded on what we might recognize as

---

[76] For details of discussions surrounding Berengarius, see Margaret Gibson, *Lanfranc of Bec* (Oxford, 1978), 63 ff. Aquinas attributes to Berengarius a symbolic understanding of the presence of Christ in the eucharist in 3a. 75. 1.

[77] See W. P. Stephens, *The Theology of Huldrych Zwingli* (Oxford, 1986), 180 ff.

[78] 3a. 75. 4.

[79] Ibid.

[80] 3a. 75. 5.

proof or demonstration. As he sees it, it is something implied by Christian faith. 'We could never', he observes, 'know by our senses that the real body of Christ and his blood are in this sacrament, but only by our faith which is based on the authority of God.'[81] Whether rightly or wrongly, Aquinas concludes that our warrant for believing in the presence of Christ in the eucharist lies in the teaching of Christ whom faith perceives to be divine and, therefore, not to be argued with. We must, he says, agree with authors like Cyril of Alexandria (d. 444). In the Synoptic Gospels Jesus says, 'This is my body', in the context of the Last Supper.[82] Aquinas holds that we must respond to these words by saying 'do not doubt the truth of this, but take our Saviour's word in faith: he is truth itself, he does not lie'.[83]

Those who defend a symbolic account of the eucharistic presence will obviously reply that 'This is my body' can be understood to mean 'This symbolizes my body' or 'This represents my body'. But Aquinas is clearly unconvinced by such a move. In his view, the symbolic interpretation of the eucharistic presence depends on it being true that bread and wine are truly present throughout the eucharistic celebration. And this, he argues, cannot be the case for several reasons. If, for example, Christ's body is what is present in the eucharist, then the bread and wine must have been changed into it since something can only become present in a place if it moves there locally (impossible in the case of Christ's body, which, for example, cannot cease to exist in heaven) or if something at the place in question is changed into it.[84] Then again, so Aquinas suggests, if the eucharist is just a matter of bread and wine symbolizing or representing Christ, the words 'This is my body' would be false since 'this' must means 'this substance' and 'the substance of bread is not Christ's body'.[85] Also, Aquinas adds, if the eucharistic bread and wine are truly bread and wine throughout the celebration of the eucharist, Christians would be guilty of idolatry. For they treat the eucharist as divine and reverence it accordingly.[86]

In Aquinas's view, therefore, what is present when the eucharist is

[81] 3a. 75. 1.
[82] Matt. 26: 26; Mark 14: 22; Luke 22: 19.
[83] 3a. 75. 1. Cf. Cyril of Alexandria, *Commentary on Luke*, 22. 19.
[84] 3a. 75. 2.
[85] Ibid.
[86] Ibid.

celebrated is not bread and wine throughout. After the words of consecration (i.e. 'This is my body' and so on) have been said by the celebrant, what is there is the body and blood of Christ. It is not bread and wine that remain on the altar. Nor do we have sanctified bread and wine, or Christ plus bread and wine. We have no bread and wine. We just have Christ.

It is, however, important to understand that in offering this view Aquinas does not mean what he is sometimes taken to mean. For he is sometimes thought to be saying that in the course of the eucharistic celebration the bread and wine are annihilated and that the body and blood of Christ begin to exist in their place, which is not his position at all. He maintains that the body and blood of Christ come to be present in the eucharist, not because bread and wine are annihilated, but because they are changed into the body and blood of Christ. In his language, the substance of bread and wine are changed into the substance of the body and blood of Christ. Hence his use of the expression 'transubstantiation'.[87] As Anthony Kenny observes:

For St Thomas there could be no sense in saying that Christ's body existed *in such-and-such a place* if the bread and wine formerly existing in the place had been annihilated. For, he would ask, how is the connection made between the body on the right hand of the Father and this particular altar? The connection, for him, is this, and only this: that the accidents of what has been turned into Christ's body are in such-and-such a place. Take away the transubstantiation, according to St Thomas, and you take away the presence.[88]

In speaking of substance here Aquinas, we should note, does not intend us to think as, for example, John Locke has traditionally and famously been held to think when he alludes to substance. According to Locke (as traditionally interpreted), individual things can be thought of as composed of knowable properties belonging to an underlying and unknowable subject. When he speaks of the qualities we 'find united in the thing called *Horse* or *Stone*', he says: 'we cannot

---

[87] Luther claimed that the term was invented by Aquinas. This is quite false. It was common in the works of Masters of Theology at Paris by 1150. It can also be found in the profession of faith which Lateran IV directed against the Albigensians. For the reference in Lateran IV see *Decrees of the Ecumenical Councils*, i. 230. For the history of the term 'transubstantiation', see James McCue, 'The Doctrine of Transubstantiation from Berengar through the Council of Trent', in P. Empie and T. Murphy (eds.), *The Eucharist as Sacrifice* (Minneapolis, 1967).

[88] Anthony Kenny, *Reason and Religion* (Oxford, 1987), 18.

conceive, how they should subsist alone, nor one in another, [and so] we suppose them existing in, and supported by some common subject; *which Support we denote by the name Substance*, though it be certain, we have no clear, or distinct *Idea* of that *thing* we suppose a Support'.[89] On this account, substance would seem to be a bare, unknowable *substratum* without any qualities underlying the properties and qualities which we can know a thing to have.[90] For Aquinas, by contrast, a substance just is an individual having the properties that it has.[91] As Kenny again observes:

According to scholastic theory, substance is not an imperceptible part of a particular individual; it *is* that individual. And it is imperceptible by the senses only in the following sense: I do not see *what kind of thing* something is with my eyes as I see *what colour* it is with my eyes, any more than I see *what it tastes like* with my eyes. For all that, substances may be perceived. I can see, say, sulphuric acid with my eyes...[92]

This means that, when Aquinas asserts that the substance of bread and wine turn into the body and blood of Christ, he means that the bread and wine turn into Christ.[93] On the other hand, however, since it does not seem that bread and wine have turned into Christ during the celebration of the eucharist, Aquinas also wants to say that the turning into here occurs without the removal of those properties which allow us to pick out particular instances of bread and wine—properties such as colour, taste, dimension, and so on. Or, as Aquinas puts it, though the words of consecration result in a change of substance, they do not result in a change of accidents. 'When the change of the bread into the body of Christ and of the wine into his blood has taken place', he says, 'the accidents of the bread and wine remain.'[94] And they do so, Aquinas also wants to say, without being the accidents of anything. They are certainly not the accidents of Christ, for he does not look or taste like bread and wine. And, since

---

[89] John Locke, *An Essay Concerning Human Understanding*, ed. Peter H. Nidditch (Oxford, 1975), 2. 23. 4.

[90] That Locke genuinely wished to defend this view of substance has, however, been questioned in recent years. See R. S. Woolhouse, *Locke* (Brighton, 1983), ch. 13.

[91] In the context of his discussion of transubstantiation Aquinas uses 'substance' to mean what Aristotle in *Categories*, ch. 5, calls 'first substance'.

[92] Anthony Kenny, 'The Use of Logical Analysis in Theology', in John Coulson (ed.), *Theology and the University* (London, 1964), 232 f.

[93] In his *Commentary on the Metaphysics of Aristotle*, Aquinas observes that 'to exist separately and to be a particular thing seems to belong chiefly to substance'.

[94] 3a. 76. 2.

bread and wine no longer exist, they cannot be accidents of bread and wine. Hence, 'We are left to conclude that the accidents in this sacrament do not inhere in any subject.'[95] All that can be said to pull them together, says Aquinas, is dimensive quantity.

Qualities are divisible not in themselves, but only because the subject in which they are is divisible. Now the qualities which remain in this sacrament are divided whenever the dimensive quantity is divided; our senses tell us that. Therefore, the dimensive quantity is the subject of the accidents which remain in this sacrament.[96]

In material things, Aquinas argues, accidents get individuated as accidents of a particular subject. And the source of individuation of accidents in material things can be said to be the subject. Since matter is the principle of individuation in material things, he continues, accidents can be thought of as individuated ultimately by dimensive quantity. And this is what individuates them in the case of the accidents remaining in the eucharist after the consecration.

Notice that on this account we have an implicit rejection of what some Christians have been very much anxious to assert. When Berengarius advanced his eucharistic teaching in the eleventh century, he was required to agree that

the bread and wine which are laid on the alter are after consecration not only a sacrament but also the true body and blood of our lord Jesus Christ, and they are physically taken up and broken in the hands of the priest and crushed by the teeth of the faithful, not only sacramentally but in truth.[97]

The idea here is that one can truly assert of Christ all that one can assert of the accidents of bread and wine after the consecration. If, after the consecration, it seems that bread and wine are moving around and being broken, it follows that Christ is moving around and being broken. But Aquinas rejects this conclusion, and he does so because he denies that the accidents present after the consecration inhere in a subject.

Breaking means dividing what is extended. But we have nothing extended and divisible here except the sacramental species, because the body of Christ is now removed from all possibility of change and the substance of the bread is no longer present.[98]

---

[95] 3a. 77. 1.
[96] 3a. 77. 2.
[97] Cf. Gibson, *Lanfranc of Bec*, 81.

[98] 3a. 77. 7.

In other words, Aquinas is clearly opposed to such things as the (once popular) Catholic devotion to 'the Prisoner in the Tabernacle'. For him, there would be no virtue in paying Christ a visit in a tabernacle in which he is bound dimensively while we can go our way. On Aquinas's account, Christ is certainly present after the consecration. But he is not in the tabernacle as I can be in my room. And he is not its prisoner. It is the accidents of bread and wine that are dimensively in the tabernacle. On this basis Aquinas can deny that the dimensions of the bread and wine are changed into the dimensions of Christ's body. It is the substance that is changed. So the substance of Christ's body and blood are present, not the dimensions of his body or blood.

When the change of the bread into the body of Christ and of the wine into his blood has taken place, the accidents of the bread and wine remain. Since that is so, it is clear that the dimensions of the bread and wine are not changed into the dimensions of Christ's body; it is substance that is changed into substance. The substance of Christ's body or of his blood is in the sacrament as a result of sacramental sign; not so the dimensions of his body or of his blood.[99]

On this account one can distinguish between the substance of a thing and its dimensions. And one can say that the substance of a thing can be changed into something else while the dimensions remain the same. And, so Aquinas adds, 'the whole specific nature of a substance is as truly contained by small as by large dimensions'.[100] So the whole of Christ's body and blood are present in the eucharist, though not in a way that involves a change of their proper dimensions. 'The direct term of this sacramental change', says Aquinas, 'is the substance of Christ's body only, not with its dimensions. This is clear from the fact that it is only the substance of the bread which passes away at the consecration, but the dimensions of the bread remain.'[101]

3. Aquinas and Transubstantiation

Does any of this make sense? Anything like a full discussion of that question is impossible here. But we can hardly ignore the fact that

---

[99] 3a. 76. 2.
[100] Ibid.
[101] 3a. 76. 4.

what Aquinas says on the eucharist has certainly found critics both
theological and philosophical. Luther, for example, attacked it. In his
view, Aquinas erroneously took belief in transubstantiation to be an
article of Christian faith. Though Luther certainly believed that
Christ is present in the eucharist, he also criticized Aquinas on
transubstantiation on the ground that his development of the notion
has no biblical warrant and is also at odds with Aristotle.

But this opinion of Thomas hangs so completely in the air without support of
Scripture or reason that it seems to me he knows neither his philosophy nor
his logic. For Aristotle speaks of subject and accidents so very differently
from St Thomas that it seems to me this great man is to be pitied not only
for attempting to draw his opinions in matters of faith from Aristotle, but also
in attempting to base them upon a man whom he did not understand, thus
building an unfortunate superstructure upon an unfortunate foundation.[102]

In recent philosophical literature, Aquinas on the eucharist has
also been taken to task by, for example, Anthony Kenny, who concentrates on the notion that after the consecration there are accidents which inhere in no substance. In putting this notion forward,
Aquinas, of course, is using terminology found in Aristotle, who
also distinguishes between substance and accidents. But, so Kenny
observes:

Among the accidental categories of Aristotle is the category of place. '... is
on the altar', for instance, is an accidental predicate. But if the accidents
which once belonged to the bread do not inhere after consecration in the
substance of Christ's body, then it appears that it by no means follows from
the presence of the host upon the altar that Christ is present on the altar.[103]

A somewhat similar line of thought appears in an essay by Michael
Dummett, who (like Luther) does not wish to deny the real presence
of Christ in the eucharist, but who finds fault with Aquinas's way of
elucidating the nature of the real presence. Dummett notes that
according to Aquinas 'the accidents of the bread and wine persist,
and attach to certain regions of space . . . And as a quite separate fact,
the Body and Blood of Christ are in some special sense present,
though not exactly as occupying those regions of space.' But, so
Dummett continues, this is a highly problematic suggestion.

[102] *Luther's Works*, ed. J. Pelikan and H. Lehman, (St Louis, 1955–87), xxxvi. 29.
[103] Kenny, 'The Use of Logical Analysis in Theology', 235.

On this account there is no connection between the two. The consecrated
elements are, as it were, merely the discarded husk of the bread and wine
earlier present, and have no more intimate connection with the Body and
Blood of Christ than that. It is as if the bread and wine have stepped aside to
make room for Christ's Body and Blood, which could not otherwise be
present, and, in so stepping aside, have, so to speak, left their mortal remains
behind. Aquinas's words read very impressively; but, as soon as we pause to
reflect upon the theory he is actually advancing, we cannot but conclude that
the conception it embodies must have gone astray.[104]

How would Aquinas react to these criticisms if they were put to
him today? The question is hard to answer. Aquinas is dead. He is
not our contemporary. We can never credibly claim to say what
moves he would make in response to his later critics. But I still think
it worth making the following points as things to bear in mind when
trying to evaluate his teaching on the eucharist.

First, he clearly respected philosophical argument. And he always
maintained that not even God can bring about that which is logically
impossible. So were it to be proved that his position on the eucharist
is logically untenable or in some other way refutable, he would,
presumably, withdraw it. Luther was wrong to suppose that he took
belief in transubstantiation to be an article of Christian faith. He
never describes it in those terms. As we saw in Chapter 14, articles of
faith are, for him, the articles of the creed, which say nothing about
transubstantiation. He also denies that true belief concerning the
eucharist is a special article of faith. He says that it is included under
the article on God's omnipotence. 'In this sacrament', he writes,
'Christ's body is miraculously contained, and in this respect the
eucharist is implicit in the article on omnipotence, along with all
the other miracles attributed to God's omnipotence.'[105] Aquinas
certainly thinks that heresy can arise with respect to teaching about
the eucharist. For him, however, as also for Luther, heresy concerning the eucharist lies in denying that Christ is present in the
eucharist, or in saying that he is present there only symbolically.[106]

---

[104] Michael Dummett, 'The Intelligibility of Eucharistic Doctrine', in William J.
Abraham and Steven W. Holtzer (eds.), *The Rationality of Religious Belief* (Oxford,
1987), 246 f.
[105] 2a2ae. 1. 8 ad. 6. Further reasons for denying that Aquinas took
transubstantiation to be an article of faith are given by Denis R. Janz in *Luther on
Thomas Aquinas* (Stuffgart, 1989), 46 f.
[106] See 3a. 75. 1.

And this is a view which can be accepted by people whether or not they agree with what Aquinas says on transubstantiation.

Second, in putting forward the details of his teaching on the eucharist, Aquinas is not so much offering an explanation of what is going on when the eucharist is celebrated as trying to say what cannot be going on. He reasons that, since Christ taught that the eucharist is his body and blood, it cannot be the case that it is bread and wine, and it cannot be bread and wine if we rightly pay it honour due to God alone. Since bread and wine appear to be present after the consecration, he continues, it cannot be the case that the appearance of bread and wine guarantees the presence of bread and wine. And since, in celebrating the eucharist, we begin with bread and wine and end up with the body and blood of Christ, and since Christ does not become present by local motion, it cannot be that anything other than a change of bread and wine into Christ has occurred. Trying to advance negative points such as these is what leads Aquinas to the details of his teaching on transubstantiation, just as advancing negative points leads him to develop his teaching on the nature of God. But we need not suppose him to think of these details as anything more than the best that can be offered in the circumstances as a way of expressing what cannot be going on when the eucharist is celebrated. Anyone reading through the discussion of the eucharist in the *tertia pars* of the *Summa theologiae* ought to see without much difficulty that Aquinas thinks of himself as talking about something which finally defies understanding. The eucharist, for him, is a mystery in precisely the sense that God is a mystery—for the eucharist, for him, is the presence of God. Writing about transubstantiation without reference to Aquinas, Elizabeth Anscombe observes:

It would be wrong to think, however, that the thing can be understood, sorted out, expounded as a possibility with nothing mysterious about it. That is, that it can be understood in such a way as is perhaps demanded by those who attack it on the ground of its obvious difficulties.[107]

As far as I can see, nothing that Aquinas writes shows that he would have disagreed with this suggestion. And there is much in what he writes which shows that he would have positively endorsed it. And, given his own expositions of Aristotle, he would most certainly have assented to Luther's observation that his teaching on transubstantia-

---

[107] 'On Transubstantiation', in *Collected Philosophical Papers* (Oxford, 1981), iii. 109.

tion is at odds with what Aristotle says about substance and accidents. As Herbert McCabe, OP, observes, and as Aquinas most surely would have agreed, 'Aristotle could have made no sense of the notion of transubstantiation. It is not a notion that can be accommodated *within* the concepts of Aristotelian philosophy, it represents the breakdown of these concepts in face of a mystery.'[108] That is why Aquinas speaks of transubstantiation as a unique change without parallel and effected by God as a miracle. One might add that it is not only in writing of transubstantiation that Aquinas knowingly uses Aristotle to mean what Aristotle could not have accepted. He does the same when he invokes Aristotelian notions of causality to conclude that God is the Creator. What he means by 'creation' is, on Aristotle's account, an impossible kind of making, just as what he means by 'transubstantiation' is, on Aristotle's account, an impossible kind of change.

Finally, it is not evident that the objections of Kenny and Dummett noted above are terribly damaging to Aquinas's overall position on transubstantiation. At any rate, there is reason to think that he did not think them damaging since he anticipates them and offers an answer. In 3a. 77. 1 he asks with respect to the eucharist, 'Have the accidents which remain no subject in which to inhere?', and one of the objections which he notes to saying 'Yes' is remarkably like the point made by Kenny and Dummett. It runs:

It seems that the accidents do not remain in this sacrament without a subject. There should be nothing out of order or deceptive in this sacrament of truth. But for accidents to be without a subject is against the natural order of things for which God is responsible. Likewise, there is something deceptive about it, because accidents are signs which reveal the nature of the subject in which they inhere. Therefore, in this sacrament, the accidents are not without subject.

Aquinas's reply takes the form of arguing (1) that there is no logical impossibility in the notion of accidents without a subject, and (2) that continuity of accident is enough for us to identify the accidents of bread and wine before and after the consecration so as to say that what was there before the consecration has been changed into something else, the presence of which is to be associated with accidents that do not inhere in a subject.

---

[108] Herbert McCabe, OP, *God Matters* (London, 1987), 146.

With respect to (1) here we can, I think, see what Aquinas is saying by noting something else to which Kenny draws attention. This is that, though one might find it odd to speak of accidents without substance (or properties without a subject),

there is nothing miraculous or even mysterious in the smell or taste of onions hanging round after the onions have been eaten. Again, the shape of my boot may remain imprinted in the snow after the boot itself, imprudently placed too near the fire to dry, has gone up in flames. In these cases the accidents are accidents of individual substances now defunct: but the colours of the rainbow, and the blueness of the sky, are colours not attributable to any substance present or past.[109]

One might say that 'part of the very definition of an accident is that it exists in a subject'.[110] But that, replies Aquinas, is not how 'accident' should be defined. Rather, we should simply say that accidents have natures suited to existing in a subject. In the eucharist we have accidents kept in being by God. And these accidents are real enough, which is why our senses perceive them.[111] This, observes Aquinas, is a miracle; but not in any sense that involves contradiction, for the accidents are genuine accidents. They do not stop being accidents by virtue of the change.

With respect to (2), Aquinas's point seems to be that we can identify bread and wine with their accidents, and, given that we have reason to believe that the substance of what we have identified has changed into the body and blood of Christ without the accidents disappearing, the presence of the accidents after the change is reason for saying that what is now present are accidents of what used to be bread and wine but is now no longer, accidents which may be held to be signs of the presence of Christ. Aquinas, of course, thinks that we *do* have reason for believing that bread and wine change into the body and blood of Christ after the consecration, for he takes this to be taught by Christ himself. For the record, he also thinks it possible to say why the presence of Christ is shown forth by accidents of bread and wine rather than by accidents belonging to Christ's body and blood.

It is obvious to our senses that, after the consecration, all the accidents of bread and wine remain. Divine providence very wisely arranged for this. First

[109] Anthony Kenny, *Aquinas* (Oxford, 1980), 37.
[110] 3a. 77. 1 obj. 2.
[111] 3a. 77. 1 ad. 2 and 3.

of all, people have not the custom of eating human flesh and drinking human blood; indeed, the thought revolts them. And so the flesh and blood of Christ are given to us to be taken under the appearances of things in common human use, namely bread and wine. Secondly, lest this sacrament should be an object of contempt for unbelievers, if we were to eat our Lord under his human appearance. Thirdly, in taking the body and blood of our Lord in their invisible presence, we increase the merit of faith.[112]

Still, as I say, a full discussion of the merits and demerits of Aquinas's teaching on transubstantiation lies beyond the scope of this book. For present purposes it only matters that we understand what that teaching amounts to, and how it fits in with what Aquinas says about sacraments as part of the lives of Christians. Looked at from that point of view, its main purpose is not to saddle the Church with a debatable piece of metaphysics. It is intended to stress that there exists a union between God and people which is thoroughly real and continuous, a union in which Christians share in the life of God as it is lived by the Son of God, who is the Father's giving of himself.

'*There exists a union between God and people which is thoroughly real and continuous, a union in which Christians share in the life of God as it is lived by the Son of God, who is the Father's giving of himself.*' This, in effect, is Aquinas's final teaching. It is what all his voluminous writings were ultimately geared to expressing and exploring. Readers who plough through his commentaries on Aristotle, or his various essays on topics in philosophy and questions of theology, may well gain a different impression. So may those with the stamina to work through the *Summa theologiae*. For, though this is his most systematic and comprehensive intellectual achievement, its details can blind one to its overall structure, as, perhaps, this book may do. But it is clear what Aquinas wanted to say in the end. And he ended his life while trying to say it. His notion of the sacraments, expounded in this chapter, was the last thing he offered to be studied and thought about by others. He died having broken off the attempt to put it forward and to spell out its implications. So it is, perhaps, appropriate that this book should finish where Aquinas himself did.

[112] 3a. 75. 5.

Select Bibliography

1. Bibliographical Works

BOURKE, VERNON J., *Thomistic Bibliography: 1920–1940*, Modern Schoolman (1921).

MANDONNET, P., and DESTREZ, J., *Bibliographie Thomiste*, 2nd edn. revised by M.-D. Chenu (Paris, 1960).

MIETHE, TERRY L., and BOURKE, VERNON J., *Thomistic Bibliography, 1940–1978* (Westport, Conn., 1980).

The *Bulletin Thomiste* (1940–65), continued in *Rassegna di letteratura Tomistica* (1966–), receives all Thomistic publications and is most useful as a research tool with respect to Thomistic bibliography.

2. Useful Selections from the Writings of Aquinas in English

The Pocket Aquinas, ed. VERNON J. BOURKE (New York, 1960).

The Philosophy of Thomas Aquinas, ed. CHRISTOPHER MARTIN (London, 1988).

St Thomas Aquinas, Summa Theologiae: A Concise Translation, ed. TIMOTHY McDERMOTT (London, 1989).

Introduction to St Thomas Aquinas, ed. ANTON C. PEGIS (New York, 1945).

3. General Material

ACKRILL, J. L., *Aristotle the Philosopher* (Oxford, 1981).

AERTSEN, JAN, *Nature and Creature: Thomas Aquinas's Way of Thought* (Leiden, 1988).

ANSCOMBE, G. E. M., and GEACH, P. T., *Three Philosophers* (Oxford, 1973).

BARNES, JONATHAN, *Aristotle* (Oxford, 1982).

BIRD, OTTO, 'How to Read an Article in the *Summa*', New Scholasticism, 27 (1953).

BOBIK, J., *Aquinas on Being and Essence* (Notre Dame, 1965).

BOEHNER, PHILOTHEUS, OFM (ed.), *Works of Saint Bonaventure*, ii: *Itinerarium mentis in Deum* (New York, 1956).

BONNETTE, D., *Aquinas' Proofs of God's Existence* (The Hague, 1972).

BOOTH, EDWARD, OP, *Aristotelian Aporetic Ontology in Islamic and Christian Thinkers* (Cambridge, 1983).

BOUILLARD, H., *Conversion et grâce chez S. Thomas d'Aquin* (Paris, 1944).

BOYLE, LEONARD E., *The Setting of the Summa Theologiae of Saint Thomas*, Étienne Gilson Series, 5 (Toronto, 1982).

BRABANT, F. H., *Time and Eternity in Christian Thought* (London, 1937).

BROWN, PETER, *Augustine of Hippo* (London, 1967).

BURRELL, DAVID, *Aquinas, God and Action* (London, 1979).

—— *Knowing the Unknowable God* (Notre Dame, Ind., 1986).

CALLUS, DANIEL A., OP, *The Condemnation of St Thomas at Oxford* (London, 1955).

CATAO, BERNARD, *Salut et rédemption chez S. Thomas d'Aquin* (Paris, 1965).

CESSARIO, ROMANUS, OP, *The Godly Image: Christ and Salvation in Catholic Thought from Anselm to Aquinas* (Petersham, Mass., 1990).

CHADWICK, HENRY, *Boethius* (Oxford, 1981).

—— *Augustine* (Oxford, 1986).

CHENU, M.-D., *Toward Understanding Saint Thomas*, trans. A. M. Landry and D. Hughes (Chicago, 1964).

CHESTERTON, G. K., *St Thomas Aquinas* (London, 1943).

CLARKE, W. N., 'What is Most and Least Relevant in the Metaphysics of St Thomas Today?', *International Philosophical Quarterly*, 14 (1974).

CONGAR, YVES, *Thomas d'Aquin: Sa vision de théologie et de l'Église* (London, 1984).

COPLESTON, F. C., *Aquinas* (Harmondsworth, 1955).

CORBIN, MICHEL, *Le Chemin de la théologie chez Thomas d'Aquin* (Paris, 1974).

COSGROVE, MATTHEW R., 'Thomas Aquinas on Anselm's Argument', *Review of Metaphysics*, 27 (1973–4).

CRAIG, WILLIAM LANE, *The Cosmological Argument from Plato to Leibniz* (London, 1980).

CROWE, MICHAEL BERTRAM, 'Peter of Ireland: Aquinas's Teacher of the ARTES LIBERALES', in *Arts libéraux et philosophie au Moyen Âge* (Paris, 1969).

DAVIDSON, HERBERT A., *Proofs for Eternity, Creation and the Existence of God in Medieval Islamic and Jewish Philosophy* (New York, 1987).

DAVIES, BRIAN, OP, *An Introduction to the Philosophy of Religion* (Oxford, 1982).

—— *Thinking about God* (London, 1985).

—— (ed.), *Language, Meaning and God* (London, 1987).

DESCARTES, RENÉ, *The Philosophical Writings of Descartes*, trans. John Cottingham, Robert Stoothoff, and Dugald Murdoch, 2 vols. (Cambridge, 1985).

DODDS, MICHAEL J., OP, *The Unchanging God of Love: A Study of the Teaching of St Thomas Aquinas on Divine Immutability in View of Certain Contemporary Criticism of This Doctrine* (Fribourg, 1986).

DOIG, JAMES C., *Aquinas on Metaphysics* (The Hague, 1972).

DRONKE, PETER (ed.), *A History of Twelfth-Century Philosophy* (Cambridge, 1988).

ECO, UMBERTO, *The Aesthetics of Thomas Aquinas* (London, 1988).

ELDERS, LEO, *Faith and Science: An Introduction to St Thomas's* Expositio in Boethii de Trinitate (Rome, 1974).

—— *The Philosophical Theology of St Thomas Aquinas* (Leiden, 1990).

EVANS, G. R., *Anselm* (London, 1989).

FARTHING, JOHN L., *Thomas Aquinas and Gabriel Biel* (Durham, 1988).

FERRUA, A. (ed.), *Thomae Aquinatis vitae fontes praecipuae* (Alba, 1968).

FOSTER, KENELM (ed.), *The Life of Saint Thomas Aquinas* (London, 1959).

FREGE, GOTTLOB, *The Foundations of Arithmetic*, trans. J. L. Austin (Oxford, 1953).

GARRIGOU-LAGRANGE, REGINALD, OP, *The One God: A Commentary on the First Part of St. Thomas' Theological Summa* (St Louis, 1952).

GEACH, PETER, *God and the Soul* (London, 1969).

—— 'God's Relation to the World', *Sophia*, 8 (1969).

GILBY, THOMAS, OP, *The Political Thought of Thomas Aquinas* (Chicago, 1958).

GILSON, ÉTIENNE, *The Christian Philosophy of St Thomas Aquinas* (London, 1957).

HANKEY, W. J., *God in Himself: Aquinas Doctrine of God as Expounded in the Summa Theologiae* (Oxford, 1987).

HENLE, R. J., *Saint Thomas and Platonism* (The Hague, 1956).

HICK, JOHN, and McGILL, ARTHUR (eds.), *The Many Faced Argument* (London, 1967).

HILL, EDMUND, OP, *The Mystery of the Trinity* (London, 1985).

HILL, WILLIAM, OP, *The Three-Personed God: The Trinity as Mystery of Salvation* (Washington, DC, 1982).

HUGHES, GERARD J., SJ, 'Aquinas and the Limits of Agnosticism', in Gerard J. Hughes, SJ (ed.), *The Philosophical Assessment of Theology* (Tunbridge Wells, 1987).

HUME, DAVID, *A Treatise of Human Nature*, ed. L. A. Selby-Bigge (2nd edn., Oxford, 1978).

—— *Enquiries Concerning Human Understanding and Concerning the Principles of Morals*, ed. L. A. Selby-Bigge (3rd edn., Oxford, 1975).

JANZ, DENIS R., *Luther on Thomas Aquinas* (Stuttgart, 1989).

KELLY, J. N. D., *Early Christian Doctrines* (5th edn., London, 1977).

—— *Early Christian Creeds* (3rd edn., London, 1972).

KENNY, ANTHONY (ed.), *Aquinas: A Collection of Critical Essays* (London, 1969).

—— *The Five Ways* (London, 1969).

—— *Aquinas* (Oxford, 1980).

KIRWAN, CHRISTOPHER, *Augustine* (London, 1989).

KNASAS, JOHN F. X., 'Aquinas: Prayer to an Immutable God', *New*

Scholasticism, 57 (1983).

KNOWLES, DAVID *The Evolution of Medieval Thought* (2nd edn., London, 1988).

KRETZMANN, NORMAN, 'Goodness, Knowledge, and Indeterminacy in the Philosophy of St Thomas Aquinas', *Journal of Philosophy*, 80 (1983).

—— 'Omniscience and Immutability', *Journal of Philosophy*, 63 (1966).

—— KENNY, ANTHONY, and PINBORG, JAN (eds.), *The Cambridge History of Later Medieval Philosophy* (Cambridge, 1982).

LAFONT, G., *Structures et méthode dans la Somme théologique de Saint Thomas d'Aquin* (Bruges, 1961).

LEAMAN, OLIVER, *Moses Maimonides* (London, 1990).

—— *Averroes and His Philosophy* (Oxford, 1988).

LONERGAN, BERNARD, *Verbum: Word and Idea in Aquinas*, ed. D. B. Burrell (Notre Dame, 1967).

LOTTIN, O., *Psychologie et morale aux XIIe–XIIIe siècles*, 3 vols. (Louvain, 1942–9).

LOUTH, ANDREW, *Denys the Areopagite* (London, 1989).

MCCABE, HERBERT, OP, 'Aquinas on Good Sense', *New Blackfriars*, 67 (1986).

—— *God Matters* (London, 1987).

MCINERNY, RALPH, *Thomism in an Age of Renewal* (New York, 1966).

—— *Being and Predication* (Washington, DC, 1986).

—— *St Thomas Aquinas* (Notre Dame, Ind., 1982).

—— *A First Glance at St Thomas Aquinas: A Handbook for Peeping Thomists* (Notre Dame, Ind., 1990).

MANDONNET, P., *Siger de Brabant et l'Averroisme latin au XIIme siècle* (Louvain, 1908–11).

MANN, WILLIAM E., 'Divine Simplicity', *Religious Studies*, 18 (1982).

—— 'Simplicity and Immutability in God', *International Philosophical Quarterly*, 23 (1983).

—— 'The Divine Attributes', *American Philosophical Quarterly*, 12 (1975).

MARENBON, JOHN, *Later Medieval Philosophy (1150–1350): An Introduction* (London, 1987).

MASCALL, E. L., *Existence and Analogy* (London, 1949).

MASTERSON, PATRICK, 'Aquinas' Notion of God Today', *Irish Theological Quarterly*, 44 (1977).

MAURER, ARMAND, *Being and Knowing: Studies in Thomas Aquinas and Later Medieval Philosophers* (Toronto, 1990).

MERRIELL, D. JUVENAL, *To the Image of the Trinity: A Study in the Development of Aquinas' Teaching* (Toronto, 1990).

MONDIN, B., *St Thomas Aquinas's Philosophy in the Commentary on the Sentences* (The Hague, 1975).

O'BRIEN, T., *Metaphysics and the Existence of God* (Washington, DC, 1960).

O'NEILL, COLMAN E., OP, *Meeting Christ in the Sacraments* (Cork, 1964).

OWENS, JOSEPH, *St Thomas Aquinas on the Existence of God: Collected Papers of Joseph Owens S. Ss. R*, ed. J. R. Catan (Albany, NY, 1980).

PATFOORT, A., *Thomas d'Aquin: Les Clés d'une théologie* (Paris, 1983).

PATTERSON, R. L., *The Conception of God in the Philosophy of Aquinas* (London, 1933).

PEGIS, ANTON CHARLES, *St Thomas and the Problem of the Soul in the Thirteenth Century* (Toronto, 1934).

PENELHUM, TERENCE, 'The Analysis of Faith in St Thomas Aquinas', *Religious Studies*, 13 (1977).

—— 'Divine Necessity', *Mind*, 69 (1960), reprinted in Basil Mitchell (ed.), *The Philosophy of Religion* (Oxford, 1971).

PERSON, PER ERIK, *Sacra Doctrina: Reason and Revelation in Aquinas* (Oxford, 1970).

PFURTNER, STEPHANUS, OP, *Luther and Aquinas: A Conversation* (London, 1964).

PIEPER, JOSEF, *The Silence of Saint Thomas*, trans. John Murray and Daniel O'Connor (Chicago, 1965).

—— *Guide to Thomas Aquinas* trans. R. and C. Winston (Notre Dame, Ind., 1987).

—— *Scholasticism* (New York, 1964).

PIKE, NELSON, *God and Timelessness* (London, 1970).

PLANTINGA, ALVIN, *Does God Have a Nature?* (Milwaukee, 1980).

PLOEG, J. VAN DER, 'The Place of Holy Scripture in the Theology of St Thomas', *Thomist*, 10 (1947).

POTTS, TIMOTHY, *Conscience in Medieval Philosophy* (Cambridge, 1980).

POURRAT, P., *Theology of the Sacraments* (2nd edn., St Louis, 1914).

PRINCIPE, WALTER H., *Thomas Aquinas' Spirituality*, Étienne Gilson Series, 7 (Toronto, 1984).

RADCLIFFE, E. S., 'Kenny's Aquinas on Dispositions for Human Acts', *New Scholasticism*, 58 (1984).

RAHNER, KARL, *The Trinity* (London, 1970).

REDPATH, PETER A., *The Moral Wisdom of St Thomas: An Introduction* (Lanham, 1983).

——*A Simplified Introduction to the Wisdom of St Thomas* (Washington, DC, 1980).

REILLY, JAMES P., Jr., *Saint Thomas on Law*, (Étienne Gilson Series, 12 (Toronto, 1990).

ROENSCH, FREDERICK J., *Early Thomistic School* (Dubuque, Ia., 1964).

ROO, W. A. VAN, *Grace and Original Justice According to St Thomas* (Rome, 1955).

SCHMIDT, R. W., *The Domain of Logic According to Saint Thomas Aquinas* (The

Hague, 1966).

SIGMUND, PAUL E., *St Thomas Aquinas on Politics and Ethics* (New York, 1988).

SILLEM, EDWARD, *Ways of Thinking about God: Thomas Aquinas and Some Recent Problems* (London, 1961).

SORABJI, RICHARD, *Time, Creation and the Continuum* (London, 1983).

SOUTHERN, R. W., *Saint Anselm: A Portrait in a Landscape* (Cambridge, 1990).

STEENBERGHEN, FERNAND VAN, *Le Problème de l'existence de Dieu dans les écrits de S. Thomas d'Aquin* (Louvain-La-Neuve, 1980).

—— *Thomas Aquinas and Radical Aristotelianism* (Washington, DC, 1980).

—— *Le Thomisme* (Paris, 1983).

—— *Siger de Brabant d'après ses œuvres inédites* (Louvain, 1931 and 1942).

—— *La Philosophie au XIIIe siècle* (Louvain, 1966).

STUBBENS, NEIL, 'Naming God: Maimonides and Aquinas', *Thomist*, 54 (1990).

STUMP, ELEONORE, 'Atonement According to Aquinas', in Thomas V. Morris (ed.), *Philosophy and the Christian Faith* (Notre Dame, 1988).

—— 'Faith and Goodness', in Godfrey Vesey (ed.), *The Philosophy in Christianity* (Cambridge, 1989).

—— 'Atonement and Justification', in Ronald J. Feenstra and Cornelius Plantinga, Jr. (eds.), *Trinity, Incarnation and Atonement* (Notre Dame, 1989).

—— and KRETZMANN, NORMAN, 'Absolute Simplicity', *Faith and Philosophy*, 2 (1985).

—— —— 'Eternity', *Journal of Philosophy*, 78 (1981).

THERON, STEPHEN, 'Esse', *New Scholasticism*, 53 (1979).

THOMAS, J. L. H., 'The Identity of Being and Essence in God', *Heythrop Journal*, 27 (1986).

TUGWELL, SIMON, OP, 'Prayer, Humpty Dumpty and Thomas Aquinas', in Brian Davies OP (ed.), *Language, Meaning and God* (London, 1987).

—— (ed.), *Albert and Thomas: Selected Writings* (New York, 1988).

—— (ed.), *Early Dominicans* (New York, 1982).

URMSON, J. O., *Aristotle's Ethics* (Oxford, 1988).

VANN, GERALD, OP, *Saint Thomas Aquinas* (London, 1940).

VILLETTE, LOUIS, *Foi et sacrement: De Saint Thomas à Karl Barth* (Paris, 1964).

VOS, ARVIN, *Aquinas, Calvin and Contemporary Protestant Thought* (Washington, DC, 1985).

WALSH, LIAM G., OP, 'Liturgy in the Theology of St Thomas', *Thomist*, 38 (1974).

—— *The Sacraments of Initiation* (London, 1988).

WEBER, ÉDOUARD-HENRI, *Le Christ selon Saint Thomas d'Aquin* (Paris, 1988).

WEISHEIPL, JAMES A., *Thomas d'Aquino and Albert His Teacher* (Toronto, 1980).

—— *Friar Thomas d'Aquino* (Oxford, 1974; republished with Corrigenda and Addenda, Washington, DC, 1983).

—— *Nature and Motion in the Middle Ages* (Washington, DC, 1985).

WHITE, VICTOR, OP, *God the Unknown* (London, 1956).

WILLIAMS, C. J. F., 'Is God Related to His Creatures?', *Sophia*, 8 (1969).

—— *What is Existence?* (Oxford, 1981).

WIPPEL, JOHN F., *Metaphysical Themes in Thomas Aquinas* (Washington, DC, 1984).

WISSINK, J. B. M. (ed.), *The Eternity of the World in the Thought of Thomas Aquinas and His Contemporaries* (Leiden, 1990).

YATES, JOHN C., *The Timelessness of God* (Lanham, 1990).

Index

Note: References to, and quotations from the *Summa theologiae* appear on the majority of pages and have not been listed separately.

Abelard, Peter (1079–1142) 59, 118, 237, 325–30
  Introductio 118
  Theologia Christiana 118
Abraham 292
action, human 220–5, 248
Adam 254–7, 264–6
agnosticism 36, 43, 57, 59–60, 111
Al Ash' ari (d. 936) 163
Albert the Great, Saint (c.1200–80) 1–5 *passim*, 15, 36, 43
Alexander of Hales (1186–1245) 125, 189
Ambrose, Saint (c.339–97) 120
analogy, doctrine of 70–4
angels 55–6, 172, 173
animals 169, 210, 216, 223
Anscombe, Elizabeth 164, 373
Anselm, Saint (c.1033–1109) 45, 104–5, 123, 129–30, 152, 200
  Cur Deus homo 322–3, 326–9
  'Ontological Argument' 22, 24
Aquinas, Saint Thomas, *see* Thomas Aquinas, Saint
Aquino, Landulf d' and Theodora (St Thomas Aquinas' parents) 1
Aristotle 46–7, 113, 153, 289–90
  and Aquinas' writings 5, 6, 26, 371, 373–4, 376
  on argument and knowledge 22, 278
  De anima 125–7, 209
  and good 85, 87, 230, 231, 238–9, 274, 285
  his concept of God 36, 131–2, 140
  and medieval philosophy 2–3, 5, 6
  Metaphysics 131–2, 210
  Nicomachean Ethics 5, 87, 238–9, 285
  Peri hermeneias 176
  Physics 5, 105–6, 160
  and the soul 129, 209–10
ascension of Christ 342–4
Athanasian creed 118, 185, 187
Athanasius (c.296–373) 251

atonement 325–6, 327
  see also forgiveness; redemption; salvation
Augustine, Saint (354–430):
  Aquinas' writings compared with 15
  De gratia et libero arbitrio 118, 166–7
  De Trinitate 192
  defining charity 290
  Enchiridion 174
  on evil and sin 89–90, 254, 255
  and the Incarnation 323–4
  on nature of God 23, 44, 45, 58–9, 118
  and predestination 166–7
  and relationship between God and his creatures 138, 251, 253, 270
  and the Resurrection 219–20
  and the sacraments 347–9, 362
  The City of God 349
  on time and eternity 104, 105
  and the Trinity 186–7, 192, 194, 200, 204, 206
Averroës (1126–98) 26
Avicebron (c.1021–c.1058) 59–60
Avicenna (980–1037) 23, 26

baptism 311, 347–8, 350, 356, 360–1, 363–4
  see also sacraments
Basil the Great (c.330–79) 251
Benedict XIV, Pope (1675–1758) 172
Berengarius of Tours (c.1040–80) 364–5, 369
Berkeley, George (1685–1753) 19
Bernard of Clairvaux, Saint (1090–1153) 179
Bible, as unquestioned truth 12, 114–17, 281–2, 299, 319
Bobik, Joseph 50
body:
  Christ's 307–8; and eucharist 364–76
  human 209–20, 295

Boethius (*c.*480–*c.*524) 104–8 *passim*,
  159–60, 301, 303
  Consolation of Philosophy 107–8, 137,
    159–60
  De Trinitate 23, 197, 200–2
Bonaventure, Saint (*c.*1217–74) 37, 179
  Itinerarium mentis in Deum 188
Bourke, David 350
Boyle, Leonard 7
Bultmann, Rudolf 345
Butler, Joseph 235

Calvin, John (1509–64) 337
'Cambridge changes' 77–8
Canon Law 17
Cassian, John (*c.*360–435) 179
causes and causality:
  divine 27–39 *passim*, 62–5, 159, 161,
    163
  secondary 163–5, 269
Cessario, Romanus 330–1
Chalcedon, Council of 297–8, 300–1,
  302
chance 159–62
change 45–9, 77–8, 101, 102–3
charity 288–96
Chenu, M.-D. 21
Christ:
  ascension of 342–4
  body of 307–8, 364–76
  and the Church 312–14, 333–4,
    361–3
  death of 298, 308, 319, 325–6,
    332–4, 352
  and eucharist 364–76
  faith absent in 298–9, 311–12
  and gift of prophecy 310
  as God the Son 203–4
  as goodness revealed 324
  grace of 308–14
  hope absent in 311–12
  human and divine 298–307
  knowledge of 314–18
  power of 318–19
  as priest 321, 330
  and redemption 324–32
  resurrection of 219, 339–42
  and sin 307, 311, 319
  as teacher 195, 298, 310, 366
  temptation of 311
  will of 309
  see also Incarnation; Trinity; Word
    incarnate

Christology 297
Church, and Christ 312–14, 333–4,
  361–3
Cicero 245
Cologne 5
Congar, Yves 361
conscience 235–7
Constantinople, First General Council of
  (381) 185
Corinthians, first epistle to 269, 274, 341
Councils:
  Chalcedon (451) 297–8, 300–1, 302
  Constantinople, First General (381)
    185
  Fourth Lateran (1215) 5, 363
  Lyons, Second (1274) 9
  Nicaea (325) 185, 275
  Orange, Second (529) 167
  Second Vatican (1962) 17
  Trent (1545–63) 346, 349
courage 244, 263
Coventry, John, SJ 276
Craig, William Lane 26–7
creation 33–9, 82–3, 86, 90
Creator, divine 33–5, 75–9, 146–9
creeds 12–13, 275, 281
  Athanasian 118, 185, 187
  Niceno-Constantinople 185, 204,
    275
Cyril of Alexandria (d. 444) 251, 366

damnation 167
death 215–20, 254
  of Christ 298, 308, 319, 325–6,
    332–4, 352
deification 251
Denys the Areopagite, *see* Dionysius the
  Areopagite
Descartes, René (1591–1650) 19, 50,
  122, 130, 208–14 *passim*
  Meditations on First Philosophy 208
despair 287
Deuteronomy, Book of 118
Dillistone, F. W. 326
Dionysius the Areopagite 231, 268, 361
  describing God 59, 62, 67, 72
  influence on Aquinas 4–5, 16, 42–3,
    59
disease 93–4, 161
dispositions, concept of 225–6,
  239–43, 271–2
divine simplicity, doctrine of 44–5, 51,
  66, 68, 100, 119, 198

Dominican order 3–4, 10
dualism 208–211, 214
'Dumb Ox', Aquinas described as 5
Dummett, Michael 371–2, 374
Duns Scotus, John (*c.*1265–1308) 322

Ecclesiasticus, Book of 175
Eddy, Mary Baker 90
Eriugena, John Scotus (*c.*810–*c.*877) 59, 167
Ernst, Cornelius 268
Eternal law 154–5, 247–9, 254
eternity 103–14
eucharist 361–76
  see also sacraments
eudaemonia 230
evil 89–97, 162, 231
'existence argument' 33–5
existence, divine 21–36, 39, 55–7
Ezekiel, Book of 320

faith 166, 266, 274–85, 288, 324
  Christ's absence of 298–9, 311–12
  and Trinity 187–93, 201
Father, God the 202–3
'Five Ways' to prove God's existence 25–31, 35–6, 39
food 228, 232
forgiveness 336–7, 339
  see also atonement; redemption; salvation
form 46–9, 126–8, 218–19
Fossanova 9
Frederick 11, Emperor of Germany (1194–1250) 1, 2
free will, *see* freedom
freedom, human 161, 167, 174–8, 184, 248, 266
Frege, Gottlob (1848–1925) 69
future:
  knowledge of 124–7
  see also prophecy

Galatians, epistle to 194, 328, 333
Geach, Peter 39, 51, 53, 77, 85, 195
Genesis, Book of 36, 83, 296
Gérald d'Abbeville (*c.*1220/5–1272) 8
Gilby, Thomas 17, 19
Gilson, Étienne 10
God:
  demonstrating existence of 21–36, 39
  describing 58–79
  the Father 202–3

as first cause 28–9, 32–3, 55, 102, 119, 131, 138, 145, 163
grace of 267, 268, 270
the Holy Spirit 204–6
intervention of 173–4
is active 110–13, 122
is beginning and end 21, 88
is Creator 33–5, 75–9, 146–9
is desirable 87–9
is eternal 103–14
is everywhere 98–101
is Existence 32–3, 55–7
is good 84–9
is immaterial 43–4, 52–4, 99, 125, 129
is incomprehensible 40–57, 58–9, 192–3
is omnipotent 121–4, 170
is omniscient 141–4
is perfect 30–1, 65, 67–9, 80–9, 129
is unchanging 29, 51–2, 101–3, 106–7, 110–17, 146–7
is unique 118–21
justice of 152–7
knowledge of 124–5, 128–38, 141–4
love of 149–52
mercy of 152–3, 155–7
providence of 158–84
and sin 123, 151–2
as the ultimate goal 228
vision of 250–3
will of 140–9
Godescalc of Orbais (*c.*804–*c.*869) 167
Grabmann, Martin 14
grace 262–73, 290–3, 308–14, 333–9, 356–7
Gregory 180
Gregory of Nazianzus (329–89) 251
Gregory of Nyssa (*c.*330–*c.*395) 251
Grosseteste, Robert (*c.*1170–1253) 1, 125, 322
Gui, Bernard 8

happiness 218, 227–32, 322
Hebrews, epistle to 109, 261, 282, 298, 343
Helm, Paul 107
Holy Spirit 204–6, 288–9, 292–3, 294
  see also Trinity
hope 285–8
  Christ's lack of 311–12
Hugh of St Victor (d. 1142) 278, 348, 350–1

Hughes, Christopher 108
Hume, David (1711–76) 19, 63, 164, 232
Ibn Sina (980–1037) 44–5
'identity theory' 208–9
Ignatius of Loyola, Saint (c.1491–1556) 16
Incarnation 111, 150, 257, 260, 297–319
  and grace 333–9
  and sacraments 350–6
  and salvation 259, 320, 334
  and sin 321–32, 336
  see also Christ; Trinity
individuation 49–51, 133, 219, 369
intellect and reason 125–7, 229–30, 232–49
  see also knowledge
Irenaeus (c.130–c.200) 251
Isidore of Seville, Saint (560–636) 349
Isaiah, Book of 115, 171, 294, 320–1

James, Epistle of 115
Jantzen, Grace 110, 112
Janz, Denis R. 339
Jeremiah, Book of 115, 261
Jerome, Saint (c.342–420) 123
Jews 259
Joel, Book of 320
John Chrysostom, Saint (c.347–407) 7
John Damascene, Saint (c.675–c.749) 41, 59,181, 316
  De fide orthodoxa 59
John XXII, Pope (1316–34) 14
John, Saint:
  Gospel of 42, 193–4, 251–2, 289, 320, 325; and Holy Spirit 109, 196–7, 268, 292, 312, 362
Jordan of Saxony (d.1237) 3
Joshua, Book of 171
Julian of Norwich (c.1342–1413) 164
justice:
  divine 152–7, 167, 327, 329, 332
  human 153, 244, 263
'justification' 335–9

Kenny, Anthony 19–20, 46, 48, 126, 226
  and transubstantiation 367–8, 371, 374–5
knowledge:
  of Christ 314–18
  divine 124–5, 128–38, 141–4

human: of God 58–9; through the senses 25, 43–4, 125–8, 214–15, 216, 233–4, 252; *see also* intellect and reason

Lateran Council, Fourth 363
Law:
  Canon 17
  Eternal 154–5, 247–9, 254
  human 246–7
  natural 244–9, 257–8
  of nature 172–3
  New 260–2, 290–2, 310, 351–2, 354
  Old 257–60, 291, 292, 351–2, 354
Lazarus 340
life, eternal, *see* salvation
Locke, John (1632–1704) 19, 367–8
Lombard, Peter (c.1095–1160) 5, 348, 349
  Sentences 5
Louis IX, King of France (1215–70) 8
Louth, Andrew 43
love:
  of God 149–52
  as Holy Spirit 206
  of self 295
Lucas, John 114
lust 224–5
Luther, Martin (1438–1546):
  and justification 335, 337, 339
  and transubstantiation 371, 372, 373–4
Lyons, Second Council of 9

McCabe, Herbert 93, 111
  and knowledge of God 41, 63, 69
  and predestination 169, 177
  and transubstantiation 374
McDermott, Timothy 256, 295, 352, 357
McGrath, Alister 337–8
McInerny, Ralph 245
Maimonides (1135–1204) 26, 36, 45, 60, 61
Malachi, Book of 115
Malebranche, Nicolas (1638–1715) 163
Manichees 8, 295
Mascall, E. L. 73
matter 46–51, 218–19
Matthew, Saint, Gospel of 7, 81, 195, 320
Maurer, Armand 10–11
mercy 152–3, 155–7, 332

miracles 169–74, 192, 269, 281, 319, 365
monophysitism 301
Monte Cassino 1
morality 232, 234, 237–9
Moses 292, 312

Naples 1
    University of 2, 3, 4
natural law 244–9, 257–8
neoplatonism 16, 42–3, 89–90, 103, 140–1
Nestorius (d. *c*.451) 304
New Law (after the Incarnation) 260–2, 290–2, 310, 351–2, 354
Nicaea, Council of (325) 185, 275
Niceno-Constantinople creed 185, 204, 275
Nicholas of Lisieux (*c*.1272) 8
Numbers, Book of 115

Occam's razor 119
occasionalism 163
O'Connor, D. J. 235
O'Connor, Edward D. 294
Old Law (before the Incarnation) 257–60, 291, 292, 351–2, 354
'ontological argument' 24, 56
Orange, Second Council of (529) 167
Origen (*c*.185–254) 137, 181

Paris 4–5
    University of 2, 5–6, 7–8, 12, 37, 126
Paul V, Pope (1552–1621) 16
Paul, Saint 109, 179, 254, 274
    and the Church 313, 334
    and faith 166–7, 280, 282, 298
    and grace 269, 333
    and the Incarnation 217, 261, 340–3
    and knowledge of God 23, 25
    and redemption of sin 320–2, 325, 328, 330, 337
    and the Trinity 194, 289
Pegis, Anton 10–11
Pelagian heresy 255
perfection, and God 65, 67–9, 80–9
Peter of Ireland 3
Peter, Saint, Epistle of 251
Philippians, epistle to 175
Philoponus, John *De aeternitate mundi contra Proclum* 37
physicalism 208–9, 211
Pieper, Josef 16

Pike, Nelson 110–11, 113
Pius V, Saint, Pope (1504–72) 16
Plantinga, Alvin 53
Plato 16, 46–7, 126, 211
Plotinus (*c*.205–70) 42, 59, 89, 103–4, 141
Potts, Timothy 233–4
power:
    of Christ 318–19
    of God 121–4, 170
    human 228–9
prayer 178–84
predestination 166–9, 307
    see also freedom
procession and Trinity 193–8, 204–6
Proclus (*c*.410–85) 16, 42, 104
prophecy 310
    see also future
Proverbs, Book of 175
providence, divine 158–84
prudence 241–4
Psalms, Book of 109, 120, 334

Rahner, Karl 353–4
Raymond of Peñafort, Saint (*c*.1178–1275) 6
reason and intellect 125–7, 229–30, 232–49
    see also knowledge
redemption 250, 324–32
redemption, *see* atonement; forgiveness; salvation
Regensburg 3
Reginald of Piperno 8–9
remotion, method of 40–57
repentance, *see* atonement
resurrection 218–20, 266, 339–42, 352
Revelations, Book of 252, 320
Richard of St Victor (d. 1173) 188
Richards, Hubert 182
rites and ritual 258–9, 347, 350
Ritschl, Albrecht (1822–89) 298
Roccasecca 1, 4
Romans, epistle to 166–7, 254, 289, 325, 330, 337, 340
Rome 4
Rupert of Deutz (*c*.1075–1129/30) 321–2
Russell, Bertrand 19, 20, 57

sacra doctrina 11–14
sacraments 346–76
    see also baptism; eucharist

salvation 167, 168, 285–7, 307
  for animals 169
  and grace 356–7
  and Incarnation 259, 320, 334
  and sacraments 338, 346, 348, 353
  see also atonement; forgiveness
    redemption
Samuel, Book of 115
'satisfaction', *see* redemption
'science' 241, 278–9
Second Coming 306
senses, experience of, and knowledge 25,
  43–4, 125–8, 214–15, 216, 233–4,
  252
simplicity, doctrine of divine 44–5, 51,
  66, 68, 100, 119, 198
sin 92, 94–7, 254
  and Christ 307, 311, 319, 321–32,
  336
  God's inability to 123
  original 189, 254–7, 266
sinners, God's love for 151–2

Solomon, Song of 320
Son of God:
  and the Trinity 203–4
  see also Christ; Word incarnate
soul 209–20
Swinburne, Richard 110, 113, 114, 188
synderesis 233–4, 235–6, 239, 245–6

Taylor, C. C. W. 18
temperance 244, 263
temptation of Christ 311
Tertullian (*c.*100–65) 346
Theodore of Mopsuestia (*c.*350–428)
  304
Thessalonians, epistle to 179, 342
Thomas Aquinas, Saint (*c.*1225–74)
  and agnosticism 36, 42–3, 57, 111
  career 5–8, 12, 15–16, 20
  Catena aurea 8
  character of 10–16
  Compendium theologiae 142–3, 333
  Contra errores Graecorum 8
  De aeternitate mundi 36
  De ente et essentia 31
  De malo 174–5
  De potentia 6, 31, 36, 41, 165
  De principiis naturae 5
  De regno 8
  De spiritualibus creaturis 6
  De veritate 284, 313

death of 8–10
as Dominican 3–4, 10
the 'Dumb Ox' 5
early years 1–5
in modern theology 17–20
and neoplatonism 16, 42–3
philosopher or theologian 10–14
as saint 14
Scriptum super libros Sententiarum 5,
  36, 179, 315, 322, 328–9, 335
Summa contra Gentiles: arguing against
  unbelievers 6, 191, 281; describing
  God 22, 31, 36, 40, 142, 165; and
  prayer 115, 182
Summa theologiae, *see* preliminary note
  to index
valued by the Church 16–17
Thomas Didymus, Saint 281–2, 298
time 105–6, 109
Timothy, epistle to 179, 320, 321–2
transubstantiation 364–76
Trent, Council of (1545–63) 346, 349
Trinity 118, 150, 184–206, 250, 253–4,
  288
  the economic 194–5, 207, 313
  the Father 202–3
  the immanent 195–8, 207, 313
  the Son 203–4
  the Spirit 204–6
tritheism 187, 198
Tugwell, Simon 14

University of Naples 2, 3, 4
University of Paris 2, 5–6, 7–8, 12, 37,
  126

Vatican Council, Second 17
Velecky, Ceslaus 196
virtues 239–44
  intellectual 240–2
  moral 242–4
  theological 263, 273, 274–96

Walsh, Liam 347, 352
White, Victor 57
will:
  of Christ 309
  divine 140–9
  human 220–5
William of St Thierry
  (*c.*1085–1148) 179
William of Saint-Amour (d. 1272) 8
Wippell, John 41

Wittgenstein, Ludwig (1889–1951)
  Philosophical Investigations 74–5
women, place of 18
Word incarnate 196–7, 203–4, 303–7,
  309, 314, 350, 357–8

see also Christ; Incarnation; Trinity
world:
  beginning of 35–9; *see also* creation

Zwingli, Ulrich (1484–1531) 365

DATE DUE
